D1348857

Adventures of a Cold War Fast-Jet Navigator

For my grandchildren
Oscar, Douglas,
William, Stewart
and
Beatrix

To the Memory of
Squadron Leader Barrie 'Wings' Chown

He taught me everything
I ever needed to know about
Flying, Navigating, Weaponeering, Drinking
and
Having a Bloody Good Laugh!

By The Same Author

The Buccaneer Songbook

Short stories contributed by the same author in:

The Buccaneer Boys
Out Of The Blue
Out Of The Blue Too

Adventures of a Cold War Fast-Jet Navigator

The Buccaneer Years

Wing Commander
David Herriot

Foreword by
Air Chief Marshal
Sir Michael Knight KCB, AFC, FRAeS

Pen & Sword
AVIATION

First published in Great Britain in 2017 by
Pen & Sword Aviation
an imprint of
Pen & Sword Books Ltd
47 Church Street
Barnsley
South Yorkshire
S70 2AS

ISBN 978 1 52670 659 1

Typeset in Ehrhardt by
Mac Style Ltd, Bridlington, East Yorkshire.
Printed and bound in India by Replika Press, Pvt. Ltd.

Pen & Sword Books Limited incorporates the imprints of Atlas,
Archaeology, Aviation, Discovery, Family History, Fiction, History,
Maritime, Military, Military Classics, Politics, Select, Transport,
True Crime, Air World, Frontline Publishing, Leo Cooper,
Remember When, Seaforth Publishing, The Praetorian Press,
Wharncliffe Local History, Wharncliffe Transport,
Wharncliffe True Crime and White Owl.

For a complete list of Pen & Sword titles please contact
PEN & SWORD BOOKS LIMITED
47 Church Street, Barnsley, South Yorkshire, S70 2AS, England
E-mail: enquiries@pen-and-sword.co.uk
Website: www.pen-and-sword.co.uk

The Adventures Of
A Cold War Fast-Jet Navigator

who was often

'Temporarily Unsure of My Position'

Tools of the Trade (J.F. Herriot)

A professional navigator is never ever lost, although he may sometimes be temporarily unsure of his position!

The Buccaneer Years

Contents

Acknowledgements

A book of this nature is never the work of one person and whilst I have done all the pen-pushing, or more appropriately these days, keyboard-bashing, during its production, it could not have been completed without the wisdom, advice and memories of many others. All of these have been good friends at some point in my RAF career, and many have become solid, good and lifelong buddies to me - my wife and my family. In an air force career that spanned almost forty years, like all of my kind, I have had more acquaintances than the average man could muster in a lifetime. Some were fleeting in a bar in a far-flung land and others just mates for the duration of a 3-year tour. To those who feature solely in that capacity in this book, and who have helped to hang my tale together, I offer my sincerest thanks to you.

To those, however, who made each and every hilarious moment complete I offer the biggest thanks. I had a ball and thank you very much for giving me your permission to relate our story amongst the *'Adventures of a Cold War Fast-Jet Navigator'*. I use no hierarchical rank listing but, as mates, merely list you in alphabetical order. So my sincere and faithful honest thanks to: Ken Alley; Nick Berryman; John Broadbent; David Cleland-Smith; Tim Cockerell; Paul Dandeker; Tom Eeles; Martin Engwell; Ivor Evans; Mike Gault; John Kershaw; Phil Leckenby; Art Legg; John Lewer; Ken Mackenzie; Len McKee; Ray Morris; Kyle Morrow; Sir Peter Norriss; Mal Prissick; Graham Seaward; Graham Smart; Colin Tavner; Frank Waddington; Les Whatling; Phil Wilkinson; Jerry Witts and Peter York. Each and every one of you had a huge influence, some good and some bad, on my RAF career!

Helen Chown I thank for the friendship that she, along with her late husband Barrie, has given me ever since we first met on XV Squadron at Laarbruch in 1972 and for her encouragement to 'write the story of what Mr Wings (and I) got up to!' Helen, frustrating as it sometimes was for you as you waited for Barrie to return from the bar, I am sure that you will realise now that it was never my fault and that he was the definite ringleader!

Sir Michael Knight has been a pillar of support and encouragement, on and off, throughout the last forty-three years. Particularly so following his acceptance of the presidency of the Buccaneer Aircrew Association, which he held for twenty years. It was Sir Mike, as my very astute station commander with his words in my final Annual Confidential Report on XV Squadron in 1974, who ensured that I never became a 'bag-carrier' in my air force career. Ironically, in my capacity as Honorary Secretary of the Buccaneer Aircrew Association, I have been his 'bag-carrier' throughout his presidency! More important than that, I very much appreciate him giving his permission for me to publish our exploits together in Nevada with the words 'publish and be damned!' There are few very senior RAF officers who would admit to being thrown out of a hotel on the Las Vegas Strip, let alone permit to have the story published! For his foreword to my memoir I am equally grateful as it describes me well and acts as an excellent scene setter.

Graham Pitchfork, Buccaneer navigator extraordinaire, and now renowned aviation writer and historian, deserves special mention for being a marvellous help in guiding me throughout the latter stages of my project and for leading me through the minefield that can be the publication process. Never once did he show any vexation or impatience when he answered his telephone to discover that it was only me on the end with another dumb question.

No aviation memoir would satisfy its audience if it did not contain a number of photographic plates that help to illustrate the words on the pages. Whilst I hold a significant stock, some of which are included, this book would be nothing if I had not managed to get in touch with and gain permission from Nigel Price, Group Editor (Aviation and History) at Key Publishing, who provided many of the excellent plates that feature the Buccaneer both in the air and on the ground. Also my sincere thanks to Rick Brewell, erstwhile RAF photographer and oft-time winner of the air-to-air category of the RAF Public Relations Photographic Competition, who provided the top quality air-to-air photographs that adorn the cover. To Fleet Air Arm pilot Clive Morrell I offer my sincere gratitude for admitting that it was he who, from the Altnacealgach Hotel bar, took the photograph of the Buccaneer at very low-level over Loch Borralan in the North-West Highlands of Scotland and for allowing me to publish it here. For the exceptional dusk photograph of Buccaneer XX901 outside its hangar at the Yorkshire Air Museum I am indebted to Ian Finch, at the museum, for his permission to use it. My thanks also go to Richard Somers-Cocks who was kind enough to provide me with the photograph that links the start and end of my RAF operational flying career, from Buccaneer to Tornado (more of which is planned in a second volume). Finally, to the late Glenn Mason, I am most grateful for his permission to reproduce the cockpit view at low-level in Glen Tilt; an image that evokes the thrill of what it was like to be down at low-level, sitting on your right wing at 500 mph.

From the moment I set out on this task I questioned in my mind whether it was readable and would be of any interest to the general public. I was delighted, therefore, when Pen and Sword Ltd took up the challenge of putting my story of my Buccaneer years into print. Throughout the publishing process Laura Hirst, the company's Aviation Imprint Commissioning Editor, has been a most helpful guide and mentor over the long months that it has taken to process the book to launch. I will be eternally grateful to her for having the faith to take my story on and to encourage me at every stage of the production process. So too Ken Patterson, my appointed editor, who has ploughed his way through it all correcting my text and providing very helpful suggestions where necessary to enhance my English. I am most grateful to Ken for his relaxed attitude to the whole affair and for putting me at my ease from the outset of our relationship.

Finally, there are two people who deserve my greatest appreciation for their unstinting support and encouragement from my very first scribblings.

Iain Ross was my first pilot in my RAF career. Sat in our Buccaneer, as students on the operational conversion unit, he assisted and encouraged this fresh-faced navigator to success and onward throughout our time on XV Squadron together. Without his encouragement, support and help, there might never have been any Buccaneer years to write about. We shared some very happy memories both as bachelors in the mess at Laarbruch and as a highly effective operational crew in the cockpit. As a result he has been a great help in the creation of this chronicle with his prompting of my memory and correcting of some facts during its production. I will be forever indebted to him for that and for permitting me to expose many of our mischievous escapades together.

My wife Jo, who had to put up with my long absences from home whilst I was serving, must have been overjoyed at the prospect of my retirement and the likelihood that we would spend more time together. Yet she complained not once when she discovered that my plan to write my memoir would find me locked in my study for days at a time whilst I battered away at my keyboard. Willingly and diligently she also took on the task of being the first person to read about what I got up to, as she acted as my editor and appraiser for each and every chapter as it came off the press. As a lay person she has helped me immensely in reducing the amount of jargon that aircrew, by the very nature of their task, use routinely to express themselves. She has been outstanding in her support throughout the project and I will always be grateful to her for that and for giving me a 'pink chit' to complete it.

Foreword

Air Chief Marshal Sir Michael Knight KCB, AFC, FRAeS

Sir Michael Knight. (*Via Sir Michael Knight*)

I t is yet another of those truths 'universally acknowledged' that, by the very nature of their professional 'trade', fast-jet military aircrew tend towards the outrageous in their off-duty conduct. This was certainly the case with the young David Herriot; though, like others before and after him, he went on to carve out a serious – even illustrious – career as a Royal Air Force navigator and weapons instructor on two fine front-line aircraft – the Blackburn Buccaneer S2 and the multi-national Tornado GR1.

Our paths first crossed (as often as not, literally so) when, as a young officer on his first tour in Germany, he had the mixed fortune to find me as his long-suffering station commander. Some years later, when we had both moved a little way up the promotion ladder, we met again at Nellis Air Force Base in Nevada, where he and his fellow weapons instructors worked hard to lead me astray in downtown Las Vegas. Not their most challenging remit, it has to be said.

In quieter times, the no longer 'young Herriot' became the extremely capable honorary secretary of the famed Buccaneer Aircrew Association, of which I was its first president. Our lives have thus been interwoven for upwards of forty years, and I can truly be said to know him well – 'warts and all'.

To say he was a lively character in his early Royal Air Force career would be an understatement. As a first-tourist bachelor living in the Officers' Mess at RAF Laarbruch, he was usually 'front and centre' when it came to high jinks in the bar after flying had finished for the day. But, in the air, he was already on track to becoming a well above average and thoroughly reliable operator who, whatever the circumstances, could get the job done. There followed three more flying tours on the Buccaneer before he transferred his highly-developed skills to the Tornado force – again in Germany.

In a career which spanned some thirty-eight years and over 3,000 hours of front-line flying, in both overland and maritime environments, there is yet ample scope for a little light relief, and the RAF's Buccaneer aircrew were ever ready to indulge in the latter. The aircraft, though greatly cherished by those who flew it, was certainly no pushover when it came to high-speed, all-weather, ultra low-level and extremely challenging operational training. That was clearly the case for its pilots; but for those sitting behind them, with no direct control over the handling of the aircraft, it was a rather different story. Lacking a dual-control variant of the Buccaneer, highly-developed crew co-operation and total mutual confidence between crew members were essential; and it was a tribute to rigorous training and constant practice that the force attained such impressive results – whether in the hands of its first operators (the Fleet Air Arm), its only foreign air arm (the South African Air Force), or the Royal Air Force, which was privileged to see out the final years of this fine aircraft.

As is the case in an ever-evolving operational environment, David Herriot's was indeed a diverse and never less than interesting career. In this book he has revealed all – or, perhaps more accurately, all that is not the subject of military confidentiality, privacy or libel. The result is a fascinating narrative of life in the fast lane as the UK and her NATO allies faced the threat of renewed conflict in Europe. Against that sombre background, the book's many episodes of light relief may appear ill-timed and uncaring, but they also have their place in restoring some sort of balance to what might otherwise have been a life of unremitting solemnity.

One last thought: When challenged by another crew member as to the progress of any flight, the 'holding' response of a navigator was, often unfairly, said to be: 'temporarily unsure of position'. In David Herriot's case, the phrase has quite another meaning; as he recalls the not infrequent occasions on which he has stood at attention, on the carpet of one or other of his seniors, to explain his part in some excessively anti-social behaviour in the Mess the previous evening. That he won through to become a respected and highly professional member of a tightly-knit 'band of brothers' says all that needs to be said of this always engaging military aviator.

Prologue

When I was a small child, like every other boy of my years, I wanted to be a train driver; steam driven in those days. By the time I was nine, however, a BBC 'fly on the wall' documentary series had encouraged me towards a career in medicine – I was fascinated by the black and white images on a friend's television screen that showed the goings on in an operating theatre in a busy hospital. When I was thirteen and at a Scripture Union camp, in a well-intentioned move to turn we early teenagers away from smoking, I was shown a colour film of a man's cancerous left lung being removed – and decided that a surgeon's life was not for me! Now thoroughly short of ideas and with no real desire to drive a diesel-powered locomotive – it just wasn't that romantic anymore – I flew in a passenger aircraft for the first time and my life changed forever.

A successful and highly entertaining thirty-eight year career as a fast-jet navigator ensued. It wasn't a job per se. To describe it thus would suggest that it might have been tiresome and laborious. Maybe even give sense to a notion that I did not enjoy it! A job is a job after all. It is something that we all have to do to put food on the table and a roof over our heads. Flying in the RAF, for me at least, was a vocation. I loved every minute of it – I got paid for doing something I loved. I went to work every morning, whether to fly or man a desk, with a spring in my step. If I was ever lucky enough to be reborn I know I would do it all again. So when my wife Jo, who has faithfully conducted the first edit, suggested that I should put my experiences down on paper for others to enjoy, I decided to do just that after I retired from the RAF in 2007.

My first scratchings I deemed suitable only for the eyes of my family. That audience, to my mind, seemed adequate. I wished purely to enlighten my children who, in their youth, yawned at the very prospect of hearing another *'there I was over the North Sea at 100 feet and 580 knots'* story! I figured that they might prefer to read it at their own pace rather than have to sit bored and with feigned interest. It was planned therefore as a short story with little embellishment, but one that might teach them more about what I got up to in my youth, both good and bad, and throughout my flying career.

As the story developed I recalled more and more of the humorous moments and events away from the cockpit rather than those in it. Tales of alcohol-infused nights on detachment in Norway, Cyprus, Las Vegas and Lossiemouth, for example, formed much of the pattern of my life in my early RAF career. Those high jinks that were more often than not shared with Barrie Chown, my drinking buddie, became a recurring theme as I continued to write.

It was not all about drinking and partying, of course. Life in the RAF is, after all, a serious business, but life in the RAF during the Cold War allowed a little bit more leeway than it does today. And what now might be described as vulgar hooliganism was then just deemed to be high spiritedness! And there was plenty of high spirit on the four operational Buccaneer outfits on which I flew and on the stations upon which I served. Much of which I had a happy knack of being involved in and not always having used my best judgment beforehand!

Through reference to my flying logbooks I managed to extract from my memory banks sortie details of missions flown far too long ago for them to be at the forefront of my aging brain. Some hairy moments in the back of a Buccaneer, and some amusing ones too, all sprang to mind as I waded through the pages of these very precious logs. As I turned the pages happy memories came flooding back. Stories began to jump off my keyboard and so the memoir grew. Life as a Cold War navigator on a two-seat fast-jet bomber squadron in the 1970s and 1980s filled much of my early career. I delighted at the memory of flying at 100 feet over the ocean searching for and carrying out simulated attacks on warships. I contemplated the hours spent idly in the Quick Reaction Alert shed for long periods of time waiting to man the West's nuclear response to a Soviet initiated Armageddon. I chuckled at the antics that my first pilot and I got up to over the plains of West Germany at 250 feet on my first operational squadron and I dwelled, but not for long, at the nerve-tingling moments sat as an instructor in the back of a Buccaneer with a student pilot who had only ever taken the beast into the air once before – and I did not have any flying controls; not that I would have known what to do with them had I had them. I laughed as I recalled the mischief and stories that sprang from my memory of life in an officers' mess on operational RAF stations in Germany and the UK. And, I blanched when I remembered some of the crazy things we did both professionally and socially on overseas detachments across the length and breadth of the NATO alliance.

My son, daughter and two step-daughters are now adults with families of their own, and hopefully, one day, they will find the time to read my story. Certainly, they will have to keep their copy on a top shelf until their children are old enough to read some of the more ludicrous and seamier adventures that their grandfather got up to in his youth, after a night on the beer! They are too young now and I need to retain some respect around here.

Jo, ever eager to support me and having now read my tale from cover to cover, has encouraged me to publish the whole story, warts and all, and so I have.

I hope you enjoy it.

Chapter One

I Learned About Flying From That!

It was just another day at Nav School but, unlike all the previous, today was the first day of the Night Flying Phase! We had completed all the astronomy lectures; learned all about MOOs and MOBs and how to apply them to our star shots; carried out Three-Position Line Fixing exercises in the classroom; studied the calculations in our Air Almanacs and endured hours handling and manipulating the periscopic sextant that we would fit into the astrodome of the Vickers Varsity T Mk1 when we eventually climbed aboard dressed, as usual, in our green Flying Suits and Black Flying 'Wellies', and carrying not only our sextants, but also the true symbol of our chosen profession, a Mk1A Flying Helmet with its cloth inner and H–Type Oxygen Mask! We were, we thought, at twenty years of age, true pioneers of the sky. A new generation of aviators destined to explore the skies of our world and defend our nation against the Soviet hordes who had only some nine years earlier sealed themselves in the East of Europe and aggressively threatened NATO and the Free World! There were medals to be won here, chaps, but first we luckless students had to get through our first Night Navex, or Exercise B14 as the staff preferred to call it, at No 6 Flying Training School, RAF Finningley!

Pete York and I had found ourselves thrown together on No 133 Course at No 2 ANS, RAF Gaydon[1] in the autumn of 1969. Having started out his RAF career as a Cosford Apprentice, Yorkie had, on completion of his initial RAF trade training, been commissioned, like me, as an officer in the General Duties (Navigator) Branch. Consequently, he had arrived at Gaydon with much experience of air force life, if not much experience as an officer. I, as a fresh out of school acting pilot officer, knew that he was a man I needed to look to for guidance and security in the fraught world that was the lot of a U/T Navigator in the traumatic training regime, where every move, both in navigation and officer qualities, was watched, checked, reviewed and considered on a daily basis. It was very much a case of 'when I say jump, you say how high' training system that existed in the RAF at that time. We shared a room in the officers' mess, drank and partied in Doncaster together, and, when invited on Sundays, even went for afternoon tea to our batwoman's house in the local mining village of Rossington. Yorkie and I were a team who worked, partied, took tea and flew together regularly.

The Vickers Varsity T Mk1 first flew on 17 July 1949, some seven weeks after my birth. Built by the same company that built the Vanguard turboprop airliner, that had

1. No 2 ANS was based at RAF Gaydon, from 1965 to 1970, when it and No 1 ANS at RAF Stradishall combined to form No 6 FTS at RAF Finningley, near Doncaster. I started my training at Gaydon and completed it at Finningley.

first stimulated my interest in a career in aviation, the Varsity was based on the earlier Viking, operated by BEA, and the Valetta – a military trainer and derivative of the Viking – to meet Air Ministry Specification T.13/48, under Operational Requirement 249, for a twin-engined training aircraft to replace the Wellington T10 and the Valetta T3 and T4. The obvious difference between the Varsity and its predecessors was that, rather than being a tail-dragger, the Varsity was equipped with a tricycle undercarriage. However, it also had a greater wing-span, a longer fuselage and a ventral pannier to allow a trainee bomb aimer to lie prone in the 'lower deck' in order to conduct practice bomb runs. This last attribute also permitted baby navigators to conduct visual low-level navigation training from the comfort of a padded bed and a panoramic window beneath the main deck of the Varsity.

For those who seek the technical specifications, the Varsity was equipped with two Bristol Hercules radial engines, was 67 feet 6 inches long with a wingspan of 95 feet 7 inches. Height at the tip of the tail was 23 feet 11 inches and the total wing area was 974 square feet. Empty, it weighed 27,040lb and its maximum All Up Weight was defined as 37,500lb. Each engine produced 1,950 horsepower and it was quaintly known by those who flew it as the 'Super Pig', which was one step up from the Valetta, which was merely 'The Pig'! Operated by a crew of four, its maximum cruise speed was 250 knots at 10,000 feet, it had a range of 2,302 nm and, although we normally flew it at medium altitude, its service ceiling was 28,700 feet! True to its nickname it had a sluggish, but not unexpected – given its design – rate of climb of about 1,400ft/min! It was capable of carrying practice bombs in an external carrier, but I never knew an occasion when that might have occurred and certainly not at Nav School! The Varsity was withdrawn from service with the RAF in May 1976.

The last ever students to be trained as navigators, or Weapons Systems Officers as they were by then called, at the Nav School at RAF Cranwell in 2011, would have learned to navigate using sophisticated aids such as GPS or INAS. However, at 2 ANS in 1969 no such technological sophistication existed, so our training focussed on learning the art of the Manual Air Plot (MAP)! This very basic method of air navigation required a continuous plot to be made of the true headings steered and the air distances flown, and the identification of the resultant track errors based on the discovery of the actual wind. Having prepared one's chart with the tracks to be flown between each turning point, a MAP required the navigator to adopt a rigorous and regular fixing cycle, and by advancing a previous position to a new one on the basis of assumed distance and direction moved, known as Dead Reckoning, a prediction of where the aircraft will be at a given time in space could be deduced. If successful, a heading correction was made in order to regain track effectively and efficiently; the method is known as 'DR'ing Ahead' and was usually based on a six-minute cycle. For it to be effective, it was essential that the pilot flew the aircraft at a constant Indicated Air Speed (IAS) which, in the case of the Varsity, was 180 knots or 3 nm per minute.

To assist the navigator, the Varsity was equipped with a number of Second World War vintage Navigation Aids, prime of which was Gee. Developed to assist Bomber Command raids on mainland Europe, Gee used a three-phase electronic system that relied on pulse transmitters which were located in the south of England. A location chosen in order to allow greater and more accurate coverage of the now erstwhile Third Reich rather than support young students in the air over the UK. It worked on the principle of measuring the difference in arrival time of pulses from two of the transmitters. The receiver in the Varsity picked up the pulses from the three stations and displayed them on a Cathode Ray Tube at the navigator's station where they were manipulated and refined to allow each arc on the 'Gee Chart' to be plotted and, from the resultant crossing point of each, a position fix could be identified and transposed onto the nav's main Mercator plotting chart. If used accurately and with strong signals from all three stations, Gee could be accurate to about one nautical mile, which in the 1940s was actually pretty acceptable, and in the 1970s was more than adequate for a U/T Nav to cope with!

The aircraft was also equipped with Rebecca Mk IV, another wartime navigation aid that worked on a similar principle to Gee, but allowed the navigator to obtain radio position lines to establish a three position line fix rather than a positive radio-beacon based fix like Gee. We also learned the art of visual navigation. Initially, this was done by standing between the two pilots to obtain a visual position line from a coastal landmark such as Land's End or Flamborough Head. However, in the latter stages of the course, we planned our route on a 250,000 scale topographic chart and 'route-crawled' from pinpoint to pinpoint whilst lying in the bomb-aimer's position on the lower deck. Of course, just as celestial navigation required the aircraft to be above cloud, visual navigation could only be undertaken when in visual contact with the ground!

One of the strangest, but simplest, pieces of aircraft navigation equipment in the Varsity was the Drift Sight, situated just inside and forward of the entry door on the port side. The Drift Sight was nothing more or less than a periscope that was set at right angles through the skin of the aircraft with a reticle scale of parallel lines etched on its lens. By using the simple technique of following two points on the ground with a pencil linked to the lens mechanically, one could use the resultant trace to calculate the drift. After landing you could often tell when a baby navigator had taken a drift sight reading as he would have black boot polish smeared around his right eye; a common jape by some of the more senior students against the junior courses! Up front, the pilot was able to keep an eye on his position by using the information received from NDBs and VORs, but these were not available to the student navigator routinely and usually only when the MAP had completely collapsed.

The Basic Navigation Course was nine months long, and for me, it started on 131 Course at 2 ANS on 7 September 1969, but lasted not more than a month initially! Attending the SMC for an aircrew medical, shortly after my arrival, the 'Doc' identified the lump in my right groin as a hernia. I too had noticed it months previously, but, as it caused me no concern or pain, had chosen to ignore it. Not so our eagle-eyed medical expert, who immediately declared me unfit for flying, grounded me and arranged a short period of residence at RAF Hospital Halton, near Aylesbury, where I was to undergo surgery to repair the hernia. In the late twentieth century, medical science and techniques had advanced significantly and such repairs were usually conducted by keyhole surgery with the patient recovering sufficiently to be discharged on the same day as the operation. Not so, however, in the dark days of the mid-twentieth century! A hernia operation then was a fairly serious affair, where an incision that required, in my case, eleven stitches to seal the skin and necessitated a ten-day sleepover under the tender mercies of the RAF PMRAFNS sisters!

The operation was due to take place on the Monday morning, so I duly reported to Halton on the Sunday afternoon and was housed suitably and comfortably in 'The Officers' Surgical Ward' – I was the youngest and most junior officer in the place and, so remote was I from my family in Scotland, received no visitors during my incarceration. However, never one to be depressed or crestfallen, I determined to make the most of my stay.

The PMRAFNS sisters were all older and more senior than me, but I was sure that I could win them over and some of the younger ones might even be winnable if I played my cards right! After all, I was 'aircrew' with an aircrew's zest for life, an innate ability to make people laugh and, inherited from my mother, a natural tendency to look on the bright side! So, having unpacked my small bag of personal belongings I climbed, as ordered, into my RAF-issue pyjamas (blue, white and grey flannel with a cord tie) and settled back on my bed to await the first contact! It was not long in coming! A very smart but burly lass, with a very starched apron and flyaway starched headdress, approached clutching a small silver tray, a loaded shaving brush and a safety razor! Instinctively I knew that this was a 'No Nonsense' moment and that submission was probably the best answer to having my nether regions shaved! Without a 'How do you do?' the covers were whipped back and I was invited to lower my pyjama bottoms. Now terrified, she must have noticed my pleading eyes, I had said not a word, because she suddenly softened, offered me the 'equipment' and told me she would be back in ten minutes. The relief I felt must have been obvious as she smiled demurely as she walked back to the nurses' station; although, thinking back after all these years, it was probably a regular joke played out in the Officers' Ward between like-minded souls! True to her word she returned at the appointed hour and, having relieved me of the equipment, thrust a magic marker in my hand and told me to write 'RIGHT' in bright red lettering on my right groin so that 'the surgeon doesn't get the wrong one'! I thought these were intelligent people who knew their left from their right, but apparently not!

The operation went without a hitch and by the Monday afternoon I was back in the ward recovering from my ordeal. The nurses were brilliant and, apart from slight nausea, I was soon on the road to recovery. When I recovered fully I became aware of a new patient who had been admitted in the bed next to me; a flight lieutenant navigator who was in Halton to have his tonsils out. He was very sociable and, delighted to discover that his new acquaintance was a U/T Nav, he soon began to regale me with tales of his time on the Vulcan and what life on a squadron was like. I was aware that he did not quite fit the mould that I had imagined an operational navigator might seem! This uneasy feeling was confirmed when he pulled back the covers from his bed in order to show me the navigator's brevet that he had stitched onto his RAF-issue pyjamas! I freaked some hours later when he got up to go to the toilet and donned his dressing gown, which also had a navigator's brevet stitched to its left breast! Just what kind of career had I chosen and could all navigators be quite as odd as this chap? My concern deepened when he called back to me, 'We all do it! You'll do it too when you graduate as a navigator!'

I next met him again some six years later when he arrived to join 12 Squadron at RAF Honington on the Buccaneer; his career there did not last long as he was subsequently taken away by 'men in white coats' after declaring to his flight commander that he would kill himself if his name appeared on the next morning's flying programme! If only they had asked me earlier I could have saved them all the time and trouble! Anyway, as this story will hopefully explain later, when you meet some of my aircrew friends, I need not have worried. His removal, however, did restore my faith in the Navigator Branch and in the 'System'!

I managed to maintain a civil if short-lived association with him in Halton before he took his leave following his, unlike mine, minor surgery. After his discharge, however, and without personal visitors it was something of a lonely existence. Nevertheless, I was grateful for the short contact and sympathy that I received from other visitors once they had been informed of my circumstance. Indeed, I became quite the most popular patient during visiting hours as they would all come to my bed to ask me how I was doing. As the days passed, however, it became apparent that the anaesthetic had had a debilitating effect on my bowel movements. I was quite constipated and, although having a pee was not a problem, anything more was out of the question! It was explained to me that I 'had to go' before I could be discharged! Remedies were explained to me and by about Day 8 post-op, the first of these was administered. Two Senna Pod laxative tablets were inserted 'PR', as my wife, the Registered Nurse, calls it, so use your imagination here folks, and I was told to make my way to the toilet in about thirty minutes when they would have had their magical effect. Always one to obey orders, I dutifully set off slowly, my groin was still quite stiff and sore, towards the toilet watched by a growing bank of concerned visitors.

I sat down to contemplate what might happen and opened my bowels only to hear the definite 'plop, plop' of two unsuccessful laxatives striking the surface of the water on their way to service the needs of a constipated mackerel somewhere downstream! Being young and naive I remained where I was imagining that something close to a new dawn would occur before very long! It did not happen; there was no new dawn for APO Herriot! Despite the discomfort of both the toilet seat and the pressure in my gut, I even managed to doze off! Suddenly, I was awakened by the voice of the senior ward sister shouting, 'Has anyone seen Pilot Officer Herriot?'

Quickly recovering my composure, I hollered, 'I'm in here!'

Promptly, I saw the bulled black shoes of the sister underneath the cubicle door, 'What on earth are you doing in there,' she asked.

'Nothing happened,' I responded. 'So I have been waiting to see…'

Before I could finish, she exasperatedly told me to wait there and she disappeared without another word. Five minutes later her hand appeared below the door clasping two more laxatives and a surgical rubber glove!

'What do you expect me to do with these?' I said, now clutching my stomach which was becoming quite tight and painful!

I kid you not, this was her response: 'Put the rubber glove on, insert the two tablets in your bottom and hold them there for thirty minutes and that will sort you out!'

Thirty minutes later I was disappointed to hear, once again, the 'plop, plop' of the laxatives hitting the surface of the water and knew, from my very recent experience, that nothing at all had been 'sorted out'. I flushed my last remnants of medical hope down the loo and started the now much slower return to my bed to the accompaniment of many 'ohs' and 'poor lad' from those visitors who had witnessed the whole horrible saga played out before them in the past two hours that constituted the visiting period that afternoon. I had been in that toilet for what had seemed like the rest of my life and nothing had changed. I felt very miserable and extremely dejected, so curled up and went to sleep!

Twenty-four hours later, a doctor appeared at my bedside during rounds and informed me that if nothing 'moved' today, then serious steps would have to be taken the following day to clear the blockage. I was too scared to ask what 'serious steps' might involve. Nothing moved that day nor did it the following morning! The following afternoon, I heard those words that I now know strike fear into the heart of the strongest man!

'We will have to give you an enema,' said the quite cheerful doctor, although he did have quite a serious expression on his face! I knew what an enema was; it had often formed the basis of schoolboy humour at the High School of Glasgow. I knew that it involved piping, jugs and warm soapy water, but I had no idea of the actual effect that it could have on the human anatomy! Consequently, I staggered along to the appointed room and to my fate under the watchful and sympathetic gaze of the knowing crowd of onlookers who were my usual concerned group of 'visitors'. The potion was duly administered, but only after a stern warning that, 'if you feel anything happening, just kick me aside and run to the 'loo'' had been given. If you have not experienced the warm glow of your bowels being filled with warm soapy water then let me tell you, you have not lived. It is not too unpleasant and, if you will excuse the pun, it is quite a fulfilling sensation.

However, there was never any chance of me suffering what must be the human bowel equivalent of a nuclear explosion during the delivery of that enema in 1969. I became aware of the nurse actually holding the last jug aloft whilst she emptied the remnants of the soapy solution into my body. 'Nothing?' she asked as she placed the jug on the table beside my head.

'Nope, not a sausage,' I joked, but she was not laughing! Having tidied myself up, I was invited to return to my bed with the encouraging words of, 'something will happen soon' ringing in my ears. The faces of the visitors and other inmates oozed sympathy as I now wandered ever slower, now with my cheeks firmly clenched, back to my bed.

Some twenty minutes later, there was a rumbling in my gut akin to what I imagine the first tremors of Vesuvius felt like to the population of Pompeii just before they were calcified into a tourist attraction for the rest of their days! I leapt from my bed and, as best I was able, positively sprinted the length of the ward to loud cheers and applause from the assembled patients and guests. I returned from the toilet area with my head held high and with a positive strut to my step; a man reborn who had just shed a very heavy load, literally! Stitches removed, I was discharged from Halton two days later and returned to Gaydon to join Yorkie on 133 Nav Course.

Before being let loose in the air, we had to spend hours and hours in the classroom understanding the principles of air navigation and becoming familiar with the tools of our trade. We had been to 'Stores' and been issued with the basic instruments that are dear to the heart of any navigator, many of which would have been second nature to any geometry student, but, as will become apparent later, not to me, as I was no mathematician during my school days! Odd, therefore, that I was now pursuing a career that had maths at its foundation! Amongst this plethora of 4H pencils, dividers, compass sets and rulers were some more exotic items such as the Douglas Protractor, which was a very sophisticated piece of plastic for measuring bearings, and back bearings, through 360°, but most unusual of all was the Dalton Computer, a circular slide rule, upon which, and based upon known inputs such as OAT, IAS and Heading, a navigator could calculate the TAS, wind vectors, drift, Mach Number and such like. Amongst much RAF memorabilia I still have in my collection the Computer Dead Reckoning, as it's technically known in the RAF, that I used on my days on the Buccaneer.

We practised MAP techniques, undertook simulator exercises, learned how to use our Nav Aids and spent interminable hours with Flight Lieutenant Stan Barrett who taught us all the radio theory, and more, that we would ever need. Stan also put us through our paces with learning, reciting and testing on the Morse code! At Nav School, students were required to be proficient in Morse and pass a test that required a 'reading speed' of eight words per minute. The Morse test was one of the most difficult exams on the basic course to pass. But pass you certainly had to, and a number of students, that included me, had to retake the test a number of times before successfully moving on. Frustrating, as I now know that I rarely had to use Morse in anger in my later career and, when I did, had plenty of time to refer to the guide on the back of an En-Route Supplement before interrogating the code being pumped out by a particular beacon or airfield ICAO identification light! Stan Barrett was not only expert in his knowledge and teaching methods, he was also one of the RAF's great characters which helped make radio theory a pleasure to learn. We undertook adventurous training in Wales, trekking across interminable stretches of moorland carrying pine poles great distances to prove our worth as leaders of men. And, of course, we drank beer!

Copious amounts of ale were consumed in the officers' mess bar at Gaydon and it seemed that, since the staff joined us in this pursuit, it was accepted as part of our new life or, maybe, we were even being given marks out of ten on our alcohol capacity! Nobody seemed to be 'chopped' following these often raucous drinking bouts, so I can only assume that drinking to excess was a requirement and was one of the training objectives stipulated in the syllabus! I cannot remember which poor student had been incarcerated in the SMC but it did seem quite appropriate and responsible during one particularly heavy drinking session to go and get him so that he could join us in the officers' mess bar. The 'patient' slept very soundly that night in the bar and was returned to the SMC the following morning before Met Brief! I suspect the fact that we did not just 'collect him', but pushed him in his bed, accompanied by all his belongings in his bedside cabinet, from the SMC down the hill, past the main gate and into the officers' mess bar for the rest of the evening was not quite appreciated by the medics and Group Captain Dawson, the station commander. However, when they did find out later the next day, nobody seemed to bat an eyelid; 'High Spirits' were alive and well in the RAF of the mid-twentieth century.

It was during one such session that I had a very interesting conversation with our course commander. Before embarking on his tour as a staff navigator at Gaydon, he had been a Transport Command navigator on an Argosy squadron. In the bar on this particular evening I had professed my long-held desire to become a fast-jet navigator, preferably in an aircraft that would take the war to the enemy and deliver bombs. I knew that my course commander was not a fan of the 'bomber boys', but was unaware that he held quite so deep-rooted prejudices against them. So it came as something of a surprise when he accosted me later in the toilet and quizzed me about my motives for wanting to 'drop bombs on people' as he put it. I soon realised that he was challenging me on the ethics of carrying out aggressive acts in time of war. I was slightly concerned that he had chosen the Gents' at Gaydon to conduct this 'interview', but was even more disturbed that an officer in the RAF, and one in such a position of influence amongst young navigators, could hold quite such strong views. Notwithstanding both the amount of alcohol that we had both consumed and that he was both my senior and my mentor, I held strong to my view that the RAF was a war-fighting service and that the first principle of such a service was to deter, by whatever means, the acts of an aggressor and defend its borders and its population when and if war came. Despite veiled but sustained pressure during the rest of the course to steer all his students towards 'heavies'[2], I managed to maintain my resolve that one day I would become a fast jet navigator.

The Flying Phase of the course commenced on 19 December 1969. The syllabus consisted of one hundred and ten hours on the Varsity followed by sixty hours on the Advanced Navigation Course, flying in the Dominie T Mk1. The two courses were, however, 'stand-alone', but the latter could only be undertaken by those who had successfully completed the basic phase. During the nine-month Basic Navigation Course, the Varsity was flown with two U/T Navs occupying the First and Second Navigator positions in the aircraft. The role of the First Nav was to complete the syllabus task using only those navigation aids permitted, whilst the Second Nav kept a 'Safety Plot' using direct fixing aids such as Gee. Occasionally, a Staff Nav would fly with the crew to both assess the work of the First Nav and monitor the 'Safety Plot'. Each student had, of course, to fly as First Nav on each of the twenty-one syllabus sorties. Second Nav sorties were, therefore, a bonus and allowed the U/T Nav to either gain a sneak preview of what was coming next or consolidate his knowledge by producing a perfect Air Plot Chart with a full Navigator's Log that demonstrated his fixing prowess to whomsoever should be interested in it. However,

---

2. A general term used to describe large fixed wing aircraft in the RAF.

since the Second Nav's work was never assessed, it was always a hope that one would first be programmed to 'follow' on a syllabus sortie rather than 'lead' and lose the opportunity of a sneak preview! I have no intention here of reciting, fix by fix, each and every mission that I flew whilst at Nav School, save to say that each placed its own demands upon me, but all were completed satisfactorily and above the pass mark required.

The Flying Phase started with a slow build-up using MAP and a Gee-based fixing process. The pressure was then increased as we were forced to abandon GEE and resort to Three Position Line Fixing using Rebecca Mk IV. Subsequently, Day Astro sorties were flown, obtaining position lines in order to familiarise us with the periscopic sextant in the air. Given the distances involved between the aircraft and the celestial body, aircraft speed, height and attitude were critical. 'Standby for Astro' was the common cry on the intercom to the pilot who would then disengage the autopilot so that he could hold the aircraft steady for the duration of the sun or star shot. Time-based calculations to compensate for movement during the 'shot' were undertaken prior to take-off, so it was imperative that 'shots' were taken at the pre-planned clock time, as even a few seconds either side rendered the resultant position line inaccurate. Movement of the Observer (MOO), the distance moved through the sky by the observer's eye during the shot, and Movement of the Body (MOB), the celestial body's relative movement in the sky during the shot, were bread and butter calculations for student navigators. It all just added more pressure on the already overworked and apprehensive First Nav.

In the latter stages of the basic course and throughout the Advanced Nav Course, position line fixing was routinely undertaken using bearings from three different sources: radio; visual; or astronomical. A Two Position Line Fix, by its very nature, is less accurate than a Three Position Line Fix. However, it is not common for three lines, once plotted on a chart, to provide the navigator with a fix where the crossing point of each line coincides at an exact and single position on the chart. The resultant triangle is thus known as a 'cocked hat'. To resolve the actual position, the navigator then has to bisect each of the three angles within the cocked hat, apply empirical correction factors to each of the three lines in order to produce the MPP of the aircraft at that time from whence he can then 'DR Ahead' and regain track as described earlier. It is also better to obtain position lines that intersect at 90°, as the more acute or obtuse the angle of intersect, the less accurate the fix would be.

So it was no easy matter learning my trade, it was complex and demanding and the enforced six-minute fixing cycle that we had to abide by made a four-hour thirty-minute sortie in a Varsity an adrenaline pumping and distressing exercise for the First Nav. I remember well being petrified every time I walked out to the aircraft to take my backward-facing seat on the left-hand side of the Varsity Nav Station. Not so, however, the task of being Second Nav, which was a breeze compared to the torture suffered when being assessed to his left. Like most piston-powered aircraft of its era, the Varsity had a distinct and unmistakable 'greasy rag' smell that filled your nostrils from about fifty feet and did nothing to calm the nerves or suppress the feeling of nausea as you climbed aboard. As the crew walked to the aircraft, each member was borne down by the equipment required to complete his task. This included, not only a bone dome and nav bag stuffed with all the documents, supplements, charts, navigational instruments and manuals required, but also a Second World War Irwin parachute harness, which restricted one's movement considerably on the ground, and a heavy parachute chest pack which was discarded once on board, but left prominent and accessible should the day ever dawn when one had to leap out the access door having first grabbed your 'chute and clamped it to the two strongly sprung clips on the chest straps of the harness. Thankfully, that day never did dawn for me, although it came close once whilst flying as Second Nav over the Bristol Channel towards the end of the Basic Nav Course.

In May 1970, Gaydon closed its doors as an RAF station for the very last time, it is now the Heritage Motor Museum, and with it so too did No 2 Air Navigation School. The Advanced Navigation School (No 1 Air Navigation School) also closed at RAF Stradishall in Cambridgeshire and students at both locations packed up their possessions and headed off to RAF Finningley in South Yorkshire, to continue their studies at the new No 6 Flying Training School, still under the command of Group Captain Dawson.

About the same time, the GEE Chain was switched off and the Varsity was re-equipped with the DECCA Navigator System as its primary navigation aid. It was a step-change from Gee, but caused many a U/T Nav heartache as they struggled to come to terms with the new charts, radio technology, and interpretation of the three dials for the Red, Green and Purple Chains, but, more importantly, trying to work out when, why and how one was supposed to interpret the fourth dial – The Spider – which had been invented purely and simply to bugger up any prospect of us getting an accurate fix at the required time. Of course, by now the senior course at Basic Nav School, we had little need of DECCA other than to carry out the Safety Plot as Second Nav – I just really did not get it!

On 7 July 1970, Mike Straw was to navigate WJ889 by the stars on our first Night Navex, with Flight Lieutenant Mike Sykes in command, from Finningley out into the North Sea, thence towards Aberdeen and back to Finningley past Edinburgh and Newcastle. The sortie was to be flown at medium altitude and at an airspeed of 180 knots, a bonus for a baby navigator, as anything divisible by sixty is helpful in terms of calculating miles flown per minute! My role in this affair was minimal as all I had to do was master the use of DECCA for the first time as Mike's Second Nav! The planning and briefing were uneventful. I had refreshed myself on the required DECCA fixing cycle, drawn the route on my Mercator Navigation Chart and produced a suitable Flight Plan. I had also checked all Mike's MOO and MOB calculations for his Astro fixes and reassured him that he was 'on song' and that the sortie would be a breeze! The crew coach pulled up outside the Ops Block and we were driven, like true Bomber Command heroes before us, out to WJ889. It was late in the evening, but not quite dark as we approached our trusty steed. The Varsity was already connected to its generator and lights glowed through the square windows of its fuselage. We lumbered from the bus onto the dispersal wearing our Irwin parachute harnesses, each nav weighed down by his bulging Nav Bag and his helmet and oxygen mask! Mike also lugged the quite heavy periscopic sextant that he would eventually ram into its location in the upper fuselage just ahead of the navigator station. Each of the five aircrew – we had a Screen Navigator – also carried a box of aircrew rations to sustain us on what was planned to be a four-hour night flight into the skies of Northern Britain. We climbed on a heading of 045° out of Finningley for 63 nm towards Flamborough Head. Given the Super Pig's poor rate of climb, it took us rather longer than that first leg to reach our cruising height of 17,000 feet.

Airspace generally is divided into below 24,500 feet, where Quadrantal FLs are flown, or above 24,500 feet where Semicircular FLs operate. Thus Basic Nav course students had to learn the principle of the former, whilst Advanced Nav course students, flying in the Dominie, followed the Semicircular principle. These principles are mandated by ICAO and are designed to facilitate safe separation between aircraft that are flying with the altimeter set to the Standard Pressure Setting of 1013mb rather than the QNH or a QFE, and who are operating under IFR conditions. The required altitude is ordered by the ATC agency providing a radar service and varies dependent upon the heading, by quadrant or semicircle, being flown. In Quadrantal terms, aircraft flying a heading between 0° and 089° are allocated 'Odds'; those between 090° and 179° 'Odds + 500 feet'; 180° and 269° 'Evens'; and those between 270° and 359° 'Evens + 500 feet'. All more 'stuff' for us would-be navigators to absorb and put into practice! All would change when we moved forward to fly the Dominie when 'Odds' covered the headings 0° to 179° and 'Evens' matched those headings from 180° to 359°.

Overhead Flamborough, having taken a DECCA Fix to ensure his position, Mike called for the captain to turn onto 001° towards our next turning point abeam Aberdeen. The leg was 180 nm long and, at 180 knots, would take exactly one hour to complete. Mike settled down to prepare himself for his first Astro Three Line Position Fix which would happen some twenty minutes into the leg. Meanwhile, I took responsibility for ensuring that we remained on the fuel plan line whilst struggling to work out just how Mike had managed to gain the DECCA Fix on the four spinning dials in front of us. I could see and understand the Red, Green and Purple indicators, but what, please somebody remind me, was I supposed to do with that bloody spider that was so essential to the accuracy of the fix!

Before I knew it, Mike was struggling past me with his sextant and ramming it into its aperture above our heads.

'Navigator to Captain, Steady for Astro,' he instructed over the intercom.

Mike Sykes responded with, 'Steady for Astro', as he slipped WJ889's autopilot to neutral and flew the aircraft manually for the duration of the fix.

After some minutes, I heard, 'Astro complete', which received an echo response from Mike Sykes as he re-engaged the autopilot and relaxed back into his seat to enjoy the mood and banter with his co-pilot on a sortie that was for them quite routine. Not so for those in the sweat box down the back.

Mike started to plot his fixes on his chart whilst, at the same time, he entered all the necessary details on his Navigator's Log. I was impressed with his work and contented myself in the knowledge that his progress on the course had been solid and that if I never managed to take a DECCA Fix that night it would not matter as he was bound to keep us 'on course' and 'on time'. I was grateful that the Screen Nav had taken himself below and was not hovering over either of our shoulders!

There was a sudden expletive from my left as the First Nav began to plot his position lines on the chart. I looked over to see what the problem might be and was surprised to see that the first two plots were not quite what he, or I, had anticipated! The first line ran quite happily down the North Sea almost parallel to track and quite adjacent to it. However, the second plot was far removed to the west and happened quite neatly to run down The Minch, which separates the Inner Hebrides from the Outer Hebrides. Mike was in mild panic and, whilst he was plotting the final position line, begged me to get a DECCA Fix in order to allow him to, 'illegally', have some idea of where we actually were. Whilst I watched 'The Spider's' erratic movements I was aware of my buddy holding his head in despair as he gazed at his final plot line, which just happened to run along the English Channel! His cocked hat had quite literally encompassed virtually all of the United Kingdom – this was going to be one hell of an MPP! I'm afraid I was not much use to him and for the first time in our flying careers we were temporarily unsure of our position; we were, in fact, lost!

Things improved from that moment on, but did deteriorate some two hours later whilst we were heading towards the English border and home to Finningley. I had mastered the DECCA fixing cycle, with some assistance from the Screen, and was content that we were heading in generally the right direction and not too far removed from the required track past Edinburgh. We were just preparing for the final Astro Fix when I heard through my earphones the dulcet tone of Mike Sykes' voice:

'Captain to Second Nav, listen up on UHF.'

Acknowledging his call, I selected the UHF button on my intercom box and listened into the conversation that was taking place between Mike and the controller at Border Radar.

'Are you aware that you are about to enter the Edinburgh Terminal Control Area?' asked the controller.

'Are we?' responded Mike.

'You are, turn right forty degrees onto one nine zero degrees and maintain Flight Level.'

'Second Nav, do you have any idea where we are?' Mike demanded.

Without wishing to display my inabilities I looked quickly at my chart, estimated where we must have been to earn an admonishment onto one nine zero and replied, 'Yeah, Captain, hold this for four minutes and then turn left onto one three zero back towards track.'

Some ten minutes later, I was concerned for my future when I heard the same voice from Border Radar state, 'You are now heading for Otterburn Range!'

Sykes responded with his estimate of what heading was required to avoid it, only to be given the instruction from Border of, 'Maintain Heading, the range is actually closed and it's full of Varsities already!'

After three hours and fifty minutes we landed back in the early hours at Finningley. Mike and I were both chastened by our experience and feared for our future, but, since my progress on that trip was not being assessed, nothing more was said about my inabilities with DECCA and I continued with the Night Phase and successfully completed my own first Night Navex without a hiccough!

Some two weeks later, on the twentieth, I became involved in my first real aircraft emergency. I was again Second Nav, but had, by then, mastered DECCA. The sortie was the final Night Navex and was designed to test one's overall capabilities as an Astro Navigator. It was the penultimate assessed sortie on the basic course. The route to be flown from Finningley was out to the south-west via South Wales, the Scilly Isles, with a return through Cornwall, Devon and the Midlands. The Screen was a flight lieutenant by the name of Marsden who had, reputedly, played rugby for the RAF and had an aggressive manner towards students to match! Whilst heading for the Scillies on 220° over the Bristol Channel, a sudden call from the aircraft captain came over our headphones: 'Starboard Engine Fire! Give me a steer and distance to the most suitable diversion, Second Nav!'

We were just past Lundy Island and, looking ahead on my chart, I concluded that RAF St Mawgan, a Master Diversion Airfield (MDA) in Cornwall, would fit the bill nicely! 'Come left one nine five for St Mawgan; distance forty-two nautical miles!' I responded quickly and the aircraft immediately started to bank as it turned towards our diversion. Marsden, who had dozed off whilst scanning *Playboy* on the comfortable lounger in the Bomb Aimer's position, suddenly found himself thrust awake. He came charging up the few steps from below and demanded to know what was going on. Calmly I explained that we had had an engine fire that was now extinguished and we were heading, on diversion, to St Mawgan. Marsden, a strong heavyweight at the best of times, dragged me from my seat and demanded to know where we were so that he could take control of the situation. In response to his, 'Where are we?' I drew my hand generally across the area of the Bristol Channel on the map and repaired below to find the *Playboy*! Unfortunately, in the 1970s, there were rather too many 'Marsdens' within the RAF's training set-up but, thankfully, none managed ever to find a chink in my armour that might have diverted me from my chosen path in life.

Success at Basic Nav School was assured after I completed, successfully, the final four sorties that included two lying in the Bomb Aimer's position doing visual low-level navigation. That was my first taste of what was to become my bread and butter in my later career. With 130 hours and 25 minutes on the Varsity under my belt, Yorkie and I progressed to the Advanced Nav Course and to the Dominie T Mk1.

The Dominie was a completely different kettle of fish to the Varsity. It was, in effect, a Hawker Siddeley 125 Business Jet equipped with a navigation suite on the rear bulkhead. It had a maximum cruise speed of 284 knots and was capable of flying as high as 42,000 feet. Equipped with two Rolls Royce Viper jet engines that each produced 3310lbs of static thrust, it was a quantum leap from the Varsity and, with its much greater cruising speed, ensured that U/T Navs could not become complacent as distances travelled over a 6-minute fixing cycle, and errors accrued, were much greater than had been previously experienced. With a wingspan that almost exactly matched its length, just over 47 feet, it was an agile aircraft that would expose many frailties amongst its students. Our course commander for the Advanced Phase was an excellent officer, Flight Lieutenant D.W. Gerrard, who was known as Gerry throughout the RAF. A bachelor, fresh from a tour as a 'Kipper Fleet'[3] navigator on the Shackleton MR2, Gerry knew how to party, knew how to drink and knew how to get the best out of his charges. He also drove a Jaguar XK120, so he was both a man to look up to and a man for the ladies! On average, only eight years older than most of his students, Gerry was like-minded and far more understanding than his predecessor on the basic course. As a result, the Advanced Nav Course was much less stressful than the period spent previously and, although we had to work hard and pass each of the ten syllabus sorties that we flew as First Nav, there always seemed to be time to party in the Finningley bar with Gerry in the lead. The three months passed far too quickly and as the final weeks – and probable success – loomed large, we began to feel comfortable enough to start looking forward to the final flying exercises, which would see us embark on our first overseas Navex and a weekend Ranger[4] to Gibraltar.

Apart from the rather too often weekend hangover, after a particularly energetic Friday Happy Hour, little of significance happened during the advanced course. I have to confess, however, that it was during my time at Finningley that, after a few mid-week beers on a Wednesday evening, I was surprised to pull back the curtains of my room in the officers' mess on the Thursday to discover that a hangar that had been clearly visible the previous day was now but a shell, having burnt to the ground! My appearance subsequently in the corridor outside my room earned me derision and abuse from my fellow students, who looked as if they had been up for hours and were more unkempt in their appearance than any officer should be before breakfast. It was not uncommon to suffer friendly banter on route to the showers, but on that morning there was more of an edge to it than usual. Justified it was, nevertheless, when I discovered that they had all responded to the very early morning and universal call-out for all personnel to rush to the hangar to assist with the extraction and rescue of the Varsities and Dominies therein!

In researching the detail of the fire for this memoir, I was disappointed to discover that there was little reference 'on-line' in the various Finningley archives. Wikipedia quaintly describes the detail as *'a Varsity aircraft caught fire in one of the hangars and subsequently destroyed 2 other aircraft by setting them ablaze'*. The actual truth was that a disenchanted airman, who had chosen to show his embitterment by defecating in Group Captain Dawson's garden, chose to respond to his subsequent punishment by breaking into the hangar to set alight a small privately-owned aircraft that he had pulled under the wing of a Varsity.

Alcohol is an excellent relaxant and one of nature's greatest soporific nectars, and on that night at Finningley it allowed me to have an excellent night's slumber. Other than my mates, nobody noticed that I was not there and nothing was ever said!

Friday, 4 December 1970 dawned, to find eight soon-to-be navigators feverishly calculating headings and groundspeeds that would take four Dominies from

---

3. Generic term used to describe the aircraft, crews and squadrons of No 18 Group, tasked with Anti-Submarine Warfare and Search and Rescue Operations.
4. An overseas training flight designed to provide aircrew with experience of 'foreign' ATC procedures and autonomy of operations away from home base.

Finningley to Gibraltar via St Mawgan to refuel and thence to Porto, in Portugal, to refuel and take lunch. With Flying Officer Parker in command and Yorkie by my side we were soon passing the top of climb and heading in a generally south-west direction towards the sun. I had been given responsibility for the legs from Finningley to St Mawgan and Porto to Gibraltar, whilst Yorkie would take us from St Mawgan to Porto. After four hours and forty minutes in the air, we successfully passed through the Straits of Gibraltar and, avoiding Spanish airspace so as not to inflame their political claim to 'The Rock' further, slipped onto Runway 09 at 'Gib'. With the aircraft safely bedded down we took ourselves off to the officers' mess and Happy Hour at RAF North Front, which would be our home for the next sixty hours.

In terms of tales to relate, it was a fairly uneventful weekend. With each of us having to undertake an assessed sortie back to Finningley on the Monday we felt less than compelled to keep up with Gerry on the Sunday, but had given him a good race on the Saturday evening which found us all in the Gibraltar Casino by the early hours of the Sabbath. There was, and I hope still is, something quintessentially British about Gibraltar. It has, much to Spanish disgust, been a British Crown Colony since 1830. Its common border with Spain was closed by the Spaniards in the 1950s, as were Spanish air routes to any British aircraft, military or civil, whose final destination was on the 6,000 feet runway that bisected the road between 'The Rock' and the rest of mainland Europe. The border was officially reopened in 1985, but despite the Spanish influence that that has unfortunately brought, the people of Gibraltar stoically resist all Spanish attempts to deny them their right to be British citizens. Gibraltar will feature further in this tale, so with NFTR it is time to return to Finningley and our graduation from No 6 Flying Training School.

The Monday dawn was met by our intrepid aviators again busily plotting the required headings and ground speeds back to base via Istres in France. Yorkie was to take the final leg into Finningley and I had responsibility for the outbound leg from 'Gib'. After two and a half hours in the hot seat, we landed safely in France and I happily handed over the First Nav's seat to Pete to take us home, with me operating the DECCA for the last time as a student Nav.

There was a week allocated in the syllabus for tidying, rehearsing and completing the necessary administration that would take us to our Graduation Ceremony on 16 December. Most importantly, there was the fretful experience of pondering one's position in the 'pecking order' of the course results. We had previously been taken to RAF Scampton to view the Vulcan B2 and learn about life as a V-Bomber navigator. Having climbed up the ladder by the nose wheel of the Vulcan and entered the black hole that was the home to the three rear crew, Nav Plotter, Nav Radar and Air Electronics Officer, I had determined that the last aircraft that I wanted to fly was the Vulcan! Those who came lower down the course pecking order were virtually guaranteed a Vulcan slot and so I determined to work extra hard and, hopefully, secure a life that did not involve working in a black hole, facing rearwards and without an ejection seat. We were all entitled to fill out a 'dream sheet' of what we would like to fly, three choices, and the student who came top of the course was guaranteed his first choice if a slot on the OCU was available. My 'dream sheet' read: First – Buccaneer; Second – Phantom; Third – Canberra. I was determined to fly Fast Jets!

On Results Day, I was delighted to discover that I had come third on the course and waited with baited breath to hear what my destiny was to be. Flight Lieutenant Al Blackwell had come first and had requested Britannias back at Brize Norton where he had latterly been an Air Traffic Controller. Flying Officer Dave Baker, an ex-airman, had asked for Phantoms as his first choice. However, on that morning nobody knew what was available or what the outcome might be. At 1600hrs Gerry Gerrard returned to Finningley with the news. Blackwell got Britannias and Baker did get Phantoms. With my heart beginning to sag, there surely could not be a 100% top three! I held my breath until Gerry put me out of my misery. The top three were exactly as our dream-sheets had requested. I had got the only slot on Buccaneers – I was to be the first-ever first tourist navigator to be trained by the RAF at the newly-formed 237 OCU at RAF Honington in Suffolk. The dream had come true, I had managed to raise my game at Nav School and, by good fortune, a Buccaneer slot had coincided with my graduation from Finningley. Yorkie was posted to Victors at RAF Marham; Bob King, who eventually came to the Buccaneer, was posted to Canberras; Dick Hansen went off to fly Gannets with the Royal Navy, with a promise of a tour on AEW Shackletons afterwards at RAF Lossiemouth; Roger Harper was posted to the Vulcan OCU to become a Nav Plotter; and Brian Hall went to the Navigation Bombing School at RAF Lindholme to learn the intricacies of the Vulcan's H2S radar system. We were not all ecstatic about the outcome, but I was over the moon and, as I hope this story will prove later, my posting to 237 OCU was to shape the rest of my life both in the RAF and subsequently beyond. Sadly for Mike Straw his efforts had been in vain, but he subsequently graduated from 135 Course.

The Graduation Ceremony took place in the Main Briefing Room at Finningley on Wednesday, 16 December; nine days before Christmas in 1970. As had happened when I gained my commission, my parents travelled by train from Scotland to be amongst the gathering of proud onlookers. The Reviewing Officer was Air Vice-Marshal Ivor Broom, CBE, DSO, DFC, AFC, RAF, the Air Officer Commanding No 11 Group, and a distinguished and decorated Second World War bomber pilot. After a short introduction, the eight RAF navigators stepped forward individually to receive their brevets from AVM Broom.

It had been a long and arduous fourteen months since I had arrived at Gaydon, but I was now a qualified RAF navigator with a brevet pinned to my left breast to prove it!

Chapter Two

Family Hold Back!

Whilst I accept that pro-lifers will say that life starts at the moment of conception, for me it started with my birth at 32 Lamington Road, Cardonald, Glasgow. The date was 26 May 1949 and, my mother told me, I took my first breath at twenty minutes past ten on that Thursday in late spring! It was an arrival that came as no surprise to me as I had been building up to it for about nine months, but, it would seem, it came as a complete surprise to both my parents.

Whilst some might say otherwise, I am not suggesting for a second that I was created by an immaculate conception. Nor, for that matter, am I suggesting that my mother lacked the intellect to realise that she was pregnant. Indeed, she had definitely had experience of the latter with my elder siblings and, knowing them as I have done now for over sixty years; I can assure you that if there had been anything immaculate about them I would have identified it by now!

It was nothing simpler than the fact that neither of my parents had thought or agreed on a suitable name for me by the time I was born and so I was known as 'No Name' for nine days until, I can only imagine, they decided that they had to come up with something if only to avoid prosecution for failing to register my birth! So, by the time of that event on 3 June 1949, I was David Rodger. The Scots, by tradition, have a habit of honouring a paternal grandmother or ancestor by giving a newborn infant a maiden name from that root. My elder brother Michael had been endowed with that of a paternal great grandmother, 'Ferme', to follow his William Michael. In the case of my elder sister Judith my parents did not follow tradition and labelled her 'Margaret' in celebration of our maternal grandmother. In my case, I was privileged to be given the maiden name of my paternal grandmother's family who lived in the Borders. David was chosen because my mother liked it and held affection for her Uncle David, her father's elder brother and a solicitor in Glasgow; perhaps she had high hopes for me in that regard.

My parents met in Tain, Ross and Cromarty, during the Second World War. My mother, the youngest of three girls, lived with her family in the school house attached to Tain Primary School on Knockbreck Road where her father was the headmaster. My father, an only child and not a native of the area, had taken a post with The National Commercial Bank of Scotland in Tain and was living in the Balnagowan Hotel at the time. They married in the Bath Hotel, Glasgow, on 20 February 1940 and within two years Michael was born at Kirksheaf Cottage in Tain, the then family home, with Judith following some two years later in October 1944. However, in 1948 the family moved from Tain to Cardonald in Glasgow, following a transfer for my father to join the Paisley branch of the bank.

I have forever been slightly disappointed that, unlike my elder siblings, I have not been able to call myself a Highlander! There is something quite romantic and at the same time sinister about that appellation that stirs my blood. I do not mean to offend the people of the city of my birth. Glasgow is a fair city and, in the twenty-first century, a prosperous and bright one. However, when I was growing up in the 1950s and 1960s, Glasgow was a dark and intimidating place to live.

My memory of the city centre as a young boy is one of damp, dank streets with an all-pervading smog that filled my nostrils as I made my way from school to catch the train home to the suburbs where we lived. As we walked from the High School, on Elmbank Street, to the Central Station, it was not uncommon to see groups of 'winos' drinking their bottles wrapped in a brown paper bag to overcome the 'no drinking in the streets' laws; poverty and alcoholism were the sad face of Glasgow. In the 1960s Glasgow was renowned throughout Britain as the country's knife capital. There were many teenage gangs roaming the streets, the most infamous being The Tongs, whose slogan of 'Tongs ya Bass' was daubed on many a city wall. To me the city was blighted. It always seemed to be damp, you never saw the sky through the smog and, because of its latitude you rarely saw the sun in winter, apart from through the windows of your classroom. We went to school in the dark and by the time we were released we went home in the dark!

Nevertheless, I am a Glaswegian and a Glaswegian I will always be! And, in many respects, the city is my root and my soul, even if I have been blessed with the soft lilt accent that comes from being the product of a Highland lass and a Borders lad.

But I'd rather have been a Highlander!

Early days in 32 Lamington Road were idyllic. My mother had formed a good and, what was to become, life-long friendship with Sheila MacLachlan, the wife of one of our two local GPs. By their contact, I formed a wonderful friendship with Iain, Sheila's eldest son, and his younger brother Roy. The friendship lasted long after our subsequent move away from Cardonald and was fortified when I eventually joined him at the High School of Glasgow. Iain and I were never out of each other's company as toddlers. We were playing either at his house, 2160 Paisley Road West, or at mine. To a 5-year-old it seemed to be a time of constant fun, exploration and excitement. There were no barriers to our enjoyment and few restrictions placed upon us, although we were not, at that age, allowed to wander much beyond the garden of either house and only to go between numbers 32 and 2160 as quickly as possible!

I lost contact with Iain MacLachlan after we both left school and I joined the RAF. He went to Medical School at Glasgow University and, like his father before him, eventually qualified as a doctor. Sadly, and undiagnosed for a significant number of years, Iain was harbouring a malignant brain tumour that eventually took his life on 14 July 2003; he was 54 years of age!

Other than my memories of Iain MacLachlan, my early life in Lamington Road is a bit of a blur and, to be honest, I lived in that house for so few years of my early life that I am surprised that I can remember anything about it at all. Moreover, the house was so similar in layout to our subsequent home in Shawlands that the two homes of my childhood have, to some extent, blended into one. There are, of course, a number of events that do still feature in my early memory, not least of which, as it is for most people, was my first day at school. My time at the High School of Glasgow will follow later, but save to say at this stage that, unlike Iain, I did not 'hit the mark' with David Lees, the rector, when my mother took me to his office to undertake the entrance exam for entry as a 5-year-old in September 1954.

So my school life started at Cardonald Primary School, forever after in the Herriot household referred to as Angus Oval, which was the street upon which it sat. On this inauspicious day, when I was for the first time forsaken by my mother, I felt temporarily unsure of my position! I cried from the moment it became clear that I was to be abandoned and was, I am told, quite inconsolable. Fortunately a young lady by the name of Louise rescued me from my emotions and, taking my hand and by clasping my head to her bosom, managed to stop the flood of tears. Like me, Louise was a fellow 5-year-old abandonee, but she was either very used to this type of happening or was made of sterner stuff than I was!

I stayed at Angus Oval for just one year and have virtually no recall of the place, my classmates, or the teacher. By the time my younger sister Fiona was born the following January, we were already starting to prepare for our move to the upmarket 'Waverley Park' area of Shawlands on the southern edge of the city. Fiona Elizabeth McCracken, for that was her handle, was named McCracken after our maternal grandfather. Now if Fiona thought she had been lumbered with a mouthful on birth, she could not blame our parents when she eventually chose as her husband a man who went by the name of McCusker!

The birth of a child in any family is a wondrous event and I recall only too vividly the emotion that I experienced when my own children, Christopher and Sarah, were born in the late 1970s. Well that's not strictly true in Sarah's case as I fainted at just about the *moment critique*! This I put down to having been laid flat for two weeks with a spinal compression fracture until the moment when my first wife announced, 'This is it'! Notwithstanding my inability to remain upright on that occasion, there is nothing in life that brings so much emotion and happiness to a man as the feelings that are exposed when he meets his own children for the very first time.

Like any 5-year-old in 1955 I was intrigued by the bump on my mother's tummy and the talk of 'new additions' that constantly percolated the conversations at home prior to Fiona's birth. In the days before this mystical event, the regular comings and goings of Doctor Forsyth to my mother's bedroom upstairs, and the arrival of the nice lady with the smart blue uniform and frilly hat were more than a young fellow's curiosity could bear. All the euphemistic talk of storks and babies meant nothing to my tender ears. I wanted to know exactly when this 'baby' would arrive and how soon afterwards I would be allowed to play with it! With Michael being seven years older than me, he had not really been a playmate for me in my early years and Judith, being distinctly disgruntled that I had been born a boy rather than the playmate sister that she had hoped for, was not ever in a mood for joining in any of my childish 5-year-old games! Frankly, I was not bothered whether the new baby was a boy or a girl. I just hoped that it would want to play in my mud piles in the garden rather than with either of my two elder siblings. I was, frustratingly, excluded from Fiona's birth moment, but I do have a distinct memory of being invited to my mother's bedroom shortly afterwards to be introduced to the 'new arrival' and being asked by Doctor Forsyth if I had been hoping for a sister – a strange question, I guess, because that's what I had got and there was not much I could do about it at the age of five, or at any other stage in my life come to think of it. Anyway, the sex of my new sibling was not important to me as long as no matter what this smiling pink blob was doing right now it just needed to be ready to dig mud and kick a ball by the morning. Fiona's arrival was a blessed relief for Judith, however, as the family was now balanced with 'two of each' and she had, at last, got somebody she could play dolls with and banish forever her nagging thought of being in the minority!

The move to 148 Kenilworth Avenue took place not long after Fiona's birth, and with it I bade farewell to Angus Oval, the kind-hearted Louise and the embarrassment of my first day at school. Waverley Park, as the sandstone frieze announces to those arriving at these large, late-Victorian, semi-detached, sandstone villas in the leafy suburbs of Glasgow, pays homage in its road names to the novels of one of Scotland's greatest writers, Sir Walter Scott. In purchasing our new home I suspect that the key issue for my father, who was an avid fan of the good Sir Walter and also one who had read all of his twenty-five Waverley Novels, was in that name – Waverley Park. My father's personal collection of the magnificent Waverley Novels adorns the top shelf of my study today. It was certainly a very pleasant suburb of the city and the neighbours were all well-set, middle-class people who enjoyed a level of comfort if not great wealth. Moreover, it was a safe haven where children could play in the street in what now seems to have been the less-traumatic 1950s.

I have vivid and happy memories of our life in Kenilworth Avenue. My parents were not wealthy and had paid a king's ransom – something in the order of £1500 – for the house in 1955. It nearly broke them doing it too. My father was a bank teller by profession and had turned down promotion and manager responsibility throughout his career to avoid further moves, thereby ensuring a settled home life for his children. I recall my mother telling me that he had earned not much more than £100 per annum at one stage of his career and I know for a fact that they both went without a great deal in order to ensure that we did not. The house had three bedrooms upstairs as well as a bathroom and an airing cupboard. The rather large downstairs accommodation consisted of a sizeable lounge that looked across the front garden and was known as 'the front room', immediately behind it was another sitting room that looked out the back which was quaintly, and not surprisingly if you have been following the story, referred to as 'the back room'. The dining room was also to the rear of the property with a single-storey kitchen adjoining it. A fourth bedroom was located in the same single-storey block as the kitchen, with access through a short passage under the stairs. There were two under-stair cupboards which were used as storage and, in the case of the larger, it was here that one could locate and use the large, black, Bakelite telephone. Having the phone locked away in a cupboard had many advantages, principle of which was that my father could not always easily get hold of you by the scruff of the neck when, in his opinion, you had 'been on long enough'! It also permitted a degree of privacy for those members of the family who wished to discuss illicit details of their relationships without parents overhearing or, worse, intervening. My parents occupied the master bedroom at the front and Judith, by now eleven, occupied the small bedroom that faced Kenilworth Avenue. Michael and I shared the back bedroom and Fiona had the room downstairs. It was a perfect family home with fun, laughter and music of all varieties playing regularly.

Until my father decided to install night storage heaters there were only coal fires to warm the home. Hot water was available either by the back boiler situated behind the fire in the dining room or, in the event of the fire going out – a regular occurrence – from an immersion heater in the airing cupboard which, because of the running costs, was very limited in the time allowed to heat the water. So we had a bath once a week, whether we needed it or not, and we invariably got dried in front of the dining room fire as the rest of the house was too cold to endure in a semi-naked state.

My mother adopted a hair-raising method of lighting fires in the house! Rather than adopt the Boy Scout approved method of paper, kindling and coal, with ignition achieved by rubbing two sticks together, my mother would use her well-practised cross-fertilisation technique! Invariably, when a fire was required in another room, she would approach the smouldering fire in the dining room armed only with an old shovel that showed marked wear and tear around its leading edge from previous abuses. With a holler around the house of 'Everybody Stand Back!' she would scoop out the burning embers from the one fire and stagger through the house to the unlit fire in another room, leaving a smoke trail hovering behind her and, very often, burning embers on the parquet floor in the hallway between the two rooms! With both fires now struggling for their very existence, damp coal from the bunker outside would be ferried to each, which only succeeded in smothering both. Consequently, sheets of *The Glasgow Herald* would be stripped off and held over the fire to seal it, thereby making a back draught that would ensure that a flame would eventually flicker and the fire recover. It was not a good idea to be in the house at the time as it was usually a case of 'all hands to the pump' to either scoop up fallen embers from the floor, man the back draught, or 'bring more coal'! All too often, a pair of inexperienced and childlike hands would be caught out as the page of *The Glasgow Herald* combusted before your very eyes and had to be ushered up the chimney to avoid the subsequent conflagration of the whole house and the burning of all its occupants to a cinder!

If you were fortunate enough to be born above the poverty line, which we were just, the 1950s and 1960s were a good time to be a young boy in Scotland. However, it was a hard struggle for my parents bringing up four children on a bank teller's salary. Nothing was ever bought if it was not needed. If something could be made, it was made rather than bought. Money was never ever wasted, which is why my mother was quite aghast when, having tasked me to buy myself a pair of cricket boots for school, I came home with a pair of doeskin boots rather than the much cheaper canvas type! I do not think my father was ever made aware of my largesse with his money on that occasion!

If you wanted a bike, you had to wait until your birthday and you could bet your last ha'penny that, if you did receive one, you were never the first person to have owned that particular bike! When we wanted an electric train set, Michael and I had to share it and again we were not its first owners. When Fiona wanted a dolls' house for her Christmas, and when she still believed in Father Christmas, my father not only made it, but made all the furniture and decor that went inside it! Having said that, my father was a dab hand at DIY. He had to be because my parents could never have afforded to pop out to B&Q – had it existed in those days – and they certainly never had the money to 'get a man in'. My parents could never have been described as squanderers and we were taught the value of money from a very early age! My mother was a fantastic baker; she had to be with four hungry mouths to feed. There would always be something baking in the oven or boiling on the stove. Shortbread, sponge cakes, Dundee Cake, tablet – we Herriots were encouraged to have a sweet tooth. There was a special cake tin in the kitchen with an 'in-case cake' therein. It was never eaten unless it was going stale and would have to be thrown out. It was there 'in case' somebody came to call! If guests arrived unexpectedly, they were always invited to stay for tea. If invited guests were staying, and we had a lot of passing musicians that took advantage of my father's classical musical leanings and our hospitality, there would never be enough to go around as the budget never increased no matter who was visiting. Gathered round the table for High Tea, I do not ever recall having 'Dinner', my mother would enter from the kitchen bearing the culinary delights whilst announcing to the assembled throng 'FHB'! I know not what our guests thought of this announcement, but I know that each of the four children were well aware of what that simple three-letter acronym meant; the budget had failed once again and there was not enough food to go round – Family Hold Back!

We never starved; there was always plenty of food on the table. Always just enough to satisfy, but rarely enough for 'seconds'. If we had toast for breakfast or bread at tea time, we were allowed butter or jam, but never both – the budget would not stretch that far! There were no fizzy drinks and rarely orange squash available during a meal. If you wanted a drink there was nothing wrong with 'corporation lemonade'[1] my father would declare – it came from the tap in the kitchen and was free! If one of the children was to ask for seconds and not much was available, my mother would say, 'Those who ask don't get!' To which Michael would always respond, 'Those who don't ask, don't want!' My mother was a good cook, although she did have a tendency to overcook vegetables, as I think most Mums did in those days. If there was a hole in a sock she would darn it, if you needed a jumper for school she would knit it. If you needed new school uniform, the shorts and blazer would both be purchased with growth in mind! There was no television allowed. Well not until 1968 when Judith, who had previously represented Scotland in the 1966 Commonwealth Games in Jamaica, was selected as a member of the Great Britain Foil Team for that year's Olympic Games in Mexico. I did not disavow my father of the fact that he might be able to watch her in action 'if only we had a television'. Before that epiphanic moment, evenings were spent sitting in the dining room doing homework, or idling, whilst listening to Radio Luxembourg on the wireless. Meanwhile, my father would

---

1. Tap water.

be in the back room listening to his classical music on his Grundig Gramophone – 'you can't play pop music on that, you'll damage the needle!' – or recording himself or his quartet on his Grundig reel-to-reel tape recorder during practice for their next concert. Both Judith and Fiona represented Scotland at sword fencing, and Judith won significant medals in an international career that culminated in a Team 'Silver' in the Women's Foil event at the 1970 Commonwealth Games in Edinburgh.

Centuries have passed since young men were dispatched aboard His Majesty's sailing ships as cabin boys. Indeed, by the time of my birth, seventy-four years had passed since an Act of Parliament had stopped the Victorians from sending young boys up the inside of a chimney to sweep it! Although slave labour was no longer tolerated in the 1960s, in the Herriot household a strong work ethic was encouraged and by the age of eight, like it or not, I was being roused very early on a Sunday morning by Michael to assist him with his paper round. My reward for this filial support was a copy of a *Beano* or *Dandy* that he would purchase from the half-crown that John Ferguson paid him for his endeavours each week; my endeavour was to go to all the top-floor flats on Tantallon Road whilst Michael sped about at lower levels delivering the news to the ground-dwelling residents! The day soon dawned, however, when, having been pulled from my deep slumber, I would depart to Ferguson's paper shop on Kilmarnock Road to do the round alone whilst Michael took forward his new passion at Cowglen Golf Course. On the first morning of this, my now solo duty, the staff of the paper shop dutifully stuffed my bag with the full round of papers and helped me pull it onto my shoulder. Still only eight, and built like a string bean, I suddenly found myself anchored to the floor, but too embarrassed to ask for help. Whilst I tried to struggle towards my bike with what seemed like the complete weekend output of Fleet Street around my neck, the rest of the staff busied themselves with the next batch of papers that were to be taken by the subsequent boy in line. They were somewhat surprised, therefore, when they turned round to load him to find Herriot Junior cemented to the shop floor, and going nowhere in a hurry! So began ten very happy years working for John Ferguson as a paper boy in Shawlands. Having started out as the most junior boy in the shop, I progressed over the years to become, by the age of eighteen, the senior dispatcher with responsibility not only for getting the news out on the streets, but also for unlocking the shop and manning the counter whilst John Ferguson chivvied his younger employees to speed their delivery. Rewards with John Ferguson for dedicated service were many and he would often take me sailing in his yacht on the Clyde as long as I had made myself available to help him scrub barnacles off its hull during the winter months! Eventually, rather than scrape hulls in the yard at Helensburgh or pull sheets on the Clyde, John Ferguson purchased an old converted fishing smack that we would take to the high seas on Sunday afternoons after our toil. Paid employment was, however, not restricted to delivering papers. My mother routinely shopped at Barrs' Grocer Shop on Pollokshaws Road and, by the time I was fifteen, I had secured a Saturday job behind the counter there working under the guidance of Willie, the manager, and his able assistant Nora. It was under Willie's tutelage that I began to learn the skills of: slicing cooked meat – 'an ye hae tae mine yer fingurs, Davy'; weighing dry foods accurately – 'Davy, man, yer losin me munny wi yer largesse!' and food hygiene – 'noo wash yer hans, laddie, afore ya touch the cheeses!' Strangely, there was never a warning 'tae wash yer hans' before touching any other provisions. It was also in Barrs' Grocers Shop that I had my first rebuttal in love. I had noticed the stunningly beautiful 'Daughter of the Manse'[2] on Pollokshaws Road previously and was delighted if ever I managed to beat Willie or Nora to the counter when she came into the shop. To my burgeoning post-pubescent youthful desires, she was everything that a young man wanted in a woman and I had heard the rumour at school about just how liberated vicars' daughters were supposed to be. She was also not averse to smiling demurely at my subtle attempts to woo her. After several encounters around the cheese board I plucked up the nerve to ask her out and was delighted to receive positive encouragement, if not a definite affirmative and a time and place set; she, being similarly fifteen years old, would have to check with her mother! I carried on with my work that Saturday morning with much vigour and a spring in my step as I awaited her return and a firm engagement. I did not have to wait long. It took her just fifteen minutes to walk to her home, four hundred yards distant, and return. My heart sank, however, when I saw her enter the shop with her mother, who had a face like thunder! According to the 'Lady of the Manse', she did not appreciate her daughter being courted by a mere shop boy and demanded that Willie take steps to ensure that I made no such approaches in future. I was doubly mortified when I realised that not only had I failed so drastically in my first love excursion, but that this was the woman who had loudly complained once before that, 'that boy has not washed his hands before handling my cheese!' I never even got to know the name of the 'Daughter of the Manse'. There would be more disasters in my search for love before 'striking gold'.

Knowing your grandparents well is, to my mind, one of the cornerstones of life. It allows you to understand where you have come from, but, more importantly perhaps, it allows you to know where your parents came from and can assist in your understanding of some of their more odd foibles! Sadly, and perhaps the biggest regret of my childhood and my life as a whole was that I never really knew any of my grandparents other than my maternal grandmother, Margaret Sarah McCracken. My mother's father, William Rennie McCracken, had been unwell for a long period of his life and had died in 1938, two years before my mother had married my father. My paternal grandfather, William Herriot, died only seven weeks before I was born and his widow, Minnie Rutherford Rodger, died when I was three and, although I had been introduced to her, she lived in my father's home town of Peebles which was some distance from Glasgow and not routinely accessible to a family that never owned a car.

An only child, my father's relations all lived in Innerleithen, a small town six miles to the south-east of Peebles, and an area with which he was much acquainted. Being a non-driver, however, he had only ever made the journey from Glasgow to visit his

2. A house provided for a minister of certain Christian churches, especially the Scottish Presbyterian Church.

aunts by bus. It was on a journey to Innerleithen that I discovered that it was not from my father that I gained my navigational DNA! I was stationed in Germany with the RAF at the time and had bought my first new car, a 'Sapphire Blue' TR6, which I had driven home to show off to my parents. When I suggested it, my father was delighted with the idea of taking a day trip to The Borders and so, with the roof firmly closed to protect him from the cold Scottish air, we set off in a south-easterly direction through Lanark and onwards, following the signs to Peebles. As we entered Biggar, my father suddenly declared that we had to turn right! It seemed logical to my sense of direction to continue straight ahead, but my father knew the area better than me and so turn right we did! As we continued to follow his route towards a T-Junction, my father declared, 'Turn Left!' Now firmly disposed to his command of the navigational situation, I did as I was told, only to discover that the next command was, 'Turn Left!' Followed shortly by a, 'Turn Right!' back onto the road we had left some five minutes previously.

'Dad', said I, trying to be respectful and disguise my twenty-two year old's disgust, 'we are back on the road we started on!'

Not one to hold his patience well, my father's nonplussed response was, 'Well I can't bloody help it! This is the way the bus comes!'

If there is one definite characteristic that I have inherited from my father it is this: he did not suffer fools gladly and could be quite outspoken when he wanted to be! He was also, quite rightly, intolerant of bad manners and inculcated in his children an appropriate approach to others in society. We were always ordered to give up our seat on public transport when the need arose and woe betide us if my brother and I did not hold a door open for a lady. A situation summed up beautifully by my father one day when he broke his journey home by bus to shop at a department store on Eglinton Road, which passed through The Gorbals. As he departed the store, he politely held the door open for a woman who wished to enter at the same time as he exited. The woman sailed past him without a word! Feeling rightful indignation, my father turned on his heel and strode after the woman deep into the bowels of the shop and found her just as she was about to pay for the item she wished to purchase. My father immediately tapped her on her shoulder: 'Excuse me, madam,' he asked politely.

'Yes?' she responded tetchily.

'I'm afraid you dropped something as you entered the shop,' he re-joined.

'What was it?' she offered. My father, however, was far too smart for her!

'If you care to come with me, I'll show you,' he answered.

Now concerned, the woman stopped her purchase and followed my father all the way back through the shop and out onto the street. Looking quizzically, and with nothing apparent on the pavement, she demanded to know what it was that she was supposed to have dropped. My father looked her in the eye and, turning on his heel, said, 'Your manners! Good day, madam!' and headed back to the bus stop to continue his journey. You just have to admire a man like that!

It is from my mother, however, that I get my intellect, even if I was loathe to put it into practice at school. Having been Dux of Tain Royal Academy, by the time she was seventeen, in 1933, Helen Whyte McCracken was already an undergraduate at St Andrews University where she studied French and German. There was always great fun and laughter at home and you could guarantee that my mother would be involved in whatever game was underway either indoors or out. She was a great sport and a great peacemaker; she had to be with four kids and an occasionally implacable husband to cope with! She is the one who gave me my sense of fun and mischief.

My mother was the youngest of three girls and so we did have aunts, uncles and cousins on the McCracken side of the family. As I review my mother's siblings here I note that it seems to have been de rigueur for McCracken girls to marry bankers. My mother's eldest sister Margaret, known as Reta, married James Lawrence who, as far back as I can recall, was the manager of the local branch of the Bank of Scotland in Grantown-on-Spey. Her elder sister Agnes, known as Nan, was wedded to Jack Shankland who was, like my father, a bank clerk in Glasgow. Of course, as we know already, my mother married John Ferme Herriot, who was born in Peebles, but was working at the time of their marriage for The National Commercial Bank in Tain.

My father, known as Ferme, was a superb, if impatient, craftsman who nurtured and educated me in his hobbies. He taught me the black art of photographic development and instructed me in what woodwork tools were used for what purpose. I spent many a happy evening in the blacked-out kitchen watching as a white sheet of photographic paper developed into one of the outstanding images that my father had captured either in Pollok Estate or on his travels around the city and beyond. He had a fantastic eye for depth and had been quite a clever artist in his youth, for example, bringing Frans Hals' 'Laughing Cavalier' to life in pen and ink. He had also built a scale model of a fully-rigged 'Golden Hind', which he subsequently refurbished whilst in his seventies. I never, however, remember a tradesman being involved in any routine maintenance around the house. If a room needed redecorating, my parents did it with the help of those from the lower ranks who were capable of assisting. Most such events resulted in hysterics amongst my mother and the subordinates, whilst my father either got increasingly frustrated by a kink in the already glued wallpaper, or my mother's inability to perform what he saw as the simplest of tasks. The air was often blue at Kenilworth Avenue when painting and decorating was underway! None more so than, following a violent outburst of blaspheming coming from the front room, when he was found at the foot of a stepladder with his foot firmly fixed in a tray of white emulsion and with the can of paint splattered across the floor, it having fallen from the top of the ladder, drenching my father from top to toe in the same way as gravity took control of its flight path! My mother and all four siblings were quite uncontrollable with our response to my father's misfortune on that occasion. He, however, was definitely not amused; 'So you think it's funny do you?' still rings in my ears today! Actually, it was bloody hilarious in truth!

The garden of 148 was surrounded by eight-foot high walls that were about twelve inches thick. They were easy to climb and, with a curved coping stone on top, were actually quite easy to walk along too! This made inter-garden games with neighbours quite enjoyable and the retrieval of balls relatively easy. It also allowed my mother and Jean MacArthur, who lived at 146, a means of attracting each other's attention should either wish a 'quick word' or issue an invitation for a coffee! Although neither of the two could see over the wall, a quick loft of a potato from one garden to the next would be enough to attract the other for a conversation – who needs a mobile phone! It was also a good method of encouraging Graham or Sheena, who was my age, over into our garden for a game of cricket or rounders. French cricket was a popular back garden summer game as the restrictive positioning of the bat against the legs and often behind the body ensured that no windows were ever broken! The rap of a potato inviting me round to the MacArthur's to practise my joined up writing with Sheena was not always as welcome as the invitation for a game of cricket!

Upon arriving in Waverley Park, and still under the cloud of having failed to impress Doctor Lees at my 5-year-old entrance interview at the High School, I was enrolled in the primary department of Shawlands Academy. The primary school was not much more than 'at the end of the road' and was situated within the school grounds and below the senior school whose large and imposing buildings faced Pollokshaws Road. I remember the primary department being a single-storey building, shaped like a flat 'V' with an open veranda and its exterior walls made from red brick. The school had a large catchment area and attracted boys and girls not only from Waverley Park, but also from many of the tenement buildings in and around Shawlands Cross and Crossmyloof. We were a mixed bag and although sometimes tensions in the playground ran high, I do not suspect that it was any different from any other playground in the land.

I had plenty of friends both in and out of school, but, after school, used to play cricket, tennis or 'kick the can' (football without a ball!) in the middle of Kenilworth Avenue with either my brother and elder sister and their friends – when they were feeling tolerant – or with Morton Stark and Sheena MacArthur – 'the girl next door'! Latterly, however, I fell in with the boy who lived at 4 Midlothian Drive, John Liddell. John was an only child and was quite possessive of his friends. Indeed, so possessive was he that he could only ever have one friend and I was to be him! That stated, John was a very loyal friend and we spent hours together at his house playing with his electric train set, his Scalextric, or learning the art of construction with his Bayko Building Set.

Improvisation was very much to the fore too. A full-scale, well for our age anyway, pirate galleon was often constructed utilising his garden shed as its superstructure. When we were able to get hold of various pram chassis we constructed 'bogeys' using an old wooden box or an orange crate that Willie, the local grocer, was only too happy to supply. A Liddell/Herriot bogey was of classic design, with a fully steerable front axle, but no brakes – that's what the heels of Clarks' shoes were designed for! As an only child, John was much better off than I was as one of four. He got pocket money every week, whereas, I might have been given a sixpence if my parents were feeling particularly flush, or I had excelled at school or helped around the house. John got a shilling, weekly, no matter what! Conscious as he was of my relative poverty in that regard, he would often share his purchases equally with me at The Candy Box. On one occasion, unable to purchase anything for a penny ha'penny each, rather than spend a threepenny bit on himself he actually dropped the coin down the drain! I was impressed with his display of devotion to our friendship, but mortified that he could dispose of a coin that was fifty per cent of my occasional income, if I had behaved myself! John and I were not sporty, but were, one day, keen to develop our high jump skills. We tied the rope at a suitable height between two washing line uprights in his garden and started to clear it easily as we launched ourselves from the lawn over the rope with a scissors kick onto a gravel path. In true Olympic fashion, the bar was relentlessly raised in order to establish who would win 'Gold' and who would not. John won, as I had to withdraw through injury! It was just as Doctor Forsyth was stitching up my chin that I heard my mother say, 'Would it not have been a better idea to land on the grass rather than on the gravel?' Sometimes Mums can be wise after the event, as can 8-year-old boys!

That was not the last time that Doctor Forsyth was to be summoned to repair a wound taken bravely in the pursuit of sporting excellence. My brother Michael, bless him, decided one evening that it would be a good idea to play rugby together in our bedroom. Although he and I occupied one of the larger bedrooms in the house, it had all the clutter of two growing lads, a large Victorian fireplace, chests of drawers and a huge coffin-like wardrobe. It also had two wooden-framed single beds and it was on the corner of one of these that, having possession, I felt the full weight of my seven year older brother as he crunched into me, swept me off my feet and directed the back of my head on to one of the wooden bed legs! Blood gushed from the wound and Doctor Forsyth once again climbed into his Humber Hawk and set off to cover the three miles from Cardonald to Waverley Park to patch me up!

Although my mother had held a driving licence previously, my father never had, and with a car being a luxury and an unnecessary expense, we were regular users of public transport. Tram, bus and steam train were routine methods of getting into or across the city for the Herriot kids. Going on holiday was equally an adventure. If we were bound for St Andrews to stay in Fionna Black's (one of the Cardonald Mums Triumvirate) flat on Bridge Street, it would entail either a journey by train or bus into the city centre, followed by a 'six-man' march with baggage to Buchanan Street Bus Station and a coach trip to Scotland's oldest university city in the Kingdom of Fife. There was a strict pecking order for mounting the Bluebird bus to St Andrews and, with Michael to the fore; I could guarantee never being first! Alternatively, if Mrs Walker's cottage in Lamlash was our destination, as it became in my teens, then we could let the train take the strain from Shawlands Station via a change at Glasgow Central and onto the Boat Train through to Ardrossan on the Clyde Coast to catch the steamer to Brodick on the island of Arran. The four-mile journey to Lamlash was then taken on one of the oldest buses ever to take to a Scottish road! There next followed a family trek, lugging suitcases from the village centre, past the putting green and the tennis courts, and onwards towards the Cuddy Dook and the half of the Walker abode that she rented out as holiday accommodation. We were always met with a cheery Gaelic '*ciamar a tha*[3]', as if we were long-lost members of the Walker family!

---

3. How are you.

Both St Andrews and Lamlash offered idyllic holiday spots for a young family. Golden beaches, beach cricket, golf, tennis, putting, and quiet evenings playing board games, although *Monopoly*, like in most families, was never quiet and resulted in many feuds! The Clyde or Fife, that's as far as we ever ventured. Foreign holidays were not common in the 1950s and 1960s and, even if they had been, we would never have been able to afford them.

I was nine, I seem to recall, when Judith decided it was time that she taught me to swim. I had no real desire to do so and have never been a confident swimmer, but Judith was determined and, having forced my rubber ring on, decided that the silver sands of the West Beach at St Andrews was as good a place as any to start! Have you ever dipped a toe, let alone immersed your body, in the North Sea? Let me assure you that woollen bathing trunks that expanded to five times their volume on contact with salt water are not the garment to be entering the North Sea in – even in the height of summer. An Immersion Suit, as provided in later life by the RAF to undertake aircrew Sea Survival Drills, is not the greatest fashion item for 'drowning' in the North Sea, but it's a damn site more comfortable than woollen pants!

Judith tried to drown me! It was a deliberate act and an effort to rid her of this impersonator who had denied her of a little sister back in 1949! Yes, she held my hand, yes, she reassured me, but she had not cleared all the debris from underneath the ocean and when I tripped on a rock she let go as I plummeted to the bottom of the briny! I must have been down there for all of five seconds before the air in the ring recovered from the shock of having to act and bring me back to the surface! I never ventured out of my depth again on that holiday and still will not unless I am confident that my flotation aid is in full working order!

At home we were encouraged to entertain ourselves, but we would often go out as a family either to the Kelvingrove Art Gallery, or to Kelvin Hall to see the circus when it came to town. My father would routinely take me to Kelvin Hall to the Ideal Home Exhibition or similar. In the summer, picnics would be taken locally in Pollok Estate, accessible by foot as long as we were all present to assist with lugging games equipment and food hampers! Easter Sunday was always spent at Pollok Estate where the large hill allowed us, and most of the local children, to roll our hard–boiled Easter eggs down the slope to symbolise the rolling aside of the stone at the door of the tomb – we were not religious, but we were educated in Christian principles and knew what was symbolic and important in the Christian Calendar.

My father had, amongst his possessions, a number of silent strip 'flick' Walt Disney cartoons and an ancient projector that was regularly set up in the front room for a 'film show'. These were very basic cartoons and, given their 1930s vintage, of very poor quality and short duration. Nevertheless, as kids we were transfixed by them. The strip of picture frames was no more than eighteen inches long and travelled from right to left past the lens, to be projected onto a sheet hung across the windows in the front room. Each lasted no more than one minute and had to be replaced by the next strip for continuity, which always resulted in an argument as to which of the four viewers would have the honour of replacing it! Mickey Mouse, Donald Duck, Pluto and many more, provided hours of entertainment in the Herriot household in the 1950s. My parents also owned a Victorian Bagatelle Board, which spent most of its life folded in half and stored underneath the sideboard in the front room. It was about ten feet long and three feet wide when unfolded and similar in purpose to a billiard table. The major difference on a bagatelle board, however, was that one end was rounded instead of square. Additionally, instead of pockets around the edge, at the semi-circular end there were nine cups, one in the middle of the semi-circle and the rest surrounding it evenly in a ring. The hole in the middle was numbered nine and the others were numbered one to eight in a semi-random order. A variety of games could be played, including one where a block of numbered tunnels was placed across the board, which required great skill and accuracy to score the high numbers as cue shots had to touch the side before penetrating one of the tunnels. Bagatelle provided hours of fun and heated competition when it was set up on the dining table at 148 Kenilworth Avenue. When my parents moved to Ixworth in Suffolk in 1980 they took the Bagatelle Board with them and placed it under their sideboard again just in case we should ever want to play once more! Sadly, when it came time to clear my parents' house, the Bagatelle Board had lost much of its shine and the green baize was somewhat threadbare, and so the decision was taken to sell it rather than refurbish it; nobody had a house big enough to store it!

Occasionally, my parents would take us 'Doon the Watter'[4] on a Clyde Steamer. Most often this was on board the RMS *Waverley*, a paddle steamer that sailed from The Broomielaw in the centre of Glasgow to Rothesay on the Isle of Bute. Because my father worked Saturday mornings, any family adventure had to be scheduled for a Sunday when, without fail, we would wear our school uniforms because a) it was the thing to do and b) we did not have any Sunday Best!

My father was proud of the fact that he only attended church for christenings, weddings and funerals and saw no reason to go on any other occasion; he viewed all 'men of the cloth' as hypocrites. That stated, although not regular church goers, both my parents believed in God and lived by Christian principles. They neither encouraged nor discouraged us from going to church and so I regularly attended the South Shawlands Church and Sunday school with John Liddell. In later life, after I had grown out of Sunday school activities, I became a member of the Scripture Union at Glasgow High School and attended The Crusaders Union meetings locally on Sunday afternoons with my brother Michael. However, unlike my elder sister Judith, who has returned to a devout Christian faith in her later years, I have to confess that I am, like my father, a lapsed Christian with some considerable scepticism of those who believe in the creationist theory and anticipate a life after death – I could get a bloody nice surprise one day!

My father was the man who taught me much of what I know about life. He worked hard to provide a comfortable, if not extravagant lifestyle, but he was not, because of his own strict Victorian-based upbringing, very emotionally attached to us as a father. He was always there if we needed him, but it was my mother who was the glue that kept the family sane. It was she who provided the comfort and emotional support

---

4. A Glaswegian expression for a river excursion on the River Clyde.

when things went wrong. It was she who encouraged us to always do our best. It was she who taught us right from wrong and it was she who would always ask, 'Well! What did you do to deserve that?' if we came home complaining about something that had happened either in class or in the playground. She was always absolutely fair and could see both sides of every argument, which was often quite frustrating when you 'knew you were right' – as most kids do when the chips are down!

Both my parents gave up a lot to ensure that we all had a sound education and I regret that I did not apply myself to academia quite as well as I might. I am not pretending for one second that I am an intellectual – hell no! However, I could have done better at school had I applied myself. My problem is that I am too much of a comedian and do not take life seriously at all. My mother did everything in her power to help me study, but I did not have the time or inclination to knuckle down to it, as will become apparent later. If I was studying a Shakespearian text, rather than sit quietly analysing it, I would be up performing all the parts and leaping from chair to chair in the dining room reciting soliloquy after soliloquy in the various voices required. *Falstaff*, *Hamlet*, *Ophelia*, and *Romeo and Juliet*, all got an airing in our dining room, and rather than discourage me and get me back into the books, those present in the house at the time would gather in hilarious and encouraging uproar. That has been my problem throughout both my schooling and my professional life – playing the fool has got me into more trouble than I care to remember, but all will be explained as this story evolves.

Chapter Three

S+ For Diligence

As you now know, my first contact with the High School was when I took the entrance test as a 4-year-old in 1954 with a view to entering Primary One in September of that year when I had passed my fifth birthday. From what I recall of the experience, it was conducted in the rector's office as an interview between my mother and Dr Lees, at which I was allowed to be present. I recall I was provided with some bricks that I thought were for playing with, but later understood that this was an early attempt to establish my mathematical genius; I was also asked to read a passage of a book to him, but was too shy to do so! Such was the imposing nature of the school to my tender years! It was all to no avail, however, as Dr Lees' opinion, which my mother supported, was that I was not ready for the delights of 'The High' and would benefit from time in a small primary school closer to home for my first few years within the education system rather than in, what appeared to me to be, the vast halls of Elmbank Street.

The motto of any school is, quite rightly, designed to inspire and encourage its pupils to greater and grander achievements. It works for those inclined, but, for the jokers in the pack, it serves only to remind them of their failings! The Latin motto of the High School of Glasgow is *Sursum Semper* and its literal translation into English is 'Up and Always', which was interpreted officially at school as 'Ever Upward', so it certainly fits the bill in inspirational terms! So, at the tender age of nine and having convinced David Lees that he should let me in, it inspired me to follow in my brother's footsteps, having at last gained a coveted place at this prestigious educational establishment, which was renowned as the oldest seat of learning in Scotland and is the twelfth oldest school in the United Kingdom. The school was founded as the Choir School of Glasgow Cathedral in the twelfth century, became the Grammar School of Glasgow in the fifteenth century and changed its name to the High School of Glasgow in 1834. It was, to say the least, well-established, and had produced many a former pupil who had taken its motto seriously and become great achievers in their lives. The four school houses were named after past luminaries: Sir Henry Campbell-Bannerman and Andrew Bonar Law, who both became Prime Ministers[1] of Great Britain; Lord Clyde, who, as a Major General, successfully defended Balaklava from a much larger Russian force at the Battle of the Alma during the Crimean War and, as Commander-in-Chief India, relieved Lucknow and pacified the north of India; and General Sir John Moore of Corunna who saw action in the American Revolutionary War and was wounded in the French Revolutionary Wars. He was wounded again

---

1. The only educational institution aside from Eton and Harrow to produce two Prime Ministers in the twentieth century.

trying to free the Netherlands from French control and again attempting to oust the French from Egypt. He was killed at Corunna during the Peninsular War. So pupils entering the High School were inculcated with high achievement and were left in no doubt as to where their destinies lay!

The opening passage in the school's 'Rules of Discipline', circa 1968, sums it up quite neatly under the title 'General':

> *'Application for the admission of a boy to the School is taken to imply that his parent or guardian is prepared to co-operate with the School Authorities in carrying out the rules and regulations actually in force, and such others as may be prescribed from time to time.* **The Corporation**[2], **on the recommendation of the Rector, is at liberty to require the withdrawal of those pupils who, from idleness or other cause, are unable to profit by the instruction given, or whose conduct is detrimental to the welfare of the School.'**

Strong words indeed and, please note, not mine, but original Bold Type! There would be no slacking, skiving, sloth or misbehaviour tolerated and those who failed to measure up to the standard required would be out on their ear – no questions asked! Read the bold type again – *Those unable to profit!* So, rest assured lad, if you do not cut the mustard it will be through no fault of the school's and the blame could only fall at your own doorstep! I wonder how many parents today would accept a contract like that for the education of their children! I would be surprised, in this liberal twenty-first century blame-driven culture in which I find myself recounting my school days, if that same passage has survived, or is allowed to survive, in the contemporary Rules and Regulations of the High School of Glasgow. In the 1950s and 1960s, however, if you did not aspire to achieve the standards set by the likes of Campbell-Bannerman, Clyde, Law and Moore, then you would have nobody to blame but yourself. Disturbing as that might sound today, it was nothing of consequence to children of that era – we had been brought up in the shadow of the Second World War and knew from our parents what it was to stand up and be counted and to work hard for reward. Much as I 'idled' my way through my studies at The High, I participated fully in all aspects of the school and thoroughly enjoyed every minute of the nine years that I spent as a pupil at the High School of Glasgow. However, if only I had read that passage in the rule book then rather than now, I might just have profited more academically!

---

2. The High School of Glasgow was a government grant-maintained fee-paying school. It came under local authority control in 1872, consequently the 'Corporation' referred to here was Glasgow City Corporation. In the early 1970s the Labour controlled City Council decided to withdraw grant-maintained funding and despite valiant efforts by Rector David Lees, supported by an army of parents and former pupils, the school closed and eventually resurfaced in 1976 as an independent co-educational school rebuilt on part of the school's playing fields at Anniesland. In 2009, *The Times* placed it as the top independent school in Scotland for Higher and Standard Grades (A-Level and GCSE equivalent).

My journey to the High School was made by a Circle Line steam train from Shawlands Station to Glasgow Central and then onwards by foot to Elmbank Street. So it was, in late August 1958, dressed in my new, bought with growth in mind, chocolate-brown blazer and shorts, and with my chocolate and gold cap emblazoned with the crest of the High School firmly stuck on my head, that I accompanied Michael, for he was in charge, to our local station and onwards on the 8.31 train for my first day at school in the city centre. I have always found rail journeys exciting, but none could compare to those first few trips into Glasgow sharing the compartment with Michael's 16-year-old peers. I was in awe! Of course I suffered the usual banter that a 9-year-old would expect from such exalted company! My cap was routinely dangled out of the window, as was my satchel, as the train steamed through Maxwell Park and Pollokshields West stations, before arriving across the River Clyde and through the grand proscenium arch that welcomed weary travellers from as far afield as London Euston and all points north on the West Coast Main Line. However, although our journey was but fifteen minutes long, I was nonetheless weary, having spent those minutes trying to rescue my school cap from the hands of those much taller and stronger as it was passed above my head and towards the beckoning void of the open window! A brisk ten-minute walk from the Central Station up Bothwell Street and into Holland Street was all it then took to arrive at school in time for 9.15. It took me only a few days to convince my mother that I could do this journey on my own and would meet up with my own class mates who caught the train further down the line and would save me a seat when I boarded at Shawlands – at least now I was able to hang on to my cap!

So it was that I took my deserved place in Miss Barrie's class in Primary V[3]. Miss Barrie was a diminutive woman who had a very caring attitude towards – and provided a solid educational base for – her flock. There were thirty-three boys in the class from various backgrounds and with varying academic ability. Sandy MacGregor, who was fifty per cent of the identical MacGregor twins, Forrest Malloch, Noah Freedman and Malcolm Swinbank, were amongst the brighter element, whilst Brian Bellamy, Peter Knight and Alan 'Cow' Clark, would all feature with me as some of the jokers in the pack in later years. 'Ike' Grant was a particularly good friend and fellow traveller on the 8.31. Ike earned his sobriquet because of his initials; his parents had christened him Iain Kevan. 'Cow' Clark, on the other hand, had no such parental consideration and had earned his merely because he could belch the National Anthem in its entirety and, once we had hit the Senior School, was prone to letting rip regularly in class, much to the consternation of the teacher who was never able to work out quite where the interruption had come from. Cow was also a prolific farter although he never quite managed to compose tunes through his backside quite like he could with the reflux in his throat!

Miss Barrie's class was a haven of calm for 9-year-old boys to learn in and although my school report has long gone I must have excelled in my first year at the High

---

3. Note – Roman numerals – clear and concise proof, were it needed, that this was an establishment that focused hard on serious learning.

School as I was streamed into Miss Pate's class for Primary VI and VII! Miss Pate was, to say the least, the exact opposite of Miss Barrie. She was a tall slender spinster of considerable age, or appeared to be so to 10-year-old boys, with swept back grey hair tied in a bun on the back of her head. She looked even more stern in her school teacher's black gown as she paraded around the classroom berating the less able in their studies to try harder and to, 'Think, boy, think!' Her classroom regime was severe and her, and therefore our, work ethic was very earnest! There was no time for 'jokers' in Miss Pate's class. She took the A-stream pupils to groom them towards success in the 11+ examination and their onward passage to the Senior School. There would be no defaulters on the way. Miss Pate took seriously that opening passage from the School Rule Book and made damned sure that none of her charges would falter!

I worked diligently for Miss Pate and my mother was extremely pleased and proud of how I had settled into The High. Indeed, my school reports from Primary VII show me to have peaked in fourteenth position in the class of twenty-nine students by the end of the first term of my final year with Miss Pate. By the time of my 11+ exams I had moved up to ninth and was scoring well in all subjects apart from, perhaps, Arithmetic, where I fell five points below the class average. However, in English, History, Geography, Latin and French I was well above the median. Some might be unkind and suggest that I was Miss Pate's pet! I would disagree, as she rarely called me David and usually referred to me as Peter! I suspect that there had been a Peter Herriot 'in her life' previously and she, for whatever reason – perhaps he had been killed in the war – just could not get his name out of her head. No matter, it did not worry me as I was glad to be noticed and did everything I could to stay on the right side of this tyrannical teacher. I had, actually, a bit of a soft spot for her and when she asked if my mother could also buy fresh eggs for her from Mr Wilson, an Ayrshire farmer who delivered fresh eggs to our door routinely, my mother and I were only too happy to oblige. If it curried favour with Miss Pate and kept me 'on side' then anything, including fresh egg delivery, was alright by me.

Miss Pate's classroom was above Miss Barrie's in D-Block and one had to climb the stairs and walk the corridor to the corner door to gain entry to it. It was thus remote from the beaten track in D-Block and no teachers would routinely pass it. It thus lent itself readily to becoming a riot scene if Miss Pate ever left the room for an extended period of time, which she rarely did! However, I do recall a particular occasion in Primary VII when we were left to our own devices for a considerable period, but sworn, on pain of death, to do nothing other than to diligently complete the task set whilst she was out of the room – woe betide any boy who failed to heed her stern words! She was gone some length of time and slowly the room dissolved into a war zone as we all took advantage of our time alone. Sadly, we had not posted any sentries and one disadvantage of the long corridor that led to her classroom was that, in the customary quiet of the block, the sound of mayhem carried a long way, and on this fateful day, met her as she ascended the stairs on her return from her errand! The explosion as she opened the door and the look of sheer horror on her face told us all immediately that we had overstepped the mark. It soon became evident that her threat upon departure was not idle and we were all soon lined up to receive two strokes of her taws before being despatched across to C-Block and Harry McGill's class for music! There was not much enthusiasm for singing that day and it took most of the music lesson for our wrists to stop stinging from her punishment. Throughout my time in Primary VI/VII, I held Miss Pate in the highest regard. She reminded me very much of my spinster great aunts and was probably of similar age and, even as an 11-year-old, I admired her as a role model and teacher. She died whilst I was a Senior School pupil and she was the only school teacher whose funeral I, and many of my contemporaries, ever attended.

Passage through the 11+ and onwards into the Senior School came easily thanks to Miss Pate's involvement and encouragement. With an S+ for diligence, and creditable marks in all subjects other than art, I was privileged and encouraged to enter Form 1A, the top stream. My parents were delighted! I have never really considered the definition of diligence before now. It is one of those words that are common in English and used routinely. To me, it means being conscientious and studious. *Collins Dictionary* offers: steady and careful application. The High School of Glasgow, in keeping with its notion of *those unable to profit* provides the following on the reverse of its 1961 School Report:

'Diligence is assessed separately from attainment, for its results do not necessarily reveal themselves in school progress or proficiency. The diligence mark recognises a pupil's assiduous attention in class, faithful performance of home exercise, and thoroughness in home preparation. It assesses character as revealed in school work.'

So, on a scale of E to U through S+, S and S-, you would think S+ would qualify for high praise. Not a bit of it:

'S+ – Under encouragement he works to the limit of his capacity, achieving by his application more than his native endowments (whether they are high or low), would lead his teacher to expect.'

Now I have heard some back-handed compliments, but wait, even E, which I thought stood for Excellent, does not paint the rosiest of pictures:

'E – Outstanding in reliability and initiative (Even with poor school attainments a pupil may reveal these qualities in his work).'

So, here we have somebody who could be thick, but is *able to profit* from being so! How does that work? Anyway, enough of this analysis, there will be time later and a need, perhaps, to discuss the merits of S and S- diligence; thankfully, it would appear from my school reports that we will not have a need to discuss a Diligence Score of U!

I would not describe my time in the Senior School at Glasgow High as being blessed with academic brilliance – more that of a plodder who was easily distracted and who soon found many extra-curricular activities to divert him from his studies. Consequently, I do not plan to bore you with each and every detail of my seven years of secondary education at the High School; the mathematically quick will have realised already that there is an extra year in there somehow! Save to say that I majored in English, Geography and Mathematics by the end of my schooling and took glancing blows at French, Physics and Chemistry on my way through the Scottish Certificate of Education Standard Grade. Given success in Latin with Miss Pate, I took it and History during my first year in the Senior School with some mixed success!

'Pa' Duff taught Classics and took Form 1A for Latin. If Miss Pate was ancient, Duguld Duff was positively prehistoric. The rumour at the time was that he was seventy-two, which I can now confirm having read Harry Ashmall's historical account entitled *'The High School of Glasgow'*[4], and that he had returned to teaching having originally retired at sixty-five. In Ashmall's record he states that, 'He taught his subject with the vigour of a man half his age: and to that end he was conscientious and without discipline problems.' From my memory, both of these statements are correct, although discipline in Pa Duff's Latin class was not 'without problems' although he had his own method of resolving issues. Small of stature and stooped with age, Pa Duff would overcome his height restriction and the fact that the 'guilty' towered over him by stepping onto the 6-inch high platform in front of the blackboard to administer the belt to a pupil. To regain the advantage in this battle of tall versus small, the recipient of the taws would step on to the platform too, thereby denying Pa Duff the 'height' advantage! Pa Duff would instruct the pupil to step off the platform, but, as soon as the taws was raised over his shoulder to administer the first stroke, the intended recipient would remount the platform. This game of 'cat and mouse' would continue until Pa Duff lost his rag and either gave up or marched the defendant to see the Head of Classics, George Chalmers, or Dr Lees himself, who would discharge the punishment and a few more besides! I excelled at Latin with Pa Duff in the autumn term of 1961, scoring eighty per cent in the end of term exam. I could conjugate Latin verbs with the best of them and was not averse to running off the occasional Amo, Amas, Amat, Amamus, Amatis, Amant in order to convince my mother and my siblings that I was destined for greatness as a classical scholar! It was the June exam that academic year that rather deflated my ego when I returned a humiliating eighteen per cent which rather undermined my ambition and finished my life with the classics!

Despite it being all about Scotland and the persecution of my fair homeland by the English in the form of the Hammer of the Scots and his like, History too failed to enthral me! So it was that by the time I entered the Third Form and the serious stuff started, I had reduced my curriculum to the six subjects mentioned above, but with the addition of Art. I did not shine in Form IIID and, having secured only 255 marks out of a possible 700 in the mid-year exams, seemed destined to fall into the unable to profit basket. With diligence marked as no greater than S, but with also two S- scores in English and Physics, it was inevitable that I had failed to make the grade

---

4. Published in 1976 by Scottish Academic Press Ltd.

and the decision was taken with my parents' blessing that I should repeat the Third Form. Devastated by this decision, but acknowledging that I would have to try harder and apply myself, I watched as the brighter members of my year group advanced to the Fourth Form, their SCE grades and subsequently their Higher Certificate of Education. The other High School jokers from Form IIID, and I, were assigned Dr Phillips as our Form Tutor to do the whole thing again and this time, hopefully, without all the joking! It was not to be. 'Cow' Clark, Brian Bellamy and Peter Knight were with me, along with Ronnie Orr who, like me, was a member of the CCF and all that that provided in terms of skiving!

'Doc' Phillips was a typical scientist who had joined the Science Department to teach Physics. From what I remember, and despite his age, following a life in scientific research in industry, his contract with the High School was his first teaching appointment. He suffered all the mischief that a group of experienced youths can bestow on a 'new boy'. From blowing down the gas tap to alter the gas mix and thereby extinguish the flame to the deliberate disruption of experiments, Form IIID was unsympathetic to Doc Phillips' inexperience. Despite this lack of familiarity with teaching, he was not averse to using his belt to sort out the troublemakers. However, like Pa Duff, the boys of the Senior School had developed a tactic to diminish its effect. Doc Phillips suffered from poor eyesight and wore rather thick spectacles as a result. So, when a pupil stood before him to receive his punishment with both palms crossed and uppermost, the remainder of the class would sit with their hands ready to clap loudly on the down stroke of the belt. At the critical moment the recipient of the taws would slide his hands apart to allow the belt to travel through the space whilst the crash of twenty-plus claps would register with Doc Phillips as a punishment duly administered. Forty-plus years later it sounds quite implausible, but I assure you that most boys escaped punishment from Doc Phillips in this manner!

There are many advantages to having a big brother progress through school ahead of you. However, there are many disadvantages for a younger sibling in an academic establishment where academic and sporting prowess are rewarded and lauded publically. It is quite understandable in such an environment that comparisons will be made. If I had a pound for the number of times that I had to respond positively to the question by staff of, 'Are you Michael Herriot's brother?' I would be a very rich man. Nevertheless, that question still haunts me almost fifty years on as the staff response was always either, 'He was much better at maths than you are!' or, 'Not as good as him at rugby, are you?' etc, etc. You get the drift, not that I am psychologically scarred or emotionally troubled by the comments, but I do still feel that it cast a shadow over my time at The High.

I do not deny that Michael is a natural sportsman and that I am not, but I tried hard. I do not think I ever enjoyed a PE lesson at school. For a start, the PE teachers were sadists and I took no enjoyment from circuit training at all. Purgatory, sheer purgatory. I played rugby and cricket in the Junior School and actually played quite well; if never quite attaining selection for the First XV or First Eleven once I had reached the Senior School. It was usually the Seconds for me in both sports. I was dedicated, however, and never missed a training session or a match and I always turned out to support the First XV and First Eleven no matter what the weather conditions. So reliable did I become that I was eventually running the line for the First XV and acting as scorer for the First Eleven. Consequently, I routinely travelled to away games with both teams and became a popular member of these groups, regularly leading the singing of rugby songs on the way back home on the bus. I played in a number of positions on the rugby field, from hooker, through scrum half and even had a spell on the wing. In cricket I was no bowler, but had a useful bat and occasionally stood wicket for the 2nd Eleven. One of the greatest advantages in winter for both the First and Second XVs was that our annual away fixtures against our school opponents in Edinburgh were deliberately arranged for International days at Murrayfield. After a pounding match in the mud at the likes of Goldenacre or Myreside, the two teams would head off into Edinburgh and Rose Street for a couple of beers, if we could con the barmen, before joining in the long trek west to Murrayfield, which then was not the magnificent stadium it is today, but had terracing and, quaintly, a 'Schoolboys' Enclosure' where we could safely watch our heroes in action. It was a fantastic privilege and one very good reason to train hard and stick close to the First and Second XVs. I saw many an outstanding game of rugby at Murrayfield in the 1960s when Scotland took on the might of the southern hemisphere on our hallowed turf – I was there when Colin Meads, the outstanding All Blacks lock, was sent off for deliberately climbing over a ruck! No yellow or red cards in those days! No disciplinary citing boards, no appeals – just summary justice duly accepted by the miscreant without a murmur!

Whilst sport was not my forte, I did discover other talents other than the infrequent success in the occasional exam! My attempts to entertain my siblings back in Kenilworth Avenue by attempting every part in the Shakespearean tragedies that I should have been studying more diligently had triggered a notion that I might enjoy acting. So, in 1966, when the school Amateur Dramatic Society was appealing for actors to take roles in their production of R.C. Sherriff's *'Journey's End'*, it seemed a reasonable ploy to me to take myself over to the auditions, which were held in the School Hall with its full stage and proscenium arch. My mother was less keen on this notion, as she had seen just how less than S+ for diligence I had become as I progressed through the Senior School. Moreover, she, more than I, had her sight firmly fixed on my O-Level examinations that were due a few weeks after the production was due to close. I, though, could see no further than the opportunity to tread the boards and so was delighted when I won the role of the Company Sergeant Major in Sherriff's masterpiece about war set in the British trenches before St Quentin in March of 1918. Unfortunately for me, the auditions were oversubscribed and I had to share my part with Bill Shooter, a good friend who had the role of sergeant created to give him a part too – he stole half my lines in doing so, but we remained good friends throughout our subsequent thespian careers at The High.

The drama club was very active and auditions were always eagerly contested. Performances were invariably very well attended and often to rave reviews, some of which would appear in *The Glasgow Herald* or *The Evening Times*. Of course, being a single-sex school, boys played leading ladies without a second thought and the costumes were always grand affairs. The Art Department pupils, under the guidance of Leslie 'Dusty' Millar, produced the scenery and mums often became involved in adapting costumes to fit, or sewing muscular young men into dresses intended for demure Victorian ladies! Mostly, however, it was the pupils who undertook the stage management, make-up, lighting and sound roles during performances.

The following year, I auditioned successfully for the part of Lady Clementina Beauchamp, great aunt to Lord Arthur Savile, whose crime we were all about to expose on stage; Bill Shooter took the part of Lady Windermere, who, in a previous life, had owned a fan! Actually, all these years later, looking at the script of '*Lord Arthur Savile's Crime*', by Constance Cox and based on a short story by Oscar Wilde, I need to question the producers,' Donald McCormick and David Menzies, our English Masters selection of that play in 1967 given that of the ten actors required to stage Savile's Crime, fifty per cent of the parts were female! Unaccustomed as I was, and still am, to wearing female attire, the only highlight of the first night, and the one that got the biggest laugh, was when I rose from the chaise longue, stood on my hem and ripped my dress from shoulder blade to backside as I turned to 'exit stage left'! Sanity was recovered in 1968, my final year at school, when I was cast as Sir Lucius O'Trigger in Sheridan's '*The Rivals*', a part I got totally immersed in, but sadly at the expense of good results in my final year exams, the Scottish Certificate of Education – The Highers!

I told you there was plenty of extracurricular activity at The High to draw a less than diligent scholar from the classroom and I found many more, not just acting! However, what acting did provide me with was a confidence and an ability to stand up and speak clearly and loudly to a gathered throng – a skill that was to serve me well in my military career to come. The downside of acting at school was that it taught me to 'play the fool'! Whilst there were not many laughs to be had in *Journey's End*, with the roles of both Lady Clementina and Sir Lucius, there dawned a realisation that I could make people laugh. In hindsight, and as I have alluded to previously, I would have been served better if I had realised when to draw the line, but you cannot turn back time and I am happy that I have had the ability to make people laugh throughout my life both professionally and socially, even if my timing, at work, was not always appropriate or appreciated by those in my chain of command!

My father was a leading light in the music world of Glasgow, particularly as a founder of the Glasgow String Orchestra and the Glasgow Chamber Orchestra. In his life he performed with: The Paisley Chamber Music Ensemble; The Paisley String Quartet; The Glasgow String Orchestra; The Glasgow Chamber Orchestra; and The Yvoriot String Quartet.

So you see I come from musical stock. Well, that is certainly true if you consider only the immediate preceding generation and my father in particular. As I am now past my mid-point, I show a distinct resemblance to my father and I was born in my mother's bed at home. So, despite what many of my friends might think or even say, my parentage is not in question. Moreover, I can crack out a pretty mean song when I set my mind to it and have been known to provide some or all of the lyrics to many a squadron song in the past. Although I have to confess that this particular attribute is better developed once a considerable quantity of alcohol has oiled my vocal chords. I get my singing voice from my mother who would often entertain her four children with the love songs of Robbie Burns, or arias from light opera, whilst preparing the evening meal. However, my father! Now that is a different story. My father was no mean violinist and a violist who mainstreamed on the viola and was, in the 1960s, both president of the Glasgow Chamber Music Society and of the Glasgow Orchestral Society. He was a well-known and oft-quoted figure in journals, both broadsheet and musical, and had developed the art of orchestration of major works that would allow his ensembles or string orchestras to modify and perform works designed by the composer for a full orchestra. As a result of his strong involvement in these orchestras, the Herriot household would entertain, routinely, a variety of people who brought their own brand of music into our home. A regular was Frank Wilson, a trumpeter with the Sadler's Wells Opera Company.

My brother Michael took up the violin and Judith, my sister, followed with the cello, whilst I, five years her junior, watched with interest from the sidelines as to how my father, the accomplished musician with a low tolerance of those less able or less diligent, would react. His often overbearing demands to 'practise, practise, practise' were very difficult to come to terms with and were made more difficult when he entered the room to berate you for either not getting the beat or intonation quite right. For a young boy or girl starting out on their paths to a musical career I am convinced that the standard being met at the time was adequate for a beginner working their way up through each of the stages. It was never good enough for our father, who set incredibly high musical standards for us all to achieve.

The High, and the Girls' High School too, had excellent music facilities and a regular stream of tutors who attended on a weekly basis to coach their charges. Not unnaturally, I was encouraged by both my parents to follow Michael and Judith on a musical journey once I had entered The High. Unlike my siblings, however, I managed to resist my father's overtures to take up a stringed instrument and with the arrival of Frank and his trumpet I saw an opportunity to satisfy my father whilst not falling into the trap of playing an instrument upon which he was a virtuoso! Fortunately, or unfortunately, depending on your outlook, my father was well known to Harry McGill, who was Head of Music at The High.

I found the trumpet an invigorating instrument to play – lots of breathing technique required, but only three valves and variations thereon to remember, but with the need to develop a pursed lip! I thoroughly enjoyed it. There is nothing like playing a brass instrument for the sheer power of its music. Of course, it can be evocative when played softly, but what 11-year-old lad wants to play soft music? Once I had mastered the scales and dabbled with a bit of triple-tonguing, I was off. Lessons were held weekly, on a Wednesday, after school with Mr Gregor Grant; a man of considerable age and no mean fortitude to a lad still in short pants. He had been a brass tutor for years and, whilst I can no longer remember his pedigree in that field, I do recall his temper and the prolific amount of saliva that he would produce when he displayed to me, on my trumpet, just exactly how the piece should be played. Had it existed, Health & Safety would have been appalled at the cross-contamination possibilities of us sharing a mouthpiece as he blasted out the Grand March from '*Aida*' that I was struggling to produce. Nevertheless, progress I did and was soon able to churn out Jeremiah Clarke's *Trumpet Voluntary Suite in D Major*!

Things were looking up in my father's eyes. Here was a musician and in his family too. Michael had already forsaken the violin and Judith's cello was getting in the way of her promising sword fencing career, which was by now taking up much of her spare time. At last, despite the fact that it was not strings, my father was happy! There was, however, a snag!

Progression in music is ordained by one's ability to read music, maintain a beat and play along with others in either an orchestra or, for brass, a band. I could maintain a beat, but if I lost the thread whilst playing along with others I was doomed! With the tune in my head and not on the paper, I had to return to the beginning and start all over again which, quite rightly, Harry McGill was not prepared to tolerate. My music career was doomed and the timing of that event for me could not have come at a better time.

At thirteen years of age I was qualified to join the school's Combined Cadet Force (CCF), which I had been hankering after since I had ventured upwards from the Primary department. How was I to tell my father that the trumpet and I were finished? I could not do both as trumpet lessons were held on a Wednesday and the Corps paraded on both Mondays and Wednesdays after school. So, in my hour of need, I turned to my brother who gave me this advice; 'Just give it back to Grant and tell him where to stick it!' Helpful indeed, but less than considerate, and it did not solve the problem with Dad! So I tried him again. This time his response was just as abrupt; 'Look, that's what I did with the violin. Gave it back and then told Dad. He won't be able to do anything about it and the heat will reduce over time. Mum will understand and douse any flames!' Michael had indeed done it before me and Judith had managed to convince him that the cello was not for her, but I knew that my father was relying on me and, whilst he did have a heart of gold, he was prone to kick off occasionally. Nevertheless, something inside me told me that I had to join the cadet force, so McGill got his trumpet back and I turned my attention to the CCF and the issue of telling my father. He did not take it well and I feel very sorry for my younger sister, Fiona, who had wanted to play the piano but, in the light of the failings in her three elder siblings, was denied for ever after the opportunity to take any music lessons whatsoever.

Joining the CCF was a masterstroke for more reasons than you might imagine. Prime, it settled my career choice, albeit the school only had an army section affiliated to The Highland Light Infantry and taught few skills that would assist directly with my later application to the Royal Air Force. Second, it allowed me to wear and maintain a military uniform from an early age and to develop my personal discipline and teamwork skills, which would serve me well if I was successful in my application. Thirdly, it provided outdoor adventurous activity both in military skill and personal development, and fourth, it provided an opportunity to once again reduce my S+ for diligence scores in academics!

Michael had also had a successful career in the CCF and had reached the exalted rank of company quartermaster sergeant by the time he left school for Ross Hall[5]. The commanding officer was a PE teacher, recognised in the CCF as Captain Thomson. As previously confessed, I was not a strong sportsman and, accordingly, I was wary of Thomson and the inevitable question that would one day utter from his lips. It never came, until one day, early in my military career and whilst heading north on a 'troop train' from Buchanan Street Station in Glasgow to Inverness, for our annual camp, I fell foul of the law for the first and last time. The train was steaming through the Highlands stuffed to the gunwales with cadets from all over Scotland en route to Fort George for summer camp. The train was well north of Pitlochry and we, at fourteen, were consuming bottled beer. Illicit as this was, the whole carriage of boys, all wearing their military battle dress and sporting various Scottish Regimental cap badges, had fallen upon an ideal means of disposing of the evidence. Now, as I write this, I do appreciate that our method would have done little to protect the environment, but, in 1963, not much consideration was given to the environment, save that littering, if caught, might cost your parents a minimal fine. So it was that the evidence of our illegal drinking was deposited 'out the window'. As our alcohol levels increased, 'depositing' turned into a game of 'how far'! No money was to change hands, but there was prestige to be had. As the train chugged north towards Newtonmore, and past Dalwhinnie, the line runs quite close to the A9 road that connects Perth with Inverness! Out I lobbed my empty bottle, only for it to be caught in the slipstream and lofted over the fence and smash on the surface of the highway – I had won, but my victory was very much tarnished when I realised that my bottle had hit the road in front of a car, forcing it to brake and swerve to avoid the debris. Thankfully, I was able to see it recover its equilibrium before the train sped round a bend and left the A9 in its wake. I remember only too well the feeling of terrible guilt that hung over me as the train continued its journey. I was devastated, my parents would be devastated if they ever found out and CQMS Herriot would be thoroughly pissed off with his little brother for traducing the family name in military circles! My mates tried to console me, encouraged me that nothing had or would come of it, but as the train began to slow as we approached Newtonmore Station, a strange sense of foreboding overwhelmed me. As we rolled to an unscheduled stop in the station all thoughts of seven days at Fort George vanished and all I could imagine was a journey back south chained to an iron parcel cage in a British Railways guards van, either with or without a police escort.

I could hear the voices of the train staff approaching, accompanied by Captain Thomson, and vowed at that stage to own up. My parents had always instilled in their children that honesty was the best policy and I wanted to ensure that I followed their guidance on this first, and hopefully last, occasion when it had been my own stupid fault and I needed to ensure that I would receive the least punishment possible. My morale, however, took a sudden dive when I realised that two burly Highland policemen were in the company of the investigation party! All thought now of ever

---

5. The Scottish Hotel School was based at Ross Hall from 1948 to 1981.

seeing my parents again vanished! My friends were aghast that such a development could have befallen us and me in particular.

'Did one of you lads throw a bottle from the train window about ten miles back?' asked one of the burly Highlanders.

I paused to draw breath and, despite their best efforts not to implicate me, realised that all my friends' eyes were cast in my direction.

'It was me,' I said, 'I am very sorry and I do hope that the people in the car are alright.'

'Name please,' said Burly 1.

'David Herriot,' said I.

'Not Michael Herriot's brother?' interjected Thomson!

'Yes,' quaked I.

There, it was out, but at least Thomson did not follow it up with, 'He'd never have thrown a bottle out of a train window!'

There then followed a ten-minute lecture from both police officers about the merits, or not, of drinking beer as a 14-year-old and of the consequences of disposing of one's evidence from a speeding train window. Thomson chipped in occasionally, but the police left without charge and the train resumed its northward journey. I was summoned to see Thomson upon arrival at Fort George, but, after quite a serious ticking off, nothing more was ever said about the incident. Certainly the school never informed my parents and I put it down to a valuable lesson learned in life! Following the train incident I endeavoured to keep out of Captain Thomson's way as much as possible, but often enjoyed his company as I progressed through not only the CCF ranks, but also on rugby trips to away games and to Murrayfield and the Schoolboys' Enclosure.

I 'marched' through the ranks well and even won the Goodwin Cup for Best Cadet in the school year 1964–65. I became a .22 and .303 marksman and gained my Signals Classification. By 1965 I had made it to lance corporal and, one year later, double jumped to become a sergeant in 1966. I can, without any fear of criticism, vouch that my happiest time at The High was when I was dressed in my military battle dress and partaking of military activity with the CCF.

Notwithstanding the venture north to Fort George in 1963, CCF camps were routinely held at Cultybraggan Camp, near Comrie in Perthshire. Cadets from all over Scotland would congregate at this military encampment, which sits on the Highland Boundary Fault Line – one of four geological faults that define Scotland's geography, which includes the Outer Hebrides. The camp was built on the flood plain of the River Earn and had been a POW Camp during the Second World War, where once had been imprisoned Hitler's sidekick Rudolf Hess. The flat lands of the plain and the adjacent mountain ranges provided excellent ground for conducting fieldcraft exercises and for honing our map-reading and leadership skills. The proximity of the River Earn also allowed some fun building and racing rafts during 'down time', if such a thing existed under the military regime invoked by the senior cadets.

The accommodation at Cultybraggan was Nissen huts, and the mess hall provided food to sustain us throughout our stay, all of which was cooked by members of the

Army Catering Corps detached to the Highlands to provide our sustenance. The toilet blocks were quite basic; troughs the length of the wall for communal urination and WCs that consisted of a sewage pipe that entered the building at one end and exited back below ground at the other. Circles, surmounted with a wooden seat, had been cut at regular intervals along the pipe to allow cadets to perch upon when the cook house fare had been put to its full use and was no longer required. Plywood screens separated one 'hole' from another, with a hessian curtain hung to the front to protect one's modesty. The sewer was flushed periodically by a tidal wave that would drag all and sundry through the pipe as it passed from one toilet block to the next.

Senior cadets, with their usual sense of fun and mild terrorisation of their juniors, developed a merry jape that would catch out the unwary very regularly. With the requirement to parade every morning in full pressed uniform, blanco'd belt and gaiters and bulled boots, boot polish was in plentiful supply at Cultybraggan. Boot polish is flammable! Experience helped the seniors identify the cycle of the flush, plus, to the trained ear, an almost imperceptible lapping preceded the arrival of the bow wave. Young cadets, unaware and not alert to why seniors might be hanging around the toilet block, were often caught with their pants down, literally, and would suffer a slightly singed bum as the flaming boot polish tin passed under their exposed posterior on the eddy current that preceded the tidal rush towards the North Sea! It was all done in good fun and nobody suffered unduly – it was part of the process of growing up. I suspect today a dim view would have been taken of it, but this was the carefree 1960s and nobody batted an eyelid, not even the junior cadets who always saw the funny side.

By now Captain Thomson had moved off to pastures new and his role as officer commanding was taken by Major Alastair Mack, who had joined the school staff in 1966. Mack, who had held a commission in the Highland Light Infantry, taught history under the leadership of Harry Ashmall. Having now spent almost forty years in the RAF and having associated with the regular army on occasions throughout my career, I can state categorically that Major Mack was a typical army officer and displayed all the eccentricities expected following a career in a Scottish infantry regiment. No matter the season, he wore a Lovat Green Harris Tweed three-piece suit to school and alternated it routinely with one of a quite bright russet hue! To accompany his suit he wore highly-polished brogues, a Viyella square-patterned heavy cotton shirt and a Harris Tweed tie. He was very much the British Army officer and conducted himself as such within the school.

In the summer of 1966, under Major Mack's leadership, and by his 'pulling in favours' from his army days, the CCF departed from routine and undertook their summer camp with the 1st King's Own Scottish Borderers at their garrison in Osnabruck, Germany. The move away from Cultybraggan was novel, but of course it had to be funded, and that inevitably fell to my parents to provide. It was, as ever, a stretch, but they were insistent that I participated, as I was, by then, a sergeant and had responsibilities to fulfil! We travelled via Harwich to the Hook of Holland and onwards to Osnabruck where we were then transported, not to the barracks, but to a local training area near Haltern, west of Munster. Here we had the delight of undertaking 'proper' mounted infantry tactics in AFV-432s, a tracked armoured personnel carrier, with 'proper' soldiers to guide and drive us. I use the word proper in its loosest sense because memory tells me that the KOSBs spent most of the daylight hours racing around the training area as fast as a 432 would go and, if confronted with a blind alley, took great delight in crashing down saplings and telegraph poles with its armour-plated ends to achieve an escape route! However, we did get the opportunity to drive the 432s and we did also drive FV620 Stalwart[6] vehicles that were newly arrived in the BAOR inventory in 1966. By night, we were entertained to the delights of the British squaddie away from home and off the leash, but only once did we have to race back to camp with them to avoid a fight with the locals following a serious altercation in a local hostelry! Thank the Lord that I played on the wing for the Second XV at the time and, like the rest of the cadets, had not consumed the vast quantities that had caused the squaddies to provoke a fight in the first place. As a result, we from The High were able to outstrip most of the soldiers and reach the camp gate long before the last troop staggered through and it was slammed firmly in the face of the leading German pursuer! All part of life's rich tapestry and part of growing up – again! Now confined to barracks by the commanding officer of Borkenburge Training Area, we were grateful when that phase of our visit to Germany passed and we moved back to barracks in Osnabruck a couple of days later.

Just twenty-one years since the end of the Second World War, Germany was an interesting place to visit as a 17-year-old. The BAOR had been established in 1945 and its primary and original purpose had been to regulate the corps districts which were running the military government of the British Zone of occupied Germany. However, once government passed to civilians, it became the command unit for British troops stationed in Germany and relinquished its administrative responsibilities. As the Cold War rhetoric increased, BAOR, along with its sister command, Royal Air Force Germany, which I would experience some six years later, took on more the role and responsibility as a defender of West Germany than an occupying force. However, this point was not always realised by its population who still saw British troops as occupiers. So the natives of Osnabruck, who had not differentiated between occupier and saviour, were not particularly welcoming, no matter that I was attempting to spend my money on their economy! Why should they be really? Most of them had lived through the war and had seen the segregation of their country by the Soviets in 1961. To them there was little to differentiate between a soldier of occupation in 1945 and the one who claimed to be a defender who drank in their bars and wooed their daughters in 1966. However, with twelve Deutsch Marks to the pound, we British schoolboys felt like kings, but, as ever, I was conscious that the money I had in my pocket had been hard earned and not by me! As will become apparent in this tale, I spent a considerable amount of my military life in Germany and when I returned in 1972 as a young RAF officer, I was quite surprised to discover that sterling had slumped to a meagre 8 DM to the pound. When I returned in 1981 for my last tour on the Buccaneer, it had hit almost rock bottom with a 4:1 ratio! Despite its defeat

---

6. A highly mobile amphibious military truck built by Alvis that served with the British Army.

in 1945, West Germany had become a thriving economy twenty years after the war ended and certainly more vibrant than that of the UK at the time.

When The High reopened its doors in August 1966 to start what should have been, had I not repeated Form III, my last year in school, Mack selected me from amongst his small group of sergeants to become his CSM. Nobody within the CCF circle could ever now compare me to Michael Herriot. I was now senior to my elder brother and with my good friend, Ronnie Orr, filling the position of company quartermaster sergeant, the corps was, in my opinion, in very capable hands. By his very manner, enthusiasm and experience, Mack ensured the survival of Glasgow High School CCF at a time when many other members of staff saw no purpose in the 'militarisation' of pupils and kids were less inclined, and sometimes discouraged, to participate in military activities. Thankfully, Dr Lees was a staunch advocate of The Corps and between the three of us we fought off all attempts to undermine and disband the popular group of pupils who paraded regularly twice a week. Major Mack led from the front and, despite his insistence in perfection from everybody and a resoluteness of mind that was difficult to challenge, he was a very popular commanding officer. Despite his eccentricities, cadets were in awe of the man who, following a particularly arduous day-long climb and descent on a map-reading exercise that year across Ben Lawers in Perthshire, decided that we would bivouac in Glen Ogle before continuing with more military activity the next day. Tents were raised, camp fires built and food cooked on hexamine stoves. After a couple of military manoeuvres in the evening sunlight, Mack decided that we had earned the right to a couple of beers in the nearby Lochearnhead Hotel. Upon our return to the campsite, and following the consumption of a small *cerry oot*[7], we all prepared ourselves for our night under canvas and were amazed to watch Alastair Mack drop a trestle table as his bed and cover himself with his kilt as he prepared to sleep under the stars!

With promotion to CSM came appointment to the School Council. Becoming a prefect was a goal that many aspired to but few achieved, as only fourteen slots were available each year and two of these were reserved for the school captain and his lieutenant. Prefects were selected predominantly from the VIth Form, but with three or four from the Vth, who would naturally retain their position when they entered the VIth; two of whom would become school captain and school lieutenant, respectively, in their final year. Selection to the school council was mandated by the rector and his chosen captain, who himself was selected traditionally because of his all-round ability, initiative and integrity. The school captain in 1966–67 was Robin MacGregor, the other fifty per cent of the identical MacGregor twins that I first met when I joined Miss Barrie back in 1958. His lieutenant was Ian Rowan, who, like me, was determined to seek a career as a pilot in the Royal Air Force. The rest of the council was made up of academics, cricketers, rugby players, swimmers and athletes and Ronnie Orr, my CQMS. Ronnie Orr, Bryan Morrice, Alan Walker and I were the four V[th] Formers amongst the twelve prefects, with MacGregor and Rowan at the helm.

---

7. Glaswegian slang for alcohol purchased at an off-licence for, generally, home consumption.

There is little point in my recounting the role of a prefect as most who read this story will know exactly what I am talking about. Save to say, at The High in 1966 we were not ALL hated! What the council room provided, however, was an opportunity to reduce even further my S+ for diligence scores. It was just too easy to find something better to do than attend class and the 'Herriot sends his apologies, Sir! He's on council business' excuse must have been wearing for the masters to hear continuously if it had not become totally transparent by the end of that year. Of course, occasionally, I would ask my messenger to change the story to 'corps business' just to protect my cover when necessary. What with council and corps business, and rehearsals for school plays, time for class and study was few and far between! Nonetheless, I still managed to score S for diligence in my June 1967 report:

'S – He works within the limits of his capacity, giving no grounds for censure or commendation.'

All that statement really means is that he is neither an academic eagle nor a dodo, but more of an ostrich content to study with his head firmly in the sand! There were too many opportunities and plenty of available excuses for me to avoid learning and I took most of them. If I was not in the CCF stores with Ronnie conducting another interminable inventory check, or counting the dozens of .303 Lee Enfield rifles in the very secure armoury, then I was involved in a council meeting or rehearsing a play in the school hall with either Donald McCormick or David Menzies. Unfortunately, the school report that was sent to my parents only indicated 'Days Absent' and 'Times Late' above the form master's signature block – I scored nil for both, so had, as far as my parents were concerned, a 100 per cent attendance record. Pity the form did not have a block for 'Classes Skived'!

Mine was not a classic and successful academic experience. Before each end of year exam, my mother would sit with me by the fire in the dining room drumming historical facts and dates, chemical equations, or mathematical formulae into my thick head in the vain hope that they would stick until they fell on the exam paper the following morning. I was not too bothered, but should have been. I wanted to fly in the RAF and whilst I accepted that some academic qualifications were required, I was confident that my seven O-Levels outstripped by two the minimum requirement for entry to the flying branches and I still had my Scottish Highers to come.

By the summer of 1967 I was ready for my final school year and returned in August ready to secure my career potential by becoming more involved in the CCF and proving my dedication to a military lifestyle. I had also made a solemn promise to my parents that I would diligently strive for success in my end of year exams.

First, however, there was a problem in the CCF and it was of my making indirectly. Whilst I could remain as CSM, both I and Major Mack felt that that would be unfair to those who, by right – had I stuck to my academics – would have had a clear path to that appointment. I had won the Dawyck Guthrie Cup, the corps' top award, as CSM, and it would have been a strange and much-questioned state of affairs if my name had appeared on it again. Major Mack, who I have to admit had seen some military potential in me, came up with the bright idea of promoting me to under officer, a cadet rank used at the Royal Military Academy Sandhurst, and to the position of unit adjutant. In other words, I would become Mack's second in command. So Mike Clark became CSM and I took on more of an administrative role in the corps. Of course, and you've spotted it already, taking on more responsibility meant less time for academics and with my very own adjutant's office on the top floor of C block, I had found yet another excellent hideaway where I could prioritise my busy schedule.

Major Mack and I got on outstandingly well together, although we did not always agree and often came to metaphorical blows in the corps office. He was an extremely hard man to please (most army officers are) and I could never do anything right when he was in a self-obsessed military mood. However, I had already made a number of applications to the RAF for scholarships, and Mack was a pillar of strength and support when I was knocked back initially. His guidance, encouragement and enthusiasm for the military made sure that I stayed focused on my career choice.

I have, still in my possession, a personal letter from Alastair Mack that he wrote to me after my departure from the school. In it he thanks me for all my hard work and acknowledges my tolerance of his abrupt manner when I was his adjutant in my last year in school. He also states that I was most often right in our heated discussions and commended my ability to contain diplomatically his confrontational approach to issues in the corps office. So, despite his demeanour, he was actually a humane and humble man underneath his severe military exterior.

In that final year, new pupils were selected from the Vth and VIth Forms to join the four of us who formed the rump of the school council from the previous year. Dr Lees, however, selected neither a school captain nor a lieutenant to lead the team initially! He informed the four of us that he wished to delay his decision whilst he contemplated what was best for the school, the pupils and the staff. To my mind, Alan Walker was the front runner. He was captain of rugby, played cricket for the First XI and for Stirling County and was an able golfer. He was a sportsman through and through, and, here I quote from the 1968 school magazine, was of 'adequate academic record'. What the magazine does not tell me is whether he was S or S+ for diligence! I, on the other hand, only had the CCF and a budding thespian career to support any bid that I might have had for the ultimate position in school. I was certainly no sportsman, as many a PE Master had told me previously when comparing me to my brother, and my academic record could never have been described as adequate. For a start, I had repeated Third Form, scraped some O-Levels and never been much better than S for Diligence! Ronnie Orr was in the frame, as was Bryan Morrice, but, coincidentally, they too had repeated years and whilst Bryan was an ace cricketer, Ronnie had been one rank below me in the CCF. Alan Walker had to be first choice and I, possibly, had a chance of being his lieutenant, but there were others from the VIth Form now present who had much greater academic records, or were outstanding sportsmen, so nothing could be guaranteed.

I was surprised, but delighted, therefore, when Dr Lees invited me into his office about three weeks into the autumn term of 1967 to ask me to be his school captain for that year; Alan Walker was to be my deputy. Unfortunately, it became apparent quite quickly that Alan Walker was not happy – he clearly felt that he was a shoe-in given the three dullards that were in competition with him! What he did not know and came as a surprise to me, was what Dr Lees told me when he invited me into his office. The CCF, I knew, had proved that I had initiative and integrity, but, unlike Walker, I doubted my all-round ability. Nonetheless, I had been selected because, out of the four he had to choose from, Dr Lees thought that I was the most level-headed! I hope that I proved him right, but it was a very difficult year for me. Alan Walker, supported by his year contemporaries, who invariably sided with him and who now formed the bulk of the school council, systematically went out of his way to undermine my authority.

It was an unhappy year for me and I was quite glad when it was all over. Whilst the council functioned effectively, it was definitely split down the middle. The corps was my sanctuary and I found myself undertaking more and more administration out of sight of most of my peers and masters whenever I could.

My duties as captain involved 'ceremonial' tasks at school assemblies and my mother was honoured with presenting the prizes at school sports day, but maintaining discipline both within the council and the school in general was a difficult task with the forever undercurrent created by Walker's supporters. Neither I nor David Lees ever did discover who had daubed the school wall with 'FUCK HERRIOT' in white distemper, but, despite the janitors' best attempts to remove it, it is still visible almost fifty years later if you know where to look!

Time moves on and all too soon my schooling was over and I was ready to seek my fortune in the great metropolis of life. By October 1968, I had in my hand a letter from the Officer and Aircrew Selection Centre at RAF Biggin Hill telling me that, subject to my continued medical fitness, I had been selected for training as a navigator, leading to appointment to a Direct Entry Commission in the General Duties Branch of the Royal Air Force. With seven O-Levels and one Higher, in English, I was on my way!

Chapter Four

Kicking My Heels

My first experience of aviation I can thank my musical upbringing for. With my father's involvement in classical music in Glasgow, our family home routinely became a lodging house for international soloists who, when on tour and in Glasgow, were invariably hosted at our house. Other than Frank Wilson, people like Erich Gruenberg, violin, Maryse Chomé, the cellist who turned Judith to that instrument, and Peter Wallfisch, piano, were regular visitors. The Wallfisch family lived in Notting Hill in London. Peter, as a 12-year-old, had escaped the Holocaust as it approached his home town of Breslau by making his own way to London via Jerusalem. Whilst Peter had been avoiding the Nazis, his future wife, Anita Lasker, had been surviving in Auschwitz as an accomplished cellist in the camp's Youth Orchestra. They had invited me as a 13-year-old in 1963 to spend the Easter holidays being shown the sites of London by their son, who was of a similar age. This presented a mild dilemma for my parents as to how to transport me, on my own, from the industrial capital of Scotland to the nation's capital some 400 miles south. Thus it was that I flew for the first time, courtesy of a BEA Vickers Vanguard, from Renfrew Airport to Heathrow. As the turboprops began to rotate and the aircraft moved from the apron towards the threshold, the excitement that beat within my 13-year-old chest was almost too much to bear and as the Border sheep got smaller and we passed through the thin lair of stratocumulus that covered the Southern Uplands on that day, I knew I had just experienced the launch of the next phase of my life. I determined at that moment that I would become a pilot in the RAF; despite the comfort of the Vanguard in the cruise I would not join the airlines. I wanted the thrill of the chase, the passion of the fight, the sheer exhilaration that I was sure the acceleration of a jet fighter would provide. Yet my first thoughts were uninformed, uneducated and certainly those of a romantic. I had no idea what being a fighter pilot would be like. I did not know the first thing about aerodynamics, propulsion systems, or air combat. What I did know was that I wanted to do it and nothing would stand in the way of my achieving it.

Michael, too, had wanted to go into the RAF and had taken the entrance tests for Cranwell and passed, but, to his amazement, had failed the aircrew medical examination because his nose had been broken two or three times playing rugby, which apparently made it too weak for him to be allowed to fly single-seat aircraft, which is all he had wanted to do. It was, probably, a very lucky 'break' for Michael. His life took a completely different path working long hours as a hotel manager for many of the big conglomerates; he ultimately became Managing Director of Virgin Hotels, working for and with Sir Richard Branson. On leaving the Girls High School, Judith worked in the computer department at J & P Coats, the thread makers, in their office in Glasgow. In 1963, computers were a very new concept and their bulk filled many rooms to provide no more output than a smart phone can provide today. At school Judith had been an excellent swordswoman and had won a number of medals in competition. This she continued after school and was fortunate that J & P Coats recognised her sporting skill and allowed her time off work to compete both nationally and internationally. She bears a number of scars from her efforts, not least of which is in her thigh, when, in a competition in Germany, her opponent's foil snapped during a lunge and penetrated her quad muscle – she has an entry and exit wound! Undeterred by this 'flesh wound', Judith eventually won representative honours at the Jamaica Commonwealth Games in 1968, the Mexico Olympics of 1970 and the Edinburgh Commonwealth Games in 1972. A true international sportswoman. Fiona, the brain of the four – and another successful competitive swordswoman – subsequently left the Girls High and ventured to Edinburgh University, where she succeeded in gaining a degree in medicine and a career as a GP.

Very soon after my Easter trip to London, posters of Lightning pilots with long-drawn g-induced faces adorned my bedroom wall and joined those of Californian Surfers; my musical taste then and now was firmly set with The Beach Boys and their evocative 'Surfing Sound' and even though I was a poor swimmer, surfing was my dream! By the time I reached sixteen I had already applied to OASC for a Sixth Form Scholarship to the RAF for a commission as a pilot. Unfortunately, David Lees had taken note of my 'S+ for diligence' scores and, with little faith in my academic ability, had informed the RAF accordingly; I was unsuccessful! Undeterred, I applied again in January 1967 for a Cranwell Cadetship and was invited to attend for selection in July that year, but with the same negative result. Once again it was my academic record that was not in my favour. I had, however, got further in the process than previously, which only hardened my resolve to succeed. So, with the re-sits of the Higher Exams behind me and the results pending, I applied for a Direct Entry Commission in July 1968 and was invited once again to Biggin Hill for assessment and medical examination. My mother, ever wise, had encouraged me to make sure that I had 'more irons in the fire', and so I also applied and was interviewed at Hamble for selection to the BOAC pilot training school there. I also applied to take part in a familiarisation visit to the Royal Military Academy Sandhurst. However, this two-day visit to Berkshire was endured whilst suffering considerable pain following a skiing accident suffered in Glencoe whilst attempting to race others back to the ski lift after only one day's training on skis! I hit a mogul at thirty-plus knots with wayward skis, which flashed and crossed before my very eyes before they dug into the deep snow! All a prelude to being stretchered off the mountain. No lasting damage was apparent and so I left for Sandhurst a few days later on crutches, but was not overly enamoured with my trip south on that occasion. I suspect that, unbeknown at the time, it was in Glencoe that I ruptured my groin, which eventually took me to RAF Hospital Halton rather than continuing with my navigation course!

RAF Biggin Hill was near Westerham in Kent. After a journey on the overnight sleeper train from Glasgow to London Euston, it was but a mere hop across the city to London Victoria and the train to Bromley, where a coach was waiting to collect the candidates. As the coach drove through the gates of this famous Battle of Britain airfield, we were confronted with a vision of what had brought us all together! There, on a pole, was a full-size Spitfire, that iconic aircraft that had played a major role in the survival of Britain in 1940. There was no doubt in any of our minds that this was the gateway to the Royal Air Force and that the next four or five days would define our futures one way or another. After a welcoming address and a briefing on what was about to befall us, we were despatched to our dormitories and thence lunch before participating in the aircrew aptitude tests.

The large group of candidates was broken into smaller syndicates and each man, there were no women from what I recall, was allocated a tabard with both his syndicate letter and an individual number emblazoned thereon. From this moment, you became a number rather than a name. We all knew, because we had prepared ourselves, that if you were successful in the aptitude tests, the medical examination, the individual and group exercises and the interview, then you stood a very good chance of going forward to the second part of the selection process. If not, then your anticipated five-day visit to Kent would be foreshortened!

Today, the aptitude tests are run on powerful computers, but follow much the same principle that they did in 1968. For me, it was clear that their purpose was designed to identify the eye-hand reaction and coordination of individuals with a view to them becoming a pilot. Following a small white dot on a black screen with two feet planted firmly on pseudo rudder pedals, whilst at the same time using a small joystick to track the erratically moving dot, is more difficult than you might imagine! Other tests challenged your numerical skills, whilst the group and individual exercises analysed both your logical thought processes and your ability to convey those thoughts to others in a team. It was, strangely, very enjoyable, although the pressure was immense, as to fail meant the end of one's hopes and dreams.

The personal interview was undertaken by a wing commander and a squadron leader together in a small room. The junior member spent twenty minutes interrogating me about my knowledge of the RAF, its aircraft and their roles, the geopolitical world situation and the command structure of the service that I one day hoped to become a member of. During this intense pressure period, the wing commander took no part at all, but sat quietly scribing notes and ticking, or marking with an X, boxes on a clipboard that he held out of view! Without a second to draw breath and with a reversal of roles, there then followed a similar interrogation by the wing commander about my schooling, my family, and my desire to become a Royal Air Force officer.

I felt comfortable with my RAF knowledge and the aircraft it flew. After all, I had been a bit of an aircraft spotter in my day and had been a regular visitor at both Renfrew and Prestwick airports. The latter often received British and American military aircraft either on diversion or on a refuelling stop following a transatlantic crossing. All sorts of military aircraft would regularly pass through Prestwick and so aircraft identification was not an issue for me. Moreover, CF-104 Starfighters of the Royal Canadian Air Force underwent major servicing in the Scottish Aviation company's black hangars on the north side of the airfield at Prestwick. So it was routine to see Starfighters inbound and outbound or pounding the Prestwick circuit prior to delivery back to the Canadians. It was also customary to see groups of youths, including me, skulking within the protected area around the black hangars in an attempt to secure the registration numbers of the CF-104s therein! Little did I realise that one day in 1975 I would break the sound barrier in one!

I had also been a fairly regular visitor at Battle of Britain Open Days at RAF Leuchars, near St Andrews in Fife, once even enduring a freezing and dark four-hour return on the back of Jim McNaughton's moped to get back home. The journey there in the September sunlight had been uneventful, but after a hard day pounding the tarmac until the gates were about to close, the journey home was not quite so enjoyable. Moreover, I had not dared tell my parents just exactly how I was managing to get to and from Leuchars! Jim was a couple of years older than me and was a fellow 'spotter' and pupil at The High. He, too, had ambitions for a career in the RAF and was successful, eventually, in becoming a Vulcan navigator.

Ian Rowan, another fellow RAF candidate from The High, held a Private Pilot's Licence and somehow had access to a Bölkow Junior two-seater aeroplane lodged at Renfrew Airport. Twice he invited me to go flying with him and we shared the delight of flying in this high wing light monoplane over The Campsie Fells and Loch Lomond for about an hour each time. He had even let me 'have a go', which only served to reinforce my desire to make flying as a pilot my career.

In the school Easter holiday of 1965 I had also managed to take part in a five day 'Flying Experience Course' at the Royal Naval Air Station at Lossiemouth in Scotland. Lossiemouth was a unit that I would come to know and love in my later career, but for now it was there to provide a taste of what I was determined to achieve. There I was, seventeen years old and kitted out with a flying suit, helmet, oxygen mask and flying boots, ready for flying in a Sea Prince C1 aircraft. HMS *Fulmar*, as it was known to the Royal Navy, was a very busy place; and the Sea Prince, the Fleet Air Arm's name for the Percival Pembroke light transport aircraft, was dwarfed by the much more powerful Buccaneers and Hunters as it took its turn for take-off on the Lossiemouth runway. Air experience sorties were flown up and down the Moray coast, and on one notable occasion the pilot bunted the aircraft such that the effect of negative-g and simulated weightlessness allowed the cadets in the rear – in his words – to feel like spacemen! It was all too fantastic, and again, just enforced my desire. We lived in black wooden sheds alongside the Ratings' Mess at Lossie and ate with the Other Ranks during our spell there. Quaintly, because we were on the ration strength of the unit, we were entitled to our 'tot of rum' each evening at 1700hrs, but, although also entitled, were never given our concession of a packet of ten cigarettes!

All this 'spotting' and flying was imperative for candidates to prove to the RAF that they had had a long interest in aircraft and flying, and whilst 'spotting' might seem a naff pastime now, it was another lever in a very competitive selection process. A successful career in the CCF was also a positive, but I had no idea how these two officers might have viewed my academic record at The High – I could only hope that I had been convincing and shown my commitment. Needless to say, I left the room in a cold sweat with no knowledge of whether I had impressed or not. Had they seen through my flannelling about my poor academic record and was my successful career in the CCF sufficient to sway them in my favour? Only time would tell; and next I had to endure the next 'Stop/Go' examination – the Medical!

The medical examination was, to say the least, thorough. Full anthropomorphic measurements had to be taken as, sadly, not every human form can fit inside a fighter cockpit – although many that you think might not, actually do! Of course, pee tests, balls and cough checks and heart and lungs were all given full functional analysis before the critical and 'dead end' tests took place. In the 1960s you could not become a pilot in the RAF unless you had 20/20 vision and were not colour blind. I knew I was not colour blind as I had undertaken the Ishihara 'card' tests many times in my life previously. However, none of us were very sure about the eyesight test. None of us wore glasses, but not many of us had had our eyes tested previously. I could read the number on a Number 23 bus as soon as it crested the hill on Pollokshaws Road, but did that mean that I had perfect vision? Definitely the most 'exotic' test was the hearing test. Throughout my RAF career, during my annual medicals, hearing tests have been undertaken in a soundproofed audiometric testing booth, which is connected to a calibrated 'read-out' printer. Not so in 1968. At Biggin Hill, in the mid-twentieth century, the hearing test was conducted with the Medical Officer standing in one corner of the room whilst the candidate and the nurse stood in the opposite one. Then, with absolute silence in the room, but no sound screening from the traffic passing outside, the doctor would whisper words at you whilst the nurse wiggled her finger in the ear that was not being challenged at that time! Quaint, but very British!

Wednesday lunchtime at Biggin was spent mostly in silence. Despite our hopes and dreams, none of us could be particularly sure of our position and whether we would still be there at the end of the day. We re-mustered after lunch to learn our fate. When your name was called out, we were told, you had to reposition in the room next door; nobody told us whether that was a good or a bad thing! My name was, eventually, called out and I passed into the other room to be confronted with many dejected faces. We sat for ages, some paced up and down, others engaged in almost hysterical conversations. I held my council, unsure whether it would be third time lucky or another rejection. At least if I was rejected this time it would not have been as a result of a damning letter from my headmaster, but through my own weakness, whether that had been medical or interview failure, or an accumulation of failures over the last two days. Would I get another chance? How many times can you apply? Was there anything that I might be able to do if I had a medical issue? Surely not, how can you reverse nature? Aptitude! What if I had failed the aptitude testing? All sorts of irrational thoughts raced in and out of my brain, but solved nothing, we just had to wait!

It seemed as if hours had passed before a corporal appeared to let us know that we had passed Phase One and would be participating in the hangar exercises the following day. We were ecstatic and decided that that night was a night to celebrate and so we took ourselves to the White Hart in Brasted, which had been a regular haunt of the Battle of Britain pilots from Biggin Hill in 1940. However, sense prevailed, and with the prospect of having to impress in the hangar the next day, serious drinking was not a feature that night. After a couple of pints we bade the landlord farewell and made our way back to our dormitory to get a good night's sleep before the Thursday morning exercises in the hangar.

The hangar exercises, still used to this day, are designed not only to identify those with a natural flare for leadership, but also to ascertain who was a willing and able follower, and who was not. In groups of six, led by a squadron leader there to assess, we worked our way through the hangar with one candidate tasked to lead each exercise. A training period preceded the actual selection process to allow us to familiarise ourselves with the types of equipment, the procedures and the safety precautions. That complete, and prior to each lead exercise, the assessor provided the leader with a verbal brief on the task and special rules for that particular exercise. Meanwhile, his fellows were positioned behind a screen so that they heard nothing of the brief nor had they an opportunity to assess the exercise and the equipment. Once briefed, the leader was permitted a couple of minutes to survey the exercise site and to move freely about the course and check whether the planks provided would bridge gaps to be crossed and to check the weight and sturdiness of drum barrels that needed to be moved from A to B. Then it was up to each leader to call forward his team, brief them on the task and guide them through its execution. It was not the time, as leader, to be bombastic, nor, on the other hand, was it time, as a follower, to try to usurp the leader's position.

The exercises were designed to test all the candidates both physically and mentally. Either the ropes and planks were too short to accommodate the plan or the 'leap distances' were just beyond the reach of the average man! However, completing the task, whilst admirable, was not the main purpose of the event. Proving sound leadership or followership was the most important aspect and so, once your lead was done and dusted, there was no prospect of sitting on one's hands, as to do so would have been instant failure!

Come the Friday lunchtime, it was all over, and after a relaxing lunch and with our bags packed, we were transported back to Bromley and, for me, onwards to the night sleeper back to Scotland. We left content that we had got through the whole process, but unaware whether an offer might one day fall on our door mats!

With my school days behind me and no career secured, I realised very quickly that I needed to knuckle down and find myself a job. I was not looking for anything other than 'short term' as my mind was still firmly set on a career in the RAF. There was plenty of time for me to seek my fortune elsewhere if the RAF rejected me again, but the confidence of youth, at nineteen, was unprepared to consider rejection as anything other than the non-option! I had been working regularly since I was eight as a paperboy for John Ferguson at his shop in Kilmarnock Road, but the wages of a paperboy, even an experienced one, were not high and I needed funds both to save my parents further financial despair and to ensure that my social life increased.

As a teenager, I had not been a great one for venturing far from shore. Whilst some of my school friends, Peter Walker, Ike Grant and Stuart Fyfe, lived relatively close, others, including David Mutch, Stuart Laing, Ronnie Orr and Peter Knight, lived to the north of the city and were inaccessible routinely without a car. My parents had never owned a car, my father never ever drove one, and so the prospect of driving myself across the city and beyond was a non-starter. David Mutch and I had, as young teens, regularly entertained each other to tea after school, but his home in Bishopbriggs was a considerable distance away and he had left The High at the end of the Vth Form and eventually took to accounting and a long career with Deloitte's in Bermuda; I lost contact with him until he emerged on Facebook in 2008. Stuart Laing's family owned Laing's the Jewellers, in Glasgow, and his career was destined to follow in the family line. Ike was in love and although we went to the occasional party together, he concentrated more on his love life than his mates. He was also in a band with Stuart Fyfe, with whom he still 'gigs' at charity events in and around Glasgow. Peter Walker and I had a very warm friendship and were regular visitors to each other's houses. However, as we both progressed along different paths at school we drifted apart, but bumped into each other in 2005 thanks again to Facebook.

As you might imagine, there were plenty of bars in and around Glasgow and when we boys got together in a group there was no fear of being thrown out for underage drinking! There was always someone able and brave enough to pass themselves off as eighteen, whilst the rest of us skulked in a crowd in a far corner. So mob-handed can be a good thing and more so if, in ignorance, you wandered into one of the less-salubrious hostelries in the city centre. The Eglinton Arms in Eaglesham was a good place to drink, but it required someone with access to wheels to get you there. 'Sammy Dow's' at Shawlands Cross was another and within staggering distance from home too. However, none of these places ever provided the drinker with much 'talent spotting', as pubs in Glasgow in the 1960s were very much a gentleman's domain – they were not all gentlemen either! Unless you went to a planned dance at the tennis club or the like, there was very little prospect of meeting young and available like-minded women. Meeting a girl in one of the few select pubs in Glasgow was also extremely difficult as the licensing laws of the day forced pubs to close at 9.30pm with 'Last Orders' being called fifteen minutes prior. So even if there was any talent available in the pub, by the time you had plucked up the courage to approach, let alone buy them a drink, the pub had closed and you were out on your ear with nowhere further to go except home!

Ronnie Orr lived in Bearsden where he had access to his father's Rover. A friend with a car is a good friend to have! So, regularly on a Saturday night, in my last year at school and afterwards, I would travel into the city by train and hike across to Queen's Street Station and onwards to Milngavie, where Ronnie would pick me up in his father's Rover before we joined up with Peter Knight and Stuart Laing for a night out. The evening would start at The Burnbrae Hotel before we headed back towards the city along 'The Switchback' road that connected Bearsden with Anniesland; an area we knew well because of the location of The High's playing fields there. There were plenty of bars along Byres Road and Great Western Road and there were no drink-driving laws or breathalysers in those days. However, even these bars were not filled with women, although some did attract many students from Glasgow University which was local. This was the 'Flower Power' era and a time of liberation and free love, but, for me, there was not much free love available and my attempt to secure some was invariably ineffective! Ronnie had the solution, however. He had heard about The Carioca Club in Bearsden, which remained open late and, happily for me, closed just in time for me to catch the last train back from Bearsden and home to Shawlands. The Carioca was a place without an alcohol licence, but was not worth visiting anyway until its mass of humanity arrived after the pubs shut! Girls galore! Women dancing around their handbags, whilst we drunks propped up the walls and watched, plucking up the courage to ask for a dance, but never sober enough to do so. The Carioca was, however, a very popular place to finish off a Saturday night. It was renowned for being the starting place for many a successful band and the place erupted regularly when 'names', *The Small Faces* to name but one, showed up to perform for the screaming teenagers! I fell in love almost every weekend in The Carioca Club, but, strangely, always found myself wending my weary way home alone!

Bill Shooter, my fellow thespian, and I had decided one day to try our luck at Paisley Ice Rink. I had never been on skates before, but it seemed a reasonable notion to give it a try and anyway, we were aware that it was a popular venue for meeting girls. We were not wrong! The place was crowded and after about thirty minutes of falling around on the ice, Bill and I set off gingerly around the perimeter with our right hands hovering above the wooden rail in order to arrest our inevitable fall to earth! It was on that circuit that we saw two girls hovering by the side with the similar angst that we had now shunned in favour of ensuring that we got value for money. Sylvia was her name, and yes, she would very much like to go to the cinema next Saturday evening if I would meet her on the corner of East Lane, where the ice rink was situated, and the Glasgow Road. I remember her name well because as soon as I told my mother she began to recite Shakespeare's poem *'Who is Sylvia, what is she'?* Sadly, I never did discover the answer to that question because, she never showed that Saturday night and I had no further contact with Sylvia!

I had attempted to woo Barbara Ann whilst I was still at The High. As a Beach Boys fan, I could think of nothing greater than having a girlfriend called 'Barbara Ann'[1]. As far as I can recall she lived on either one of three roads in Giffnock: Newlands; Monreith; or Carlaverock Drive. But, frankly, these three roads on my paper round were all very similar and, after almost fifty years, have melded into one. Save to say now that the houses on each were vast Victorian villas with a long winding path to the front door and were owned by the select of that suburb of Glasgow. I parked my bike against the garden wall, dumped the paper bag on the pavement and made my way up the long drive to push a copy of *The Glasgow Herald* through the letterbox. Whilst thinking about nothing in particular, I looked up to see a vision of loveliness, about seventeen years of age, standing full in a bedroom window pulling a school blouse over her, as yet, only bra-restrained breasts! Now there's nothing better than the female form to send a young man's passion racing. If it is semi-naked, then so much the better. It was not long before I had managed to extract some intelligence on Barbara Ann whilst on my next train journey to school. Ike knew her through the Clarkston Tennis Club and he offered to arrange an introduction if I wanted to

---

1. One of *The Beach Boys* hits was entitled *Barbara Ann*.

attend the next dance there where his band would be performing. You cannot get luckier than that! Sadly, the introduction proved fruitless as she informed me that her mother would only allow her to go out with tennis club members whose parents were known to her family. So, despite my best efforts and as a non-tennis club member, there was little hope of any romance there. I saw Barbara Ann regularly afterwards and we became quite good friends. She travelled on the same train into the city to attend Park School and often shared the same compartment as Ike and the rest of The High gang. Sadly, and despite further attempts, I never wooed her, she was by then 'goan steddy'[2] with a lad from the tennis club. What with 'mothers of the daughters of the manse', 'mothers of the tennis club' and 'Sylvia who refused to let me find out what she was', my love life was virtually non-existent as a teenager!

Whilst awaiting news from the RAF, I applied for, and gained, an appointment in Copland & Lye's department store on Sauchiehall Street, next door to Pettigrew and Stephen; these were two of the most prestigious stores in Glasgow. The latter was where my mother had to fork out to buy my school uniform. Both stores were Victorian in origin and nothing much had changed in the ensuing years. Very posh would be an understatement and the premises were occupied by gentile ladies on both sides of the counter! Customers were treated as god-like and woe betide any member of staff who caught the eye of the floor walker! I can only imagine that the scriptwriters of the BBC comedy *Are You Being Served* studied Coplands whilst undertaking their research.

My role was 'below stairs', working in the Despatch Department! The job description was pretty simple. Receive orders from the shop above and segregate them into cages for distribution by the appropriate driver, who would then flash around Glasgow in the distinctive brown vans with gold lettering that were Copland & Lye's trademark. Occasionally, I would be called upon to visit departments and collect parcels that were for express delivery. No loitering was allowed by the despatch staff once they reached the shop floor. On my first visit to the Ladies' Fashion Department I happened to notice a young girl who was busy with a customer. Thora Storie was eighteen, I was a year older. She was divine! I became infatuated with her very existence and wanted to see her whenever I could manage to slip out of the cellar. I would find any excuse to leave my post and sneak out of 'despatch' on the pretext of running a store errand just to catch a glimpse of her. She, too, began to notice me and before long I had plucked up the courage to talk to her, but it had to be discrete as the floor walker took a very dim view of staff consorting together and especially a boy from 'below decks'. Her cute, coy smile twisted my heart into knots every time I saw her. I was head over heels in love, but I had to know if she felt the same. When given a tea break, I would head quickly for the canteen to conduct a recce to see if Thora was there. If she was, I would contrive to sit beside her and if she was not, I would rush back downstairs indicating that there was a very long queue and that I would try later. The tactic worked reasonably well and quite often I would share my break with the woman of my dreams.

---

2. Glasgow slang for being in a relationship.

Then tragedy struck! I was promoted! The despatch manager, either working on a tip off or out of the kindness of his heart, decided that my future lay not in stacking shelves in cages, but in acting as the delivery boy in one of the vans. Davey, my driver, and I became 'Kings of the Road'. On Mondays and Thursdays our routes took us to Newton Mearns and Mearnskirk to the south of the city on the road to Kilmarnock and out past the Eglinton Arms at Eaglesham. On Tuesday and Friday, we had the task of delivering to Bearsden and Milngavie – The Carioca Club did not ever look quite so inviting in daylight as it did on a Saturday night after sharpeners at The Burnbrae! These small towns and villages, with their expensive properties and moneyed owners were all outside the city boundary and so it was a day trip for Davey and me. Regular lunch breaks were taken in the van sat outside The City Bakeries in either Bearsden or Newton Mearns. Lunch always consisted of a piping hot Scotch Pie, its bowl filled with baked beans and topped off with creamed potatoes! Luxury and all washed down with a can of Irn Bru. Total luxury! Wednesdays were for visiting Ladies' Fashions and contrived tea breaks!

By mid-October I had received my letter of offer from the RAF and the time to take my leave of a very happy six months at Coplands was getting ever closer. Thora and I were now dating and falling, well I was, desperately in love. She invited me to a school dance at her old alma mater, St Columba's in Kilmacolm, and I took her to see *The Beach Boys* at the Odeon Cinema in Glasgow when their European Tour hit my home town on 10 December 1968. We were getting very close, but the prospect of me heading south for a military career was very difficult, for her at least, to come to terms with. Ever optimistic, I was convinced that it would make no difference to our relationship, as I reckoned I could get home regularly and she could come to see me; neither of us had a car or access to one! Surely there was no problem. However, being far more pragmatic than me, Thora made the sensible decision to break up. Just three weeks after *The Beach Boys* concert I bade her farewell and headed south for my career as an airman; she subsequently married the store owner's son!

Sensibly, my parents thought it would make sense if I were able to drive before I departed for the RAF. My mother had gone back to teaching at the age of fifty when all four children were settled and frankly, the money helped. One of her teaching friends lived locally and her husband, Stuart, was the proud owner of a Humber Hawk in which he was prepared to give me free lessons. My father knew nothing of driving and my mother had last driven when she was a young woman. Consequently, the fact that the Humber was an automatic meant little or nothing to them and they envisioned a simple few hours with Stuart and I would be on my way, automotively speaking! My instructor, sensibly, had other ideas, and once he had taught me road etiquette, how to follow the Highway Code and where to position the car relative to the kerb and the white line, he persuaded my parents that I should now undertake lessons with a driving school and in a conventionally geared car before applying for my test. All went swimmingly well and, without a scratch on either vehicle, I applied for my driving test, which was allocated for 26 December 1968! I have long since lost the piece of paper that was thrust into my hand by the examiner on Boxing Day after the test was completed, but I will never forget his words, 'Well, Mr Herriot, you've passed, but you've still got a hell of a lot to learn!' Wise words indeed, but with the piece of paper in my hand I headed home with a happy heart. I may not have owned a car, but at least I had a piece of paper to allow me to do so when I could afford one. It came just in time, as the next five days were to be filled with the final preparations for leaving home.

I had read that letter from the RAF again and again and again. I had passed the selection process, but with a significant caveat to my offer of acceptance. As far as I could ascertain, my aptitude scores for pilot had been less than the RAF's accepted average standard, but my aptitude for navigator training had been marked as exceptionally high. I could either accept or decline the offer. There was no decision to be made really. First and foremost I wanted a commission in the RAF and I wanted to fly! What difference could there possibly be in whether I sat in the front or the back seat of a fighter aircraft? None, well at least none that I could think of as a 19-year-old whose head was firmly and literally in the clouds! With my obligatory trilby hat firmly on my head, I left home on 2 January 1969 and headed for the Aircrew Officer Training School[3] at Church Fenton near York.

3. In 1968 AOTS was established at RAF Church Fenton when No 1 Initial Training School closed at RAF South Cerney. AOTS subsequently closed in 1969 when officer training in the RAF was consolidated at RAFC Cranwell and the Officer Cadet Training Unit at RAF Henlow. The AOTS role was purely to train and commission Direct Entrant Aircrew for the RAF.

Chapter Five

Per Ardua Ad Astra

The RAF selection process for commissioning, and for aircrew in particular, is rigorous. It can afford to be. In the year 2000, when the RAF was 52,000 strong, some 6,000 UK citizens applied to be officers, but only 1,500 were successful in being filtered through to the selection process at OASC at the RAF College at Cranwell in Lincolnshire. Of these, only six hundred were selected for training; ten per cent of those who had applied. Of these six hundred, only one hundred and forty were pilots. In the late 1960s, when the RAF's footprint spanned the globe and its numbers were twice those in the year that started the new millennium, it was equally difficult, but I did not need to read another word of that letter, I was in! OK, so I had failed the pilot tests, but navigator was good and if I made a fist of it, I could still fly in fighters and do aerobatics and drop bombs!

The train eased off its brakes and, as the power built up, it slid forward on Platform 2 of Edinburgh's Waverley Station to begin its journey south to Great Britain's capital city. Tucked comfortably in Second Class, I waved farewell to my parents who had escorted me from Glasgow so that they could see me off on the last leg of my journey to a new life. Southwards I journeyed, alone with my thoughts.

With Christmas looming, my mother and I had had a frantic few weeks ensuring that all the required civilian items had been purchased. Now my whole life, it seemed, was packed in the suitcase in the rack above me and although excited by the prospect, I was a little unsure of what lay ahead. The required kit list had been comprehensive, but little seemed to be required in terms of casual wear. A 'sports jacket with slacks and tie' was understandable, as was a 'gentleman's suit'. But a trilby hat? I was quite accustomed to wearing headgear; the regulations of The High demanded that school caps were worn by boys up to and including the Third Form. I had also routinely worn a Tam O'Shanter as part of my Highland Light Infantry CCF uniform, but I did not routinely wear a hat for 'walking out'! Oh well, I was sure that everything would be explained by the time I got to RAF Church Fenton and I had no doubt that the RAF staff would clarify and answer any questions or misgivings that we new recruits might have!

As the train continued its journey south towards the English border, I read again the joining instructions. '*You must arrive by 1400 hours at York Railway Station where a coach will be waiting to convey recruits to RAF Church Fenton*'. It was nearly 11 o'clock and we still had not reached Berwick-upon-Tweed. Surely York could not just be two hours further south! It was in England, which made it many miles away for this rarely-travelled south of the border Scot! I began to panic that my first contact with the RAF, as a recruit, was going to be as a latecomer! My parents had been adamant that the 10.30am train out of Edinburgh would be more than adequate to get me to York on time, but as the River Tweed singularly failed to materialise out the carriage window, I began to suspect that today was going to be a disaster. I have always loved the thrill and romanticism of a train journey and whenever I needed to travel anywhere, no matter by what means, I have invariably ensured that my departure took place first thing in the morning to ensure that I arrived in plenty of time. What purpose is there in life of wasting heartbeats sitting waiting to depart when one can already be safely at one's destination and ready for whatever is about to take place!

Before long, however, the wonderful scenery of the Northumberland coastline was passing on our left-hand side and, with the ticket inspector's reassuring words that we were 'on time for York', I settled back to read the joining instructions again. '*Upon your arrival at the Aircrew Officer Training School you will be met by a group of officer cadets who will escort you and settle you in to your accommodation*'.

The train arrived in York and I soon found myself alone in a strange world and a sea of faces, none of which I recognised, and certainly none wearing RAF uniform or even looking remotely military. It was not yet 1.30pm and I had over thirty minutes to kill before the arrival of the scheduled transport to Church Fenton. The first Thursday that year was a particularly cold one and a railway station is never the warmest or welcoming of places. After a quick look outside the concourse to ensure that there was no coach waiting, I found a draught-free corner to sit out my wait and attempted to spot others who might be about to share my fate.

There were only ten of us on the coach that left the station promptly at 1400 hours. We looked around at each other quizzically, each with our own thoughts, but, before long, excited chatter ensued as we introduced ourselves and told a little about where we had come from. The main topic of conversation, eventually, was, 'Why do you think we need a trilby hat?' and, as Church Fenton drew closer and we pulled off the A162 that became, 'Do you think we ought to be wearing them?' Given the size of the RAF we all felt that ten recruits for 250 Course AOTS seemed a rather inadequate sum necessary to fortify the aircrew echelons of the RAF – little did we know!

True to their word, ten cadets awaited our arrival at the guardroom and, having introduced themselves to us, escorted us to our barrack block explaining they were cadets on 248 Course and that each would be a mentor to one of us during our initial weeks in officer training. My mentor went by the name of Dave Hurley and, like me, he was hoping to become a navigator when he graduated in two months' time. As we entered the barrack block I was amazed at the effort that somebody had gone to to make the place so pristine. You could almost see your face in the highly burnished floor and the toilets were spotless; even the taps gleamed. Quite a welcome and frankly, there was no need to have gone to all that effort! The barrack block had a dormitory at one end and we soon found ourselves claiming beds and unloading suitcases! I selected a bed fairly close to the centre of the room and began to sort out my belongings. Dave informed me that just putting them all in the cupboard was not *exactly* how it worked, but, since we were only going to be there for a few days initially, all would be explained after we returned. 'Returned from where?' I enquired. 'Scotland,' he responded. 'I've just come from Scotland, what are you talking about?' By now a small gathering of interested ears had gathered around my bed. 'Has nobody told you?' 'Nope!' 'Told us what?' 'Your course does not start for another month, but you ten have been selected to attend the Moray Sea School[1] in Scotland! You leave on Sunday! Tomorrow you will be attested into the Royal Air Force, have a briefing about the Moray Sea School, be issued with railway warrants, and on Sunday morning, you will be taken back to York to catch a train for Aberdeen and beyond! Anyway, right now you need to get your bed spaces sorted out and then get yourselves dressed for dinner in No 2 Officers' Mess. We'll see you all in the bar at five!'

There was a neatly squared pile of blankets and sheets positioned at the end of each bed, all wrapped in one blanket. It seemed a great shame to unravel it as somebody must have gone to a great deal of effort to make it look like that, but if we were going to get any sleep on our first night in the RAF, beds had to be made! The barrack block was shaped like an 'H' and the ablutions were situated in the central corridor. Soon we were all booted and spurred and ready for the bar, but we were all conscious of the need to show some propriety on our first night in the Royal Air Force. We were, of course, all potential aircrew and as such, had a propensity not only to drink, but to enjoy ourselves too. Apart from me, others in our select group were: Ray Brooke, who eventually became a supply officer, having failed navigator training and retired as a wing commander; Ed Golden, a successful C-130 navigator who retired as a squadron leader; Graham Richardson, an F-4 navigator who completed his Direct Entrant commission and retired as a squadron leader; and Graham Gillett, who was unsuccessful at officer training. Dave Hurley and his fellow mentors bought the first round and explained that we would each be given a bar number tomorrow, which would allow us to buy alcohol without having to carry money on our person routinely. That sounded like a recipe for disaster to me, but became reassured when Dave pointed out that the maximum mess bill permissible each month was £10! Anybody who broke that rule would suffer the ignominy of an interview with the station commander, which was guaranteed to be a 'one-way chat with hat on!' Our mentors explained more about the training process and let us know that they were on Red Course, which, in their estimation, was the best and only course. The intermediate course, No 249, was White Course and we, once we got going in February 1969, would be on Blue Course. That night in the bar at Church Fenton was an eye-opener. For a start, the price of beer was so amazingly cheap compared to pubs outside that I imagined that you could get very pissed very easily every night and still stay well within the station commander's £10 limit! More importantly, however, it became very obvious very quickly that we were all like-minded souls and, as a result, conversation flowed very easily! When the bar closed we dragged ourselves back to our dormitory slightly light-headed, but sure in the knowledge that we had made the correct career decision. Dave Hurley eventually flew Phantoms and, like me, retired as a wing commander. Our paths crossed occasionally throughout our careers and we always remarked back to the happy time that we had spent together at Church Fenton in 1969.

1. This was the first Outward Bound School in Scotland, situated close to Gordonstoun and focusing on sea activities. It was opened in 1952 and, in 1977, moved to Loch Eil.

The following morning, bright and early, we were up and at it. We had not yet been issued with uniform, but we were soon finished with breakfast and ready to be attested into the Royal Air Force. Our mentors had directed us to Station Headquarters where we were met by Flying Officer Sunderland, who explained the process to us. In simple terms, we would each swear an oath of allegiance to Her Majesty the Queen, sign a piece of paper which was effectively a contract and then sign The Official Secrets Act. Attestation was secured by means of an RAF Form 60, which bore the title:

ROYAL AIR FORCE
NOTICE TO BE GIVEN UNDER SECTION 2(1) OF THE AIR FORCE ACT, 1955, TO A PERSON OFFERING TO ENLIST IN THE REGULAR AIR FORCE

It was all very official. But as I signed on the dotted line, there was no doubt in my mind that I was committing my life to service in the RAF for at least the next eighteen years and, if they would have me, for as long as they wanted me. Nothing doubted the commitment in my mind.

With bible clutched firmly in my right hand, I then took the oath of allegiance:

'I, David Rodger Herriot, swear by Almighty God that I will be faithful and bear true allegiance to Her Majesty Queen Elizabeth The Second, Her Heirs and Successors, and that I will as in duty bound, honestly and faithfully defend Her Majesty, Her Heirs and Successors, in Person, Crown and Dignity against all enemies, and will observe and obey all orders of Her Majesty, Her Heirs and Successors, and of the Air Officers and other Officers set over me.'

On the Sunday we happy ten boarded the same RAF coach to retrace our steps to York Station and, for me, onwards on the reverse journey taken four days earlier back to Edinburgh and thence to Aberdeen, the Granite City, which I had learned about at school, but never visited. Its nickname stems from its grand architecture and the rock from which it is built. Some, however, refer to Aberdeen as the Silver City because, as we discovered on our arrival, the granite crystals do actually glisten in the sunlight! After a short break in Aberdeen, we were soon entrained again and heading west along the Moray coast to Elgin and four weeks at the Moray Sea School run by the Outward Bound Trust.

The Trust is an educational charity that bases its learning in the outdoors. Its aim was, and still is, to assist young people with their personal development and realise their potential by creating a challenging environment for learning – in the main – about their own capabilities. It was founded in 1941 by Lawrence Holt and Kurt Hahn and was intended primarily then as a survival school for merchant seamen. However, it soon became apparent that its methods could provide a useful process in making individuals more independent, resilient and self-aware.

Hahn had founded Gordonstoun School in 1934 and had developed it along the lines of his *Schule Schloss Salem* that opened in Germany in 1919. Exiled to Britain by the Nazis in 1933 for his outspoken criticism of fascism, Hahn bought the lease of the nascent, but financially floundering school in order to serve only as a short-lived example of his academic vision. The school survived and, although evacuated in 1940 to serve as a military barracks, by the end of that decade pupil numbers had risen to two hundred and fifty. Hahn's vision for Gordonstoun and his so-called *Salem System* was replicated in the Outward Bound Trust and one of its primary sites in 1969 was the Moray Sea School, near Burghead.

Our course, M185, at Burghead, brought together a broad cross section of British society. As well as our RAF contingent were young men from industry, the banking sector, civil servants and, strangely, a significant number of young offenders; a total of about sixty personnel! Amongst them was David Eales, a friend from The High, who was there at the start of a banking scholarship. Of note was the fact that the majority of us were of a similar age. Certainly, at our pre-departure briefing at Church Fenton, it had been explained that the RAF had identified our group as being the youngest members about to join 250 Course at AOTS and that it had been felt that the ensuing four weeks could only be to our advantage in our personal development and would undoubtedly be great fun! Would that the RAF could afford such luxuries in 2017!

Well, first, somebody needs to explain the definition of *Great Fun*! I could agree that rock climbing, seamanship and expeditions in the Scottish Highlands are most invigorating and bloody good fun, but having to run the five miles from Burghead to Gordonstoun for swimming, and back again, is hardly my idea of fun and as for swimming, what fun is there in that when you have an inbuilt loathing of the deep end! I did not enjoy my runs to Gordonstoun. Nor was I very keen on the intensive PE sessions that we had to undertake!

The beds at Burghead were adequate, but there was not a great deal of warmth oozing from the few radiators that January. The ablutions too were pretty basic, which was perhaps the reason that good old Hahn had mandated that the day had to start with a brisk run down the beach and a dive into the Moray Firth! There is a reason that people of a Scottish persuasion are less than keen on sea swimming and that, in its simplicity, is because when God created his most wonderful kingdom north of the English Border. He surrounded it with the coldest bloody water on earth! Thankfully, the staff at the Moray Sea School that January had taken the sensible decision that the sea was too cold for early morning bathing and that we, on M185, could have the privilege of starting the day with a shower – there was, however, no hot water ever available, which also made shaving a particularly unpleasant affair.

The four weeks passed rather too quickly and, despite the frugal washing facilities, were outstandingly good fun. Seamanship training was conducted from Burghead harbour in large seagoing rowing boats, where we all took our place in the engine room pulling on our oars to overcome the Moray Firth swell once we had left the shelter of the harbour wall. Rock climbing and abseiling were conducted on the cliffs to the east of the school and was a true test of your will and an excellent tool for overcoming fear and realising your potential. The most enjoyable exercise, however, had to be the expedition in Glen Affric in the Scottish Western Highlands. Glen Affric has often been described as the most beautiful glen in Scotland. It stretches for thirty miles from its westerly extremity near Kintail almost to Cannich in Strathglass. The mountain streams that tumble down the side of the glen form two major streams in the valley floor that are a source of life for the most wonderful plants and wildlife, which includes significant numbers of red deer. Together, these two streams form the River Affric that flows through Loch Affric and Loch Beinn a' Mheadhoin to Fasnakyle in Strathglass, where it becomes a tributary of the River Glass. Truly outstanding countryside and very well worth a visit. Our expedition lasted five days and required keen map-reading, leadership and followership skills, as well as good physical fitness and stamina. Whilst I had enjoyed some ability in these in my days in the CCF at Glasgow High, now on Outward Bound, and working with people from all sorts of different backgrounds, I was able to develop them further.

Performance on the course was graded as Honours, Merit or Membership! Thankfully, there were no diligence scores attributed on Outward Bound! My scores on my report read: Expedition – Merit +; Seamanship – Merit; Physical Education – Merit +; and Rock Climbing – Membership! The note below the course photograph, in which I do not appear for some unrecalled reason, in my contemporary photograph album, states simply 'VERDICT – EXCELLENT'! I guess it must have been then.

Back at Church Fenton, after two weeks of gratis familiarisation with our new employer, we assembled on Sunday, 16 February, with the remainder of the cohort of 250 Course, which would commence the following morning.

Immediately prior to the outbreak of the Second World War, aircrew recruiting for the RAF had assumed such large proportions that it had been deemed appropriate to establish specialised units to receive and provide initial ground training to prepare aircrew recruits for the various stages of their flying training. These units were called Initial Training Wings. By 1943, twenty-one of these wings were in operation, located mainly at seaside resorts where accommodation was readily available. By the end of the war, however, their task had been completed and the majority of these wings were closed. Those that remained had been moved to permanent Royal Air Force stations inland and, by December 1945, only the wing at Bridgnorth, in Shropshire, remained. In June 1946, the Bridgnorth training wing was renamed No. 1 Initial Training School (ITS).

No. 1 ITS lived a peripatetic existence as each airfield closed its doors in a reducing post-war air force. By 1957, the school was situated at RAF South Cerney in Gloucestershire and, on 1 January 1967, it was renamed as the Aircrew Officer Training School. The following January it moved to RAF Church Fenton, where it remained for some eighteen months before a reorganisation of officer training within the Royal Air Force resulted in all non-RAF College officer training being conducted at the Officer Cadet Training Unit at RAF Henlow.

The course at AOTS, which was only fifteen weeks long, was very much shorter than the cadetship course run at the RAF College at Cranwell. Nevertheless, the syllabus at Church Fenton still managed to cram all the necessary basics to turn people like me from feckless civilian to military officer. The course was designed primarily to prepare us for life as leaders in the RAF. But before all that could commence we had to be militarised. The first action was to get uniformed and in the military there is only one way as a recruit to get from barrack block to Clothing Stores! We marched! Well marched is not an appropriate verb to use for what 250 Course achieved at our first attempt and whilst it seemed to amuse many of us, Sergeant Rhoose took a different view. The air turned blue and we quickly realised that drill was a serious business. Drill, as defined in *Encyclopaedia Britannica*, is designed to:

> '*Prepare soldiers for performance of their duties in peace and war through the practice and rehearsal of prescribed movements. In a practical sense, drill consolidates soldiers into battle formations and familiarises them with their weapons. Psychologically, it develops a sense of teamwork, discipline, and self-control; it promotes automatic performance of duties under disturbing circumstances and instinctive response to the control and stimulus of leaders.*'

There were no obvious *disturbing circumstances* in our attempts to cover the short distance between our accommodation and 'Stores' that February morning in 1969, but we clearly lacked discipline and Rhoose made quite sure that we all understood that that was a situation that was likely to change! As we lined up in alphabetical order in Clothing Stores, I found myself confronted by a large pile of clothing, some of which I had anticipated receiving and some which I had not. Amongst the expected RAF blue battle dress jacket and trousers, beret, collarless shirts, rigid detached collars and black tie were plimsolls, and dark blue 'Shorts PE' and 'Vests PE', which, although not welcome, were an obvious necessity for the arduous PE sessions yet to come. What I had not anticipated were the RAF pyjamas, vests, underpants, a multitude of black socks and the RAF blue military style raincoat that were thrust forward. The pile of clothing also included two pairs of overalls for field work. As Direct Entrants for commissioning, we had been attested into the RAF as airmen for the duration of the course and so were issued with 'Shoes Black – Airman Pattern'! Everything in the military inventory is catalogued back to front for ease of storage and re-identification. However, to we civilians it seemed an incongruous method of marking our new-found wardrobe that we stuffed into our 'Holdall – RAF blue' in order to convey it all back to our block.

Once unpacked, Sergeant Rhoose, now adopting a more conciliatory approach, demonstrated how each item should be displayed in our small wardrobe before every inspection. In the military there is a place for everything and everything should be in its place! He also provided a practical lesson, for those who needed it, on how to iron a military shirt! Now it might seem simple and sufficient to flash an iron across the front and back and throw it on, but not at AOTS. Whilst the front and back were simple enough to smooth, making sure that the crease in each arm was uniform and that the shoulder to shoulder crease was exactly the right drop from the collar were more difficult to achieve. We were then informed that each morning, we would be inspected and so would our bed spaces. The floor needed to be gleaming and for this a floor bumper was provided. For those brought up in the technical age of computerised vacuum cleaners and floor polishers, and who might never have been acquainted with a 'floor bumper', I can assure you that this was a task to be avoided when it came to 'bull nights'. Polishing vast areas of linoleum with a bumper is heavy work. The ablutions needed to be pristine and that included making sure that the WC was scrubbed and spotless. Any dust would result in an appropriate sanction levied against the transgressor. If any aspect of the inspection did not meet the standard in a common area then a sanction would fall on the whole course, which inevitably would entail some sort of physical exertion. Not keen on physical exertion at the best of times, I did my utmost to ensure that my 'space' was immaculate and encouraged others involved in the 'bumping' and 'loo scrubbing' to do likewise.

There were, amongst our merry band, a number of officer cadets who had served time as airmen (Other Ranks) previously and they were good men to know. They knew just how best to polish a pair of shoes such that the Drill Sergeant's face was reflected in the gloss. They knew just how best to get a knife edge crease into a battledress sleeve. And they knew just how much, or in reality how little, you could get away with on room inspections! Masters of the 'Box Blanket', they were able to reassure we novices that it was possible to turn one's bed sheets and blankets into 'a neatly squared pile of blankets and sheets', but I, for the life of me, found it a very difficult task to achieve initially. Military blankets and sheets were marked with two (sheet) or three (blanket) pencil-thin lines centred and parallel to their long edge. The sheets and blankets had to be folded such that these lines were visible in the centre of the fold and directly above each other. Stacked blanket, sheet, blanket, sheet, they then had to be wrapped in the third blanket with its own lines exactly in line with those of the already folded bedding. This all had to be achieved after climbing out of bed, and whilst trying to also fit in a shit, shower, shave and shampoo without soiling any of the previously beautifully prepared ablutions, or dripping water on the burnished linoleum! The ex-airmen were, like Yorkie at Nav School, a godsend!

Drill continued apace and was intermingled with Physical Education during the initial weeks of our training. After my time in the CCF, drill held little fear for me and I quite looked forward to Rhoose's 'friendly banter' on the parade square. He had a withering put-down line for any cadet who stepped out of line. 'Don't call me sir, Mr ------, I'm not a fucking officer, I'm a fucking sergeant!' was a regular response when a quaking cadet tried to dig himself out with a humble apology of, 'Sorry, Sir!' One, perhaps apocryphal, story about Rhoose occurred during a practice parade where a cadet had been tasked with raising the RAF Ensign on the parade ground. Unfortunately, he managed to get it stuck halfway up. 'Mr ------, you are an idiot, bring the fucking thing down and start again!' So down came the Ensign and the whole process started over. Again it snagged halfway up and the poor officer cadet, now in a mild panic, was struggling to get it to shift either up or down when he heard Rhoose shout, 'The fucking thing's upside down now!' and, clearly exasperated, he threw his pace stick on the ground, whereupon it broke into many pieces. He was absolutely livid but, like all good Drill Sergeants, eventually saw the funny side of the affair.

Drill, inspections of room and self, physical training, and leadership training, were the core skills in the syllabus. Other less obvious skills, perhaps, were the development of officer qualities, quaintly always referred to in the military as OQs, general service training and, surprisingly and worryingly for me, English, Mathematics and Aeronautical Science!

My syndicate director was a very pleasant chap by the name of Flight Lieutenant Bill Howard. Bill was ten years my senior and a Shackleton pilot by trade. My time on Blue Squadron was a happy one, but with my less than satisfactory academic diligence scores still haunting me from The High, my time on 250 Course soon came to an end! My 'Week Six' report dated 31 March 1969 reads:

'Herriot is a cheerful and personable young man who has settled down well at AOTS. His appearance and turnout are always good and he accepts discipline well.

'Academically, he is experiencing some difficulty. His maths results are poor and his science is far from spectacular. His overall maths result after Progress Test 2 is 43% but because he has made obvious attempts to improve (30% to 56%) a formal caution was deemed unnecessary at this time. However, he must show improvement at PT3 if he is to stay with the course.

'Always pleasant and cheerful in his manner, Herriot is a popular member of the syndicate. It is to be hoped that he can master the academics syllabus as he seems to have good potential in other aspects.'

Sadly, it was not to be and with further lack of progress in Maths and Science at PT3, I left 250 Course to join, in Dave Hurley's words, the best and only course to be a member of at AOTS. I was now a member of B Syndicate on 251 'Red' Course!

There were forty-one officer cadets on 251 Course distributed almost evenly in five syndicates. B Syndicate was led by the very spirited Flight Lieutenant Ivan Hughes, a search and rescue helicopter pilot by training and a character well suited to the AOTS environment. By that I mean he had a sympathetic approach and a sense of humour!

251 Course had commenced on 24 March and had already lost one of its number voluntarily after just one week of training. Although some people have an absolute desire to fly, when the reality of military training strikes them they realise, sadly, that they are just not cut out for it. I was happy, as his departure had made way for me on Ivan Hughes' syndicate. There was also a friendly face from home on 251 Course. Ian Rowan, my school friend and Bölkow Junior pilot, had followed me to the RAF with an aspiration to become a fighter pilot.

Now settled on Red Course, I vowed to knuckle down and exorcise my mathematical and aeronautical science demons! It was clear from my time on Blue Course that I would never be aircrew if I did not overcome the academic portion of the Initial Officer Training Course. By the time Week Six assessment came round again, Ivan Hughes had assessed me somewhat differently from the report at the same point on Blue Course.

'Herriot is a quiet personable young man who has settled down well with his new course.

'In academics he has shown a big improvement and provided he keeps it up, should have few problems in the future.

'In Officer Training, Herriot's progress has been quite satisfactory. Possessing plenty of drive and enthusiasm, he is a good team member and constantly strives to improve his performance. A good prospect for the future.'

Leadership training was conducted at Wathgill Camp near Richmond in North Yorkshire. Here we learned the art of pine pole carrying, river crossing and other such arts to test our leadership skills. All the exercises were timed and required the selected leader to brief, lead, accomplish the task and debrief his team. Distances had to be covered and the North Yorkshire terrain made this in itself a difficult task without the addition of the very heavy pine poles that required at least two men to carry the lightest of them. The tasks were complex and required a great deal of skill by the leader to maintain the morale of his team, whilst at the same time proving to the ever-present Directing Staff that he had what it took to lead a team of men. Of course, leadership task completed, it was impossible to relax back into the team and rest on any possible laurel that might have been offered by the staff debrief of your lead. We all had to show good followership and help the next leader just in the manner that, hopefully, he had helped you. It was all quite knackering, as each leader pushed his team along to meet the exercise schedule and maintain hopes of passing the next progress point in the course that followed our return to Church Fenton. Despite these muscle-flagging exercises, there was still an air of relaxedness amongst this aircrew body of men. The staff, too, showed us just how aircrew can enjoy themselves by arranging a full silver service dinner in the field at which some of the cadets, me included, volunteered to serve as waiters. There sat the ten staff members of Red Course, including Sergeant Barnes the Drill Instructor, with some of the mess silver adorning the trestle tables and we few volunteers rushing from field kitchen to tented dining room with steaming plates of food and bottles of wine! Dave Hurley had been right; Red Course certainly seemed to know how to enjoy itself!

Back at Church Fenton the course ground on. It is quite amazing just how long fifteen weeks can last when your whole life plan rests on its completion! As part of our physical training we had to master the Assault Course with and without our 7.62mm SLRs. The purpose of the Assault Course was to build both confidence and teamwork. Many of the obstacles were difficult to overcome and relied heavily on the assistance of your peers to get up and over. A six-foot wall can present a particularly difficult barrier when laden down with military kit, back packs and an SLR, but a deft punt up from a buddy can make it feel just like a low picket fence. High beams, rope swings, scramble nets and ground-level tunnels, were there to prove our mettle! On an exceptionally cold day, I was having particular trouble getting across a rope swing that had a deep water-filled ditch that was about twelve feet from shore to shore. After a number of attempts, my strength gave way and I slid off the rope and floundered into the deep pond beneath me. The water was foul and freezing cold. It was not a place to be immersed, especially for a non-swimmer! Happily, once I had recovered my composure and was back on dry land, Ivan Hughes ordered me back to the block for a hot shower whilst the remainder of the syndicate finished the exercise and followed me. My overalls were drenched and caked in a rather putrid slime from the bottom of the pit so I took myself straight to the showers, turned one on and stepped fully clothed into it to both clean my overalls and warm myself quicker. Once my core temperature had recovered I started to slip the overalls off, only to see a stickleback jump from within my clothes and down the plughole! I was still laughing when the rest of B Syndicate arrived to hose themselves down!

As aircrew we had to be able to swim a minimum of twenty-five metres before we could graduate from AOTS. That, in itself, was a pretty tall order for me! RAF swimming proficiency classifies individuals as either X, Y or Z. The X category covers most aquatic animals and humans with webbed feet! The Y category means that, whilst you may not have webbed feet, you can swim at least twenty-five metres unaided. The Z category, by the very implication of that consonant, meant that if and when you dared to enter deep water, you had no alternative but to sink to the bottom unaided! I was a Z category swimmer and was likely to remain there given my avid fear of water when I arrived at Church Fenton! I dreaded the weekly visits to the Yearsley Swimming Baths on Haxby Road in York on a Friday morning. Much as I tried, I never managed to reach the required distance which would mean that I never had to enter a pool again! Once in the water, I always looked forward to returning to the coach and the wonderful smell of chocolate that emanated from the Nestlé factory just across the road from the pool. The smell of chocolate was overpowering and strangely warming after time wallowing in the shallow end of the pool. As graduation approached I doubted my ability to succeed. The Warrant Officer PTI had a different idea, however, and, having coaxed me previously to succeed, came with the course to the baths to administer his own foolproof method of getting an anxious officer cadet through this mandatory test. Once the session had completed and the rest of my peers were showering, he encouraged me to remain in the shallow end and, with a bamboo pole held firmly in his hand and positioned just above my nose, I began to propel myself on my back through the water and towards the deep end of the fifty-metre pool. Every time I attempted to grab the pole, he pulled it just out of my reach and, with words of encouragement, nurtured me through the water until I touched the wall at the deep end. There were loud cheers from the rest of my syndicate who were lining the wall and, as I pulled myself out of the water, the warrant officer shook my hand vigorously with a, 'Well done, Mr Herriot, you've passed! You swam fifty metres!'

'Not without your help, Warrant!' I beamed, and shook his hand equally vigorously. I was a Y category swimmer and was now qualified to be aircrew.

It was not just all work and no play at AOTS. There was an obligatory period at the start of the course when we were confined to barracks to overcome any temptation by unhappy cadets of going AWOL and running home to their Mum. Once that four-week quarantine period was over, we were permitted to leave camp at weekends and head for the flesh pots of York. There was only one rule, however, and that was that all officer cadets departing camp in civilian clothes had to walk past the guardroom and be wearing their trilby hats! You had to be smartly dressed and look like an officer and evidently, wearing a trilby hat was all that was needed for that transformation to occur! Needless to say, all trilby hats at Church Fenton looked like they had been crushed to death in a pocket. However, their malleable construct did allow them to be reshaped for the walk past the guardroom, both outbound to, and inbound from, a night out in a local hostelry.

We were paid £8 per week as officer cadets and, other than ensuring that our monthly mess bill remained below £10, had little to spend the residue on during the training week. Saturday nights at the discotheque, The Wharfedale, in Tadcaster, were always popular and with a pint of beer costing about two shillings, or ten pence in decimal, an officer cadet could have a pretty good time on his weekly wage. Beer was even cheaper in the officers' mess bar! We rarely spent Saturday evenings in York as Tadcaster was smaller and closer to home. In our 'officers' mufti'[2] we looked somewhat conspicuous and felt more comfortable in 'Taddy' where, at least, the local girls recognised us for who we were rather than some odd balls from out of town. The Tudor Tea Rooms on Jubbergate in York was a popular and regular haunt for afternoon tea on a Saturday. Not because we were tea connoisseurs, but more because the waitress was an absolute stunner. You will sympathise, I am sure, that as we were deprived of female company routinely at AOTS, we felt the need to ogle a beauty! Even if it cost us a pot of tea and some cream cakes, I can assure you that this beauty was well worth ogling!

Once we reached the halfway point of the course we were encouraged by the Directing Staff to organise a mid-course party. As ever, it was all very well organising a party, but, although some of the erstwhile serving airmen were married, few of us had an actual girlfriend that we could invite. I made a futile attempt to encourage Thora to travel south, but she had already moved on and was 'unavailable'! The staff, who had seen this dilemma previously amongst their young charges, stepped up to the plate and provided the telephone number of a good and responsive contact at Ripon Teachers' Training College. They turned up in their droves, by coach, all feeling the same hormonal deprivation as we did in our cloistered environment. The party was a great success and some private arrangements were, no doubt, cast for those who would move closer to Ripon to undertake their pilot training. Not for me, however. I never did have much luck in an open competition environment when it came to the fairer sex!

For one lucky cadet, it turned out to be a particularly fortuitous evening. Well, that was until he and his conquest were discovered *in flagrante delicto* across the billiard table by a member of staff! After a quick straightening of their attire, and a calling forward of the Ripon bound coach, the mid-course party was over. We innocents repaired to our beds and the unfortunate cadet sweated until the Monday to discover his fate! In true aircrew style, little, if anything, was said. He knew his behaviour had been inappropriate and he knew that the sweating it out had been punishment enough. I do not doubt his card had been marked, and there would be no second chances were he to step across the line between gentlemanly and ungentlemanly behaviour again.

---

2. Mufti (slang for 'civilian attire'): refers to plain or ordinary clothes, especially when worn by one who normally wears, or has long worn, a military or other uniform.

The RAF employs a Duty Roster system three hundred and sixty-five days a year to maintain an out of hours presence on every unit. The SDO is, routinely, the station commander's representative and, in the early period of my career, he was supported by an Orderly Officer, an Orderly Sergeant and an Orderly Corporal. Others, like the Duty Clerk, were on hand to provide support if required. Whilst the SDO took charge of this 'overnight' team, the Orderly Officer had a number of tasks to perform. Prime amongst these was to be present to salute the RAF Ensign in the evening and morning when it was lowered and raised respectively by the Orderly Sergeant, but there were other duties and it was never guaranteed that the Orderly Officer would get a full night's sleep. In the latter years of my career, on most units, the Orderly Officer post was done away with and his duties were undertaken by the SDO.

I met my first Royal Air Force 'character' whilst under training at Church Fenton and filling the role of Orderly Officer Under Instruction. The RAF is renowned for having had many characters in its short history and I met many more during my career, and one in particular who became a great friend. Whether these characters were World War Aces or just really entertaining individuals it did not really matter. The RAF required a special breed of men to fly their aircraft and that attracted many high-spirited chaps into the Service. This particular high-spirited chap was Flying Officer Dai Heather-Hayes, the Orderly Officer on the night in question and tasked with guiding me through my duties.

We met outside the guardroom at 1755hrs for the specific purpose of lowering the Ensign at 1800hrs precisely. The lowering and raising of the Ensign on every RAF Unit at two specific times in the day is a serious and solemn affair. The Ensign is treated reverently in the Service and its raising and lowering signifies the start and end of the official working day. Before the Orderly Sergeant raises or lowers it, he gives one sharp blast on a whistle to which everybody outside and within earshot must stop what they are doing, turn to face the Ensign and stand to attention. Officers salute, and people driving must stop and wait whilst the ceremony is signalled to be over by two sharp blasts on the sergeant's whistle. With the Orderly Sergeant in position at the base of the flagpole, the Orderly Officer is to march smartly to a position in front of the Ensign and salute for the duration of the period between the whistle blasts.

Stories about Dai Heather-Hayes were legendary around the RAF and, because of his presence at Church Fenton, had even leaked to us mere cadets on AOTS! One such tale relates to his days as a Hunter pilot in the Middle East[3]. In front of the officers' mess on this desert airbase was an oval rose garden that was bisected by a path that pointed directly at the front door of the mess. During Happy Hours, and one imagines after much alcohol had been consumed, Dai had taken to riding his motor bike around and around the rose garden, which seems innocuous in itself as long as no injury befell anybody! However, having revved the motorcycle up to almost as fast

---

3. In the years following the Second World War the RAF was a global force with stations spread across the world under the command of regional HQs. These were designated: Far East Air Force (FEAF); Middle East Air Force (MEAF) and Near East Air Force (NEAF). FEAF closed in 1971, MEAF in 1958 (subsumed into NEAF) and NEAF in 1976.

it would go, he would then cut down the bisecting path and leap up the steps straight into the mess reception area, where he would park his motorbike on the entrance hall carpet, much to the delight of his squadron peers! It had become his party piece and was a much-anticipated event once the beer started flowing. These things usually are. Characters usually have a particular party piece and, once the party starts, everybody there is waiting in eager anticipation for the moment to arrive.

The PMC, however, had become a little sick and tired of Dai's Friday night antics and took the initiative to place a concrete bollard at each end of the path through the rose garden. Dai took exception to this authoritarian act and decided to remedy it. Furnishing himself with a pneumatic drill, he dug up one of the concrete bollards and re-cemented it in the open door of the PMC's office inside the mess!

Heather-Hayes was, at the time of our meeting, a QFI on PFS at Church Fenton. The role of PFS was to introduce student pilots, with no previous flying experience, to the delights of flying in the Chipmunk and prepare them for undertaking Basic Flying Training on the Jet Provost Mk3, which was the RAF's basic pilot trainer at the time. As part of the RAF's Foreign and Commonwealth training programme, young Iraqi trainees were assigned to PFS to learn the basics with RAF instructors. Perhaps following his experience in The Gulf, Dai did not take kindly to being given a young Arab pilot to practise approaches against a cloud. It would seem from the story that was going around Church Fenton at the time that the poor lad was not good enough to practise doing approaches to the runway even with a QFI behind him! Having eventually had enough, Dai hit the transmit button on his radio and said, 'I'm pissed off!'

The Approach Controller exclaimed, 'Who said that? Callsign please.'

To which he received the prompt reply, 'I'm not that pissed off!'

On another occasion in a Chipmunk, Dai stood in the back cockpit and saluted during a flypast on an Air Officer Commanding's Inspection Parade. The story goes that he had persuaded his student in the front to crouch on the floor and steer with his hands whilst he flung the canopy fully back, stood up and gave a rigid eyes right!

All apocryphal, perhaps, but these stories were certainly alive at Church Fenton when I met the man on the steps of Station Headquarters to undertake my training stint as Orderly Officer. As I stood there, immaculately turned out in my No 2 Battle Dress uniform, I spotted him approaching from No 1 Officers' Mess, which was across the main road that bisected the camp from the married quarters site. He had thick flowing strawberry-blonde hair and a ruddy complexion. His SD hat was worn at a jaunty angle and forced the overabundance of flowing locks out from under its rim – it had seen better days, and by its tired and threadbare appearance, had to have spent many an hour rammed in the back of a Hunter cockpit! He ambled up, introduced himself and then sauntered, whilst I marched, towards the Ensign. Once the ceremony was complete, he asked if there were any questions and ambled off back from whence he came, agreeing to meet me again at the guardroom at 2200hrs to do the 'Key Check'. I never saw him again, he never showed for the 'Key Check' and I was excused the Ensign raising ceremony the following morning as we had to depart early for the dreaded swimming session in York!

Dai Heather-Hayes was a character and a half and very much a legend in the RAF in the 1960s and 1970s. I learned little from him on my training duty, but to have met him, albeit briefly, has at least allowed me to put a face to the name of one of the RAF's great characters.

As I look back now over my RAF career, I can see that being an officer recruit at AOTS was a privilege. For those fortunate to have their careers start at Church Fenton under the mentorship of fellow aircrew such as Ivan Hughes was a huge advantage. Whilst the purpose of the school was firm and grounded, its attitude to life generally was very typically aircrew; it could be nothing else given its construct. There was a light-heartedness at Church Fenton that I do not think existed elsewhere in the RAF training machine. It first manifested itself to me when my very good friend Taff Paines arrived in the staff headquarters building for an interview with Ivan Hughes one day. In a loud and unmistakable Welsh accent, Taff hollered out to those cadets already present, 'Where does Hughes hang out?' To which he received the response from within, 'Flight Lieutenant Hughes 'hangs out' in here, Paines!'

Not at all subdued, Taff entered Ivan Hughes' office, saluted as smartly as his prop forward frame would allow and, stepping forward to take the proffered seat, put his right foot firmly into the metal waste-paper basket, which stuck firmly to his oversized 'Shoes Black – Airman Pattern'! Hughes smiled, conducted the interview without comment and watched, bemused, whilst Paines departed with the waste basket firmly attached to the bottom of his right leg! Taff had played rugby for the Welsh Schoolboys and might have won an international cap had he not, whilst he was undergoing the conversion course at RAF Lossiemouth, been killed in a Buccaneer S1 following a starboard engine explosion and aircraft fire at 2,000 feet just after take-off on 8 December 1970. The aircraft crashed on a wooded slope five miles from Lossiemouth and both crew ejected. However, Taff's seat malfunctioned and he died still strapped into it. Subsequent investigation discovered that the Navy had fitted an unapproved modification to deflect broken Perspex from lodging in the top of the seat as it passed through the canopy. Unfortunately, a sailor tasked with servicing the aircraft had inadvertently stood on the plate and bent it, which prevented the scissor shackle from opening and thereby denied the deployment of the parachute that would then have released Taff from the seat!

We had been prepared for such eventualities during our training at AOTS. At the time the RAF owned an ejection seat rig that was mounted on the rear of an articulated truck known for some reason as a 'Queen Mary'! As potential aircrew we all had to 'take a ride', so with our overalls and our 'Shoes Black – Airman Pattern' on we marched down to the hangars at Church Fenton on 30 June to view this latest challenge that had been set before us. From what I recall the mechanism consisted of a thirty-foot rack and pinion system that, for transit, lay horizontally on the back of the Queen Mary with an ejection seat fitted at its bottom end. For 'the ride' it was cranked upwards to an angle of about 10° short of the vertical and a third of the normally prescribed charge was fitted. Basic ejection seats are driven by an explosive charge that propels the occupant and seat out of the cockpit and into the slipstream of the aircraft where, by various mechanisms, a parachute is pulled from the top of the seat to stabilise it in flight and eventually the occupant is released from the seat with his parachute harness to float happily down to the ground. In training aircraft like the Jet Provost, which pilots trained on in the 1970s, this simple mechanism was sufficient to ensure safe release, assuming that the aircraft had a forward velocity of more than ninety knots. Faster aircraft, like the Buccaneer, were fitted with a rocket pack underneath the seat that allowed the occupant to be projected much faster and clearer from the cockpit before the explosive charge fired, which then propelled him well clear of the fast approaching tailplane! These seats were known as zero–zero seats; in other words, zero height and zero forward velocity!

Our 'ride' at Church Fenton, however, was nothing more than an opportunity to feel what it might be like to eject should that day ever dawn. Eventually it was my turn to strap myself in, and now, fitted with flying helmet inner and outer, I braced myself for the thrust that would propel me thirty feet into the Yorkshire sky! Having never done it before, and happily never since, the short one-second pause that had been briefed seemed very long after I pulled the face blind and before the bang that sent me skywards. Although nothing more than an 'experience' check, I never ever in my subsequent flying career had any doubts that if I did ever have to 'go with a bang' I would pull the black and yellow handle without a second thought!

The end of June was fast approaching and our graduation was scheduled for 4 July 1969; Independence Day! Yet none of us knew or could be sure that we would graduate and be commissioned into the RAF's General Duties Branch. We felt like aircrew, we had the manner of aircrew; we had even been measured up on 8 April to ensure that we could physically be aircrew and fit in a cockpit! We had undertaken a hypoxia demonstration in a decompression chamber and knew just how to identify a lack of oxygen and the effect that it had on our ability to think straight. We had, however, lost almost one third of our peers to various failings along the way, but that did not mean that there would not be a final cull before graduation – anything was possible, including a return to civilian life! Most of those we had lost along the way had, like me before, tripped on the academics and found themselves following along behind, but some had been recoursed for OQs and PQs. Two had even been returned to civvie street for failings in these areas! None of us could relax. My week 12 report, written by Ivan Hughes, was helpful in quelling my graduation nerves, but it was not the final report that would be written and three weeks was a long time to survive under the assessment spotlight:

'Herriot's performance over the last six weeks has improved markedly. He has shown himself to be a forceful and enthusiastic young man capable of plenty of hard work and capable of achieving sound results.

'His performance at camp was above average, showing him to possess many sound leadership and personal qualities. This, combined with his enthusiasm for a Service career, makes him an excellent prospect for the future.'

My parents were already making plans to travel by train from Scotland for the graduation parade. Parade rehearsals had started and one final room inspection was required. As the course had progressed we had moved from dormitory arrangements to shared double rooms and then, as the senior course, into single room accommodation; each with a sink to scrub, polish and maintain. I had been fortunate that my room had never failed to pass inspection and was well prepared for this final hurdle. As Ivan Hughes and Sergeant Barnes approached, I came smartly to attention outside my room and waited whilst they entered and carried out the inspection of my spotless personal space. White-gloved fingers swept across the top of door frames and windows, but returned no evidence of shirking on my part. The sink passed muster and then I heard the fateful word, 'Herriot!' Hearing your name being called meant trouble! It was a summons to join them in your room to be shown where you had transgressed. I entered, trying to think desperately what I had missed and whether tonight would mean a defaulters' parade for me! Sergeant Barnes was standing by my bedside lamp! He had pulled the plug from the wall and was demanding to know when I had last polished the prongs of the plug! I was devastated! I had never for one moment imagined that anybody would consider that to be a task to be carried out during the bulling period before an inspection. I was stuttering to get inadequate words of excuse out when I looked them both in the eye and realised that they were smiling! With great relief I smiled back, and as Ivan Hughes left my room he winked and said, 'Well done, your room is, as usual, in excellent shape!'

Twenty-eight officer cadets from 251 Red Course, including Ian Rowan, Taff Paines and I, were successful in our goal to hold Her Majesty's Commission and become aircrew under training in the RAF. Preparations were now in full swing for the graduation parade and drill was, once again, the main activity of every day in the last week of the course. We all had final fittings for our No 1 Dress Uniforms, which we would wear on the day, and for the No 5 Mess Dress that was to be worn at the graduation dining-in night on the preceding Wednesday and just two days before our Friday graduation.

Formal dinners in the RAF are splendid affairs and our dinner on 2 July 1969 was no exception. We gathered in the anteroom of the officers' mess at 1900hrs for pre-drinks and at 1930hrs prompt were summoned to the dining room to take our places for dinner. Polite conversation ensued over the four-course meal with wine until, once the tables had been cleared and the Port and Madeira decanters were presented, the youngest member present, Mr Vice, was called upon by the PMC to propose the Loyal Toast. Once complete and Her Majesty's health had been drunk, smoking was permitted at table, speeches were made and general antics were allowed to ensue. As potential graduates from AOTS, I recall no antics at the table that night! After dinner, protocol has it that the top table should leave the room before the general rabble are allowed to depart under the policing of Mr Vice. Once back in the anteroom, and with copious amounts of beer available, all sorts of antics were permitted. The Red Course staff encouraged us now to let our hair down for the very first time at Church Fenton. We, the student body, were less inclined to take them up on it for fear that this might just be the final trap!

The anteroom wall in No 2 Officers' Mess at RAF Church Fenton was made of unrendered brick. It was some eighteen feet high and had the occasional brick sticking out about half an inch from its flat surface. Ivan Hughes and his equally exuberant mate, Peter West, who was an Air Electronics Officer in his previous RAF incarnation, challenged the cadet body in general to climb the wall and touch the ceiling. Now this would have been a difficult task sober, but with wine, port and beer now sloshing inside, it had the potential to be a very unbalancing act in more ways than one! A small group of cadets had gathered and listened as the gauntlet was thrown down. To prove it could be done, Pete West shimmied up and down the wall before you could say, 'Mine's a pint of Sam Smith's, please!' Ivan Hughes, now positively encouraging one of us to take the challenge, turned to me directly and said, 'Go on, Herriot, you can do it.'

I started gingerly at first. The toe grips of a pair of 'Black Patent Leather Dress Shoes – Officers' were not the ideal footwear to climb the north face of the Eiger, but they seemed just adequate to manage the vertical face of the anteroom wall! Up and up I went with the encouraging comments of my peers egging me on! I got to the top and, just as I stretched out to touch the ceiling with my fingertips, my right toe grip gave way and I fell backwards onto a G-Plan coffee table that was there to break my fall. All four of its legs gave way with the impact and it and I ended up in a heap on the floor with an almighty bang. There were loud cheers from the assembled throng of both staff and students, but I felt awful! I knew that that was it! My dream was over! My parents were on their way south in the morning for nothing! I had embarrassed myself, had broken mess property and would suffer the consequences in the morning with a hat on interview with Ivan Hughes at best and the station commander at worst. I felt devastated, and more so when I spied the chief instructor, a wing commander, coming from the bar to find out what all the noise and commotion was about!

'Sir, I'm sorry, I'm very, very sorry!' I blurted out as a last form of defence for my stupidity and in a contrite attempt at mitigating the inevitable sentence. 'I'll pay for whatever damage I've caused. I'm sorry.'

'Sorry! No need to be sorry, lad!' replied the chief instructor, 'the squadron fund will pay for the damage. Well done! Well done! That's just the sort of thing we expect from aircrew, well done! By the way, did you get to the top?'

I was safe; my parents' journey would not be in vain. I was bought drinks for the rest of the night and we all staggered back to our beds about 0200hrs knowing full well that we had indeed made the right career choice – we were all cut out to be RAF aircrew; we had passed the test.

The graduation parade, which was reviewed by Group Captain D.A. Maddox RAF, went off without a hitch, apart from the fact that at the dress rehearsal, on the Thursday, one of our number had managed to bring his elbow down on an exposed bayonet during a 'right dress' which precluded his participation at the main event and forced him to watch from the sidelines. After an excellent lunch in the officers' mess, with no antics afterwards, my parents left for Scotland, and after I had packed my kit and forwarded it to my next unit, I followed them on the Saturday for a few weeks of well-deserved leave. I had finished tenth on 251 Course and was posted from there to the RAF Aircrew Holding Unit at RAF Topcliffe. They, in turn, sent me to RAF Upwood in Huntingdonshire, where I worked with the Officer Commanding General Duties Flight until I started at No 2 Air Navigation School at RAF Gaydon on 7 September 1969. There I would meet Yorkie and the Varsity T Mk 1.

Chapter Six

Bring Your Own Towel

With the Velcro patch removed and my navigator's brevet now firmly stitched to the left breast of my No 1 Dress Uniform, I packed all my possessions into my Morris 1000 and turned out of Finningley's main gate and headed for the A1. I had a posting notice that would take me to RAF Honington in Suffolk to join No 9 Course on 237 OCU and the Buccaneer S2, but that course did not start until 17 May 1971. In the meantime, I had leave over the Christmas and New Year period and was not scheduled to return to work until I joined No 10C Pre-OCU Course back at Finningley on 8 February. As the main trunk road that connects London with Scotland's capital hove into sight, I indicated, turned right and headed north towards Scotch Corner and home.

After AOTS, my parents had come to the conclusion that with the remoteness of RAF airfields generally and the amount of kit that I had already accrued, a means of transport, other than at the whim of British Rail, was a necessity. My Morris 1000 cost £98, but that was over twelve weeks of a cadet's salary and I just did not have that kind of money to pay for the car outright; nor did my parents! When my brother Michael heard of my plight – and without prompting – he presented me with £80 towards its cost. The remainder was covered by my parents. It may have been a feeling of guilt for splitting my head open in the bedroom during his 'tackling lesson' that encouraged him, but whatever it was or was not, it was a very kind gesture out of his hard-earned salary as a hotel manager, and for that, I will be eternally grateful to him. The car was a godsend during my time at Gaydon and Finningley and became more so during the peripatetic life that I led in the months that followed, as I undertook a number of short training courses to lead me in to the Buccaneer.

Christmas and New Year came and went and 1971 dawned, as it always did in Scotland, after a very happy Hogmanay. My father, who was a very good amateur photographer, had taken pictures of me in my flying suit from every possible angle. He had even taken 'still life' photographs of all my navigation equipment too. It was all very relaxing and tranquil compared with the self-induced, but ever-present, 'have to succeed' environment that had overshadowed my life over the previous two years. Then the phone rang!

'They want to speak to you,' my father said.

'Who is it?' I queried.

'Someone from the RAF,' was his unnerving reply!

I entered the under-stair cupboard and tentatively took the phone from my father. I identified myself, 'Acting Pilot Officer Herriot.'

'Ah, good afternoon, David,' said a polite voice at the other end.

I am afraid I cannot remember his name, but his purpose was devastating. He was on the staff at Training Command Headquarters and he was talking about a problem with my posting to Strike Command and the Buccaneer!

'It is our understanding at headquarters that you are a Z category swimmer! I am afraid that it has been decided that you cannot be posted from Training Command to Strike Command unless you are at least a Y category swimmer!'

My head was spinning; I was a Y category swimmer! I had swum fifty metres on my back at Yearsley Baths. The warrant officer PTI had held a pole above my nose and jerked it away whenever I had tried to grab it! My colleagues on B Syndicate had cheered when I got to the deep end. What was this man talking about!

'I am a Y category swimmer,' I said confidently. 'I passed my swimming test at AOTS and have a certificate to prove it.'

'I am afraid that there is nothing on your training record to support that fact!'

My heart sank. 'I have a certificate,' I implored, but to no avail.

'I am afraid I can only go by what is on your training record and there is no indication that you ever passed your swimming proficiency test. After you complete your pre-OCU course, a room has been reserved for you at RAF Cranwell on 28 February. You must pass your swimming proficiency or your posting to Buccaneers will be cancelled! Please report to the College Gymnasium at 0800hrs on 1 March.'

And with that he was gone. I went straight upstairs and started to sift through the paperwork that I had, by now, strewn across my bed! There was no certificate! The most vital piece of paper ever issued to a non-swimmer had vanished! Without it, I was back to being a Z category swimmer and no amount of pleading was going to change that!

The Pre-OCU Course was designed to provide newly-qualified navigators with a short introduction to low-level flying and air combat, sorties were flown in Jet Provost Mk3 training aircraft and were, on average, no longer than sixty minutes in duration. Day One of the course was spent meeting the instructors, being briefed on the JP3's performance, its ejector seat and preparing maps. The pre-1979 UK Military Low Flying System comprised a number of LFAs in largely rural areas, linked by a system of routes and corridors. Within these areas and corridors military aircraft were cleared to fly down to 250 feet AGL. The normal cruise speed when operating at low-level within these areas for aircraft like the Buccaneer was 420 knots, but this would increase to 500 knots or more for target runs and combat evasion. With a maximum speed of about 300 knots flat out, our low-level sorties on 10C Course were flown at 240 knots, which conveniently equated to four nautical miles per minute. Two hundred and one JP3s were delivered to the RAF for basic pilot training and remained in service throughout the 1960s before being replaced by the JP4, and subsequently, the JP5. Those few remaining were allocated to 6 FTS at Finningley in 1970 as the 'lead-in training' workhorse for potential FJ navigators.

The aircraft was fitted with a single Armstrong Siddeley Viper 102 engine, which was the same engine that powered the Dominie T Mk 1 that I had flown on the Advanced Navigation Course. However, whilst the Dominie required two engines to get it through the air, the JP3, being smaller and lighter, required just one. With its 'cannot exceed' cruise speed, it was often described as having 'Constant Speed and Variable Noise'!

My allocated instructor for the first few sorties on the course was Flight Lieutenant Reg Drown. He had been commissioned in May 1944, almost exactly one year before the end of the war in Europe, and was just short of his fiftieth birthday when I met him at 6 FTS. He had thousands of hours in the air and was well suited to his role coaxing new navigators in the art of low-level navigation and air combat. His engagement in the RAF was termed 'Specialist Aircrew', which meant that he specialised in flying, took no responsibility for other 'extra-curricular' duties and forsook, therefore, any prospect of promotion to high rank. His tour at Finningley allowed him to do just that and receive an enhanced rate of flying pay whilst flying an aircraft that would rarely bite, and, if it did, he was experienced enough to ensure its safe recovery to Terra Firma – if not, it had two 90 knot ejection seats located side by side in the small cockpit. To my tender years and comparatively insignificant flying experience, Reg was a flying god!

The two closest LFAs to Finningley were designated as LFA 11 and LFA 8. LFA 11 covered an area of the East Riding of Yorkshire from just south of Flamborough Head, north along the coast to Whitby, and west to the approximate line of the A1 trunk road, but avoiding the RAF airfields in the Vale of York. LFA 8, on the other hand, was an H-shaped area to the west of Finningley that took its eastern boundary from the River Trent as it flowed north to the Humber and covered much of the Derbyshire Peaks. I pulled the necessary 250,000 scale maps from the drawer in the Planning Room and set about planning low-level navigation routes in both areas.

'There's no need for that map,' I heard Reg say over my shoulder.

'I'm sorry! What do you mean?' I replied.

'No need for LFA 11,' he responded.

'Why not?' Thinking this was a trick; 'Don't we need a weather alternative?'

'With a name like mine, I'm never going to fly over The Humber!' he laughed.

I knew that Reg and I would get on swimmingly; he was clearly not a Y category bather!

The syllabus consisted of two familiarisation sorties that, for me, were flown on one mission lasting just over one hour. Their purpose was to introduce me to the JP3 and the two LFAs, over which I would eventually be assessed as to my navigational expertise and my airmanship. This sortie was not flown with Drown, but with a Flight Lieutenant Mike Miles. However, with complete cloud cover and poor visibility at low-level, no sight of the ground was achieved and so, alternatively, we carried out some gentle aerobatics to test my stomach lining! The sortie was categorised as a Duty Carried Out (DCO) by Miles, which is surprising, given that part of the duty to be carried out was to introduce me to some of the 'Dog's Balls' navigational icons in LFA 11 and LFA 8. There is no mistaking Knapton Granary in the Vale of Pickering or the 'Dambusters' Dam in the Derwent Valley in the Peak District and once seen never forgotten! On my familiarisation sortie, they were totally obscured below cloud!

Despite this early disadvantage, the course progressed suitably and satisfactorily for the next two weeks although, after only four sorties with Reg Drown, I continued to fly with Miles for all but the last three sorties. Miles was a humourless man who adopted the previously identified Marsden approach to instruction! Whereas Reg Drown had adopted a friendly instructional manner in the cockpit, Mike Miles' approach to flying training was less instructional, but more of an airborne interrogation – at least that is how it felt at the time and as I look back over my sortie reports it would seem that little leeway was given by Miles in his understanding of how much experience I actually had in a small two-seat training aircraft. I felt consistently under pressure flying with Miles and was relieved when I flew with three different pilots for the last three course sorties. Instantly, my scores improved and I left 6 FTS for the last time with an Average assessment as a low-level navigator who, *'should cope with the OCU'.*

Yet the OCU was still a long way off. Before any thought of getting airborne in a Buccaneer could be entertained I still had a number of hurdles to overcome. First, and at the forefront of my mind, was Training Command's demand that I now make my way to Cranwell to be submerged in the College Swimming Pool until I could swim! I was not looking forward to it when I arrived at Trenchard Hall Officers' Mess on the evening of 28 February 1971. At Mess Reception was an ominous message from the PEdO: *Report to the pool at 0730 hours on Monday, bring your own towel.*

Breakfast was a quiet affair and consisted of just cereal and coffee. The thought of what was to come was enough to stifle my appetite! Slowly and despondently I made my way along Cranwell Avenue towards the College Gymnasium and arrived with ten minutes to spare. I was met by a very cheery PTI and ushered into a side office.

'Sir, it is our aim to ensure that by the end of the week you will have passed the swimming classification. If you succeed before Friday, then you will be released back to your unit. You will be in the water four times each day for about forty minutes each time and you will have your own dedicated instructor.'

'OK,' was all I could muster in reply.

'What swimming experience have you had and what problems have you experienced?' he asked.

It did not seem the appropriate time to tell him that my sister had attempted to drown me at St Andrews. Nor did it seem a suitable moment to admit that I was a complete inadequate if the water ever immersed my face!

'I just lack confidence,' I said. 'I actually did manage to swim fifty metres on my back at AOTS, but it was never recorded on my training record!' I did not, for whatever reason, mention the warrant officer and his pole!

'Oh well, should be easy then! Shall we get started?'

And with that we were off, changed into trunks and into the pool.

He had not lied! Four times a day I was in that Cranwell pool and despite my success at Yearsley Baths, it was not *'easy then'* to recover my previous proficiency. What is more, there is nothing more discomforting than climbing into wet, cold swimming trunks three times a day, or to regularly have X category swimmers, who shared the changing room, staring at you wondering what the hell your problem was!

It was not an easy fix and I felt literally quite washed out by the time the Friday morning came. Just as in York previously, this was crunch time. Swim twenty-five metres and fly Buccaneers, fail and kiss goodbye to a flying career in the RAF! There was no bamboo pole, but the PTI did walk along the side of the pool offering 'mild' words of encouragement. Lying on my back, I set off with the side wall just inches away from my grasp. Kicking my legs as best I was able, I passed through the water like a thrashing barn door, desperately hoping that the demon in my head would go to sleep before I got out of my depth! He did not. He was there in an instant. '*You can't stand up now!*' I could hear him saying. '*You're going to drown!*' He told me. And before I could stop myself, my backside began to drop and my natural buoyancy departed and I started to thrash about in the water grabbing the side in my panic as I felt myself submerge!

'Out you get, Sir,' said the PTI as he grabbed my flailing left arm and hoicked me upwards. 'Go and get dressed and we will try that again later! You were going really well, what happened?'

'The deep water demon,' I mumbled, and took myself off to the changing rooms and a quiet contemplative coffee in College Hall Mess.

Back in the water at 1100hrs, and after a few confidence building widths in the shallow end, I was off again along the side wall heading for the deep end and another probable encounter with the deep water demon. I was going well. Not much water was being splashed over my face and I felt a sudden surge of confidence. I tried desperately to ignore the fact that the water below me was deepening and just kept pressing on for the far end. Suddenly, I felt my hands hit something solid and I panicked! My bottom went down and I again started to thrash about in distress. Then the penny dropped. It could not have been the side wall that I hit as both hands had come into contact with it. I paused, looked up and realised that I had done it. The PTI was smiling as he reached down and helped me from the water.

'Not the prettiest stroke I have seen, Sir, but there is no doubt that you have swum twenty-five metres!'

'Thanks, Corporal, and thanks for your help!'

I glued and sellotaped my new Y category swimming proficiency certificate into my Flying Logbook and left Cranwell after lunch, on Friday, 5 March 1971, happy in the knowledge that nobody now or in the future could ever try to question my new found swimming prowess! There was no way that anybody at Training Command or elsewhere was going to deny me my rightful place on the Buccaneer OCU now.

Since the previous day I had been on the strength of 237 OCU at RAF Honington in Suffolk. Honington had been reopened and refurbished to take the General Dynamics F-111, which the UK Government had planned to purchase to replace the cancelled TSR2. However, programme costs within the development and production programme in the USA had forced its cancellation too. Consequently, Honington had become the Buccaneer's RAF home and 12 Squadron, the RAF's first Buccaneer squadron, had been operating in the ASuW role from there since October 1969. As I turned onto Cranwell Avenue and headed for the A1 again, I looked forward to my first sight of the place and the aircraft that would come to play such a large part in my life.

Honington lies almost equidistant between the East Anglian towns of Thetford and Bury St Edmunds. As I turned off the A134 and followed Green Lane round and past the threshold of Honington's 09 runway I suddenly realised just why it was that I had been so keen to fly the Buccaneer. There, sitting at full power against their brakes, were two 12 Squadron S2As about to launch. As my 'Moggie' eased left with the sweeping curve of the narrow road that led to the main gate, I could only stare in amazement as it dawned on me just how potent and how threatening the Buccaneer looked and how in the world was I ever going to manage to navigate such an awesome piece of aviation hardware. I pulled over to the side of the lane to watch as the black smoke from their two Rolls Royce Spey engines increased and, as the pilots eased their breaks off, they began to roll down the runway together and launch themselves into the spring sunlight that bathed the airbase that Friday afternoon. It was an amazing sight. There are many military jets that are potent and capable, but few actually looked as menacing as the Buccaneer did. I could not wait to get started.

237 OCU had been formed four days previously under the command of Wing Commander Tony Fraser and, after checking into the guardroom and finding my room in the officers' mess, I soon discovered that there was to be a 'Welcome Barrel' in the bar at 1700hrs that Friday night – it seemed churlish not to attend.

RAF instructor crews who had been serving with the Navy's 736 Squadron at Lossiemouth formed the bulk of the initial OCU staff and, as I introduced myself in the bar, I discovered the wonderment of being their first student to arrive at Honington! There is an advantage and a disadvantage in being the most junior member on any military unit. The advantage is that nobody expects too much of you initially and the disadvantage is that all those senior to you – that is everybody – will always be able to find a 'Silly Little Job' for you to undertake! As the night went on and more beer was drunk, more and more SLJs were promised for me when we started work on the Monday morning. The bar was packed. As well as the few staff already arrived on 237 OCU, the whole of 12 Squadron were there and the one thing that became apparent very quickly was that Buccaneer Boys could drink! I have little recall as to what time the bar closed or what time I got to my bed, but I know I had a good night. One of the most recent arrivals on 12 Squadron was Mike Heath, who had been on Red Course at AOTS with Dave Hurley and, on 736 Squadron at Lossiemouth, he had been on the same course as Taff Paines when he had been killed. Mike and I had a lot to talk about that night and we became firm friends throughout our RAF careers.

At work on Monday, we all soon set about preparing our accommodation on the airfield ready for the first course, which I was to be a student on, commencing on 17 May. The Ops Room had to be fully equipped with chinagraph boards, briefing rooms had to be prepared, telephones needed to be ordered and a coffee bar had to be built. Also, with only a few Buccaneers currently available, those qualified to fly them had to maintain currency by taking time out from building to go flying. I, too, had commitments away from Honington. I had still to undertake Sea Survival Training at RAF Mount Batten and attend the AMTC at RAF North Luffenham to undertake another hypoxia demonstration and be issued with all the necessary aircrew equipment for flying in the Buccaneer. I also had to go to RAF Lindholme in

South Yorkshire to undertake two sorties in a Hastings using the H2S[1] radar as part of my lead-in to low-level and medium-level radar appreciation.

The month of March 1971 was a very busy one, but as more people arrived to form the OCU staff complement, my tasks became fewer and easier to complete. The next student to appear was John Kershaw, a fellow navigator, who was the only person to ever fly the Buccaneer from both the front and back seats whilst wearing the appropriate flying badge for that seat. JK, as he has always been known in the Buccaneer world, had started his flying career as a pilot in the Royal Navy. As a student pilot on 736 Squadron, he had been tasked with carrying out dive bombing on Tain Range; it was the first time he had ever flown the profile. It was winter and there were some vicious snow storms in the area of the Cromarty Firth and the Black Isle. The attack profile required the aircraft to be flown straight and level towards the target at 400ft and 460kts. At 3.5nm from the target the pilot was required to initiate a ten-degree pull to 900ft where he then commenced a bunt manoeuvre to acquire and track the target. When the bomb, which was released automatically, had left the aircraft, he then had to pull 4G until the nose of the aircraft was at thirty degrees above the horizon and climb to a downwind height of 2000ft. Not a particularly easy manoeuvre for a new Buccaneer pilot; made more difficult by the number of snow storms in the area on that day. A large snow shower covered the base turn by Tarbet Ness lighthouse. Keen to pick up the visual cues that would lead him towards the target, JK was momentarily distracted, when all of a sudden he saw through the starboard quarter light heavy snow and a rough sea coming towards him. An aggressive recovery manoeuvre brought the nose up, but he felt he had lost elevator authority. He called for his observer[2], Pat Cummuskey, to eject and, with the aircraft now in a nose down attitude, followed him out with little time to spare.

Whilst no less professional, the FAA took a less serious view about flying accidents than ever did the RAF. Whilst Buccaneer XV346 had been lost and John spent a few days in hospital recovering from his ordeal, the Navy attitude was to put JK 'back on the horse' and take him flying in a Hunter T7 three times before inviting a 'trapper' from Yeovilton to assess him in the air. It was all for nought and, without a Board of Inquiry to establish the facts, JK found himself out of the Royal Navy and eventually into the RAF as a navigator. He had followed me through 6 FTS and had now pursued me to Honington as the second first-tourist navigator that would be trained by the RAF at Honington.

Next to arrive on the scene was Iain Ross. Like me Iain was a Scot and, with his father having been a high-ranking RAF medical officer, was a former boarding pupil at Strathallan School in The Highlands. Having already spent a few years flying Hawker Hunters with 208 Squadron in Bahrain, unlike me, he was not about to embark on his first RAF tour. Those were his true formative years and for me they were going to

---

1. H2S was the first airborne, ground-scanning radar system. It was developed in Britain during the Second World War for the Royal Air Force and was used in various RAF bomber aircraft from 1943.
2. To avoid confusion between those who navigate in ships and those who navigate in aircraft, the Royal Navy classify the latter as observers rather than navigators.

become a very important part of my ascendancy in becoming a worthwhile member of the FJ world! He was the inimitable DFGA pilot, and whilst our time together initially was in the erection of chinagraph boards, I would be delighted to discover later that he was to be my pilot through the difficult months of the OCU course and onwards to XV Squadron.

The RAF had been supporting the RN's diminishing Buccaneer Force for a number of years with pilots and navigators to bolster their squadrons' aircrew numbers. These aircrew were trained on 736 Squadron at HMS *Fulmar*, near the town of Lossiemouth in Moray, and, with the advent of the Buccaneer into RAF service, had been training those RAF crews who would form the first operational squadron at Honington. Accordingly, RAF conversion courses were established within 736 and by the time I arrived at Honington in 1971, seven RAF courses had been completed in Scotland. Nos. 8 and 9 Courses, the first on 237 OCU, were planned to run in parallel and were staffed by a mixture of experienced RAF Buccaneer aircrew, along with a few RN chaps, to support the few Naval pilots and observers still passing through to 809 Squadron, which was the only surviving FAA Buccaneer squadron serving on the last remaining conventional aircraft carrier, HMS *Ark Royal*.

No. 8 Course was designated as a 'short' course whose students were all experienced on previous operational aircraft types. Nick Berryman, a Canberra recce pilot, had arrived from the recently disbanded 58 Squadron at RAF Wyton and was crewed with Colin 'Kabong'[3] Tavner, who was a very experienced ex-sergeant navigator who had started his operational career on Meteor night-fighters, the first British operational jet fighter, then Canberras, and had come to Buccaneers from a tour as a Victor navigator on 139 Squadron, one of the RAF's Blue Steel equipped strategic deterrent squadrons. Kabong was a vastly experienced navigator and one from whom I could learn a great deal both professionally and, as it would turn out, socially too. The other crew on No. 8 Course consisted of Rob Williams, a Vulcan pilot by previous employment, and Neil McCrimmon, his navigator, who had also served with the V-Force. No. 9 Course was earmarked as a 'long' course to allow us, the inexperienced aircrew, to find our feet.

Before long, and working as a well-oiled team, we soon had the Operations Room serviceable and ready for use. Aircrew are renowned for their ingenuity (or ability to double deal), and by devious means we had persuaded various departments around the station to part with sufficient wood, bricks and mortar to build a coffee bar in the room designated to be the 'crewroom'. Plumbing was a little more difficult to overcome, but again, with strong powers of persuasion, we managed to coerce the staff at the local MPBW to provide the necessary manpower and equipment to fit us out with sink, taps and boiler.

---

3. Taken from the Quick Draw McGraw cartoon character who would assume the identity of the masked vigilante El Kabong. His introduction went as follows – "Of all the heroes in legend and song, there's none as brave as El Kabong"! As El Kabong, Quick Draw would attack his foes by swooping down on a rope with the war cry "OLAYYYYEEEE!" and hitting them on the head with an acoustic guitar (after shouting "KABOOOOOONG!"). No! I do not understand either!

By mid-March work had to stop as we all headed south-west to undertake our Sea Survival Training at RAF Mount Batten, near Plymouth in Devon. Mount Batten had been a seaplane base operating Short Sunderland flying boats on ASW and SAR missions during the Second World War. By 1971, however, flying operations had ceased and it was now the home of the RAF's Marine Craft Training Unit and the School of Combat Survival and Rescue. It was to this latter establishment that the students of Nos. 8 and 9 Courses were bound and, for this only just Y category swimmer, with some trepidation! At Mount Batten, we met the final two members of our course. Wing Commander Ashley was intended to be the next commander of 12 Squadron at Honington, whilst Dave Symonds, a first tourist, was to become JK's pilot on No. 9 Course.

Lectures introduced us to the Buccaneer ejection seat system, its ancillary equipment (aka a parachute) and its PSP. We also covered the Mae West, which was part of the so-called torso harness that all FJ aircrew were required to wear. The torso harness was a wonderful piece of kit that did away with the multitude of straps that had been required previously to strap oneself into a jet fighter. Designed specifically for rapid response crews, of which we Buccaneer aircrew were destined to become on Nuclear QRA, it allowed one to strap oneself into the 'bang seat' quickly and methodically, and perhaps more importantly, eased your exit by a simple and simultaneous flick and click of a 'Koch' fastener just below each collar bone if and when one was being dragged either overland or through the ocean post a rapid exit upwards from the cockpit! Hmm! Being dragged through the ocean was to take place in a few days' time and I was more than uncomfortable about the prospect! We learned about the salt water immersion-operated McMurdo Light on our Mae West that would indicate our presence to passing ships if we were unfortunate enough to find ourselves in the ocean in the dark! We found the whistle to attract attention and, most importantly, we discovered how to locate and activate our SARBE, which was probably the one, and only, piece that would bring assistance! We emptied the contents of the PSP and marvelled at just how much 'stuff' had been rammed into it to aid our survival. Boiled sweets, can opener, dry pack rations, fishing line, waterproof matches (not that handy at sea!) and much, much more; all the sort of things you might need if you had had to abandon a fast jet and survive for any length of time! Most importantly, inside the PSP was a single man dinghy! How a man had managed to package all this kit into what was the seat box portion of the Martin Baker Ejection Seat still beats me to this day!

We practised deploying the dinghy and inflating it automatically by a sharp, but even tug on its metal handle. We slid ourselves into and out of our dinghies on dry land, which was too easy, but we knew that it would be much more difficult in waterlogged clothing in a sea swell off Plymouth Sound. We deployed the sea anchor and we simulated bailing out! We ensured that the canopy was inflated just enough to give us protection from the elements, but not so much that it acted as a sail, and we thought about capsize drills; I thought about them a lot!

Our next port of call was the swimming pool where we put what we had learned on the gymnasium floor into practice in the pool. Fully decked out in flying overalls and skeletal harnesses, we lined up along the side of the pool – not confident about my prowess in the water, I took position cleverly at the end of the queue and close to the shallow end! I was comfortable that the Mae West would do what it was designed to do, but there was no point in putting myself at risk, was there?

'Right, gentlemen,' said a friendly instructor. 'Would you all make your way down to the deep end and form a line behind the diving board please.'

Uh oh, I thought, there's no getting away from what is about to happen here!

Diligently I followed my leader to the far end of the building and prepared myself for the first time in my life to jump off a diving board into the deep water beneath!

'Now, gentlemen, remember the pre-water entry drills we went through in the classroom,' said the friendly instructor. 'Look up, check the canopy! Remove oxygen mask and discard! Look down and check height! Check PSP connection to harness and, just before your feet impact the water at about 10 feet up, release the PSP by turning and squeezing the QRB!'

This was all very fine, but it was the bit that came next that I was less than interested in!

'Once in the water,' he continued, 'release your Koch fasteners, deploy the dinghy and start surviving!'

So simple, so very simple and essential training if you want to become FJ aircrew. Probably quite enjoyable if you like and are accustomed to submerging yourself in water, but for your average Y category swimmer it was all a bit of a nightmare. Nevertheless, I could not show my fear and I had to get on with it. Then he said the words I feared the most.

'Remember, gentlemen, don't inflate your Mae West until you're in the water!'

What! He had to be kidding! Jump into the deep end without any buoyancy aid! Oh bugger!

I slowly meandered my way towards the diving board as each man before me took his turn at jumping into the water. Shouts from the staff encouraged each with reminders of what was the next task on their individual agendas as they followed the briefed routine. 'Bail out, sir!' to one. 'C'mon, sir, you need to deploy the sea anchor!' to another and 'Are you not in yet?' to someone struggling to overcome the natural drag of his sopping flying suit and the weakness in his arms from having failed to get on board after a number of attempts.

It was my turn. I looked across the surface of the water at my chums who were all, by now, 'surviving'. I looked down into the deep water and pondered my fate. I looked at the staff and realised that they were all watching and waiting, and, with that silent encouragement, I pulled the inflation valve on my Mae West and jumped!

'Oh bloody hell, sir!' I heard as I surfaced, 'I said don't inflate your Mae West until you're in the water!' And from that day to this, during each annual Dinghy Drill, I have always 'forgotten' not to inflate my Mae West until I am in the water! It worked for me, even if it did frustrate the hell out of every PTI who witnessed it.

On the last morning we were motored down to the harbour side at Mount Batten to board one of the RAF MCTU's rescue launches and head out into Plymouth Sound. It was late March and the sea temperature was below 10°C, so instead of wearing flying suits we were fully protected from the elements and the sea in immersion suits.

Once we had rounded Rame Head and were well clear of the coast I stood in line and waited my turn to jump off the stern and into the ocean below. This time there was no opportunity to inflate my Mae West as I and my Koch fasteners were firmly attached to the stern of the boat by a parachute harness. This was almost for real and I was about to be dragged through the swell to simulate the effect of an inflated parachute and a howling gale.

Back on the boat after some forty-five minutes alone in the English Channel, with a tot of rum and a mug of piping hot Scotch Broth in my hand, it all seemed to have been so remarkably straightforward! I had survived, which was the most important point. It had not been as terrifying as I had anticipated and I had coped quite well with the whole thing. As soon as I surfaced I realised that I was moving quite swiftly through the swell and that it was time to release the Koch fasteners, which I did at my second attempt. I pulled the PSP towards me and with one almighty tug released and watched as the dinghy inflated before my very eyes. What a welcoming sight it was and although the immersion suit was keeping me relatively dry and warm I could not wait to climb aboard. Not as easy as it might seem in a rolling swell and with cold wet hands. Try as I might, I could not locate the grab handles on the upper skin of the buoyancy chamber. I knew they were there, I had checked them out in the pool only yesterday, but for some inexplicable reason I could not reach them whilst being thrown about by the swell. Eventually, I grabbed the right hand one and attempted to haul myself in. No luck. The briefed method is to grab both handles and pull the whole dinghy underneath your body whilst at the same time kicking with all your might to propel yourself forward. A single-handed action merely had the effect of throwing the dinghy off to the opposite side and away from my thrashing body! I tried again with the same result. After about ten minutes I did manage to stabilise myself and the dinghy, and with both grab handles secured, thrust myself forward onto my floating home. I quickly turned round, located the sea anchor which I threw into the sea, and very quickly the dinghy cocked, as briefed, into wind. I pulled the canopy loosely over my shoulders to provide added shelter and started to locate my SARBE in its pocket in my Mae West. I pulled the pin to initiate the beacon and, having clipped it onto its storage point on the left lobe of the Mae West, shoved its antenna through the prepositioned hole in the canopy and thought about relaxing if only for a moment. Although my vital actions were complete, my task had not finished. Packed as it is with all its survival goodies, the PSP has one significant disadvantage for the survivor if it is not pulled aboard and stowed in the dinghy. Made of fibreglass and with its seat cushion attached it is quite a dead weight even when empty; with all the goodies on-board it acts more as an anchor and has a tendency to pull one corner of the dinghy down towards its unmarked Plimsoll Line. With it now safely stored on board I began the task of bailing out. Bailing out a rubber dinghy, whose hull sits no more than eighteen inches above the water surface – with a flat rubber bailer, is akin to playing a violin whilst Rome burns! It is, perhaps, the most inefficient task that I have ever had to undertake. Whilst the morale-boosting sound and sight of water leaving one's craft in tea cup amounts does fill you with encouragement, the sight of it rolling back in over the gunwale because of the body effort required to move in the confined space of one's surroundings does moderate the delight! However, what bailing does do is keep you focused, keep you exercising and, therefore, keep you warm – so it is worth every second in a survival situation. Before long, I had everything done, the canopy was up over my head, the McMurdo Light was shining brightly and I had time to call to my fellows with the whistle provided! Of course, aircrew being aircrew, we had to invent a game to occupy our childish minds, and so it was not long before we were all pulling on our sea anchors in an attempt to get together and form one huge raft! Of course, that earned us our first bollocking! We were supposed to be doing this ourselves, all alone in the ocean simulating an ejection and more importantly, as a clutch of dinghies, we ran the risk of causing damage to ourselves from the downdraft of the SAR helicopter if we were all tied together. We separated and slowly drifted apart and sat in solitude with eyes peeled on the horizon for the bright yellow Whirlwind that would pluck us to safety from the jaws of death and deposit us back on the launch. I was fortunate to be one of the first few to be picked up from the Channel. As the winchman was lowered from the gaping door above me I prepared myself for rescue by pushing the canopy away from my head and shoulders and sitting more upright in the dinghy. Having earthed himself in the water, the winchman then walked across the water's surface and without any hesitation placed the strop over my head and under my armpits. Then, with his legs straddling my body, he and I ascended from my watery home into the bowels of the helicopter. The dinghies were left below to be collected by the launch before we sprinted back to Mount Batten for a final night in the bar and the next morning's low-level graduation ceremony. Soon, we were back at Plymouth railway station and heading back towards Honington for a well-deserved weekend and lots more drinking. On Sunday we had to head off to North Luffenham for more pre-OCU training and the issuing of Buccaneer-specific flying kit.

All in all, it seemed to have been all worthwhile and quite rewarding! Jumping off the boat had not been half as petrifying as I had imagined and the English Channel seemed quite a friendly place given all the survival aids and equipment that had been provided. I felt confident that, should the awful day dawn when the guy in the front shouted, 'EJECT! EJECT!', I had the training, equipment and now the confidence, to not fear the worst as I soared skyward on top of my rocket-powered escape system. More importantly, the last shout of the instructor on the Marine Craft had been: 'Now remember, gentlemen, unlike the swimming pool, this is the closest thing to the real thing, so make sure that you inflate your Mae West as you jump and before you enter the water!' Some words just have a habit of warming your heart at the worst possible moments in your life!!

The AMTC was commanded by a senior RAF Medical Officer, who was supported by a team of medical officers and technicians who had responsibility for fitting and instructing aircrew in the use of flying protective clothing and equipment. Instruction in medical aspects of high performance aviation included practical experience of hypoxia and exposure to sudden explosive decompression of an aircraft cabin. This was carried out in a complex of RAF Mark V decompression chambers installed on the site for aircrew training and research purposes. It was at AMTC that we Buccaneer aircrew would receive all the necessary Buccaneer-specific equipment necessary to fulfil our operational task. The joining instructions specifically recommended the use of a motor vehicle to remove all the equipment that we would be issued with during our visit. So, on Sunday, 28 March 1971, I set off in my 'Moggie' to cover the two-hour journey through Cambridgeshire and Lincolnshire towards North Luffenham.

RAF North Luffenham was located in the heart of England and in the smallest county, Rutland. What real relevance is its specific location to this story, I hear you ask. Well, those beer connoisseurs amongst you will know that Rutland was the home of one of the best small breweries in England. The brewery was established in the county in 1858, and in 1912 was bought by John Ruddles, who gave the brewery its name. Situated in the village of Langham, some nine miles west of North Luffenham, it was not too far for the officers' mess to obtain its eagerly consumed supply of Ruddles County Ale. Apparently, it was the local Langham well water that gave the beer a unique character and quality, which many an airman would testify to throughout the rest of his life. Whether it was the ability of aircrew to consume vast quantities on a three-day sojourn at AMTC, or keen advertising by the Ruddles Brewery, its beer became renowned in the UK and earned the status of being only one of three beers to achieve Protected Geographical Indication. For aircrew, however, its taste and colonic capabilities were two of its most important facets during time spent at North Luffenham.

After a night on 'The County', we gathered for breakfast and readied ourselves for the three days that would see us equipped with a Mark 3 Flying Helmet, suitably sized flying suits, an immersion suit, flying boots and a skeletal harness. The 'bone dome' was sized then fitted tightly to one's head by a technician who seemed to take great delight in squeezing what brain cells remained after our night in the bar! Once securely fixed, we were invited to spring the tightening clips forward to tension the inner straps – my head was already pounding from the effects of Mr Ruddles' best ale and now it was just a matter of seconds before it exploded once and for all! I was asked to keep my head still whilst the technician attempted to remove the helmet without undoing the tension straps or the chin strap.

'You're fine, sir, that'll not come off in an ejection,' he surmised, 'how does it feel?'

'Great,' I replied, 'feels fine!' I lied, my head was about to detonate, but I knew that I had nothing to compare the tightness to, he was an expert and my head would recover once I was back at Honington and eighty-five miles removed from AMTC and the effects of Ruddles County.

Next came the torso harness fitting, which was a much more pleasant experience as it required absolutely no contact at all with my head and I was permitted to remove the offending bone dome whilst the fitting took place. It was a simple process to get into the harness. Two steps, one into each of the lap straps, followed by a push with each arm through its armholes secured the harness onto your body, a bit like a loose hanging overcoat. The lobes of the Mae West covered the frontal area secured within a blast-proof nylon sheath and the stole of the inflation tube passed behind your head. It all seemed very comfortable and even with the metal breastplate done up felt perfect on my body. The technician made a few adjustments by tightening and then sealing a few straps to ensure that the Koch Fasteners sat in the correct position just below my clavicles and confirmed that I was comfortable. I was, and without my helmet on my head was making something of a recovery! I could walk upright and unaided and, although there was no mirror available, I was sure that I looked very much the part of a steely Buccaneer navigator!

'Ok, sir,' he chimed in to wake me from my romantic reverie, 'that's the way it's worn when you walk to the aircraft, but, before you climb the ladder, you must tighten these two straps by your groin. They'll tension the whole harness and, once sat in the cockpit, you'll find it quite comfortable.'

I pulled on the straps and was amazed how my body just seemed to double up whilst, at the same time, my private parts et al protruded from the tight V that had formed in my groin. It was not my head that was throbbing now!

'How does that feel?' I heard him say. He could not be being serious and I was not about to tell him!

'Fine,' I croaked, almost convulsing with laughter as I looked around the room at the other eight hunchbacks who were trying not to laugh also!

'Right, sir, just wait in line and take your turn on that bang seat and we'll strap you in. Once that's done, you can take it all off, sign for it all and have an early lunch.'

I was not sure at all about an early lunch, or any lunch for that matter – a long ice-cold drink was what I needed and not one that had anything to do with Ruddles or its county home!

The afternoon was spent in lectures with a medical officer who attempted to explain to our weary bodies about the physiology of man, the effects of hypoxia and how to recognise its onset before becoming comatose and how various aircraft are pressurised to overcome breathing difficulties and temperature reductions at height. Of course, all this led to the introduction of the next day's programme that would include a hypoxia demonstration in one of the unit's decompression chambers and a simulated ejection on a rig similar to that that I had done during my time at Church Fenton.

There is nothing in an afternoon of lectures that cannot be cured by a night of excess on John Ruddles finest beer! So it was back to the bar at 1700hrs and, following dinner, a continuation of a habit that seemed to be very much a part of being Buccaneer aircrew.

The following morning dawned like the previous one and, not surprisingly, with another dull thudding deep within my cranium. Our group of would-be Buccaneer aircrew had been split in two and I very much hoped that we, the No. 9 Course representatives, would be first in the chamber rather than first on the ejection rig – I did not really fancy being fired thirty feet in the air with that tight bone dome encapsulating my now mildly throbbing brain. Fortune favours the brave and the relief amongst the four of us, who had been uncommonly quiet over breakfast, was tangible as we ambled towards the decompression suite watching gladly as Kabong, Nick and the rest of No. 8 Course dragged their feet towards the ejector seat rig.

Once again we found ourselves in a classroom confronted by a Medic and now listening, through thick heads, to the safety precautions and procedures for the hypoxia demonstration. 'Enter the chamber with helmet on, but oxygen mask off your face', 'find a seat', 'pilots sit opposite their navs', 'simple tasks', '100% oxygen', 'chamber will increase altitude by reducing air pressure', etc, etc, etc. He droned on and on, and some of it managed to get through the fuzz that was my weary brain!

We were all ready to go and on the Medic's instruction we all clamped our oxygen masks to our faces and checked in on the intercom. With a thumbs up to the technician on the outside, the Medic signalled our preparedness for ascent. With the steady sound of breathing over nine 'hot' microphones the cabin pressure began to reduce and the chamber began its simulated ascent. The altimeter passed through 3,000 feet and on towards 10,000 feet where we knew, from our lecture the previous day, that there was insufficient oxygen in the atmosphere for a man to breath easily and that without an oxygen supply, his ability to perform efficiently would start to deteriorate. Upwards we went.

'OK,' said the Medic, 'pilots pick up the pencil and paper and start doing the simple arithmetical calculations you have been given. At 15,000 feet please release your oxygen masks and turn off your oxygen/air mix supply at the regulator. Navigators, for the time being, you stay connected and monitor your pilot's behaviour.'

Iain started to do the calculations swiftly and methodically as the chamber climbed towards 20,000 feet, but slowly and insidiously his manner began to change and I could see that he was having to think really hard to do the simplest of additions. As the chamber headed towards 25,000 feet, his head began to nod, there were long pauses with no activity when suddenly, and almost without warning, his head dropped forward and he was out! His lips had developed a rather obvious blue hue, which was a clear sign of a lack of oxygen.

'OK Number 2, quickly reconnect Number 1's mask and select 100% oxygen for him,' the Doc called over the intercom.

I responded rapidly and watched as, within just a few seconds, Iain raised his head and recovered to his normal alert position. Surprisingly, he carried on doing his sums as if nothing untoward had happened at all.

'You OK?' I enquired.

'Yep, fine, why?' he responded. He had been completely unaware that hypoxia had set in and did not even know that he had been unconscious!

Noticeably, a strange aroma had pervaded our sealed chamber as we had ascended to 25,000 feet. Not too unpleasant, it had a familiar odour and one that we had all recognised very quickly!

'Let me explain the smell,' said the friendly Doc. 'As an aircraft ascends and the pressure in the cockpit decreases, the human bowel expands and any trapped gases are expelled. It's a common phenomenon and a natural hazard for airline passengers, but the worst thing you can do when flying is attempt to prevent the escape of these noxious gases. Just let it rip!'

As the chamber descended back to ground level there were wry smiles all round.

'It's alright for you guys,' said the Doc, 'think of me, in here twice a week with you guys after a night on Ruddles County!'

It was not quite colonic irrigation, but it was probably the next best thing!

It was now the turn of the navs to undertake the arithmetical quiz and so the chamber began to ascend once again with JK and I tasked with removing our masks, switching off our regulators and doing simple calculations. As we passed 20,000 feet I began to feel very light-headed and I began to stumble over the arithmetic. I was aware that it was happening and I remember looking up and smiling at Iain, but there was nothing I could do about it! I attempted to carry on doing the sums, but it was in vain.

Then I heard Iain say, 'Alright, Dave?'

'Yep, I'm fine,' I replied, as if nothing had happened, but it had. The unidentifiable effects of hypoxia to the victim are frightening and can easily kill the unwary. It is no wonder that military aircrew are drilled in conducting regular O2 checks whilst airborne, particularly when at high level, as the cost in both expensive hardware and aircrew lives could be an excessive price to pay for the unheeding.

As we opened the door and cleared the chamber of the odour, I realised that oxygen has more value than just saving one's life at altitude! The effect of 100% oxygen, I had discovered, has the rewarding skill of clearing a hangover within minutes of its selection on an aircraft's O^2 regulator – it was a lesson that I, and many others like me, would put to good use over many hours in a Buccaneer cockpit!

The ejection rig went smoothly both literally and metaphorically, and the following morning, as a combined group, we were taken up to 50,000 feet in the chamber and then 'exploded' back down to 30,000 feet. Not for the fun of it, but so that we would recognise an explosive decompression if ever a Buccaneer managed to scrape an extra 11,000 feet above its service ceiling of 39,000 feet and its canopy somehow became detached. In truth, it was unlikely to happen to Buccaneer aircrew, but it was part of the syllabus for all fast-jet aircrew, some of whom would be destined in 1971 to fly Lightning interceptors. It was quite an experience to fart your way to 50,000 feet and then have your world implode as the chamber plummeted back down again as if its cabin had been pierced and a gaping hole had appeared in its simulated fuselage.

We left North Luffenham that afternoon, well trained in the consumption of Ruddles County, but fully conversant with the problems that an overindulgence of alcohol can have on the human anatomy when flying. But now we were also fully educated in the accepted methods of self-medication whilst airborne! My 'Moggie' was laden down with my newly-issued personal flying clothing and in my hand I clutched yet another qualification certificate to nail into my logbook!

The final words of the senior Medic at AMTC were ringing in my ears as I drove through the main gate at North Luffenham. 'That kit's bloody expensive; I strongly recommend that you get it insured!'

Back at Honington I unloaded my new-found wealth at the Flying Clothing Section and headed back to the Mess for High Tea. Back in the bar that night I found myself chatting with a group of 12 Squadron aircrew who had not long arrived, having been at Lossiemouth on 736 Squadron as some of the last RAF crews to train with the Navy. They were from the same cohort as my good friend, Taff Paines. Amongst the group was a chap by the name of Bill Cope, who, upon hearing that I had never flown in anything faster than a Jet Provost, offered to take me for a spin in a Hunter T7 and true to his word, he rang me two days later on 2 April 1971 and told me to get on over to 12 Squadron as he had managed to find a Hunter that was looking for a sortie to fly. I grabbed my hat from its peg and following a quick call to Flying Clothing to ensure that my new helmet was ready, covered the ground between 237 OCU and the 12 Squadron hangar as quickly as my legs would carry me.

As all Buccaneer aficionados know, the aircraft was never built with two sticks and the first time that a pilot flew it was the first time that a pilot flew it! Unlike its contemporaries, like the F-4 Phantom, there was no method available to check pilot confidence or ability by flying a QFI in a fully capable rear seat. Consequently, each Buccaneer unit was equipped with a number of Hunter T7As and T8Bs that were fitted out with the same IFIS as the Buccaneer, but, of course, did not have the same handling characteristics as the operational aircraft. They were, however, perfect for conducting instrument ratings, night checks and many other tasks that two pilots could not achieve together in the Buccaneer. They were useful squadron 'hacks' and perfect as a 'bounce' aircraft for harassing formations when the Buccaneer was doing what it did best in hugging the sea or land to get through to its target.

Bill Cope and I were going to conduct GH, IF and CT over East Anglia and the North Sea, part of which would include a PD to RAF Marham in Norfolk, which was at the time home to the RAF's Victor K1 and K2 tanker force. Sat in the right-hand seat of this airborne Formula One speedster, the acceleration down the Honington runway on take-off took my breath away. I had never experienced anything like it in my life and to be strapped into one of Her Majesty's world-famous fighter aircraft that had equipped almost the whole of Fighter Command from the mid-1950s to the early 1970s was a dream beyond any comparison; the last Hunters left RAF service along with the Buccaneer in 1994.

We climbed to 15,000 feet in a matter of moments and before I knew it, we were wheeling and turning, conducting aerobatic manoeuvres, each of which Bill named in turn so that I could recognise them later. Aileron Rolls, Barrel Rolls, Loops, Wing-overs and Rolls off the Top spilled from his lips as he threw the aircraft around the brilliantly blue sky over Norfolk that day. It was all over too quickly and very soon we were arriving at the Low-Level Entry Point for Honington that was situated above an L-shaped campsite at Kessingland on the Suffolk coast. A feature to remember, according to Bill, as it would be a lifeline in poor weather on a low-level VMC recovery to Honington. Today, however, the weather was glorious and as we called 'Low-Level Entry Point Inbound' on the Honington Approach frequency, we turned onto west and Bill pushed the throttle forward until the Hunter settled at 420 knots for a 'run and break' at its home base. It had lasted only sixty minutes, but I now had my first fast-jet hours recorded in my logbook.

Two weeks later, JK and I found ourselves travelling at a much more sedate pace in a Hastings T5 from RAF Lindholme's 'Bomber Command Bombing School'. The Hastings was routinely used by the RAF to train V-Force[4] Nav Radars in their art

---

4. A 'catch-all' term used by the RAF to describe the Valiant, Vulcan and Victor aircraft that comprised the United Kingdom's strategic nuclear strike force.

before being posted to the requisite OCUs of the Vulcan, Victor and previously, the Valiant. It was a dark and miserable place in the back of a Hastings and it reminded me very much of my time on the Varsity at Nav School and of that 'kick in the pants' visit to RAF Scampton when I peered into the back of a Vulcan and decided to work harder to avoid life as a radar navigator on the V-Force.

Now here we were, mid-April 1971, and I was trudging through the sky in the darkened fuselage of a simulated V-Bomber staring at an H2S radar screen and trying desperately to work out what all the squiggly green patterns meant! Did I need this? I was going to fly an aircraft with a large Perspex canopy that was designed to attack ships at sea, which surely would glow incandescently on the Buccaneer's radar when the time came. I certainly did not need to be buckled into the back of this ancient, darkened, urine smelling, piston-driven sweatbox for any longer than was necessary. We were encouraged to attempt to interpret the radar against the 250,000 scale map that we had plotted our route on. It was almost impossible and became even worse when the staff navigator covered the 360° display with a template that turned it into a B Scan radar to simulate the Buccaneer's Blue Parrot screen. We flew two sorties at both low-level and medium-level, but it did not make much difference and I for one was rather pleased when the two sorties were over and I was back on the A1 heading south to Honington for a weekend amongst people of like minds who believed that eyes were for looking out of the cockpit and radars were for those less able than we steely-eyed aces on the Buccaneer Force – at least that is how I see it some forty-five years later!

I was ready for the OCU and, with preliminaries completed, all that was required was for the clock to turn the requisite number of times to get me to and through the groundschool and the necessary simulator sorties that would release me for my Fam 1[5] in a Buccaneer S2.

---

5. Familiarisation – the first five sorties on the OCU syllabus were designated as familiarisation (there was no Fam 4 for navigators). These were followed by High Level Navexes.

Chapter Seven

Panache Et Precision

When Tony Fraser took command of 237 OCU, he inherited a unit with some historical record, but no squadron badge, and consequently, no motto. Formed at RAF Benson on 31 July 1947 as the PR OCU, the unit trained aircrew to conduct these tasks using de Havilland Mosquito and Supermarine Spitfire aircraft until it was disbanded only four years later at RAF Bassingbourn in Cambridgeshire and subsumed into 231 OCU, the English Electric Canberra training unit. In 1956, the unit re-emerged for just thirteen months as a stand-alone PR Canberra conversion unit before, once again, it was swallowed up by 231 OCU, by then at RAF Wyton. It had been dormant for thirteen years until the Air Force Board decided to give the nameplate to the Buccaneer OCU on 1 March 1971. With the assistance of we students who had been holding at Honington before the start of Nos. 8 and 9 Courses, 237 OCU was ready to do business, but it needed an identity.

Groundschool began on 17 May 1971, nine days before my twenty-second birthday. It was clear from the outset that the planned two weeks of this phase of the course were going to be intense. I was not the youngest student, as Dave Symonds had been commissioned only two months after his eighteenth birthday and was only just twenty-one when the course began. I was, however, the most inexperienced. As a recently qualified pilot, Dave had at least some knowledge of aircraft fuel, electrical, hydraulic and flying control systems, which were subjects that were not considered necessary for would-be navigators at 6 FTS in 1970. Without the background of operational experience, or the advantage of pilot training at 4 FTS,[1] I knew from day one that I was going to have to study in the evenings to get my head round the technical aspects of the Buccaneer. But then it was also evident from day one that to be a part of the Buccaneer Force required one to be not only studious, tactically minded, operationally able with strong airmanship, but also, as the 'Meet & Greet' proved that evening, to be capable of holding your drink and being up for all sorts of pranks as the alcohol flowed more freely and the spirits grew even higher!

The barman at Honington in 1971 was a very biddable chap who went by the title with surname of Corporal Ward. I never did know his first name, as, in those days, there was a definite and strong divide between airmen and officers; they would never consider calling an officer anything other than 'Sir' and we would never ever embarrass them by referring to them by their first name – even if we did know it, which was unlikely. Ward was a man of impeccable character and one who well knew how to attend to his officers' needs. When it came time for the bar to shut, Corporal

---

1. The advanced flying training school for pilots destined to fly fast jets; it was based at RAF Valley in Anglesey.

Ward, knowing full well that he was going nowhere, would move to make fast the bar for the evening; whilst those remaining, usually a high number of drunken aircrew, would make to hold the shutters aloft to prevent him from doing so. Then the shout would go up.

'Belay the shutters, Corporal Ward!'

'Right, Sir,' came the respectful reply from the airman. 'What time would you like me to belay the shutters until, Sir?'

'Can we have another hour, Corporal?' It being 2300hrs by this stage, and we having no intent of going to bed before 2359hrs at the earliest.

'Of course, Sir.' Would reply the good corporal as he stowed the shutters once again and started to pull ever more beer whilst knowing full well that the next action would be a Dimple beer mug being passed around to 'Fill the Pot for Corporal Ward'. He was a wonderful and tolerant man who lives on in the memory of all those aircrew who served at Honington in the early 1970s. However, he was responsible in many a way for my inability to keep to my word and knuckle down to my studies during groundschool, and subsequently during the flying phase of the course.

Now I know it is important to some of you and I suppose that we might as well get it out of the way now as leave you gasping for the detail later. The technical facts that we had to learn in groundschool were mind-numbing, especially for those who lacked a technical brain. The theory of electricity had left me cold at the High School of Glasgow in Doc Phillips' physics laboratory and, as you will remember with some glee, I had not faired too well during the mathematics and aeronautical science lectures at AOTS. However, I did have the guiding hand of Iain Ross to help me through and, like my mother with history dates before him, of an evening, and before we renewed our acquaintanceship with Corporal Ward, he would din into me the necessary technical aspects of the Buccaneer fuel or hydraulic system if we knew there was to be a test the following morning.

The Buccaneer S2 was a robust airframe that measured sixty-three feet five inches from the tip of its radome to the point of its petal airbrakes at its rear. It had a wingspan of forty-four feet and stood sixteen feet three inches above the ground at its highest point at the top of its tailplane. For ease of storage on aircraft carriers its wings folded to give it a span of one inch short of twenty feet and, with its nose cone folded open and its petal airbrakes fully extended, the aircraft could be shortened by just under twelve feet. Empty, it weighed a massive 32,000lbs and could carry 23,000lbs of fuel with UWTs, BBT and, once retrofitted in the early 1970s, it's BDT. With, in the 1970s, a weapon load of either eight 1000lb GP bombs or BL755 CBU on its wing stations and bomb bay, the Buccaneer was a potent weapon system, and one well-placed to fill the gap left by the cancellation of both TSR2 and the American F-111. When I joined the force, additional weapons in its inventory were 2-inch rockets and, to illuminate the sky on a dark night over the ocean, LEPUS flares. Now, and for those who need this kind of information, the two hydraulic pressures that I can remember were 3300PSI in the flying control system and 4000PSI in the hydraulic system. If you need more information than that, then I can assure you that there are better books than this that will provide you with all the technical knowhow you might seek, and quite rightly – as it is not in the gift of a navigator to talk easily about these things – are written by pilots!

Groundschool, of course, did not just consist of technical blah about hydraulic pressures and wiggly amps, or FNA Valves and TRUs, it covered much of the navigation equipment too and the techniques to be employed as navigators at both high and low-level. As navigators we had to cover 'How to Speak on the Radio' which, and despite it sounding rather prosaic in its title, I really appreciated, having had no opportunity to do so in my previous training. The one moral I learned from 'How to Speak on the Radio', was to engage brain before opening mouth, a lesson that has served me well throughout my career both in and out of the cockpit. We learned our 'Bold Face' emergency drills and practised our 'Challenge and Response' cockpit checks until we knew them off pat. Iain and I exercised each other in both and I was very grateful to him for his patience in guiding me through it all.

As the end of groundschool approached, I did have to get out of the bar and into my books in order to attempt the end of groundschool examination. The pass mark was set deliberately high and there would be no excuses for faltering at the first hurdle on 237 OCU, no matter how much you could drink or socialise in the bar. It was worth the effort, as Iain and I passed with flying colours, and I knew that had David Lees been the CI he would have given me a Diligence mark in my report of:

'E – *"Outstanding in reliability and initiative" (Even with poor school attainments a pupil may reveal these qualities in his work)*.'

Good old Doctor Lees, an academic of great stature who would have been hopelessly at sea in the educational environment that existed on the Buccaneer OCU!

Groundschool over, there followed a further two weeks of intensive simulator flying. The simulator was, however, still at Lossiemouth and therefore required a deployment to the delights of the north of Scotland, and a week or so sampling the merits of pints of 'Heavy' and the local bars of the small fishing port on the Moray coastline. We were fortunate at the time that the RAF had decided to locate a squadron of Avro Shackleton MR2Cs at Honington for a twelve month period that covered my time as a student on 237 OCU. 204 Squadron added much to the ambience of the officers' mess bar at Honington whilst fulfilling their role as part of the RAF's MR force and, in particular, on detachment at Majunga, where they provided RAF support to the UN sanctions and trade embargo established in the wake of Ian Smith's Unilateral Declaration of Independence from the UK; known as the Beira Patrol.

The squadron also provided a perfect taxi service to take the students and accompanying staff from 237 OCU to Lossiemouth to undertake simulator training. As we climbed up the steps at the rear of our trusted steed and took our allocated seats I was aware of the very familiar smell that had welcomed my every trip on the Varsity at 2 ANS. There is something about the aroma of a piston-engine aircraft that I find difficult to put into words, but anyone reading this who has flown in such an aircraft will know exactly what I am talking about. The aircraft had a crew of ten and was equipped with four Griffon engines that drove six-blade contra-rotating propellers. It was often colloquially described as 'ten thousand rivets flying in close formation' and as we took off from Honington and headed out towards the North Sea at our cruise speed of 240 knots, the vibration that set in quickly made me realise just what people meant by that statement. However, and despite the loss of another opportunity to see the magnificent Northumberland coast from the comfort of a second-class seat on British Railways, it was a better and – as the Shack crew carried out a training exercise on the way – a cheaper method of getting us in position for our simulator rides in 'the box'. With the Beira Patrol being largely ineffective, the squadron was disbanded on 28 April 1972, but not before we and they had enjoyed many a Happy Hour at Honington, where the beer and banter flowed routinely. There were two exceptionally gifted humorists at Honington on the Buccaneer Force in 1971 who regularly poked fun at the Shackleton chaps and particularly their pilot flight commander, who was a diminutive individual by the name of Ken Miles. One of these comics was the CFI on 237, David Mulinder, and the other was Squadron Leader Operations, Jock Gilroy, who sadly lost his life in a Buccaneer accident at night on Jurby Range in January 1972. This was their typical bar repartee:

'Ken, why is the Elsan[2] at the back of a Shackleton?'

'No idea!' would reply the long-suffering Ken whilst preparing himself for the inevitable withering punch line.

'So that the turds at the back balance the turds at the front!' would come the response to much gales of puerile, but alcohol-induced laughter from the assembled Buccaneer chaps who outnumbered the Shackleton guys by about two to one.

The simulator was housed in a large building near the airfield at Lossiemouth and some distance from the wardroom. Other than the simulator cockpit itself, the building housed the hydraulic system that gave 'the box' its full motion capability, plus various classrooms, a crewroom, technical area and the model room. Unlike today where military simulators rely on computer technology and CGI to convince aircrew that they are airborne, in 1971, technology was less advanced and the simulator relied on an actual scale model of Lossiemouth airfield, the local area and a model aircraft carrier positioned in the Moray Firth to allow students to make carrier approaches in the safety and comfort of a cockpit that was firmly fixed to terra firma. Accordingly, the largest room in the simulator building was the model room and over the model itself 'flew' a small video camera that received inputs from the cockpit and 'simulated' real flight over familiar terrain to the crew in the cockpit. When the Royal Navy left Lossiemouth and 809 NAS redeployed to Honington, they brought the simulator with them and so, for years afterwards, those who flew the Buccaneer and trained on the simulator, no matter their home base location, always simulated out of Lossiemouth!

There were ten simulator sorties to be passed as part of the 237 OCU syllabus and they grew in intensity from basic cockpit familiarity to full mission exercises, with emergencies thrown in to test crew knowledge and aircraft handling. We had to know

---

2. Chemical toilet.

our Bold Face Drills verbatim, and action them quickly and efficiently to ensure progress through the course and on to the flying phase, and all this whilst ensuring that we kept our end up in the bar every night and bantered equally with the staff who had accompanied us north.

By the third mission in 'the box', Iain Ross and I had begun to get our act together. We had mastered the challenge and response Pre-Take-off Checks without hiccough, and the necessary tasks to get airborne were becoming second nature. I enjoyed my time in the cockpit with him and we felt comfortable with each other and our roles, which was critical if we were to become a capable crew once airborne in the real thing. A lot can go wrong in an aircraft that is designed to fly close to the surface of the Earth and at speeds of up to nine miles a minute! The Buccaneer, in particular, depended upon strong crew cooperation and we began to learn that fact in the simulator when things were made to go wrong by the staff on the instructors' console outside 'the box'. At the press of just one button they could ruin your day, but it was better to master the emergency there and walk away from the simulator, rather than be incapable of doing so when it happened for real. From the adrenaline pumping engine failure during take-off, to the relatively more mundane hydraulic failures, as a crew we had to react. Together we had to overcome the emergency whilst ensuring that we followed the drills accurately. My role was, primarily, to support Iain with formal, and occasionally informal advice, whilst he concentrated on flying the aircraft and made whatever cockpit switch selections were required to defeat the emergency! In a dire emergency my job was to get on the radio and let the world know that we had a problem and might need assistance or rescue!

Some emergency drills had to be second nature, and when the SWP illuminated and the clangers sounded, Iain would have to react with no input from me, other than for me to hear what the emergency was – there was no SWP repeater in my cockpit – and turn to the correct page in the FRCs. For example, whilst his immediate action drills for an engine fire would be to shut the HP Cock, switch off the Master Cock and reduce speed to 250 knots, if practicable, and then press the appropriate engine's fire extinguisher button, my role was to turn quickly to the correct emergency drill in the FRCs and make sure that he had followed the correct sequence by going over it with him once he had completed it and, hopefully, the fire had gone out! However, and importantly, if the Fire Warning Light was still illuminated after thirty seconds we would both try to check for signs of fire, and if confirmed, there was only one way that we would be getting back to earth – Martin Baker's very efficient exit system! Whereas, for a GS Pump MI Cross Hatched with HYD/GS indicated on the SWP, things would be taken at a much more sedate pace and Iain would respond to my reading of the actions from the emergency section of the FRCs. The end result for such an emergency would be a prompt landing into the approach end RHAG and, accordingly, the first action would be to reduce our AUW by jettisoning fuel until we reached an acceptable landing weight. Whilst fuel was being pumped overboard I would start to read from the checklist and Iain would respond by repeating my words whilst he selected the appropriate switches to complete the necessary actions:

'Undercarriage (Below 225 knots)… DOWN (button fully in) 3 greens
Arresting Hook… DOWN
Airbrakes… ½
Flaps, aileron droop and TP flap… 0-10-10
Adopt single proportioner failure drill
Land 45-25-25, blow[3] on into cable.'

Simple really, but these things never happen when nothing critical is happening in the cockpit and with instructors watching your every move from the console, it was inevitable that they knew exactly when you were off guard or distracted and they always took their advantage. The unwary could be caught out quite easily if they did not actually notice the MI going cross-hatched, and the longer it took them to become aware of it, the more compound the situation was likely to become as emergencies were loaded one upon the other.

Iain and I survived it all, and by the end of our time at Lossiemouth I had learned a great deal about flying in a complex aircraft with a competent pilot and he had become accustomed to sharing his experiences in the air with a GIB (Guy in the Back) who was there to ease his task and assist with much of the management of the aircraft and its systems.

Back at Honington after a further two hours and twenty minutes in the back of one of 204 Squadron's aircraft, we repaired to the bar and another session under the watchful eye of Corporal Ward. One of the instructors on the OCU, who became a very good friend over the years of my RAF career, was a flight lieutenant pilot by the name of Tom Eeles. Tom's father had been commandant of the RAF College at Cranwell and Tom, like Iain Ross, but unlike me on my Direct Entry Commission, had undertaken the full three-year cadetship course there before embarking on an operational flying career that took him initially to Canberra B(I)8 bombers at RAF Laarbruch in Germany. He then volunteered for loan service with the Royal Navy and found himself at Lossiemouth flying Buccaneer S1s, first with 801 NAS on HMS *Victorious*, and then as an instructor on 736 NAS, from whence he arrived at Honington as one of the first RAF instructors on the OCU. Tom was a character. He was an ocean-going sailor, with a yacht on a mooring at Aldborough, and a bachelor! He knew how to enjoy life and he knew how to drink his beer too. Quaintly, for a Buccaneer pilot, he owned a parrot by the name of Charles Peace, after an infamous Victorian murderer. Whenever Tom was on a bender Charles Peace would accompany him and, like an elder statesman, take up his usual position at the end of the bar. Tom's partner in crime was a fellow bachelor by the name of Pete Bucke and between the two of them they would ensure that there was never an opportunity for any 'liver-in' to go to bed when the bar was still open. With Corporal Ward on duty, you will recall, bar

---

3. Blown flaps are a powered aerodynamic high-lift device used on the wings of certain aircraft to improve low-speed lift during take-off and landing; sometimes called a boundary layer control (BLC) system. Air is taken from the engines and literally blown over the leading edge of the wing to improve handling at slow speed.

closures were something of a rarity until we could sup no more or stand no longer! Of course the bar had to shut eventually, but for those hardy few, which always seemed to include Iain and me, there was always the offer of hospitality in Tom's room in the mess where he had a plentiful supply of malt whisky, usually Glenmorangie, and a floor to sit on whilst we imbibed long into the night and long after Corporal Ward had dropped the shutters and gone home to count his new-found wealth! Tom had a plentiful selection of LP records, but insisted on playing only one on his turntable during these sessions – The Bonzo Dog Doo-Dah Band's '*Gorilla*'! Consequently, these sessions became known as The Gorilla Club, which, with all due respect to these gentle primates, was quite appropriate given the state of our bodies and minds by the time the shutters came down and the shout went up, '*Gorilla Club!*' The Gorilla Club became de rigueur after a long Friday Happy Hour, but could quite easily happen during the week if the flying programme was slack either due to weather or function for Tom and Pete. When Tom married in 1972, Charles Peace was not welcomed into the marital home and found new lodgings with Bucke!

With the ten simulator missions behind us, Iain and I began to prepare ourselves for our Fam 1 sorties, which were planned to take place during the second week of June. As no two-stick Buccaneer existed, and his first time in the front seat in command would be his first time in the front seat in command, Iain had to undertake a number of sorties in a Hunter T7A or T8B with a QFI to familiarise himself, and prove that he was happy with the IFIS of the Buccaneer with which our Hunters were equipped. I, on the other hand, would fly a couple of Buccaneer flights with a staff pilot whilst Iain then completed three in a Buccaneer, firstly with a staff QFI and then two with a staff navigator. We would next meet for our first crew sortie, which was designated Fam 4. I flew my Fam 1 with Jerry Yates, who was a larger than life character who had completed the FAA's AWI course and was vastly experienced in the front seat of the Buccaneer. I was in awe of him whilst at the same time very slightly intimidated by his experience and ability – he seemed the sort of person that I could get on with as long as I did not make a complete arse of myself from the outset. My Fam 1 was scheduled for 8 June 1971, and I diligently ensured that I had the necessary maps prepared and was ready for whatever emergency or curve ball he might throw at me!

The first sortie for a navigator on any conversion unit is designed purely to familiarise him with his environment and the capabilities of the aircraft. Accordingly, our plan was to undertake a SID from Honington and commence a climb to height where Jerry would show me some of the handling characteristics of this immensely robust bomber. This was to be followed by a descent to low-level, a charge around over the sea off the Norfolk Coast, and thence round to the LLEP at Kessingland to conduct a run in and break at Honington before engaging in some circuit work and a GCA to land. The whole thing would take about an hour and a quarter!

The Buccaneer was designed in the 1950s to meet the threat posed by the latest warship to join the Soviet Navy's inventory. Fourteen Sverdlov cruisers, each displacing 16,640 tons fully laden, were built between 1948 and 1955, and were the last conventional cruisers to enter service with the USSR. With a crew of 1,250 officers and men, a top speed of 32 knots and a range of 9,000 nautical miles, and bristling with twelve 152mm guns, twelve twin-mounted 100mm guns, thirty-two 37mm anti-air cannon and ten torpedo tubes, it posed an enormous threat to the forces of NATO, and the United Kingdom in particular, a nation dependent upon free-flowing sea lanes to maintain its prosperity. The Cold War was not yet out of nappies when the first of these vast ships took to the high seas in 1951 and with an original Soviet requirement for thirty ships, the British Government needed to act quickly to counter the threat posed.

A detailed specification was issued by the Ministry of Technology in 1952 as Naval Staff Requirement NA.39, demanding a two-seat aircraft equipped with folding wings and capable of flying at 550 knots at sea level. The requirement called for a combat radius of 400 nautical miles at low-level and 800 nautical miles at high altitude. A weapons load of 8,000 pounds of conventionally-armed bombs, as well as a capability to deliver a 'bucket of sunshine' when required, was central to the navy's need to combat the Soviet Navy. The Blackburn Aircraft Company's design won the tender in 1955 and the first prototype took to the air for the first time on 30 April 1958. However, the Buccaneer S1, equipped with Gyron Junior engines, was distinctly underpowered and many were lost throughout its short life in FAA service between 1962 and 1970. The Buccaneer S2, a much beefier aircraft equipped with Rolls Royce Spey engines that provided 8,000lbs more thrust than the two Gyron Juniors, was brought quickly into naval service in 1965 to replace the less than convincing S1! The S2 was more reliable, and, unlike its predecessor, its Spey engines would happily consume anything organic that got in their way!

Whilst the RN was attempting to equip itself to combat the Sverdlov threat, the RAF, as was its want, was refusing categorically to have anything in its inventory that might have been chosen first by the Royal Navy! To be fair, the Air Ministry sought a supersonic aircraft to replace its Canberra Force and the British Aircraft Corporation had on their drawing boards the TSR2, which was designed to penetrate a well-defended forward battle area at low altitude and very high speed. Once through the defensive shield it would attack targets in the rear with nuclear or conventional weapons. Some of the most advanced aviation technology of the period was incorporated in order to make it the highest-performing aircraft in the world in its projected missions. The aircraft first flew on 27 September 1964 and was planned to enter service by 1967. However, rising costs, inter-service bickering, and a desire by the Labour Government's Chancellor of the Exchequer in 1965, James Callaghan, to provide support for the ailing British car industry, resulted in funds being pulled from TSR2. The project was cancelled and the aircraft jigs destroyed!

This left the RAF with no plan, no Canberra replacement and no possibility of regenerating TSR2 should the government be ousted at the next election. The US Government was, at the time, re-equipping with the F-111, a high-performance multi-mission bomber, and offered this swing-wing aircraft as a low-cost substitute to TSR2. A total of fifty F-111K were ordered from the Pentagon on 1 February 1967, but by early the following year the order was cancelled because of rising project costs and technical difficulties.

Enter the Buccaneer S2 into the argument! The aircraft seemed to have all the requirements to match the TSR2 and the F-111; albeit its design shape would preclude any thought of a supersonic dash at low, or for that matter, high level. The Royal Navy had already proved that it was capable of high subsonic speed at very low-level. It had a robust airframe that would cope with the diverse flight envelope that the RAF planned for it. Indeed, many components were milled from solid billets of aluminium. It had an area rule design to reduce drag at high speed, which, as a bonus, provided ample space in its aft section for the black boxes that would give it – for its 1950s design – a complex avionic system. Its folding wings, part of its naval requirement not needed by the RAF, but convenient for hangar storage, were equipped with high lift devices that were provided with bleed air from its two Spey engines that delayed the onset of stalling speed and reduced the approach speed to 127 knots. From an Air Ministry perspective it was not the ideal solution, but it would now have to do until the recently-projected MRCA could be brought into service. An initial order was placed and, as a money saver, these would be made up initially from those aircraft being cast off by the navy because of the withdrawal of the majority of its aircraft carriers and the concomitant run-down of its fixed wing force in the late 1960s. Thus, the RAF's initial inventory of Buccaneers was made up of re-worked FAA jets that were refurbished and repainted, and delivered to Honington in October 1969 to form the RAF's first Buccaneer unit, 12 Bomber Squadron.

Have you ever looked in a Buccaneer cockpit? It is, and has often quite rightly been described as an ergonomic slum! However, despite Blackburn's philosophy for the avionic boxes and cockpit switches of 'throw them all up and screw them in where they fall', they did get one thing right in their development of a low-level fast-jet bomber that no other aircraft manufacturer has done since. The front seat in the Buccaneer is offset very slightly to the left, and the rear seat is similarly positioned slightly to the right and above. This allowed the navigator to see fully forward, over the pilot's right shoulder and through the right quarter-light of the windscreen. It also allowed the GIB a clear view of many of the important dials on the right-hand side of the pilot's cockpit and a clear sight of the 'Blow Gauges', which had to be critically monitored during approach and landing.

As well as navigating, the navigator's role was to: a) identify radar targets; b) manage the weapons system; c) manage electronic countermeasures; d) manage the fuel system; e) work the radio; f) 'Check Six' and everything between two and ten o'clock in the rear hemisphere; and g) mop the pilot's fevered brow (metaphorically) when things got tough! To do this, Ferranti had secured a contract with Blackburns to provide the rear-seat occupant with a multitude of navigational aids to ease the workload! Prime amongst these was the 'Blue Parrot' radar, designed primarily for the detection of maritime targets, and the 'Blue Jacket' Doppler radar, which encompassed everything in a Ground Position Indicator system that a first tourist navigator would require to keep him 'on track and on time'! Well, it would have done if the ground position Eastings and Northings counters had not jumped up to a mile in no pre-known or particular direction (of their choosing) as soon as they were selected 'On' during the take-off run! An Inertial Navigator they most certainly were not, and the result was that they were so unreliable that many Navs were 'unsure of their position' pretty much as soon as they were airborne, had they not learned quickly to disregard them and use the Mark One Eyeball, the most reliant of NavAids, to secure positions on route. I concede that had I ever flown 'off the deck' I might have had to become more reliant on the Blue Jacket, but, never having had that privilege, I very quickly became circumspect about its utility for navigation.

In 1971, additional NavAids included a 'moving roller map', which required about sixteen hours of preparation, glue, a sharp pair of scissors and an 'out and back' mentality in the planning stage to give it any value. OK, I lied about the sixteen hours, but it took so much time to prepare and, given it was fed by the Blue Jacket, it was very quickly deemed 'bloody useless' and soon gave way to the Radar Warning Receiver control panel in the ergonomic slum! Some bright spark had also deemed it a good idea to provide the Buccaneer Navigator with a fold-down table (about eighteen inches square) that he could use to do his high level chart work on; yeah that'll be right! It had to be folded away in the 'up' position at low-level as it prohibited access to the bottom handle should one have to leave in a hurry! The Navigation Suite was completed with an S/X-Band Wide Band Homer system that provided directional information should it ever lock on to a Soviet maritime radar in the final stages of an attack!

Having checked and signed the 'Authorisation Sheet' on the OCU's Ops Desk, and having declared us 'Walking for 270' to the Duty Authoriser, Jerry walked me through to the 'Line Desk' to check through the aircraft serial XT270's Form 700. The F700 is a controlled document that bears witness to anything and everything that ever happened to the aircraft from a technical viewpoint whilst on the ground or, indeed, whilst airborne. It contains the servicing and flying records for each aircraft and is, in effect, the aircraft's historical flying and servicing record. The Line Desk is the hub of the maintenance regime on any squadron. It is where the engineers control servicing activity on the aircraft sat on the line being prepared for flight. Before accepting the aircraft from the engineers and signing to take responsibility for it, the aircraft captain – in the case of the Buccaneer, the pilot – must check the recent servicing record, ensure that the aircraft has received either a T/R or B/F servicing and, finally, make sure that he is content with the Red Line Entries – snags that can realistically be carried, but that will not affect the safe flying or operational ability of the aircraft to complete the mission planned and can therefore be delayed. Unlike many other aircraft, in the Buccaneer world this was a two-man responsibility, so Jerry talked me through each of the pages that were required to be checked by us in the thick volume before he then signed for the aircraft. I felt as if I was walking on air, I was wearing my torso harness and my anti-g suit, my kid leather flying gloves were in my kneepad pocket and my Mk3 Flying Helmet and Nav Bag were held firmly in my right hand. I was about to become Buccaneer aircrew – officially!

As we signed for the aircraft and left the hangar to walk the 200 metres towards the very large ASP built prematurely at Honington to take the now cancelled F-111s, the assembled Buccaneer ranks of 237 OCU's fleet and those of our neighbours, 12 Squadron, were arranged neatly before us with each of those about to fly connected to a Houchin electrical generator and with a Palouste air starter connected to their port engine. Each aircraft had a team of three mechanics, routinely two SACs and one corporal or JT, tasked with supporting crew strap-in, and the start and taxi of each aircraft in turn. As we approached, Jerry explained that another idiosyncrasy of the Buccaneer Force was that the navigator would always carry out his own 'Walk Round' of the aircraft before mounting the cockpit. The routine was for the Nav to travel independently clockwise around the aircraft whilst the pilot did likewise checking off items in the FRC that would, eventually, become second nature! On my Fam 1, however, I was to accompany Jerry so that he could explain what I was to look out for.

We started at the front checking that the folding nose was closed and that its handle and indicator were flush, then to the ADD probe to ensure that its cover had been removed, it was undamaged and that it was aligned centrally. Into the wheel wells to make sure that the undercarriage locks had been removed and that the MASB was connected. A quick check to make sure that the airframe was intact on all surfaces and that aerial covers and any intake blanks had been removed. A quick shufty down each engine intake as we came to it to check the integrity of each of the HP compressor blades and that there was no obvious damage or indication of prior birdstrike ingestion. By the same token, a look up the aft end of each engine to check its condition and, as bird debris had a habit of going straight through causing nothing more than a foul (no pun intended) burning smell in the cockpit air conditioning system, whether there was any evidence of organic pollution on the sooty deposit of the engine tailpipe! A check of the aileron droop and tailplane flap, and a note of its position, and we were just about there. Was the tailskid down and the airbrake fully open? And that was it. Confirming my contentment, I prepared to mount the six steps of the crew entry ladder that would take me up ten or so feet above the ground and into the ergonomic slum!

I completed my Internal Checks from the FRCs, and with the Blue Jacket ready and the Blue Parrot warming up, I prepared myself to monitor Jerry through his Engine Start checks. Whilst I was comfortable with the tasks at hand, I could never lose sight of the fact that I was a student, Jerry was staff and, although his role was to train me, the RAF system was such that I could not afford to slip up or be caught out by not following the necessary procedures, either now or at any stage in the future, and certainly not before I was declared Combat Ready on my first operational squadron.

'Ready for Start?'

'Ready for Start!' I responded, and turned my attention to his monotone voice and his actions that he was now dictating and I was monitoring on the cards in my right hand.

'Port Engine starting…3 seconds on the button…LP light flashing…port throttle to GROUND START,' he voiced proficiently as I heard the recognisable sound of the left-hand Spey winding up, and he continued on and I followed.

LP rotation light… Out
RPM … 50%
TGT… 420°C
LP RPM… 25%

On we went together, Jerry checking each item and me ensuring that each accorded with the words on the card. Complete, and with the port engine at idle and the Palouste now connected to the starboard engine, we prepared to go through the whole routine once again.

'Ready for Starboard?'

'Ready for Starboard!' And back into the FRCs.

'Starboard Engine starting…3 seconds on the button…LP light flashing… starboard throttle to GROUND START.' And back into the post-engine start checks for the right-hand Spey.

With both engines now 'turning and burning' and the Palouste disconnected, I followed Jerry through the rest of the Functional Checks and readied myself for taxi. Outside the cockpit the three airmen were busy tidying up the Palouste air starter's tube that had been used to blow air into the engine to initiate the start sequence and the Houchin's very heavy electrical cable that had provided electrical power to the aircraft until its generators had come online.

'Ready for taxi?'

With the excitement mounting in my stomach, I informed Jerry that I was ready to go.

'Honington Tower, Lima Yankee Romeo Two Seven is ready for taxi.'

'Lima Yankee Romeo Two Seven, taxi, Runway 27, QFE 1007.'

'Two Seven, Roger, SID 5 on departure climbing Flight Level 310.'

'Roger Two Seven, one ahead on a low-level departure.'

'Roger, Two Seven.'

Without a pause for breath, Jerry then intoned.

'Pre-Take Offs please, Dave.'

Trims… 15-10-10
Airbrakes … In
Autostabs… Set
Yaw Damper… Off
Autopilot… Off, MI Off
Aileron Gear Change… High Speed and Down

Etc, etc, etc, through the routine that invariably lasted the length of the taxi to the Holding Point for Runway 27 at Honington.

Wings… Spread and catch engaged
Canopy… Closed, Locked, light tested and out
Flying Controls… 3300, full and free movement

With the Take-off Emergencies Brief completed, and with a final tug on my straps, we were ready to go!

'Tower, Lima Yankee Romeo Two Seven is ready for take-off.'

'Two Seven, cleared take-off, surface wind two three zero at 5 knots, SID 5, contact Honington Zone on Stud Three once airborne.'

'Roger, Tower, Cleared Take-off and to Zone on Stud Three once airborne.'

And without further ado, other than a quick 'Ready' to me in the back seat, Jerry pushed the throttles forward together and when he released the parking brake, XT270 surged forward and I felt myself being pushed back into the parachute pack that formed the back of my Martin Baker rocket-assisted ejection seat. With my head reeling at the force of the acceleration I quickly tried to think, 'what next'! I know, I remember. The runway was streaking past and as I felt the aircraft lift from mother earth, I stretched forward and flicked the counters switch on the Blue Jacket to 'ON'! The buggers jumped at least one nautical mile north-east, the roller map followed and instantly I was temporarily unsure of my position, but more from the thrust skywards than any incapacity in my navigational skills.

'Two Seven is airborne to Zone.'

'Roger, Two Seven, Stud Three.'

Jerry had already moved the button on his UHF radio control box two clicks to the right from Stud One.

'Zone, Lima Yankee Romeo Two Seven, airborne SID 5, passing fifteen hundred feet in the climb for Three One Zero.'

Are we? I am still struggling to remember what my next action is! I had heard Jerry intoning his After Take-off checks, but I was not too sure that I had actually monitored them and, apart from the wandering off of the Blue Jacket counters, I had hardly started my own and, significantly, I had not yet flicked the switch to start the UWT fuel feed to the main fuelling gallery in the fuselage!

'Roger, Two Seven, continue climb, call passing Flight Level Five Zero.'

'Roger, passing Five Zero on Ten Thirteen now.'

Are we? Bloody hell! This is not going well!

'How you doing, Dave?'

'Great, I've got everything fired up and I've been following you through your checks and radio transmissions!' I lied, but he did not need to know that I was feeling maxed out already and fearing for my future.

'OK, just sit back and relax. Normally you'd take the radio after take-off, but for now I'll hang onto it while you enjoy the ride!'

Bloody hell! Could he see through my oxygen mask? I had a grin that spread from ear to ear and I felt wonderful as we continued the climb through 10,000 feet and upwards to our cleared height of 31,000 feet, or Flight Level 310 in aviation speak!

It takes the Buccaneer about ten minutes to climb to height, and as we levelled off Jerry initiated a fuel and oxygen check before he began to tell me what would happen next. He had briefed me on the ground beforehand, but, I suspect, an experienced instructor knew that most baby navigators had lost all sense of reality by the time those first ten minutes in a Buccaneer had passed.

We stooged around at FL310 for about ten minutes whilst I became accustomed to the NavAids, looked at the Norfolk coastline on the radar and generally became comfortable in my new surroundings. Then, with a short warning from Jerry, he closed the throttles to 'Idle' and flicked the airbrake out to 'Full' as he rolled the Buccaneer over and pointed its nose towards the North Sea. As we passed FL245, he called to Eastern Radar that we were going VFR and chopped to Stud 7, the OCU's own discrete frequency. With 400 knots set, we plummeted at about 16,000 feet per minute towards Earth! The heights were passing so rapidly that I found it difficult to keep up with my required height calls, but Jerry was content as I seemed to get the important ones out! We levelled off at 5,000 feet and carried out another fuel and oxygen check before he briefed me on the next phase, which was to be an acceleration to 580 knots followed by him slamming the throttles closed whilst selecting 'Full Airbrake' to prove the effectiveness of the pen nib slab of metal that made up the very rear of the Buccaneer. It took about twenty seconds for the aircraft to reach 580 knots from the almost standing start of three hundred and as we cruised across the sea at almost ten miles a minute I was astounded just how quickly the small ships on the surface came and went by! Then the throttles slammed shut, the airbrakes went out and I was thrown forward in my harness as we hit a metaphorical brick wall. We stopped on a tanner (sixpence in old money)! The speed agility of the Buccaneer was phenomenal.

Back up to ten thousand feet and Jerry began to perform light manoeuvring to show just how the aircraft could perform in the air. Aileron rolls, barrel rolls, accelerations, 5G pulls left and right, steep climbs at full power and a short ten-second burst of inverted flight which the aircraft was limited to by the amount of fuel held in its engines' recuperators for just such an eventuality. As I hung in my straps looking through the top of the cockpit at the sea below, all the dust, dirt and detritus from previous sorties began to float in front of my eyes. Jerry pointed out that if I ever dropped anything on the cockpit floor then flying inverted was a guaranteed way of retrieving it without too much muscular effort on my part. I was loving my first flight in a Buccaneer and I was loving flying with Jerry Yates, who did not seem to come from the 'Marsden School' of RAF instructors; some of whom I had met previously!

Then the bombshell came. It was not subtle in the way that it played out, but I was ready for it!

'OK, Dave, let me show you a loop.'

Ah ha, thought I, the Buccaneer is not cleared for a loop because the mainplane would blank the tailplane as the aircraft went over the top of the loop, which would likely induce a flick and subsequent spin! There was no way I was going to be caught out by this one!

'The Bucc's not cleared to loop,' I replied.

'Oh really! Watch this and keep calling out the height to me!' came his ready reply.

I recall we entered the loop somewhere about 5,000 feet at about 530 knots and I remember the pressure increasing in my anti-g suit as the g increased to four. As the height increased and the speed reduced, the AOA increased towards the onset of buffet, which Jerry held until 20 units of ADD was reached. I have no recall at what height we topped out despite my chanting of every 1,000 feet as we passed through it. However, and without the power to recall our bottoming height, I do remember that it was somewhat below our entry height! The whole thing passed in a blur as it was the first time that I had experienced quite such a period of sustained g! Exhilarated by the experience, I settled back to preparing myself for the recovery to base as we approached Kessingland at 1,500 feet for a visual join back at Honington.

'Pre-joiners, please!'

'OK'

Autopilot… Off, MI Off
Blow Selector… Auto
ADD… On
Jettison Selector… Set
Weapon Switches… Safe

'And the Variation is set in the back,' I said, as we completed the checks.

'Honington Approach, Lima Yankee Romeo Two Seven is Kessingland, fifteen hundred feet for visual join.'

'Roger, Two Seven, call Tower Stud One when 5 miles out and visual the field.'

'Two Seven.'

At 420 knots it took no more than five minutes to cover the thirty-five nautical miles between the caravan park at Kessingland and the runway at Honington and during those few minutes Jerry took the opportunity of pointing out the necessary visual cues that would lead me back to the airfield if the weather was any less clear than it was on that beautiful early summer's day in 1971.

The debrief went well and Jerry had few points to make with regard to my performance, such that I felt that honesty would be to my advantage should I ever be found wanting in the future.

'Thanks Jerry, I enjoyed that immensely, but I should tell you that I forgot to switch on the Under Wing Tanks after take-off and only remembered when we were halfway up the climb!'

'It didn't matter,' he replied.

'Really?'

'No, take a walk back out to the aircraft and you'll realise!'

As I walked through the crewroom and out the door towards the line, I heard his joking voice calling behind me.

'We didn't have any external tanks fitted, Dave!'

The OCU flying course continued apace and, before very long, Iain had caught up with me and by the end of the month we were airborne together doing a High Level Navex across the length of the UK. Early July found us at low-level at 420 knots and 250 feet back in the low flying system that I had been introduced to by Reg Drown in a Jet Provost. However, with much greater speed and much more fuel, we covered greater distances and could often be found across the Humber over Yorkshire and Northumberland, or, if we ventured west into Wales, flying down the A5 Pass where you could fly legally at 250 feet AGL below the trunk road that took summer holidaymakers from England to the North Wales resorts, and past Betws y Coed through Bethesda and on towards Bangor and the Menai Bridge. LFAs 11, 12 and 7 became our backyard, and with Tactical Link Routes connecting all the LFAs in the UK, the whole sortie could be flown at 250 feet above the ground. As I had tried to explain to my course commander at 2 ANS, low flying in a two-seat fast jet was the sport of kings and I was now doing it regularly!

Once we had mastered low-level in the Bucc the syllabus continued throughout July and into August with formation flying, and two or three visits to local bombing ranges, first with staff and then with Iain to try out each of the weapon delivery modes carried out by the Buccaneer. Four types of conventional bomb delivery were practised: 20° MDSL; 20° ADSL; LLADSL; and Laydown, as well as 10° 2-Inch Rocket deliveries and Long Toss, to be used for real to deliver the WE177 nuclear weapon, when and if that sad day came when the Cold War failed and 'buckets of sunshine' were being thrown about by both sides in the final days of Armageddon! Of course, we only dropped practice bombs that weighed 28lb, simulating free-fall weapons, or 4lb retarded weapons in the laydown mode. The only difference between MDSL and LL/ADSL was that the crew decided the release point in the former, whereas the computer took on that responsibility in the latter!

The integrated weapons system in the Buccaneer was controlled from the rear seat through a 'box of tricks' called the Control & Release Computer (C&RC), an 8-Way Bomb Distributor and a clockwork Pre-Release Timer. It is important to remember that all of these pieces of avionic wizardry were designed in the 1950s and therefore were analogue and not digital. With digital comes accuracy, but with analogue you are in the lap of the gods! The rear seat was also equipped with a strip altimeter that was fixed to 1013mb, the ICAO Standard Pressure Setting. Very useful, I hear all you aviators out there cry! Well, not really, and I know you were only being sarcastic! With an analogue weapons system comes built-in lag. Take the side off the C&RC and you will find cogs, string and pulleys! Very high specification cogs, string and pulleys I grant you, but, nonetheless, not renowned for their accuracy if the pilot or navigator conduct weapons attacks without paying full attention to the accuracy of their delivery parameters. So it was, therefore, that the role of the navigator during a weapons delivery was, in dive attacks, to call out the heights as the aircraft descended pointing at the target. Whilst it went some way to avoid target fixation by the pilot and prevent the aircraft becoming a 'tent peg', its prime function was to allow the pilot to hear the rate of descent and equate that to his understanding of the required rate for any given dive angle and adjust accordingly! Can you believe that? You will not believe it further when I tell you that all this was established by conducting a pre-range 'height check' over the sea at 100 feet and at attack speed to allow the navigator to etch a chinagraph mark on his altimeter to ensure that the 1013mb was superseded for the range detail of the day by a local pressure setting mark! Accurate? Well it would have been if the chinagraph mark had not been about '100 feet' thick! Some bright spark came up with the notion that a simple 'angle of dangle' meter made out of a piece of string, a scale and a weight would improve accuracy during dive attacks. Great in theory, but it took no account of the necessity for the navigator to focus on other aspects of the cockpit rather than on a piece of string wavering about on the side of the canopy! Needless to say, it never took off!

So the role of the navigator in the Buccaneer was not a particularly easy one, but it did ensure that we were trained on the OCU to be masters in the low-level world and could outfight most threats, maritime or over-land, because our very lives did depend upon it. What all this meant, of course, was that the Buccaneer was most definitely a 'crew cooperation' aircraft. The guy in the front could not function without the guy in the back, and the guy in the back was dependent upon the front-seater for getting them through successfully and back again. It became very apparent very quickly on the OCU that operating the Buccaneer was the responsibility of both crew members and that one could not and would not do it without the full support and agreement of the other. What this meant in reality was that there was no room for prima donnas in either seat, and that mutual respect was the be all and end all of Buccaneer operations! Pilots and navigators crewed together were, generally, good mates. You had to be, as life in a Buccaneer cockpit, despite its fore and aft construction, was and had to be very intimate. In fact, if you were inclined to do so, you could actually hold hands by stretching through a gap underneath the Blue Jacket. More importantly, however, if things did go awry with the intercom system it was possible to pass handwritten notes through the gap. Moreover, and perhaps more importantly, if the pilot failed to act on the Nav's directional consultancy instructions, then it was possible to give him a good clout on the side of his helmet with a MOD Store Reference 6B/349 Nav Ruler[4]. It was a stretch, but it was effective if used appropriately!

By early August, with much of the weapon phase completed and under our belts, we prepared for the dreaded Night Flying Phase! I have always believed and publicly stated that if birds do not fly at night then there surely was little or no need for man to! My words, only ever raised in the mess bar, always fell on deaf ears and so it was that I prepared myself for my Night Fam with Iain on 10 August. Other than the fact that it is quite bloody dark out over the North Sea on a night with no moon, which is rather disorientating, there is not much one can say about a night flight in a Buccaneer from a navigator's perspective. As long as you do not flood the canopy with the available cockpit lighting and, thereby, kill the pilot's long sought after night vision and hazard the aircraft, it is pretty much like day flying! Of course, there are fewer visual navigation references available and you have to keep your eyes peeled if you are VFR over the sea because other silly sods are very likely out there doing the same thing! Other than that, and keeping your pilot alert with words of encouragement, the Nav's role as a singleton on a basic Navex was easy. However, that was but the first and only night sortie on the OCU that can be thus described!

The second sortie was somewhat more complex as it involved two aircraft taking to the night sky for Close Formation practice! As usual on the OCU, for either the pilot or navigator, the first sortie was always flown with an instructor, and on this occasion I was programmed to fly the sortie with the CFI, David Mulinder, on 18 August, with Iain and his staff navigator following behind to formate on our wing once we had climbed to about 5,000 feet. However, that Wednesday night in 1971 had not been my

---

4. A 21-inch length of plastic marked with nautical miles and issued to all Navs to measure distance on either a 1/500,000 or 1/1,000,000 scale chart.

Author with his Mother: 1949. (*J.F. Herriot*)

Author with his Father: 1950. (*J.F. Herriot*)

'Herriot Siblings' – Judith, David, Fiona and Michael: circa 1957. (*J.F. Herriot*)

'Trumpet Practice' – Under the watchful gaze of my father's lens. (*J.F. Herriot*)

'Best Cadet' – Lance Corporal D.R. Herriot: 1965. (*J.F. Herriot*)

'Senior Cadets' – Glasgow High School CCF. Corporal 'Cow' Clark (3rd from left back row); Sergeant Ronnie Orr (1st from right back row) and Company Sergeant Major David Herriot (Centre front row): 1967. (*Author's Collection*)

'The Rivals' – Sir Lucius O'Trigger dictates *The Challenge* to Bob Acres (Bill Shooter), Glasgow High School Drama Club: 27 March 1968. (*Author's Collection*)

'Graduation Day' – AOTS Church Fenton: 4 July 1969. (*Crown / RAF Church Fenton*)

'Joining the Navigators' – Receiving my Navigator's Brevet from Air Vice-Marshal Ivor Broom: 16 December 1970. (*Crown / RAF Finningley*)

'Graduation Day' – 6 FTS Finningley. L to R: Dave Baker, Al Blackwell, Brian Hall, Dick Hansen, Roger Harper, The Author, Bob King and Pete York: 16 December 1970. (*Crown/RAF Finningley*)

'Buccaneer Students' – No. 9 Course, 237 OCU, Honington. L to R: Author, Iain Ross, David Symonds, John Kershaw: 17 May 1971. (*Crown/RAF Honington*)

'The Ergonomic Slum' – Blue Parrot (L), Blue Jacket (R), Control and Release Computer (C). (*Hawker Siddeley Aviation Ltd*)

'The First Eight Aircraft' – XV Sqn: 1972. (*Crown / RAF Laarbruch*)

'XV Squadron Officers' – RAF Laarbruch (Author 3rd from right, Middle Row): 1972. (*Crown/RAF Laarbruch*)

'My Pride and Joy' – Home on leave in Glasgow. (*J.F. Herriot*)

'XV Squadron Tones it Down': 1973. (*Crown/RAF Laarbruch*)

'Before the Ban' – L to R: 'Blind' Tom Bradley, Barrie 'Wings' Chown, Nick 'Abe' Berryman and Colin 'Kabong' Tavner enjoy a relaxing 'softie' at the Fortes Pool Bar: 1972. (*Author*)

'XV Squadron Beach Barbecue' – Wings and Kabong monitor the cooking. (*Author*)

'Strike QRA' – XV Squadron on Alert, RAF Laarbruch: 1973. (*Crown / RAF Laarbruch*)

'My Man up Front' – On route to Cyprus: 13 April 1973. (*Author*)

'The Original Selfie' – Over the Med at 35,000ft: 13 April 1973. (*Author*)

'Loading the Bomb Bay!' – 18 Demijohns of Cyprus Wine and Brandy for a Squadron Party at Laarbruch: 16 April 1973. (*Author*)

'Closing the Summer Ball' – The Author, RAF Laarbruch: July 1973. (*Author*)

'Winter Survival Course' – Press Release Photograph, Bad Kohlgrub, Bavaria: 12 March 1974. (*Crown/JHQ Rheindahlen*)

'Surviving!' – Beds out to air, A–Frame parachute! Breakfast on the hob! What's not to like!: 12 March 1974. (*Author*)

'Taking the Sun' – 12 Sqn aircrew relaxing on the roof of the RAF Luqa Officers' Mess. L to R: Tim Cockerell, 'Wings', Tom Eeles and Ray Morris: May 1974. (*Author*)

'Standard Bearer' – Receiving the new 12 Squadron Standard from Air Marshal Sir Nigel Maynard: 21 February 1975. (*Crown/RAF Honington*)

'Taking on Gas' – From a Victor K2 over the North Sea. (*Author*)

'Nav's Eye View' – Air-to-air refuelling over the North Sea. (*Author*)

'Procedure Alpha' – HMS *Fife* sails up the Garonne towards Bordeaux. I'm there, somewhere near the bridge: 6 June 1975. (*Crown / HMS Fife*)

'Exercise Dawn Patrol' – Back L to R: Martin Wistow, John Lewer. John Huggett, David Ray, Tim Cockerell. Front: Howard Lusher, Author, Ray Morris, Rick Willey, Julian Flood: June 1975. (*Author*)

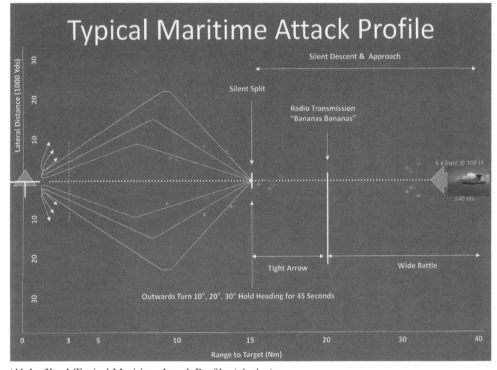

'Alpha 3' – A Typical Maritime Attack Profile. (*Author*)

'Exercise Mistico' – XV168 heads for Aberporth Range with its ready-to-fire TV MARTEL: 6 October 1975. (*Author*)

POSN	PILOT		NAV	
DESCENT PT	DESCENDING HDG 296M ⚡MISSILE		MODE NAV TERM PHASE OFF	
			FUSE MODE 2 BREAKAWAY PORT APERTURE WIDE	
-5	HT 3000' SPD 420 KTS ATT SEL MAN R/R WPN SEL MARTEL		SPEECH TAPE ON TMG 151T 160M 155G LOCK LITE OUT (GISMOS NOW ON)	
-4	HT 1500'		PRESENT LAMP ON	
-3	HT 1000' CONTINUE TO BFS HT		WSPR RECORD TERM PHASE OFF	
-1	TACAN OFF		UP/DWN SWITCH - UP (INST IN DLP -ON)	
-30	HT 200' SPD 420 KTS IAS		MODE MANUAL TERM PHASE OFF	
-15	TRIGGER LIVE		RDY LITE - ON (STOP IF NO LITE)	
-10	HDG NOW CONSTANT			
-5	NO MORE BANK 5°		TERM PHASE OFF	
ZERO	RANGE ⚡ CLEARED		TO FIRE	
LAUNCH	TRIGGER + 3 SECS		⚡FIRING FIRING NOW START WATCH	
MISFIRE +3	RELEASE +TRIGGER SAFE & "MISFIRE"		⚡ STORE AWAY IF MISSILE GOES	
+10	HDG 250M FOR 1 MINUTE		⚡ MISSILE LAUNCHED + H/C CONTINUE STBD TURN IF MISSILE GOES	
+/-10s	WPN SEL OFF ATT SEL LAYDOWN		SPEECH TAPE OFF DIVERT VALLEY	
VALLEY CCT	MISS SEL OFF(NAV)		LOCK LAMP OFF NB JETTISON IF HYDRAULIC U/S	

'Exercise Mistico' – Navigator's Crib Sheet: 6 October 1975. (*Author*)

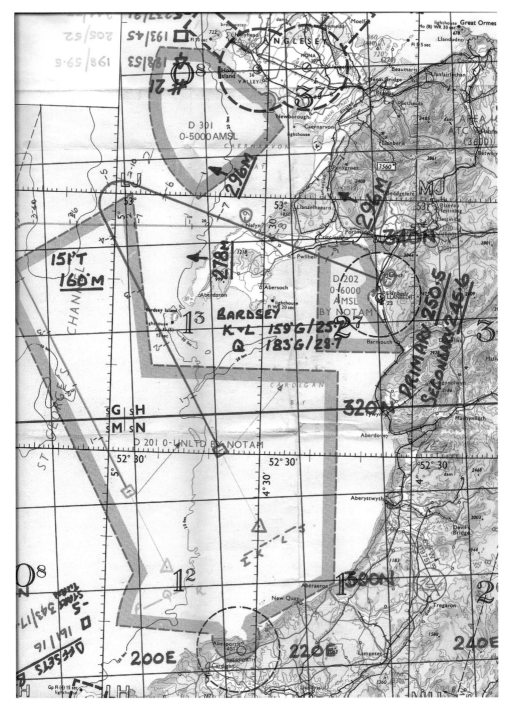

'Exercise Mistico' – Attack Map Aberporth Range: 6 October 1975. (*Author*)

first attempt at night formation. Two days prior, I had strapped myself into another Buccaneer with Tom Eeles in the front seat and headed for Runway 27 at Honington, with Iain taxiing about one hundred yards behind to follow us into the sky. The sun had set at about 1930hrs and, unusually on that Monday night, the airfield was very busy by the end of Evening Civil Twilight, some thirty minutes later; it was a very dark night, overcast, no moon, and no twinkling stars visible from ground level. Particularly, an Andover with a cargo of paratroopers on board was killing time doing circuits, overshoots and rollers, whilst it awaited its 'drop time' on Stanford Battle Training Area to the north of Honington. It had been bashing the circuit for about forty minutes when we eventually called Honington Tower for permission to taxi. As we taxied along the southern taxiway towards the 27 Holding Point, going through the Pre-Take-Off checks, Tom mentioned that formation flying was not going to be too easy for Iain following behind us, as without a moon there was unlikely to be any residual ambient light to assist him! The Andover once again touched its main wheels on the runway, rolled forward as it accelerated and nosed back into the sky for another circuit. As we turned off the taxiway and approached the threshold, the Visual Controller instructed us to hold whilst the Andover made its final 'touch and go' before it departed for the training area. It gave me a few moments to check round the cockpit and ensure that my kit was 'hot to trot' and that I was ready to launch into the darkness that enshrouded the aircraft – in 1971 the Buccaneer was not equipped with a landing lamp, so it was an eerie dark silence that covered the aircraft as we watched the lights of the Andover descend towards the runway before us. With a final jolt of the troop carrier on the runway, Tom and I were instructed to line up and hold. Clearance for take-off would come as soon as the Andover was established with a positive rate of climb and was turning to depart for Stanford.

Also in 1971, the local Flying Order Book stipulated that only one Buccaneer was allowed to line up on the runway in the dark. This meant that our departure procedure as a 'pair' and our join up in formation would be stretched out as Iain would not be cleared to line up on the runway until we had got airborne. Tom had briefed a 30-second stream take-off, but there was every likelihood, given the constraint in the order book, that our Number 2 could be airborne anything up to a minute after us. Frustrating, but rules are rules and on that particular night it was probably just as well!

Cleared for take-off, I looked over Tom's right shoulder into the inky blackness and could see nothing apart from the lights at the side of the runway. As Tom pushed the Speys up to full power and released the brakes, the Buccaneer began to accelerate down the darkened strip. Everything was happening as normal. Despite the fact that we could see little ahead, I was confident that the experienced and capable Tom would be on instruments as soon as the aircraft eased from the runway and took to its natural environment. I looked down at my strip TAS indicator and noted that it was functioning normally and that the speed was approaching 100 knots. I surmised that we must by now be approaching the middle of the runway, so I stood ready to flick on the counters on the Blue Jacket, as with few visual clues in the dark, my main challenge this night would be the safe navigation of the aircraft back to Honington once the formation exercise was complete!

There was an almighty bloody bang and at the same time – although initially imperceptible – a smooth deceleration to a full stop, but with the aircraft still at full power and straining to march forward! Now a creature of habit, I flicked the counters on the Doppler to 'On' and watched them jump the anticipated mile and a half, this time in a south-westerly direction!

'Dave, call Aborting!' shouted Tom over the intercom.

'Delta Two Nine is aborting!' I transmitted quickly on the radio.

'Roger, Two Nine,' replied the local controller, 'do you need assistance?'

With the aircraft now at a full stop in the pitch dark and convinced that we were still on the runway, Tom hit the transmit button.

'Two Nine, call you back.'

Tom checked around the front cockpit and confirmed that he had not, as had been his first inclination, lowered the arrestor hook by accident! The rest of the instruments showed normal, there were no warnings on the SWP or 'clangers' sounding, and with the throttles now at idle, it all seemed a little surreal as we sat in the darkness wondering just what the hell had happened to force our unexpected stop! Tom's next call to the tower was less than informative.

'I seem to have become stuck on the runway!'

I was of no use to him whatsoever – this was a brand-new experience for me! Air Traffic's response was not an unnatural one and they, and I suspect the Duty Pilot who by now must have been stifling a guffaw or two, came to the decision to send the ATC Land Rover out to take a look and offer advice. They were all bound to be thinking that we had dropped the hook by mistake!

As the headlights of the Land Rover approached, the runway ahead of us became a little clearer, but still gave no indication as to what might have happened. Two men jumped from the cab of the vehicle and rushed forward, illuminated by their own headlights. They stopped suddenly and without a 'Hello', 'By the way', or 'Bloody Hell', they turned quickly on their heels and doubled back into the Land Rover and drove off. I remember thinking, 'That's helpful', and must have conveyed my thoughts to Tom who expressed deep dissatisfaction with regard to the service that they had provided – well, that is the polite version of what actually took place in that particular intercom exchange between front and back seat! Air Traffic, however, were quick to inform us to shutdown, not to unstrap, and no matter what, we were not to attempt to vacate the aircraft until outside help arrived. If this had been a cartoon there would, by now, have been a very large thinks bubble showing above our helmets!

Eventually, and after what seemed an interminable age, still strapped to our bang seats, but with nowhere to go, blue lights started flashing far in our eleven o'clock and it was clear that the 'blood wagons'[5] had been despatched to save the day. First on the scene was Crash One, a long-wheelbase Land Rover fire tender, equipped with ladders and first aid fire appliances. The firemen jumped from the vehicle as it came to a stop and one, having pulled a long silver ladder from its position along the vehicle's roof, walked slowly forward and propped the ladder against the starboard

---

5. Emergency vehicles.

side of the cockpit, climbed up and spoke to Tom. With the engines shut down and no Houchin connected to provide ground power, we could not talk to each other! I was still in the dark both physically and metaphorically. As the fireman climbed back down the ladder, Tom stood up onto his seat and turned and spoke to me over the top of his ejection seat, which by now had been made safe.

'Apparently we've taken the approach end cable with our nose wheel leg! The cable is at full stretch and we are sprung in it! Make your seat safe and follow me down the ladder.'

I did just that, and once at the bottom all became clear. The RHAG was indeed wrapped round the nose wheel leg and was stretched to its absolute limit like a giant catapult. It appeared as if our Buccaneer was about to be launched, backwards, into the wilds of East Anglia! By now the station commander had arrived in the tower demanding to know just who might be responsible for this latest cock-up on his station. He was not tolerant of those who either played the fool or acted irresponsibly and somebody's head would doubtless roll once blame, as was inevitable, had been apportioned! In the darkness of the night, and without floodlighting of the area, blame and identifying the reason and the culprits would have to wait until the morning! Keen not to be embroiled in any of the ongoing discussions, Tom suggested that there was no better place to be that night than being cared for by Corporal Ward and as we drove back to the officers' mess and a pint of Double Diamond, he murmured just two words in my ear: *'Gorilla Club!'*

The following morning, with an embargo on flying whilst the carnage at the end of the runway was cleared up and an investigation commenced, the truth of the incident very quickly unfolded. Our Buccaneer had been removed the previous night to the OCU hangar where impact damage on the port UWT and superficial damage on the nose wheel leg had been discovered. However, at the RHAG, it was quite clear what had happened and why we had engaged the cable with our nose leg. Beside the runway was found the shattered remains of a wooden stand that the fire crews had manufactured without authorisation to facilitate their rigging and de-rigging of the cable. Each cable has an up and a down position. When it is up, rubber grommets hold the cable sufficiently high off the runway to allow an arrestor hook to catch it and thereby retard an aircraft with a hydraulic emergency. When it is down, the grommets are moved to one side of the cable manually such that the cable lies flat to the runway and those aircraft cleared to do so can trample it. Unfortunately for the hapless firemen at Honington, who were about to feel the full force of the station commander's wrath, they had decided that the task of rigging and de-rigging could be simplified, less back-breaking and quicker if they supported each end of the cable with a three-foot wooden tripod at either side of the runway. Blame was quickly apportioned and action taken against those concerned. Tom and I were innocent, if a bit hung-over after the excitement of the previous night!

Whilst the story written here some forty-odd years after it happened might seem amusing, there was a serious side to it. The Andover bashing the circuit that night was cleared to trample the cable. The fire crews on duty had been tasked to be on the runway to rig the cable in the up position for Buccaneer night take-offs. With the unscheduled arrival of the Andover to do touch and goes, the fire crew had been ordered to quickly vacate the runway, but, in their rush to comply, had forgotten to take their tripods with them. The local controller, in full knowledge that the Andover was cleared to trample the cable, had permitted the aircraft to conduct roller landings, but what he did not tell the captain of the Andover, because he could not have possibly known, was that the cable was sitting three feet above the ground and just about the height to connect with the top of a Buccaneer's nose olio! Thankfully, the Andover landed well beyond the cable on each of the rollers that it carried out that night. Had its captain chosen to land on the threshold of Runway 27 then there might well have been more carnage than just a few broken planks of wood! There by the grace of God!

By the end of August 1971 the main part of the Night Phase was complete and graduation was looming within the following month. Sorties became more complex in their content and the number of aircraft involved. Before very long Iain and I found ourselves becoming targets on STRIPRO sorties as we built up towards the final complex Dummy and Live Strike sorties that, if successful, would see us being qualified to join the RAF Buccaneer Force! In 1971, and for some considerable years afterwards, the Buccaneer was denied any air-to-air capability; no gun and no heat-seeking air-to-air missile. There was good and sound reasons for this. The aircraft had been designed as a Strike/Attack bomber and its concept, shape and manoeuvrability did not lend itself to tangling with agile fighters or interceptors. What it was good at, however, was sitting low to the surface of the earth and holding very fast speed, up to 580 knots, for not much of a fuel burn penalty. At normal cruise speed of 420 knots and 250 feet, a Buccaneer would burn one hundred pounds of fuel a minute. Increase it to 580 knots and the penalty increase in fuel consumption was just a further twenty pounds per minute. STRIPRO was the Buccaneer's equivalent of Fighter Evasion and, given our sustainable straight line and high speed ability, our evasive tactic was to progress towards the target until such time as a fighter might, a very big might, catch us up – particularly over the sea where a fighter with a look-down shoot-down capability would have had to get below us to obtain a firing solution. Getting a fighter below thirty feet over the ocean just to kill a Buccaneer was, we hoped, a pretty tall order for even the best Soviet fighter pilot!

My three 'Dummy Strike' missions took place on 9 & 10 September 1971, and the first 'Staff/Student' sortie was once again with Jerry Yates, with Iain on the wing, to LFA 11 in the East Riding of Yorkshire. I had planned the mission Lo Lo[6] from Honington, out over East Anglia, where we coasted out at Wells-next-the-Sea on the north Norfolk coast, and turned for Flamborough Head. Once over the sea, Jerry dropped the aircraft down to our cleared height of two hundred feet and took up my offered heading of 344°, which would take us to a position some fifteen nautical miles off this obvious headland that would, I knew, stand out on the Blue Parrot and allow me to give Jerry proper estimates of our ETA at our coast-in point. After only twelve minutes over the sea, Jerry climbed to 500 feet to avoid any possibility of a bird strike as we coasted in at Flamborough and we then settled down at 250 feet and

6. Low-level mission to and from the target.

I started to map-read our way towards our target, which was a small bridge across a not very large stream in the Vale of Pickering. With only minor adjustments along the IP run to the target, Jerry eventually called that he had the bridge visual and that we were cleared for simulated switches and, as we did so, he rolled the bomb door open so that our simulated load of retarded 1000lb bombs could leave and head for the target. Meanwhile, Iain and his staff navigator had split to ensure that they passed the target forty seconds after us in order to avoid taking fragments from the detonation of our simulated weapons. Mission accomplished, we headed back towards the coast at Whitby and turned on a south-easterly heading for Blakeney Point and a visual recovery to Honington. Whilst over Yorkshire, one of the OCU's Hunters had positioned itself out over the North Sea and close to our track to intercept us on our way home, so it was eyes out like organ stops and heads up for the Bounce[7]! After a few good spots of the Hunter and a few counters left and right to put him one eighty degrees out, we managed to buster ahead for the Norfolk coast and home.

Debrief over, I prepared to do the whole thing again that very afternoon with Iain in the front seat and in formation with a staff crew in the lead. This time, however, the mission would be a Hi–Lo–Hi[8] to LFA 12, and the delights of low flying around Northumberland and the Cheviot Hills where a Buccaneer was loitering to act as the Bounce. Dummy Strike 3 followed the next morning to Wales and was quickly followed that afternoon with the penultimate sortie on the course, a Lo Lo Strike mission through the LFAs, with a Bounce, and culminated in a timed FRA at Holbeach Range in The Wash. I flew with Jerry again whilst Iain did his thing on our wing with a staff navigator in his rear seat. The sortie went well, our bomb struck pretty close to Target 2 at Holbeach and was only a few seconds late. It was a Friday, and Friday means Happy Hour, and Happy Hour, once Corporal Ward has taken himself home, means *Gorilla Club*!

The following Thursday, Iain and I strapped ourselves into XT287 and flew our last student sortie together on 237 OCU. The Hi–Lo Strike sortie to Holbeach Range went extremely well and we landed happy at the end of what had been a gruelling and occasionally nerve-wracking four months of our Buccaneer conversion course. Final exams followed and were passed with flying colours. We were the first course to be trained by the RAF and we had succeeded. The only student to fall by the wayside had been the wing commander who had joined us at Mount Batten for our sea survival training. He had been a long time away from the cockpit when he had been designated to become the second Buccaneer boss of 12 Squadron and did not cope with the Buccaneer and the harsh environment in which we operated it.

On Friday, 24 September 1971, Wing Commander Tony Fraser held a small graduation ceremony in the OCU crewroom and presented us with our certificates, which in my case stated:

---

7. One or more aircraft tasked and briefed to act as fighters to intercept other aircraft on route to and from a target in order to practice fighter evasion or STRIPRO.

8. The sortie would require a measure of fuel conservation because of the distance of the target from the aircraft's base. Consequently, a high-level transit to, and recovery from, would be planned and flown with a low-level 'burst' phase immediately prior to and after the target.

> *'This is to certify that*
> *Fg Off D.R. Herriot*
> *Has successfully completed No 9*
> *Course on 24 Sept 1971*
> *And is qualified to join the*
> *RAF Buccaneers'*

The certificate was emblazoned with Tony Fraser's chosen crest for the OCU that had been endorsed by the *Chester Herald* during my time at Honington. It depicted two crossed cutlasses surmounted by a mortar board. The crossed cutlasses were the SOP symbol for Battle Formation and the mortar board indicated the instructional role of the unit. Wanting something other than an English or Latin motto, he chose French – *Panache et Precision*! We certainly had proved that we had panache and, having secured six DHs with Dave Scott on my first attempt at LLADSL at Holbeach Range on 20 July 1971, I had proved that we had precision too!

I had flown sixty-nine hours and thirty-five minutes in the Buccaneer and had accrued thirteen hours in 'the box'. I had passed my weapons exam and my general papers exam, and, despite my initial worries about lack of experience, had beaten both of these papers with a very high mark in my aircraft systems exam. I had a posting notice to XV Squadron at Laarbruch in Germany and I was going there with Iain, JK, Dave Symonds, Nick Berryman and Kabong Tavner. Life could only get better and, it being Friday, the only realistic thing to do was to go and say farewell to Corporal Ward and a final *Gorilla Club*!

Chapter Eight

When XV Came to Laarbruch:
What a Happy Day

Ileft two of my first loves behind at Honington when I headed to Luton Airport to check-in for the Britannia Airways 'Trooper' flight to RAF Wildenrath. Despite my having fitted a Gold Seal engine to it when its original 'big ends' went whilst I was at Nav School, my Morris 1000 was not robust enough to tackle my first venture onto the autobahns of Europe and was left forlornly in the tender hands of my other Honington-based love, Alison Field. Alison, whom I had met at a mess function and wooed for the last few months of my OCU course, was the elder daughter of the wing commander in charge of engineering at Honington. It had, I suppose, been my first intense love affair. However, Alison was only eighteen and, at twenty-two, I was not ready to settle down with the first girl with whom I had had a lengthy and meaningful relationship! Despite her unequivocal and oft stated desire to be with me forever, I had taken the difficult decision to cut my ties in the UK and head for a new life in Germany unattached, footloose and fancy free.

This new adventure had started with our last Gorilla Club where Iain Ross, JK and I agreed that our new life in Germany merited the need for a moustache growing competition. Dave Symonds, who lived on 'the patch' with his wife Jenny, when informed of this No. 9 Course task, readily signed up to the challenge. Three days into the competition, as we all boarded the MT coach bound for Luton Airport with our portable belongings, there was little evidence to suggest that we had packed our razors in our 'heavy baggage' boxes that would follow us to Germany by military air freight. The flight took just under an hour and we were quickly through the Main Gate at Laarbruch and unpacking our belongings in Block 13A, one of three two-storey single accommodation blocks that stood to one side of the officers' mess.

In October 1971, Laarbruch was the home to three operational squadrons and the nascent, and yet to be declared to NATO, XV Squadron that we were destined to join. One, a detachment of 25 Squadron, was based just to the west of the threshold of Runway 09 and was equipped with Bloodhound Mk2 surface-to-air missiles to provide air defence of the airfield in the event of an air attack by Warsaw Pact forces. XV Squadron occupied the adjacent south-western corner of the airfield which, at that time, had not been provided with hardened protection for personnel or aircraft. At the other end of Laarbruch, on the south-eastern corner, sat 2(AC) Squadron equipped with F-4 Phantom FGR2s, declared to NATO in the photo reconnaissance role, and opposite them was 16 Squadron, the last remaining Canberra B(I)8 squadron in RAFG declared to SACEUR in the Strike/Attack role. Thus, there was a mixed bag of aircrew living in the officers' mess and, on our first night in town, we were about to meet them.

An officers' mess on any RAF station is a lively place to be, but an officers' mess on a fast-jet flying station is usually livelier than most! However, in 1971 you would have been hard pressed to find a livelier place to visit than an officers' mess on an RAF station in Germany. And with its motley bunch of mid-20s 'Livers-In'[1], Laarbruch had the absolute potential to be a career wrecker. With bags unpacked in my room in the accommodation block and without my 'heavy duty' items, i.e. flying kit, to unpack, it seemed that the only logical enterprise was to meet my fellow 'new boys' in the bar. No matter the day of the week, a mess bar always opened at 1700hrs and there was usually a crush at the bar fifteen minutes later. Laarbruch was no exception and particularly so on this October night as XV Squadron had made a point of being there in force to welcome its new crews! Heineken and Carlsberg flowed freely as we met and were introduced to the Boss and the rest of the XV Squadron team. The squadron hierarchy consisted of Roy Watson, the Boss, who was ably supported by two flight commanders in Bob O'Brien and Bas Williamson, along with 'Big Louis', Mike Bowker, who was the navigation leader. The remainder of the squadron aircrew was made up of eleven junior officers and a newly-promoted squadron leader, David Cousins, known to everybody simply as 'DC'. Those of you who are accomplished mathematicians will have calculated that that makes eight crews and so we, the new boys, were to become marked as Crews 9 and 10! But there was a problem and as the beer continued to flow that problem became more apparent without anybody actually mentioning it. Aircrew are pretty good at keeping secrets – they need to be – given the serious classification of some of the targeting papers that they have to read to complete their operational task. However, they are also pretty good at skirting round a problem and giving you just enough information to allow you to work it out for yourself. XV Squadron only had six aircraft and, until more were delivered from the production line at Brough, there were insufficient to allow any more than eight crews to fly them and remain current.

The following morning, before we were formally welcomed onto the squadron, we were told the bad news officially by Bob O'Brien, OC A Flight. Nick Berryman and Colin Tavner, by their earlier completion of the OCU and arrival at Laarbruch, had beaten us to the cockpit and we, unlike they, would be seconded to Mission Planning Flight[2] until the New Year to assist the staff there with producing operational maps and charts in preparation for the squadron's war role. Over the next three months we were to become very familiar with East Germany and all the WP targets and early warning and air defence systems. However, the good news was that we were most definitely members of XV Squadron and would be invited to participate in

---

1. Those of officer status who lived in single officer accommodation and dined/drank in the officers' mess. It included school teachers, weather men, MOD-sponsored civilians as well as officers, either single or serving unaccompanied by their spouses and families.
2. A unit within Operations HQ tasked with the preparation, maintenance and briefing of all operational planning maps and procedures for pre-planned Strike and Attack missions.

everything that the squadron got up to whilst we worked in the Ops HQ Bunker during the day.

Now there is only a very limited amount of enjoyment that can be had sticking red, yellow and blue dots onto a 500,000 scale low-level navigation chart! Red dots equalled SAM sites; yellow dots signified EW radar sites; and blue dots were WP airfields that operated combat aircraft. In addition, the IGB had to be delineated on each map and there seemed to be hundreds that we had to complete in our three month sabbatical from flying. Once each map had been marked up, it had to be covered with Fablon, which needed to be a two-man job if bubbles were to be avoided. Whilst this might seem to have been a vast *Blue Peter* project with coloured paper, stick-on dots, coloured pens and sticky back plastic, it had a far more sinister purpose. The maps we were preparing would be used for real if ever the Buccaneer Strike/Attack Wing went to war. When XV Squadron was eventually declared CR to SACEUR, these maps would form the basis of the immediate readiness folders for a number of pre-planned options that the squadron would be tasked with. However, for now, the squadron was working itself up to be declared in the Strike[3] Role and, once that task was complete, it would prepare the crews and aircraft already in situ in the Attack[4] Role. The first task had to be completed promptly as the disbandment date for the Canberra outfit had already been declared and XV Squadron would, before that date, have to assume their nuclear capability role and mount QRA should Armageddon be thrust upon us.

The squadron was defined as being dual capable. In essence that meant that it could, and would if war broke out, deliver nuclear weapons in the Strike Role and conventional weapons in the Attack Role. Accordingly these pre-planned options, that the crews would have to study regularly and routinely to familiarise themselves with the detail, had to be held at immediate readiness. Knowledge of the routing to and from the target, the enemy defences inbound and outbound, the IP[5] and the 'dog's balls' features on the IP to Tgt[6] run had to be consigned to memory so that, when SAMs were flying towards you and flak was cutting the airspace in front of you, the last thing you needed to worry about as a crew was where you were in space and time and just where the target was in relation to you and your formation of Buccaneers. Strike missions were flown individually and targets were deep inside enemy territory generally. The pre-planned conventional missions, however, were flown in formation in order to both ensure that the synergistic effect of all the weapons inflicted the required Probability of Kill – referred to as P_k – on the target and provide mutual security from, and the avoidance of, marauding AD fighters. The Buccaneer was tasked to undertake conventional missions in Offensive Counter Air, Air Interdiction, Battlefield Air Interdiction and Close Air Support roles. The first and last of these

---

3. Nuclear Weapons.
4. Conventional weapons.
5. The Initial Point (IP) is a readily identifiable navigation feature, usually with vertical extent, that can be easily navigated to and overflown on a pre-ordained heading straight to the target.
6. Initial Point to Target Run – Aircrew expression that defined the last phases of an attack usually navigated on a 50,000 scale map.

required the preparation of the pre-planned options that we were working on in MP Flight at the same time as we worked on the Strike Mission Folders.

It was the first time that I had seen let alone handled classified documents. With their distinctive blood red covers, documents marked TOP SECRET often passed through my hands and had to be handled, read and protected inside a secure room known as 'The Vault'. All the Strike Mission Folders were held and prepared in The Vault and were accessible only to a few individuals with the highest security clearances. After a day in The Vault, a day working on the shop floor handling SECRET or CONFIDENTIAL maps and charts was very light relief. The pre-planned OCA mission for XV Squadron was a co-ordinated attack against a WP airfield in East Germany; it was known as Option Alpha and would have been one of the first missions ordered by SACEUR on the outbreak of hostilities. It was designed to prevent enemy aircraft from taking to the air to attack NATO forces, and all the NATO air forces with an OCA capability would be in the sky at the same time heading east! Options X-Ray, Yankee and Zulu were pre-planned CAS missions intended to prevent a breakthrough of enemy land forces on the IGB and, as the name implies, when NATO ground forces are locked in combat with the enemy. Option X-Ray was planned on the IGB, Yankee was just east of the IGB and Zulu was west of the IGB once a breakthrough had happened and NATO ground forces were attempting to stem the tide of the 3rd Shock Army[7]!

Notwithstanding the seriousness of the task, working in MP Flight allowed for pretty relaxed working hours and, therefore, time to become familiar with our surroundings and life on an operational station. There was no real demand for us to turn up at 0800hrs and, as long as we did appear before about 0900hrs, nothing was ever said. These working hours lent themselves wonderfully to taking full advantage of life in the officers' mess. The Canberra squadron was in full run-down mode and the younger members of the squadron were intent on making the most of their few final months drinking duty free booze! It seemed churlish, therefore, not to join them in the bar at 1700hrs after work and stay the course for as long as possible before making a quick dash back to Block 13A for an 'aircrew shower',[8] to then catch dinner just before the dining room closed and thence repair back to the bar where we would remain until closing time.

The bar at Laarbruch was manned by three civilian bartenders. Gunther was the notional boss, a quiet and diffident German with a not so good command of English, but a readiness to please – he was, I suspect now, the locally employed East German spy, but nobody ever had any evidence or desire to challenge his allegiance! Gunther was ably supported by two characters, one German and one Italian! Rolf was a cheerful fellow with a ready and willing manner, whilst Franco exuded typical Latin flare and a self-confident manner that endeared him to all he met across the bar.

---

7. A field army of the Red Army formed during the Second World War. The 'Shock' armies were created with the specific structure to engage and destroy significant enemy forces, and were reinforced with more armoured and artillery assets than other combined arms armies. Where necessary the Shock armies were reinforced with mechanised, tank and cavalry formations and units.

8. A liberal dose of deodorant!

These three had seen it all before and, much in the mould of Corporal Ward, were instant friends of all comers in their bar at Laarbruch. I took an instant shine to them and they to me, and, when I became Entertainments Officer in the mess, found this now deep-rooted relationship extremely advantageous when it came to organising functions in the mess.

Living on the upper floor of Block 13 were a number of single women, defined as 'schoolies'[9]! These young women were employed by the British Forces Education Service to educate the population of school-age children who were resident at Laarbruch with their parents. Many of them enjoyed a good party too! It was not uncommon, therefore, to find a mixed bag of aircrew, station officers, schoolies and others looking for entertainment after the bar had been shut for the night. So, rather than a Gorilla Club shout, the call would go out for a Block Party and we would all drunkenly troop off to one of the three accommodation blocks to continue drinking into the early hours of the morning.

One of the Canberra force's characters was a bachelor by the name of Tim Price, who eventually joined the Buccaneer Force. Tim lived on the ground floor of Block 13 and, for reasons that none of us should ask or need know, owned a shop window mannequin! After one particularly good session in the bar, Tim was careering around Block 13 'after hours' and we were all getting stuck into the ready supply of Carlsberg! Without much warning Tim, with my able assistance, dragged the mannequin into the bathroom across the corridor from his room and, having temporarily removed her head, inserted a lit thunderflash into the cavity that formed her body! Replacing the head and quickly exiting, we held the door firmly shut as we both called the countdown to detonation! After a few seconds there was an almighty bloody bang and as is often the case as one's ears recover from the shock, a deathly silence. Gingerly, Tim opened the bathroom door to inspect the damage – there was no mannequin! A faint cloud of dust, permeated with the occasional small piece of plaster of Paris, filled the entire space, whilst a distinct smell of cordite filtered into our nostrils. The door was very quickly closed firmly on the debris and we carried on drinking as if nothing untoward had happened at all. I knew then that I was going to enjoy my tour.

True to their word, not long after our arrival, we were informed by XV Squadron that we would be expected to attend a Station Dining In Night on the following Friday. I had been to plenty of these affairs before and could always be relied upon to be involved in any high jinks that was taking place, but I had not anticipated the directive that came from Colin Tavner before my first dinner night on an operational station.

'Bring your tin hat and gas mask!' Kabong informed the four of us.

'What?' We asked in perplexed unison.

'Don't ask any questions, just bring 'em', he responded.

Dinner Nights are routinely timed as 1900 for 1930hrs. On this particular night in question, XV Squadron had been allocated the right-hand leg of the tables set

---

9. Government-sponsored school teacher working under, and for, the Service Children's Education Authority.

in an E and we had been told to report to the dining room at 1855! There we found Kabong marshalling his troops and ensuring that everyone's tin hat and gas mask were securely hidden under the table.

'What are these for?' I ventured, but got no reply; only time would tell!

Pre-dinner drinks went without a hitch, and the meal and the Loyal Toast were over pretty much by 2130hrs. Following a short pee break, we were all back in our seats and ready for the speeches, and on this particular evening a 'welcome to XV Squadron recently arrived'. One little idiosyncrasy of dining-in nights at Laarbruch, I discovered, was that by request the waiter would leave a full bottle of wine by your chair leg! I got quite pissed quite quickly and only just managed to realise that the command had been given by Kabong to don gas masks and tin helmets. Quickly securing my mask to my face and my helmet to my head, I was astounded to see and be involved in the upending of our tables to create a trench-like barrier. With squadron silver cascading to the floor, I was passed a flour bomb and encouraged to throw it at the 'recce pukes' who were preparing themselves similarly on the far side of the room. The result was carnage, there was flour everywhere and it took some time for order to be regained and the speeches commenced. Strangely, neither the PMC nor the station commander batted an eyelid or sought sanction subsequently. It was all part of the routine of life at Laarbruch.

Once the speeches were over we all repaired to the bar where the three musketeers, Gunther, Rolf and Franco, had already pulled enough half litres of Heiny and Charlie to ensure that none of the hundred or so diners would have to wait to be served. Before long the station commander announced that there was to be a Mess Rugby competition between the flying squadrons. For those dedicated followers of the Six Nations, let me tell you from the outset that there were no rules to mess rugby. There were no colourful strips to differentiate the teams and the only consideration to the conventional rules of the game invented in Warwickshire by William Webb Ellis was that one was permitted to remove one's jacket before kick off! A piece of soft furnishing, a cushion in this instance, was secured as a ball! The station commander, loosely defined as the referee, threw the cushion into the middle of the anteroom and as one, the mass of XV Squadron drunks charged the mass of drunken 'recce pukes' from 2 Squadron and pounced on the target lying passively on the carpet in the middle of the room. All hell broke loose – a mass brawl! People were dragged out of the melee by any limb or means possible, the rending of golf ball shirts could be heard amid the shouts of, 'Get off my bloody leg!' or 'Arggh my balls are being crushed!' from the middle of the pile. The object, of course, was to be the first team to secure the cushion and score a 'try' by touching it against the opposing team's wall at the far end of the large rectangular room. The initial brawl lasted about five minutes as one hand after another was prised from the cushion and replaced with that of an opponent. Of course, we were too pissed to know quite who was who or whose hand was in charge at any specific time, but it did not really matter, we were all enjoying the melee and nobody ever really got injured as we were sober enough to know when a shout of pain needed a release of pressure. XV Squadron came away victorious in our first encounter and after a ten-minute lull, whilst we licked our wounds and watched the next semi-final, we were again thrust back into the fray against 16 Squadron. Up went the cushion, forward went the charge and once again I found myself at the foot of a maul with just the corner of the cushion grasped in my right hand. It was soon wrestled from my grasp and the knock about continued until eventually the more experienced Canberra aircrew won the day! Sweating profusely, and with shirts being tucked back into trousers and jackets replaced, we returned to the bar to carry on with the evening's festival.

My shirt had taken a bit of a mauling and a small rip had appeared in its back, but with it tucked into my trousers and my jacket back on my upper torso, nobody would ever have been able to tell. I resolved the following morning not to repair or replace it as it would only suffer again in future battles and whilst it might appear odd when I divested before the next kick off, it did not seem sensible financially to do anything other than wash it, iron it and wear it. By the end of my tour at Laarbruch, and after far too many mess rugby games to count, I routinely turned up at Dining In Nights wearing the original golf ball shirt which, by then, had a front, a collar, two cuffs connected to the shoulders by a thin strip of cloth, but absolutely no back! It was a bit of a surprise to the opposition when I took off my Mess Dress jacket and lined up to face them, but drunk as we all were, nobody really showed any concern whatsoever and it very soon became part of the mess rugby proceedings and my accepted practice at Laarbruch Dining In Nights!

There were plenty more games played at Mess Nights at Laarbruch, but I am sure that an imaginative reader who was not brought up in a closet can work out most of them – especially if they played rugby at school! Whether individual or team, they all required a great deal of alcohol consumption beforehand and one even demanded that each member of the team down a pint before upending his/her glass on their head before the next team member could proceed to do likewise! There was always more beer in your hair and on the carpet than ever went down your gullet if you participated in the schooner race!

Attempting to place coloured spots accurately on a map is not the best cure for a hangover, but the level of banter in the bunker was always enough to brighten your day if the soul was flagging and the task felt insurmountable. There was always the prospect of another night in the bar and a Block Party to lift the spirits. So the routine became simple and easily abided by without too much effort if you had a thick head. Get up, shit, shower, shave, shampoo and race to catch the last remnants of breakfast. Meander to the bunker, trying to focus on any passing airman who might be looking for a salute response. Get a mug of coffee. Stick dots on maps, soak up the banter, get another coffee, stick dots on maps. Go for lunch, attempting to avoid the bar in the process. Meander back to the bunker feeling regenerated and responding promptly to any salutes offered. Get a coffee. Stick dots on maps, soak up the banter, get another coffee, stick dots on maps. Race back to the mess and start drinking at 1700 prompt. Grab a last pint at 1900 and down it quickly, race to Block 13A, throw uniform on the bed, spray deodorant liberally over torso and armpits, dress in blazer, trousers, collar and tie, and RV in the bar for a quick G&T before making dinner just as last orders were being taken at 1945. Drink BritMil 'jungle juice'[10] with dinner in an attempt to rehydrate and then back to the bar. Leave bar at 2330hrs having finished last Heiny ordered as Franco tried to pull the shutters down. Block Party until 0200 and then hit the sack, sweeping neatly folded uniform onto the floor in the process! Wake groggily as the batwoman knocks at 0700 with delivery of a cup of tea and nicely polished shoes. Get up, shit, shower, shave, shampoo and race to catch the last remnants of breakfast. And so it went on – it was far too enjoyable to refer to it as Ground Hog Day, but each day was very much like the last, until eventually we were told that sufficient aircraft had been delivered fresh from the factory at Brough to allow us to say farewell to MP Flight and take our rightful place as full members of the squadron.

First, however, came Christmas and New Year. Every year of my life before 1971 I had spent Christmas and Hogmanay in Scotland with my family, but such was the family spirit at Laarbruch that it seemed only right to stay where I was and experience my first Festive Season in the military family. XV Squadron aircrew, being a small outfit at that time, had a habit of inviting every squadron member to any party that was organised in an individual's married quarter. So when Colin Mugford invited the four new boys to attend his Roman Orgy Party in his married quarter just before that first Christmas, we were all delighted to accept. White linen sheets were pulled from our single beds in Block 13A and the requisite togas were manufactured for the occasion.

It was a crisp and crystal clear night on 10 December 1971, and, following the first winter snowfall, a blanket of about twelve inches covered the landscape in Nord Rhein Westphalia. Colin had cleared the sitting room in his quarter and loud music pumped from his new tax-free stereo system as we entered. German married quarters were all built with a cellar, which was not a bad place to store beer and, on his instruction, we ventured below ground to help ourselves from the crates of Heineken and Carlsberg that were stacked in the corridor of the cellar. Everybody had made a great effort to come dressed appropriately for an orgy and most had done the same as us by wrapping a sheet around themselves – the men in an ungainly fashion and the women with flare that showed off their curves and the fact that they were probably sober when they got dressed. Once we were all assembled and the party had been in full swing for about forty minutes, it was pointed out that the squadron character and his long-suffering wife were not present. Barrie Chown, who became a huge influence in my life both professionally and socially, had failed to show. Nobody had heard that he was not coming, indeed the exact opposite had been reported. As he and his wife, Helen, had to drive in the poor road conditions from Asperden, some ten miles away, we were beginning to fret that something might have befallen them. After a short discussion that took the form of mild panic amongst the blokes, who were all now at least on their second beer, there was a faint knock at the front door and Colin went off to investigate. Helen's distinct northern Scottish accent and giggle could be heard in the hallway and we all began to relax as we realised that the weather conditions

---

10. A foul concoction of powdered fruit flavouring and water under the guise of 'orange squash!

had probably delayed their arrival. Helen appeared in the sitting room clutching an already prepared glass of Gluhwein, but with no sign of Barrie behind her. There was, however, the distinct sound from the hallway of furniture being knocked into. Eventually, but with much difficulty, Barrie began to appear through the doorway. As he sidled into the room it became quickly apparent that with just a loin cloth, a crown of thorns and fake blood dripping down his face and torso, he had decided to come to the Roman Orgy dressed as Jesus Christ. However, being strapped to two six-foot planks of wood that formed a cross took his fancy dress costume to a new and much higher level, even for Barrie! Such was the irreverence of military humour that gales of laughter filled the room as 'Christ on his Cross' attempted to manoeuvre himself into a corner where he could cause least damage! What was most amazing about the design of his outfit was that he had persuaded Helen to fit a four-foot length of rubber piping from his mouth along his right arm into his right hand, which now firmly grasped a bottle of Heineken. Drawing the beer through the pipe got Barrie very pissed very quickly – much to everybody's delight!

The party continued long into the night and before long it took the form of its plan with drunken Romans stretched out across the few pieces of furniture that had been left for our comfort and fruit being thrown at the sitting room wall that separated the married quarter from its neighbour. The occupant was a squadron leader who had arrived with his wife at Laarbruch that very day to take up the post of OC PMS in Station Headquarters; a man charged with looking after all the station's personnel, their documentation and administrative needs, which included managing any disciplinary action that was required! Although he and his wife had been invited to the party they had chosen to decline, but then, by continuously banging on the adjoining wall, chose to complain about the noise that we were creating. After a while and around about midnight, with enough alcohol now in our system to dull our senses and decision-making processes, the team determined to put a stop to these loud interruptions that were affecting our boisterous and good-humoured shindig.

Chown, still attached to his cross and now very intoxicated, was manoeuvred through the hallway, outside into the cold night air and towards the neighbour's front door. There his cross was shoved into the snow bank that had been created during snow clearance operations and he was left high and dry with a soft moon glow illuminating his head and its crown of thorns. The last man to leave the scene took the initiative to ring the neighbour's doorbell and then pelted back into the sanctuary of the Roman Orgy. About thirty seconds later there was a very loud scream from next door followed by total silence for the rest of the night! Barrie was recovered from his ice-cold perch and, after a warming brandy and a rub down with a warm towel, carried on as he had done before he had been hijacked to play his role in this re-enactment of the Crucifixion – not one person mentioned that it was Christmas rather than Easter in two weeks' time!

The 'new boys' had agreed at Honington that our attempts to produce facial hair would be judged at the Christmas Draw and once the winner had been crowned, those who chose to shave it off could do so. With Iain Ross and JK being follicularly challenged, my main competitor was Dave Symonds. Iain's attempt was, frankly, pitiful. Of the six hairs that adorned his top lip by the end, three ventured downwards, two paralleled his top lip, but in opposite directions, and one was clearly attempting to join those occupying his nasal cavity. He did not come last, however. JK, having got fed up with his moustache shortly after our arrival at Laarbruch, had withdrawn from the competition by removing the offending article one morning when he was sober enough to do so. Dave was sporting a formidable array, but with an abundance of tawny whiskers that ventured south over my mouth towards my chin, I was declared the winner. I decided to keep it.

With Christmas over and January 1972 dawning bright, we bade farewell to MP Flight and took our rightful places on XV Squadron. There was a significant amount of ground work to be done before we flew and this was established in a CR training programme that each crew had to undertake. Primary was the need to make regular visits to The Vault to undertake 'Target Study'. We were required to be familiar with our Strike target such that we could describe without reference to its features, the route to and from and the IP to Target Run, if and when quizzed by a NATO assessor. Without the knowledge we could never be declared Limited Combat Ready and be qualified to sit on QRA for twenty-four hours at a time. There were ASIs, an FOB, a Hot Poop[11] Folder, and other such regulatory documents that had to be read, understood and signed. Our flying equipment had to be checked, serviced and badged with the XV Squadron shoulder flash before we could take to the air. The official squadron badge would only be awarded after we had been declared fully CR and would necessitate a visit to the mess bar to drink the 'Op Pot'.

From a military low-flying perspective, the weather in northern Germany in January and February can be a bit iffy to say the least. It was not uncommon to wake in the morning to find the whole airfield shrouded in thick fog and the airfield Colour State declared as 'RED', or less than 800 metres visibility and/or significant cloud base below 200 feet. Whilst in those circumstances one might be tempted to roll over and go back to sleep, it would not be impossible to fly in these conditions, albeit much of the sortie would have to be flown above cloud. A sensible flying authoriser would, however, probably hold out for a minimum forecast of YELLOW[12] or better GREEN[13] before risking launching any aircraft and then he would probably release only Green Card[14] instrument rated pilots to do so. There is nothing worse than launching the fleet only to find that it was a 'sucker's gap' and the weather closed in, sealing the airfield for recoveries as soon as your chickens had left the roost!

January 1972 was no different and it would seem from the entries in my logbook that February followed January in like form that year. Consequently, with Nick

---

11. Information held in a folder on the squadron operations desk. It contained vital and recent additions to both technical and operational orders and procedures.
12. 300ft/1.6 km.
13. 700ft/3.7km.
14. Instrument ratings for all pilots were introduced in 1950. Pilots were rated on their instrument flying ability and awarded, in ascending order, White, Green or Master Green cards. Pilots were assessed through flight tests and ground examinations, with trainee pilots required to hold at least a White card. Instrument flying is important for flying in low visibility conditions.

Berryman in my front seat, my first Buccaneer sortie on XV Squadron was a bit of an anticlimax on 11 January 1972. Having got airborne from Laarbruch with Iain and Colin Tavner on our wing, we trudged around northern Germany at high level for an hour and forty minutes before recovering back to Laarbruch. We achieved not very much other than re-familiarising me with the aircraft and introducing me to the delights of speaking on the radio for the first time in my life to people who did not have English as their first language. With no change in the weather, the following Monday Iain Ross and I ventured up to 35,000 feet and repeated the whole exercise again, but this time on our own. By mid-February the weather had improved sufficiently to allow us to get down into the German low flying system and get used to the landmarks and bombing ranges that would become our bread and butter over the next two years. The low flying system amounted to seven sizeable LFAs that covered some of the less-populated areas of West Germany and were connected by low flying corridors. Thus, we used to take off from Laarbruch and head north-east at 500 feet towards the Wesel mast before crossing the Rhine and descending into LFA 2 at 250 feet, where we would remain until we passed through Nordhorn Range before recovering back to Wesel at 1,000 feet for a visual recovery back to base. Of course, that was all very well if the weather was WHITE[15], BLUE[16], or better, but if not, there would undoubtedly be a need to seek radar assistance from Clutch Radar and then Laarbruch itself to get us back on the ground.

Daily, in early spring, late autumn and winter, we would launch into a pea-soup with few recognisable features on the ground to direct us north-easterly to the Osnabruck Ridge. I never did know or meet the benevolent German restaurateur who placed the retired Douglas DC-4 'on track' in the lee of 'The Ridge' that indicated, as near as damn it, the point at which to turn left past the extremely tall 'Smokey Joe's' chimney and into the safety of the North German Plain. However, I am, like most 2 ATAF navigators, eternally grateful to him. With 'The Ridge' and Smokey Joe's behind you, the only thing that you were likely to hit from then until you left Nordhorn Range was a Starfighter lurking around VFR keeping his eye out for meandering Buccaneers. Occasionally, we would venture into Holland to visit Vliehors Range, or across the North Sea to the bombing ranges in The Wash, but Nordhorn Range was routinely the daily focus for 2 ATAF sorties. As a new navigator, it did not take long to realise the importance of the church spire at the Nordhorn IP. Preparatory stories disclosed in the bar about what could happen to you if you did not find 'the church' left most baby navigators heaving, retching wrecks, swathed in sweat by the time the Koch Fasteners were passed over their shoulders during start-up, me included. I am bloody sure to this day that the world came to a full stop about two hundred yards beyond 'the church' on a south-westerly heading and that you would come to a full stop too if you missed it. Anyway, as it turned out, I was introduced very early on in my career to the 'Nordhorn Church Secret' and ninety-five times out of a hundred after that very helpful tip I never failed to stumble upon it. On the other five per cent

---

15. 1500ft/5km.
16. 2500ft/8km.

of occasions I bounced from side-to-side between Meppen Range and the Dutch border, eventually working out that I had missed the last cottage on the right; had a desperate need to find the Crow's Foot; before being cudgelled into selecting Bombs Alpha by old bright eyes in the front seat who had had the target (and probably the whole IP run) in his sights for about twenty seconds.

I was extremely lucky to be crewed with Iain Ross, with whom I flew almost every sortie during my tour on XV Squadron. It is rare to see any other name in the 'Pilot' column of my logbook other than Iain's throughout that tour. Indeed, if I wanted to take leave I could only take it if Iain agreed to take leave at the same time. We were very much a team and a team that was determined to excel on the Buccaneer. With Iain having served his first tour on Hunters in Bahrain, a DFGA outfit, he was in that mould and it did not take long before he had inculcated that attitude into me; before long I was, to a great extent, a DFGA navigator. Helpfully, the mind-set on XV Squadron at the time was quite DFGA too, which presented a minor problem bearing in mind that we were all conscientiously endeavouring to complete the Strike work-up syllabus and SACEUR needed us to have the capability to deliver 'buckets of sunshine' in the dark if required. But in 1972 what was wrong with delivering our nukes visually – we all knew that the Blue Parrot radar was not designed for, or capable in, the overland role! Laydown, 20° Dive MDSL, 5° Dive Retard bombing and SNEB[17] rocketry at Nordhorn Range were all routine tasks for the crews working up on XV, and all delivered visually. Our task, come the day, would be to deliver nuclear weapons in a level Laydown mode after all.

To reach LCR status, we were required to fly a number of sorties at low-level as singletons around Germany for fifty minutes before releasing a Laydown 4lb practice bomb onto Target One at Nordhorn Range, both accurately within the NATO required standard and on time! Not the easiest of tasks given that the weather often baulked your route, and every Luftwaffe Starfighter in the sky would try to avenge the Battle of Britain by treating you as a target and attempting intercepts that forced you off track and away from your timeline. If the Lightnings from RAF Gutersloh caught sight of you then, again, you had to do a runner in the full knowledge that they would run out of fuel before you did!

By mid-April 1972, Iain and I had completed all the necessary Strike work-up missions and, but for one little hurdle, were ready for QRA. Having done what we had done successfully by day, now was our chance to prove that we could do it in the dark with equal success! The German low flying system closed at 1700hrs each day and, in its place, routes were established at 1500 feet that would allow us to fly safely to Nordhorn and drop a bomb using the radar to identify the target. Miserably we were about to be DFGA no longer and were to be introduced to the RBSU situated on the Osnabruck Ridge and the trickery of delivering a Laydown bomb at Nordhorn without actually being able to acquire the target visually. Given the limitations of the Blue Parrot overland, the task seemed insurmountable, but, thankfully, after two successful night missions to the range, we achieved the standard required and before

---

17. A 68mm air-to-surface rocket system of French manufacture.

long were drinking at Happy Hour to celebrate the fact that we were LCR and ready for QRA.

We were now settled well into the squadron and were trusted to be let loose around 2 ATAF in the north of Germany and its southern neighbour 4 ATAF, which was populated predominantly by the USAF. With our LCR tick on the board we were already well into our CR work up, which required us to achieve the NATO standard in conventional bombing and rocketry on Nordhorn and Vliehors, which was on the Dutch coast, ranges. Flying at 250 feet in four-ship formations was quite the most exhilarating experience and the adrenaline rush in the bombing pattern, where my responsibility was to monitor the speed and height, call out the heights in the dive to allow Iain to assess his dive angle, and call 'NOW' at the weapon release point, kept me alert and focused on the task. Setting the weapon switches into an eye-pleasing fashion so that a bomb would be released was equally energising! There was nothing worse than calling 'Off Hot' to the RSO only to receive, after a short delay, a 'No Spot' in response indicating most likely that somebody had made a switch pigs in the cockpit!

My mentor for the CR work-up training, and a like-minded soul when it came to the squadron social scene, was the aforementioned Barrie Chown. Barrie carried the affectionate sobriquet of 'Wings', for that was how he addressed everybody, no matter their rank or position, although, if senior to him he would quickly add an: 'Oops, my error, Courtney!' There was absolutely no disrespect or malevolence in his attitude to senior officers and they all took it in their stride and always with a broad smile. Mr Wings, as he came to be known, had been a sergeant signaller on the Blackburn Beverley C1 and, subsequent to obtaining Her Majesty's Commission and 'elevation' to navigator, had found himself being one of the RAF's first navigators to convert to Blackburn's other great triumph of the air, the Buccaneer. This he had done with the FAA at Lossiemouth where he had remained on 809 Squadron from 1969 until his arrival on XV Squadron some two years later. Wings was the class comedian, but a more professional aviator would have been hard to find. Work hard, play hard was his motto and he excelled at both. He had a quick quip for every situation and an antic in his fun locker for every occasion. If he was not turning up at parties in the most outrageous costume, he would be careering around the mess pretending to be a deep sea diver with flippers on his feet, mask and snorkel on his face, and a cylinder Hoover strapped to his back with which he would suck beer from your glass! If no props were available, he would entertain the assembly with demonstrations of how a one-armed man could fill his pipe and count his change (he used his finger as an imitation penis through the fly of his trousers to tap his pipe or sort through simulated coins), or he would strut straight-legged, puffing on that pipe, imitating Douglas Bader. He and I got into many drunken scrapes, but it was always put down to high spirits and never taken too seriously by the powers that be. He was, thus, much more experienced than me both in the air and in the bar and I think it would be only fair to acknowledge here that Wings taught me everything I know. It was he who was responsible for leading me astray in the bar and that, Sir, is my actual and honest defence! He was to become a huge part of my Buccaneer life story and remained a solid and good friend until his untimely death in 2014.

Pining for my Moggie, I sought Wings' assistance to venture to Autohaus Janssen in Straelen to purchase a VW Beetle to get myself mobile again. The car I chose was second hand, white and with a black vinyl roof, but it took seven days for the garage to prepare it and for it to be checked by the BFG test team to make sure that it was roadworthy. On the way back to base Wings recounted a tale about his own Beetle ownership before I had arrived at Laarbruch. At 0815hrs every morning, all station aircrew had to attend Met Brief in the Ops Wg HQ building where HQ staff would cover not only the weather forecast for the day, but also relevant NOTAMs and local hazards. The brief lasted about fifteen minutes and, once complete, attendees would disperse to their normal place of work. At the time, XV Squadron was located in temporary accommodation in a hangar on the north side of the airfield. To get to the site, personnel had to cross the threshold of Runway 09 which was controlled by traffic lights. Wings, and his fellow drivers, had developed a simple race to get them back to the squadron. The competition involved nothing more than driving their cars as fast as they could as they approached the runway where, on gaining a 'green light', the rules of the game dictated that the driver was obliged to shut down the engine as he passed the green light and cruise to a standstill outside the squadron (some four hundred yards further, through at least one ninety-degree starboard turn). Judicious use of the doors as airbrakes would ensure the finest of finishes and the adoration of the watching crowd. The winner was the one with the shortest walk to work! However, Wings, who would always take a game to its next natural level, decided one day to not only switch his ignition off, but also to take the key out of the ignition; unfortunately for Wings he managed to drop the keys on the floor! He was thus surprised suddenly to find himself heading off into the bundu unable to steer his car and remain on track! It was his first introduction to a vehicle with a steering lock which had been standard fit in German vehicles long before British Leyland cottoned on to the idea!

Despite all this frivolity, partying and intensive flying, the task at Laarbruch was a serious one! Station exercises were routine and the 'hooter' was a regular arouser of the five thousand or so personnel who inhabited the married quarters and single accommodation blocks! All NATO assigned units were charged with undergoing a TACEVAL[18] by a dedicated team sent by SHAPE on an eighteen-month cycle to assess the unit's wartime capability. TACEVAL was split into two parts which involved, firstly, a no notice station 'call-out', usually at some ungodly hour in the dead of night, and, secondly, a pre-ordained and nominally four-day exercise that would test the station's ability to mount its war plan in support of SACEUR. In order to prepare for TACEVAL, the station ran its own regular MINEVALs throughout the year and when the station became 'TACEVAL vulnerable' the HQ at RAFG would pounce with its own MAXEVAL to ensure that the RAF was not going to embarrass itself in front of its NATO allies.

---

18. A military acronym for the evaluation of tactical planning and operational assessment of a unit within the NATO structure.

Having dragged us all from our slumbers and into our places of duty, Phase One required each unit on the station to meet a target of seventy per cent of personnel to respond in a specific and short timescale. At the same time, squadron aircraft had to be generated to meet the number of Strike Lines allocated and, whilst we relaxed in the crewroom, the engineers sweated in the hangar in an effort to bring the necessary number of aircraft on line with weapons loaded for war. I do not recall us ever failing to meet the deadlines imposed in either UE or AE and whilst the ground crew beavered away, we, once awake, full of egg banjos[19], bored with playing Uckers or recounting war stories and on our fourth caffeine inject of the morning, would be tasked with 'accepting' each strike-laden aircraft from the engineers. The handling of nuclear weapons required the implementation of the 'Two-man Principle'[20] and, as with anything of a classified nature, the adoption of the 'Need to Know'[21] rule. The first ensured that there were always two people involved in the handling of a nuclear weapon and as such, the integrity of the weapon system was maintained whilst the latter made sure that only those directly involved knew anything about the aircraft, its weapon and its target. The aircraft and its weapon were securely guarded by RAF policemen and a 'No Lone Zone'[22] was established around the aircraft within which a minimum of two security-cleared individuals were permitted at any one time. Each individual had to be conversant with the role of the other and remain visible to the other and in visual contact with the critical component that required the area to be designated as such throughout their time within the NLZ. Our purpose in entering the NLZ was to carry out the pre-flight checks and set the GCU on the weapon to match our individual target and weapon delivery profile; a task upon which we were subject to examination by RAFASUPU annually. No corners were ever cut when handling nuclear weapons and procedures were always followed scrupulously. The task of accepting the aircraft took about thirty minutes and, once complete, it was back to more Uckers and more coffee whilst the Boss, SEngO and the squadron's Warlord sweated against the timeline.

'What the hell is Uckers?' I hear you all cry. Well, dear reader, it is an adult version of Ludo oft played by bored aircrew when the weather is poor and flying has been cancelled. It was played in those halcyon hours between the metaphoric 'black flag' being hoisted up the squadron's allegorical flag pole and some smart ass, career-minded officer suggesting to the flying supervisor of the day that ground training might serve a useful purpose. It was also the best of time killers during a 24-hour stint of duty in QRA. Of course I realise that as soon as I say 'adult version', those of you with a perverted mind will have conjured up unnecessary pornographic images

---

19. Bacon and fried egg sandwiches.
20. A control mechanism designed to achieve a high level of security for especially critical material or operations. All access and actions require the presence of two authorised and qualified people at all times.
21. Used to describe the principle that classified information will only be given to people who need it to do a particular task.
22. An area into which entry by a single individual is prohibited; commonly areas with accessibility to a nuclear weapon.

in your heads. Nothing could be further from the truth! Uckers is Ludo, but with shouts of 'Blob', 'Mixiblob', 'Eight-piece Dicking', 'Sucking', 'Blowing' and 'Syph on yer Donk' thrown into the mix!

With the Strike generation complete, the TACEVAL team packed their bags and headed for the main gate, leaving us to hand back the weapons to the ground crew to download and then recover the weapons to the SSA. Once ENDEX was called there seemed only one suitable place to go and Gunther, Rolf and Franco were always primed by the mess manager to be ready for us.

With Phase One out of the way, work did not stop as the station now had to gear itself up for the pre-planned conventional phase of the war that would happen in a more orderly and controlled fashion at a predetermined date some two months hence. Phase Two started with the aircraft being prepared in the Attack role to fulfil Option Alpha. Four aircraft were loaded with one 1000lb HE GP bomb fitted with a No 117 retard tail and a No 951 fuse on each of the four conventional weapon stations in the bomb bay, and another on each of the outer wing pylons, the inner pylons being fitted with UWTs to provide that extra Radius of Action[23] to get us through the IGB and into and out of the target. Whilst this work was being undertaken by the ground crew, we aircrew spent our time studying the route maps and IP to Target runs that we had prepared during our time in MP Flight. Once the generation had been accomplished successfully, the live weapons were downloaded and returned to the ESA and the aircraft were regenerated with practice bombs and the equivalent sortie would then be flown around the German Low Flying System with a pre-booked attack on a German Air Force base such as Aalhorn or Hopsten on the North German Plain. AD aircraft would be tasked to intercept us on route to our target and so, once airborne, it was all eyes out of the cockpit and ears peeled for the call of 'BUSTER'[24] or 'COUNTER'[25] by the first guy to spot a bogey and get us away either by accelerating to 580 knots or turning into the threat to disengage from his missile firing solution. If the call was 'BREAK'[26] it was a sure indicator that it was a late spot and somebody was surely going to die! Thankfully, none of the opposition forces were loaded with live weapons and so any looming finality would be nothing more than an acknowledgement over the radio that you had been 'shot down'.

Phase Two of TACEVAL lasted about four days and the intensity of flying increased as the simulated war scenario unfolded. OCA missions were flown to suppress enemy air activity and, as the days passed, additional tasks in AI and BAI were undertaken in an attempt to stop enemy second echelon forces and crucial enemy supplies making

---

23. The maximum distance an aircraft can travel away from its base along a given course with normal combat load and return without refuelling, allowing for all safety and operating factors.
24. A radio call to a formation of aircraft to execute a rapid acceleration to full power in an attempt to outrun an attacking aircraft.
25. A radio call given to get some or all aircraft to execute a level turn, usually towards the attacking aircraft, in order to offset the attacker's firing solution.
26. A call given in extremis to get some or all aircraft to execute a break turn (maximum permissible g and full power), usually towards the attacking aircraft. It will occur after a late sighting of an attacking aircraft and is usually 'last ditch'!

it to the front line. No matter the scenarios set in these exercises, we never seemed to be on the winning team and before long, with enemy forces flooding through the Fulda Gap, we were tasked with Options X-Ray, Yankee and Zulu. Throughout the 'war', Laarbruch was subject to wave upon wave of enemy air attacks which were always preceded with a klaxon warning and the stern words over the station tannoy, 'EXERCISE, EXERCISE, EXERCISE! AIR RAID WARNING RED! AIR RAID WARNING RED! ALL PERSONNEL ARE TO DON RESPIRATORS AND TAKE COVER! EXERCISE, EXERCISE, EXERCISE!' You had nine seconds to get your gas mask on and woe betide you if you did not, as it was certain that just before an air raid members of the TACEVAL Team would congregate in the squadron crewroom to time your response!

As it became inevitable that 'the war' was lost, single crews would disappear from the crewroom and be isolated in the Ops Room or the Nav Room whilst a Selective Release aircraft was generated to undertake a one-off nuclear mission. The proverbial gloves were off and it would not now be long before conventional ops were suspended and another Strike Generation would take place in advance of R-Hour; the general release of nuclear weapons – Armageddon! Again, whilst the strike weapon load took place, we aircrew would spend many a long hour awaiting the call to cockpits to deliver the nuclear response option that we had practised so regularly before. Hours spent regaling each other with more 'war stories', more games of Uckers, more 'egg banjos' or, in the case of Iain Ross and me, hatching a plot to ensure that, in the unspoken competition to be the first one airborne, we were it!

The R-Hour hooter sounded, and in true Battle of Britain style, the XV Squadron crews leapt to their feet, ran from the crewroom and scattered across the unhardened dispersal to their pre-prepared jets. Those with aircraft close to the crewroom had the advantage, but could easily be baulked in the race by an unanticipated exercise inject, or an engine that required 'grollying with a broom handle'[27] to get it working! Not so for the determined Ross/Herriot combo who, on one particular exercise, found ourselves at the front of the queue racing along the southern taxiway for Runway 27 and the wind over the wings that would lift our Buccaneer into the 'Deutsche Luft'. Airborne, first, but now working out what the take-off time should have been to match our designated TOT at Nordhorn. I was happy, Iain and I had done this so many times before that I knew that he would get us to the Wesel Mast and into LFA 2 on track, whilst I depended on my O-Level maths to get the timing right! And indeed, he did! In the Buccaneer there was none of the modern avionic suite that twenty-first century aircrew enjoy. Mark one eyeball; a stopwatch; infinite crew cooperation and guile were what were required to get a bomb on time in the Buccaneer! No digitised green writing to follow, no time early/late indications of later years and no radar worth speaking of overland. In the ergonomic slum of the Buccaneer cockpit, there was nothing worth putting your trust in navigationally over the North German Plain. Now back with the navigation and happily on track, we decelerated to about 360

---

27. Occasionally an engine gearbox would not engage on start-up, but a quick bash with a broom handle was usually sufficient to get it to comply!

knots to gain our timeline and our position in the middle of the stream of Buccaneers heading north-eastwards across Germany. Past the Coesfeld Mast and on towards the Osnabruck Ridge! Buccaneer after Buccaneer passed us in its attempt to gain its rightful place in the stream. Soon the stream settled, one minute apart, a long gaggle of aircraft at 420 knots and 250 feet in the German low flying system.

'Right, everyone settled?' said Iain from the front seat. 'Let's have some fun!'

Up went the throttles until we were cruising at 540 knots! One by one all the aircraft in front of us drifted behind until we were once again leading the field! After a minute or two to create doubt in their minds, back went the throttle and back went the speed to 300 knots, until slowly all the aircraft behind us ended up in front and we became Tail-End-Charlie! Loiter for two minutes and back again to 540 knots until we got to the front and then, you've got it, back to the rear! You could almost see the bubbles of confused inter-cockpit conversation that we were creating amongst our fellow aircrew. Five or six times Iain and I marched up and down the column until the unmistakable voice of the Boss echoed across the ether: 'Ross and Herriot!! Get back in line and stop arsing about, you're confusing everybody,' which had been the general idea – and it seemed to have worked!

With TACEVAL behind us it was time to look forward to the next great adventure on my first tour – my first overseas detachment. Routinely, RAFG squadrons deployed to AWTI Decimomannu on the island of Sardinia for our annual APC. The base was managed by the Italian Air Force and was used by the ItAF, the USAF and the Luftwaffe to drop weapons on Frasca Range, or conduct air-to-air training over the Mediterranean Sea. I deployed to Decimomannu three times with XV Squadron in my just over two years flying on the squadron and there are so many tales to relate about our antics both in the air and on the ground that they could fill a chapter on their own. However, some are too embarrassing to tell and others shall be left out to protect the alleged guilty parties. But some were so entertaining or hair-raising that they have to be included here.

As we lounged in the sun waiting to fly, simple entertainment was had by capturing two praying mantises to watch them copulate and then monitor the carnivorous end of the smaller male. One of us had the bright idea of releasing her third conquest before she could get her fangs into him so that he could rush off and tell his mates what it was like! Simple things please simple minds.

The base was spartan to say the least and maintained to a typical Mediterranean standard – 'Domani, we do ze work domani!' The air conditioning in the Ops Room never worked effectively and, on one oppressively hot day, I innocently asked the Ops Officer, Master Pilot Cole, what was wrong with it and got the memorable reply 'The fucking fucker's fucked, sir'! From that day on he was known as Master Pilot Wally Fucking Cole. The RAF accommodation blocks lacked the comforts of modern living even by 1970s standards. There were two metal-framed beds in each room and, in the true brotherhood of crew cooperation, we shared the room with our pilot or navigator. One sink made mornings a bit of a hassle if you were on the first push to the range, but with Iain's follicley challenged top lip, he was kind enough to have a lie in whilst I had a shave! The ablutions were at the far end of the corridor, which meant a bit of a trek in the night after a few beers as, with shared rooms, the sink was very much 'off limits'. The only decent establishment on base was the Italian Officers' Mess (known as the Spaghetti Palace by we Brits, but pronounced Palachi in our vain attempt to Italianise it) and the only 'place to be' was the British bar, The Pig and Tapeworm, in our officers' accommodation block. 'The Pig' was an establishment of dubious reputation. Adorned on its walls were various cartoons of squadron emblems and in its fridges was a plentiful supply of beer, which was provided by the most junior officer and consumed in copious amounts by his seniors and charged for by means of a 'tick chart'. The Spaghetti Palace was a much more refined hostelry with a good menu and a veritable unending supply of Flaming Sambucas provided by the Italian conscript barmen who tended our every need until 'Ze bar she ees close-ed!' There were no Corporal Ward types in Italian military culture! Nevertheless, it was a good place to meet our American cousins and the occasional German who passed through its portals for a night cap or four!

The flying was excellent at Deci and the weaponry on Frasca Range concentrated, which allowed us all to hone our skills during our two-week camp in the sun. The trouble with Frasca Range however, when related to the Buccaneer, was that the targets were not at sea level. It is all very well having a range on the top of a hundred foot cliff, but if the poor back-seater has only a 'strip True Air Speed' and a 'strip Altimeter' that is fixed to 1013[28] millibars, then placing the targets on top of a cliff is going to do nothing for the accuracy of the weapons. Is it? Moreover, if the peninsula is less than three kilometres wide in the target area on the attack heading, then it is not really giving the poor GIB much of a chance to 'zero' his altimeter directly over the targets. Well, I ask you, is it? Furthermore, the rear seat of the Buccaneer being offset to provide only a clear view to the right of the pilot's head whilst at the same time trying to etch a 'zero' line on the 'strip Altimeter' in your low, left nine o'clock, range three feet, with a blunt chinagraph pencil, is less than conducive to bombing accuracy. It's true, isn't it? Finally, if the range is split, on the attack heading, into 'Left' and 'Right' Range with either Left or Right Traffic, at the Italian RSO's pleasing and your pilot is employing you as local interpreter, then it is clearly acceptable that you missed your mark and that you would be eternally grateful if we could do it all again please! Well, of course it is!

Now if you add to that, the fact that Frasca is but ten minutes flying time from Deci through Point Golf via Alpha North (Runway 35), there is not a lot of time to settle to the task before you find yourself hurtling earthwards in a twenty degree dive. However, since our time together on the OCU and our work-up on the squadron, Iain Ross and I knew each other and our airborne habits well; we were a team. He understood me and I understood him. On this day in history, we were bound for Frasca as Number 4 in a four-ship to conduct MDSL bombing. For those who have never had the delight of doing MDSL (or any other DSL for that matter), MDSL was conducted from a pattern height of 4000 feet and release was initiated by the Navigator's 'NOW' call as the Buccaneer passed through 2150 feet on its

---

28. Standard Pressure Setting.

way towards the ground. Highly accurate over a flat calm sea – on Frasca Range – see above!!!! Following a very short hold at Point Golf, we descended towards the coast to be low-level over the sea as we turned onto the attack heading. During the routine 4G turn in arrow formation, my ejection seat dropped unexpectedly by about two inches with a quite solid and noticeable 'CLUNK'. Time waits for no man and, by the time I had panicked, fiddled and failed to ascertain what the problem was with the bang seat, the four aircraft had joined the range and broken into the circuit, and my height mark had been, to all intents and purposes, non-existent. Now was the time to call it a day! We were now downwind at 4000 feet for MDSL and I was unable to rectify the problem. However, what I had discovered whilst joining the range was that I could not talk on the intercom or radio and the first panic breath only resulted in my oxygen mask clamping itself firmly to my face. Undeterred, and now breathing cabin air, I wrote on a scrap of paper, 'Bang seat dropped 2 inches; can't breathe, can't speak. Dave!' – I signed it just in case there was any doubt! Then, having stamped my feet to gain attention, passed it to Iain through the gap above the Blue Jacket where the roller map used to be. By now, we were established in the dive and my poor pilot was struggling to assess his dive angle without the usual calls from the rear seat; he pulled off dry! Now without the use of dialogue, it is very difficult to translate one's emotions and a sense of urgency on a scrap of paper and I had clearly failed.

Once downwind, Iain passed the paper back with the message, 'Never mind, we'll stay dry!' Now, anxious that my bang seat was about to do what it was designed for, I was not so keen on this course of action and, using 'curt terminology', advised my friend, in writing, that I was less than happy with this proposal! Of course, the flying of the aircraft and the passing of notes takes time and now two more patterns had passed and my straps were tightened to breaking point in preparation for the inevitable. However, like all good crews, our sense of airmanship prevailed and we soon departed the range for Deci where, unbeknown to me as I had no comms, Iain had alerted ATC to our predicament. With my straps being pulled ever tighter, we completed an uneventful straight in approach and, apart from being chased down the runway by a stream of bright yellow Italian 'blood wagons', an uneventful landing followed. Upon reaching the northern ORP, the canopy motored backwards and my now frantically gesticulating pilot indicated that it was time for me to depart the aircraft by conventional means – sliding down the starboard UWT. No sooner was I safely on the ground than, without another word, my Buccaneer disappeared back to dispersal! I was stranded! Until, and here's where it pays to socialise in the bar, a familiar Luftwaffe F-104 Starfighter pilot beamed from his cockpit and gesticulated that I should jump on to his wing and sit astride his drop tank. Five minutes later, back on X-Ray Dispersal, I was deposited amongst my fellows and soon, back in the Palachi, regaling all who would listen to my tale of adventure.

Oh! The bang seat? Yes, it had dropped two inches and in the process it had managed to disconnect the lower seat portion of the PEC which was beyond my sight, thereby breaking the electrical connections for the radio and intercom and sealing off the oxygen flow to my mask! Nothing really and, with 20/20 hindsight, easily identifiable had I investigated the problem thoroughly. But hey! Why spoil a good story when it can keep you in beer for a good twenty-four hours.

Weekend trips out to the beach at Villasimius for a squadron barbecue, or forays into the island's capital, Cagliari, for a spot of shopping were routine. But jaunts to the fairground in either Decimoputzo or Poetto presented much more fun than could be had on base, and weekends in Fortes Hotel Village were outstanding opportunities for relaxation and excitement at one and the same time – until Wings was banned for life from every Fortes establishment in the world!

It was never going to have a happy ending. One of our number had discovered that Fortes Village was situated on the south coast of Sardinia about an hour and a half away from Deci. Although it was high season, he had also ascertained that there were just enough rooms available to accommodate about sixteen of us on the following Saturday night. Checked in and bags dropped in our chalets, we were intent on having a good time on the beach, in the bars, around the pools and in the nightclub! The remainder of our cadre decided to day trip on both the Saturday and, if it worked out, the Sunday. Fortes did not know what hit them. It was a riotous assembly and by the time we half-dozen hardened party goers left the nightclub at 0100hrs on the Sunday morning, a fair amount of alcohol had been consumed and the walk back to our chalets was a navigational nightmare. As we passed the Reception area, a light glowed from a garage that housed the electrically-powered golf carts that were used to transport guests and their baggage on arrival to and from their chalets. In the gloom, two unlikely looking, but familiar characters were bent over the cockpit of one of the carts! Suddenly, and without much warning the golf cart sprang to life and the two 'mechanics' jumped on board and sailed silently past the watching drunks and into the night air. With the driver's foot firmly to the floor, the vehicle and its two occupants sped off down the alleyways in the general direction of our chalets with the rest of us in hot pursuit. We were not quiet. It is difficult to maintain a low profile and utter silence when you are already topped up to the gills with beer and your adrenaline levels are high! Before long, with the cart careering along at some speed, a Fortes security man hove into sight and, unable to grab the speeding vehicle, gave chase too! Accelerating downhill towards the central bar and pool area, the cart disappeared from sight. We followed it somewhat out of breath and, in an effort to disassociate ourselves from the two felons, we tried to engage the now two security guards in polite conversation. They neither understood nor spoke English and their demeanour suggested that any attempt to placate them would be pointless. It became even more futile when we turned the corner and saw the golf cart, without occupants, who had by now disappeared into thin air, floating on its left-hand side in the swimming pool. We scarpered before the guards could gather their thoughts and grab our collars.

There is some confusion forty years later as to who exactly had manufactured the screwdriver into a key that had turned the electrical ignition. There is also some confusion as to whom it actually was who drove and who rode shotgun. Certainly, if you ask the people who were there, even after all this time, they will not talk about it. Save to say that the following morning, Barrie Chown stepped forward when asked about the incident, presented himself at the general manager's office and was banned from every Fortes establishment anywhere on the Globe for the rest of his life!

Our attendance at a local festival on our last Saturday night in Sardinia had also started out so innocently. The officers of XV Squadron had been invited to attend a traditional Sardo (that's a word!) evening of gaiety and laughter atop the Nuraghe Club in Poetto on a hot summer's night back in 1972. The Boss and his executives had declared earlier that they had had a private invitation to dinner at OC Ops' house in Poetto, but promised to join us later on the rooftop of what was the NAAFI Club in Downtown Cagliari. I recall that we were briefed that whilst we may not have wanted to attend this function, there was no alternative for fear of offending. Traditional Sardo dancers and musicians were booked to perform and a 'full-up' Sardo barbecue washed down by buckets of Ichnusa would be available; that did it for me! Ichnusa was not the best beer in the world, but it did come in rather oversized bottles and, ice-cold, you could not taste it anyway! Needless to say, the party was an unmitigated flop! The dancers were, I am sure, very good in a Sardo kind of way, but were never going to be properly appreciated after the third Ichnusa. The food, however, was appalling! A Sardo barbecue consists of cooking the four quarters of a sheep's head over a charcoal grill and then dishing it up with a beef tomato salad smothered in olive oil! I received, but did not eat once I realised what it was, the upper right-hand quadrant complete with molars and eye socket of what I am sure was a very attractive sheep during its grazing days. By now the Ichnusa was slipping down a treat and was beginning to compensate suitably for the lack of available and palatable (no pun intended) solids. Nobody was eating, but, with the Boss's words ringing in our ears, all were embarrassed by the mountain of food that was left and the desire not to offend! By now a group of feral dogs, three floors below, had picked up the scent of the Sardo Fayre and were barking loudly to gain attention. Problem solved! If we were not prepared to eat the erstwhile wool provider, then we had a bloody good idea who would!

When the plates were eventually cleared and the dancers had gone home, with the immediate Ichnusa supply exhausted, we took our leave, thanking our hosts vehemently, and descended to meet the replete hounds of Poetto and to continue our merrymaking at the funfair that had been erected close by the Nuraghe Club.

Now this, of course, was what any rational aircrew chap would have wanted to do from the outset of the evening and it was still sufficiently early to make the most of it. The fair was lively and there were as many varieties of stall as one would expect to find in a fairground in any town anywhere in the world. The only difference was that the majority of people there spoke Italian and we, the minority, did not! However, we had consumed enough beer to convince ourselves that we were bilingual. One of the first 'attractions' that we stumbled upon was the dodgems, and it seemed quite sensible to climb on board until we realised that you needed plastic discs to start the machine and that these were available from a kiosk. As we paired off I found myself next to Pidge Holme.

'I'll get the washers, Dave, if you get some hot dogs!' said Pidge.

'Good call, Pidge, I'm bloody starving,' I replied.

By the time we had RV'd, Pidge had a large handful of washers and I had two hot dogs each clutched in my hands. When the dodgems stopped we rushed forward.

'You drive, Dave, I'll feed the washers,' said Pidge, as we jumped into the nearest free car. I had no idea how many washers he had, but it looked like we would be there for a while.

By the time we started we had both consumed one hot dog each and I was manfully stuffing the next one into my mouth whilst I tried to steer a clear path around the circuit. Pidge, on the other hand, was ensuring that the majority of the washers were secured in his pocket rather than concentrating on his evening meal. I just caught a glimpse of the vehicle coming at us in our eleven o'clock when there was an almighty collision, we both jolted forward in our seats and, as Pidge's fists clenched with the shock of the impact, the sausage ejected from the roll in his right hand and fired forward striking our assailant on the cheek! We carried on for about fifteen minutes with Pidge extracting more and more washers from his pocket every time the electricity was cut from the wire mesh above our heads and, eventually, washers spent, we climbed out and looked for the next bit of fun. As we wended our way through the fair we came upon a bit of an aggressive stand-off involving one of our pilots, Gavin Knox. Gavin was standing beside a rather large Italian who was holding a larger mallet than is customarily seen in one's toolbox. Between the two of them was a 'test your strength machine' and the body language suggested that it was Gavin who was going to have to prove his strength first. Before we could scoop the drunken pilot up and move him out of harm's way, he had stripped to his waist and taken the proffered mallet in both his hands, and, with one mighty, almost over-balancing swing, he managed to smite the button at his first attempt. We were impressed. We were even more impressed when the striker rose high up the column heading for the bell at the top which, after a deathly and silent pause of a few seconds, it failed to reach. Up strode the muscular Italian and wrenched the mallet from Gavin. He started to swing the mallet recklessly above his head and we, with Gavin in tow, started to take our leave. But before we could slip into the shadows there was a mighty thwack, followed very quickly by a resonating clang, that signalled our local hero's winning of whatever bet had been set! We quickened our step.

It was then that I spotted it. A Methuselah! A full six-litre bottle of champagne dangling by a thread and a swarthy Italian beckoning us forward. After some considerable hand waving, we worked out that he who shot the thread with the air rifle not only would drink the complete contents at his leisure, but would also be ordained with cult status in Poetto and probably as far afield as Rome for evermore. It seemed too good to be true, and although I had never tried to shoot whilst full of Ichnusa before, it could not have been any different to a belly full of Tennant's Lager! Could I hit that pesky thread? Lira note after Lira note passed from my pocket to his, but still my aim did not improve! Of course, it never would, would it? The sites were bent – it was a con! Now suitably begrudged and drawing attention to those closest to me, I lowered the site, not thinking for a second that there would be anything more than a ricochet ping from the neck. How wrong can you be? The detonation was deafening as Old Methuselah shattered into a thousand pieces showering the swarthy

Italian in champagne and attracting a sizeable crowd from across the fairground. First on the scene was the local champion from our previous encounter! It is amazing just how much common sense a group of Buccaneer aircrew can have when cornered! Negotiate? With whom? Nobody spoke a word of Italian other than '*quattro birre per favore*', which did not seem appropriate under the circumstances. We were not renowned for our physique, but could see that the enemy had come prepared! What we did have, however, was military guile. So, without a word of command, we legged it, with an angry horde of Sardo men hard on our heels! We had no idea just what he was screaming behind us in Italian, but whatever it was we did not see any point in waiting around to find out. The pounding of Italian footwear fell behind as we raced back to the safety of the Nuraghe Club and we found sanctuary behind its locked door. God only knows how my parents did not lose the second heir to their throne on his first Op, but I survived!

As the end of that first detachment approached, we were all informed that we would fly home in the aircraft that we had brought down to Deci. It was a cunning plan by the squadron executives who, knowing that XW531 was unserviceable and needed a double engine change, had decided that Iain and I, the only bachelor crew, would not be concerned about getting home to enjoy a weekend with our families. First, however, engines had to be airlifted from Laarbruch to Decimomannu, fitted and ground run over the weekend before any thought of getting home could be considered. It all went smoothly from an engineering perspective, and on Monday, 17 July 1972, we took off from Deci and climbed to FL300 and headed north-west towards Alghero on the Costa Smeralda and the French FIR boundary. 'Do the air test in the climb,' the authoriser had said, which seemed logical as we would still have been well within range of Deci if either of the engines had failed to relight after we had shut it down as part of the test. If all went well, we would have covered the first forty minutes of our flight and be over the Med heading for the French coast once it was complete.

We were well past Ajaccio and settled – heading for Nice – by the time it was complete. We were looking forward to the home comforts of our own beds in Block 13A and a night well away from the Pig & Tape! Then I remembered it was XW531! The TACAN[29] had not worked on our journey down, but then we had relied on our leader to do the navigation and talk to French Air Traffic Control. I had not snagged it because 'who needs a TACAN on a ten minute VFR hop to Frasca Range'. So it had not been fixed! The Blue Parrot radar worked, but the latitude and longitude counters on the Blue Jacket Doppler ground position indicator were, as ever, marching themselves steadily eastwards. This was my problem. I had to navigate us home to Laarbruch and I had no NavAids to assist me in the process. The French controller was making all sorts of guttural noises and I could see on the radar that we were homing to a point that appeared to be halfway between Genoa and Toulon,

---

29. A tactical air navigation system, commonly referred to by the acronym TACAN, is a navigation system used by military aircraft. It provides the user with bearing and distance (slant-range) to a ground or ship-borne station.

but had nothing significant to describe it better on the radar screen. We coasted in and turned for Lyon! What now, I thought. We were GAT over France with not a NavAid to speak of, but damned if we were going to give up despite the protestations of Monsieur Le Controlleur (MLC) on the ground. The only thing going for us was that it was gin clear and we had good visual contact with the ground below. Then Iain had a brain wave.

'Get the En Route Supplement out, Dave.'

'What's Lyon's runway?' He asked.

'18/36,' I replied.

'Length?' he responded.

'Eight thousand five hundred feet,' I told him.

'Great,' he said, as he turned northwards for Dijon, our next reporting point, over an airport with a reasonably long runway that was definitely pointing in a N-S direction. But that was not all! To see the runway and make sure it really was Lyon, Iain had to stand the aircraft on its side so that we could check properly. It was far too hard to see the correct orientation and runway length from straight and level at height. Aerobatics at 30,000 feet or so was not something that the Buccaneer really liked.

Now onwards to Dijon and brimming with confidence, we provided MLC with our next estimate; then cloud appeared below us! Luckily it broke just as our ETA overhead Dijon approached and, following more aerobatics, we dutifully turned for Luxeuil in Dijon's overhead using our now tried and tested method of runway spotting. On the next leg, however, the cloud thickened up to 8/8ths[30], which prevented any sight of the ground. We were scratching our heads wondering just how reliable the forecast winds would be and whether we were still close enough to our route not to cause a fuss, when we heard an RAF Phantom from Brüggen calling 'Luxeuil overhead, Dijon next' and 1000 feet above us. Excellent! The leg was three minutes long and exactly ninety seconds later an F-4 Phantom passed directly overhead on an opposing heading.

'On track on time,' I declared to my man in the front seat.

It was about Zweibrucken that the starboard engine decided to quit, but we had had enough of being away from home and, although we discussed diverting, we quickly dismissed the thought and turned left onto 340°. Laarbruch was in sight, well almost in sight, well about 300kms actually, but we nursed it home, all the while losing height and wondering whether we would actually make it, but we did, for an uneventful single engine landing and a little white lie that the engine had quit at the top of descent – well it had, almost!

Flying continued apace and there were many NATO exercises to participate in, or Open Days to provide a static aircraft at. Iain and I had the privilege of doing just that at the Hopsten Air Day in late September 1973, and enjoyed fully the opportunity to mix with our NATO allies on what was a truly enjoyable weekend. So enjoyable that, a few days after our return to Laarbruch, we decided to pay Hopsten another visit

---

30. Full cloud cover.

whilst we were flying close by the airfield on a 2 ATAF low-level navigation sortie. An airfield attack by a Buccaneer is quite an impressive affair for those on the ground and an exceedingly enjoyable experience for those in the cockpit.

'Hopsten Tower, Mission 4271, request airfield attack?' Iain called over the radio.

'Mission 4271, cleared airfield attack, call two minutes,' replied the airfield local controller.

'4271, Roger, north to south.'

'Give them a two-minute call, Dave.'

We were within that already so I called, 'Hopsten, 4271 is two minutes for airfield attack.'

'Circuit clear, 4271, cleared attack.'

Iain pushed the throttles up and very quickly we were at 580 knots and heading straight for the threshold of Runway 19 at Hopsten. As we passed over the threshold he dropped the height to about one hundred feet and pulled hard right, and then hard left to fly over the loop of aircraft dispersal pans at the north end of the runway. Back to the runway, still at about one hundred feet, he cranked the Buccaneer back onto a southerly heading, flew below the glassed windows at the top of the control tower and pulled us around again to repeat the exercise at the southern loop!

'4271's departing and going on route; thanks Hopsten!' he called as we cleared the southern airfield boundary.

'Clear on route and thanks for a great show – welcome back, by the way,' said the controller as we cleared their frequency and entered LFA 2, heading for the Wesel Mast and home. We had clearly made our mark twice on our recent visits to Hopsten.

Unfortunately, that was not the view of the Hopsten Base Commander whose office window faced his airfield. His telephone call to our station commander had ricocheted on to OC XV's desk long before our wheels touched the deck at Laarbruch and, without time to even grab a cup of coffee, we found ourselves on the Boss's carpet having the merits of crew responsibility and airborne hooliganism explained to us in no uncertain terms!

Socially, life began to pick up for me at Laarbruch. I volunteered to become Mess Entertainments Officer with the responsibility for organising all mess functions for a six-month period. Roy Watson, knowing how ill-disciplined I could be, was not too keen on my taking on the role and viewed it as an impending disaster. In a sense he was right; it was uncommon to give such responsibility to a mere flying officer. Whilst I was on QRA one day he arrived to investigate, with OC Police Flight, how someone had managed to scratch a 'Ban the Bomb' symbol in the grime on a loaded aircraft's UHF aerial whilst it was inside the NLZ. Whilst there he informed me that he had already told the PMC that I was a poor choice for the entertainments job and that I would likely organise a band for a Friday when the party was to be on the Saturday. He was wrong; so successful was my tenure of office that I held the post of Ents Member for eighteen months at Laarbruch and all the functions organised, including two Christmas Draws and two Summer Balls, were well supported and thoroughly enjoyed. So enjoyable were the functions that I organised that there was always a large crowd that refused to go home at the end of the evening, which was

The fences, for there were two, were made of fine, but solid mesh about three metres high. Minefields, dog runs, searchlights, trip wires, screens to blank off the view from buildings in the east, observation posts and watchtowers with armed guards ordered to shoot to kill, were spread liberally within a five kilometre exclusion zone that ran the length of the IGB. By 1969 the Soviet Union and East German governments had completed the building of: 1,105 bunkers; 838 observation towers; 734 miles of single barbed-wire barriers; 59 miles of metal mesh fence; 485 miles of minefields; 311 anti-vehicle ditches; 162 miles of dog runs and 53 miles of banks of floodlights along the 836 mile Demarcation Line that had been drawn at the Potsdam Conference in 1945. The Soviets and their German allies did not want people to leave, but very many tried, some succeeded, but many lost their lives in doing so. The first thing that we noticed during our visit to the border was that the fence did not follow accurately the line drawn at Potsdam, which was indicated by a short white post about every fifty yards or so. Close by the post and facing west was a tall black, yellow and red post with the coat of arms of the DDR at its top. Quite significantly, the fence was often nowhere to be seen and, we were told, was usually located two or three kilometres behind the border marker. On occasions, we stopped our vehicle when we found East German soldiers guarding a work party, always women, who were clearing scrub by hand from a wooded area to the west of the fence, but within the border delineated by the white posts. It was explained that the woods were being cleared to allow the fence to be brought closer to the actual boundary and these women were doing the work because the men were working in manual labour jobs in factories – it seemed that there was no shortage of manpower in East Germany, albeit I doubt there was much pay offered for hand-clearing scrub from the land! As we stood watching these poor people, we noticed that an East German warrant officer was monitoring us through a pair of powerful binoculars whilst dictating our clothing and, one presumed, our badges of rank, etc, to a soldier who had a small textbook in his hands. We were no further than twenty feet away from him. It was all quite intimidating, but we decided to upset their Soviet spy plan. At the next stop there was a watchtower very close to the road and before we pulled up we could see that we were being observed from above by yet another powerful pair of binoculars. With our plan set, Iain and I jumped from the front of the car – badgeless! Quick as a flash, we threw open the rear doors of the car and out smartly stepped JK and Dave Symonds who was wearing all of our rank tabs on his shoulders! Iain and I threw up the smartest salutes we could muster and stood to attention as Dave strode smartly forward, with JK at his heel, to inspect the men in the watchtower who were watching them! 'Find that in your bloody Noddy's Guide to RAF Uniforms' we all thought as we wandered off down the fence to look at a village that had been cut in half by this cruel barrier to family union. There we stood very close to the fence and looked towards the houses on the other side of the border. Suddenly, a curtain twitched in a window and we saw a woman waving at us whilst trying to conceal the fact from any border guards monitoring her actions. Apparently, there were stiff penalties for anybody caught 'communicating' with people in the west. We were beginning to realise just what being in the Cold War meant. East Germany was an authoritarian state that subjugated its people and shot to kill anybody attempting to leave its borders. In fact our BFS guide told us that were we to step past the white marker posts and head into East Germany, no action would be taken against us by the guards. However, when we turned on our heel to return to the west, we would instantly be shot in the back as we were 'leaving East Germany'. Such were the rules, and their strict adherence, that no consideration would or could be given to the fact that we were not and had never been residents or citizens of the oppressive regime. Our last stop on the border, before we left the Iron Curtain to return to Laarbruch and contemplate better our role as aircrew assigned to offensive operations in this Cold War, was at the rail bridge crossing that connected West Germany with West Berlin. As we stood there looking east, we saw an East German trackman walking towards us, occasionally striking the track with his long-handled mallet. There was no fence, no gate and no barrier to stand in his way as he headed resolutely towards the west, just a tall and very imposing manned watchtower. Step after step he approached us, tapping the track as he advanced. As he came closer and closer we hatched a ridiculous plan – we had all read far too many spy novels – to snatch him across the white line in the centre of the bridge that marked the IGB. Once across, it would not be possible or permissible for the guards to shoot him! Closer and closer! Tap, tap, tap! He was within twenty feet. Tap, tap, tap! Ten feet! Tap, tap! He was at the white line and, with a hollow glance towards the assembled rank of RAF officers, he turned on his heel and headed home to his family! Tap, tap, tap! We had just come face-to-face with our very first, but not our last, card-carrying communist!

In 1973, Iain and I decided to visit Berlin together. As with the Iron Curtain visit, British military personnel were encouraged to exercise their right of passage down the corridor from Helmstedt to Berlin either by car, or on the military train that plied back and forth each day from Braunschweig, near Hamburg, to Charlottenburg Station in West Berlin. We chose to drive, in my TR6, to show the communists just how capitalist we could be. But first we needed to complete application forms and gain approval, be briefed by the RAF Police on what to expect, and how to behave if stopped by the Soviet or East German authorities. Before entering East Germany we had to report to the BFS Control Office at Helmstedt to be briefed all over again. Our journey was authorised over seven days commencing on Friday, 9 November 1973. We set off early that morning in order to make good time at Helmstedt and leave sufficient daylight to then negotiate the route that would pass along the autobahn through East Germany to Berlin. We were booked into Edinburgh House, the British Forces hotel in Berlin, and were looking forward to a few nights of partying in what was then, probably, West Germany's most decadent city. West Berlin, in the 1970s, was a glitzy, neon-blasted, capitalist sanctuary set in an ocean of a stark, dark, communist wasteland. Its main thoroughfare, Kurfürstendamm, was the party capital of Europe and set as the city was, abutted to the bleak contrast of East Berlin, it was designed deliberately to overshadow the communist idyll. Our journey would take us behind the Iron Curtain and past many of the targets that we had studied back in the squadron at Laarbruch and, on exercise, prepared to attack.

Something started to go wrong with the engine of my TR6 as we headed north-west on the autobahn towards Bielefeld. It was clearly not firing on all of its six cylinders and maintaining speed became increasingly difficult. We soldiered on in the vain hope that it would sort itself out, but it did not and by the time we approached Hamelin, it had become clear that something would need to be done to resolve it. Not being a carburetted engine, neither of us had a clue where to begin! Fortunately, we found a British Leyland garage in Hamelin and handed over the keys to allow them to investigate the problem. It was a quick diagnosis. One of the fuel injectors had broken, but it was repairable – but 'not today' as they did not have the part available and, with the weekend approaching, it could not be repaired until Monday at the earliest.

Our long weekend in Berlin was disappearing fast! Whilst I used my pidgin German to analyse further whether the car could be driven, Iain used the garage telephone to talk to Laarbruch to see what options were available to resurrect our leave plans. There was good news. The car was driveable and, if we wanted to delay our travel, clearance paperwork and accommodation could be regenerated for a later arrival in Berlin. The thought of breaking down in East Germany assisted our decision making. There was no option other than to drive the TR6, now with a temporary repair, back to Laarbruch, whilst the paperwork was regenerated so that we could set off later in Iain's car back to Helmstedt and the journey along the communist autobahn.

Iain's car, a Citroen Dyane, was only slightly more upmarket than the East German Trabant, but not, I am happy to say, made of cardboard and with a two-stroke engine! It had, however, no petrol injectors that might fail and it made good time to Helmstedt on Remembrance Sunday 1973, where we checked into the same gasthof that we had stayed in for our border visit and readied ourselves for our journey east the following morning.

At 0900hrs, dressed in civilian clothes, we were being briefed by BFS staff on the vagaries of 'driving the corridor'. Their orders were explicit and left no room for either misunderstanding or the consequences of ignoring 'the rules'.

Rule 1. Ignore all East German Border Guards, East Germany is not recognised internationally and so they have no authority to stop you as a member of the Occupying Powers.

Rule 2. Drive straight past the East German vehicle checkpoint and head to the Russian checkpoint.

Rule 3. One of you take your paperwork and RAF ID Cards into the Russian guardhouse, but do not leave the car unattended as the Russians will place a bug on your car and listen to your conversation all the way to Berlin.

Rule 4. You must abide by the speed limit on the autobahn and take no longer than two hours and no less than ninety minutes to complete your journey. Any shorter and you will be charged with speeding, any longer and you will be charged with spying!

It seemed all very cloak and dagger, but we were ready to take leading parts in our very own spy novel.

We crossed the border and drove straight past the East German guards who were shepherding lorries and cars heading east into search laybys at the side of their checkpoint; they did not give us a second glance. We pulled up at the Russian checkpoint where a dour-looking Russian conscript was stood, wrapped from the bitter November air in a scruffy greatcoat and with his Kalashnikov strung over his shoulder. A lit cigarette drooped from his lips and his Ushanka, with its hammer and sickle badge, was lodged firmly on the top of his head with its ear flaps fastened under his chin to keep his pate safe from the biting wind. We agreed that Iain could take the paperwork in whilst I stayed in the car. He was gone at least twenty minutes and, in that time, the conscript and I exchanged frosty stares as he circled the car eyeing up his enemy.

'Touch these!' Iain exclaimed as he thrust our ID cards and the paperwork into my hands upon his return.

'They're warm. What happened?' I enquired.

'They've been photocopied! It's just a small office, with an opaque window that has a very thin slit at its bottom,' he said, 'I stood for a few minutes waiting and then fingertips appeared below the opaque window and drew the papers in – nobody said a word!'

'Nothing else?'

'No, not a word spoken, the papers came back stamped and now we are clear to go!'

As we gave the conscript a withering last glance, Iain put the Dyane into gear and we eased out onto the autobahn and headed east to Berlin.

'You go in when we get to Berlin, it's quite fascinating,' he offered as we set off trying to identify targets and looking out for WP aircraft or armour that we would easily have recognised given our training responsibility on the squadron.

The journey to Berlin was uneventful, we saw nothing of military interest along the way and we completed it within the allocated timeframe. I left Iain in the car at the Russian checkpoint outside West Berlin and headed into the office armed with the necessary papers. My heart was beating fast, but it was a DCO as briefed with nothing exceptional to report.

We had three great days in West Berlin. On a wet Wednesday afternoon, we had watched on television the marriage of Princess Anne to Captain Mark Phillips in Westminster Abbey. We had walked through Checkpoint Charlie into East Berlin in our No 1 Uniforms, another privilege for members of the four Occupying Powers. We had spied on the Soviet Army as they guarded the Soviet War Memorial in West Berlin. We had marvelled at the construct of the Berlin Wall and stood in silent contemplation before the crosses that marked the execution points for those brave souls who had attempted to escape to freedom in the west. And we had caroused up and down the Kurfürstendamm into the early hours of the morning.

Only one spot of bother had caused us any heartache. Very late one night, and with plenty of beer swilling inside us, we decided to enter a club just off the Ku'damm. It took some effort as the door was locked, but was eventually opened by what seemed to be a nice young woman who gladly relieved us of a considerable number of Deutsch Marks for the privilege of entering her establishment. There was a cabaret in progress and Iain and I settled down to watch. It was an intimate setting with low-level lighting, silk drapes and mellow music to waft your mind as the woman on the stage danced and gyrated provocatively. A glass of champagne was thrust into our hands by a waitress.

'Dave,' Iain whispered, 'It's a bloke!'

'What! Who's a bloke?' I responded.

'The woman on the stage! It's a bloke!'

'Bloody hell! Are you sure?'

'Quite sure, and so is the waitress!'

I looked around and suddenly the penny dropped! They were all blokes! We had found a transsexual bar in central Berlin! We downed our champagne and attempted to leave, but were very quickly assured that leaving was not on the agenda! This was tricky and it took all our diplomatic skills to persuade these 'women' that we had inadvertently stumbled into the wrong bar and had no intention of staying or enjoying whatever sexual fantasy that they had in mind for us! After some few minutes, which seemed like hours, we found ourselves back on the street with our virginity intact and heading back to Edinburgh House.

'OK. When we get to the checkpoint outbound, let's both go in and see what happens!' said Iain.

'What about the car?' I asked.

'We don't know any secrets so they can bug us if they like,' he laughed.

So we abandoned the car in the tender care of another conscript with his Kalashnikov, Ushanka, greatcoat and fag, and headed into the Russian guardhouse. Same routine – fingertips and paperwork gone! Ten minutes passed and nothing happened. Fifteen minutes. Twenty minutes. After thirty minutes we were disturbed by the arrival of a woman who was clearly in a hurry.

'Hi, are you guys heading back to West Germany?'

'Yeah, we are,' Iain intoned quietly.

'Just been visiting?'

'Yeah.'

'I'm posted back to the UK! I hate this bloody city and can't wait to get out of it!' she exclaimed loudly.

Iain and I looked blankly at each other. Who was this woman? Did she not know the rules? Did she not understand the military code? She was clearly military or she would not have been travelling the corridor.

'I'm a QARANC sister and this city sickens me,'

'Oh!' We responded almost in harmony as her paperwork reappeared and she left the office!

We looked at each other unsure of whether she was telling us the truth or whether she was a Soviet plant! Why had her paperwork beaten ours through the scrutinising process! Our suspicions were rising when suddenly a door by the opaque window opened and out stepped the tallest man I had ever seen. He must have been over six feet tall, but his high-peaked Russian officer's cap made him look at least a foot taller. He walked past us and turned on a television that just happened to be showing an English league football match.

'Do you like football?' he asked. And before we could answer followed it with, 'You might like to sit down, your papers will be some time yet.'

'We're fine,' said Iain.

'By the way, I should introduce myself,' he said, 'my name is Pyotr and I come from Leningrad.' Our spy novel was now in fast forward.

'I'm Iain,' said my pilot, 'and this is Dave.' We all shook hands. There seemed no harm in giving him our names as they already knew them from our papers.

'Are you Royal Air Force?'

'Yes,' Iain responded. There was no point in denying it as they had our RAF ID cards.

'Where are you based?' The questions were becoming more difficult to answer, but we would not have been standing there if we were not stationed in West Germany and so the response was easy if evasive from Iain, who had taken the lead in talking to Pyotr.

'West Germany.' Non-specific and satisfactory as it turned out as our seven-foot captain changed his tack slightly and opted for a more direct approach.

'Do you fly?' Oh God! What do you say to that!

'Yes,' Iain offered, knowing that the pictures on our ID cards showed his pilot wings and my navigator brevet.

'What kind of aircraft do you fly?'

'Jets,' replied Iain as he grabbed our paperwork from under the glass and we both hurried from the room with a swift 'Goodbye' thrown over our shoulders. We laughed all the way back to Helmstedt.

The journey westward was again uneventful and we were soon back at Laarbruch regaling our tale to anybody and everybody who was happy to listen to our encounter with our second ever card-carrying communist!

In March 1974, as part of our preparation for war, Iain and I were selected to participate in the RAF's Winter Survival Course at Bad Kohlgrub in Bavaria. Stories about the course were legendary and some, no doubt, apocryphal. What we knew, however, was that it lasted ten days, and the syllabus consisted of seven days skiing and three nights surviving. So, in true RAF style, the balance was about right.

We travelled by rail to Munich and on to Bad Kohlgrub where we were accommodated in the Zur Post Hotel, which was also the headquarters of the Winter Survival School. No sooner were we there than activities started. Skis, ski boots, sticks and black ski suits were issued. Iain and I had both skied before on Exercise Snow Queen, which was run by the British Army, relied on Army skiers to do the instruction and was based in an old cheese factory high in mountains above Oberjoch, close to the Austrian border. Winter Survival was something different, however, and so when we were split into groups by skiing ability, we opted to join the beginner's group with Horst, the owner of Zur Post, who was a lifelong skier and a professionally-qualified instructor. We spent all day on the piste, and the hour after dinner in class learning how to trap, how to fish and how to escape and evade behind enemy lines. We learned about our available equipment and how to improvise. School over for the day, it was into the bar and the delights of Hackerbrau, the only beer that I have ever drunk in vast quantities that came without a hangover the following morning – or maybe that had something to do with the crisp mountain air and the regular exercise!

The weather was quite mild for the time of year and by the time the '*Schwartz Teufel*', the black devils as we were called by the locals, left the slopes and headed for the hills, the weather had become quite spring like and the snow in the survival area had dissipated quite markedly. The first day was spent constructing A-frame shelters from logs bound with parachute cord, a parachute draped across and with bracken and moss to waterproof our home. Our clothes were wet, so the later hours were spent scavenging for wood to build a fire and logs to erect a screen to reflect the heat from the fire into the A-frame. Snares were set up along 'lines of communication' to trap unwary animals and fishing lines, and nets were set in the river in the hope of catching trout for dinner. We spent a reasonably comfortable night in our A-frame; albeit a little hungry as no traps had been sprung or fish ensnared. The following day consisted of maintaining the campsite and also an introduction in 'How to deal with a furry animal once caught', or, in more blatant text, 'How to kill, skin and cook your rabbit!'

On our course, the Open University, in concert with the BBC, had asked if they could send a film crew along to shoot part of their '*The Physiology of Man*' undergraduate course, to which the powers at RAFG had agreed. But the BBC, in their inimitable wisdom, had limited their spending on the project by sending just a BBC producer, whilst they had recruited locally a German cameraman and a soundman to deal with the technical bits. Our instructor was one of the RAF's great characters. Master Aircrewman 'Geordie' Platt, unsurprisingly, had a marked Newcastle accent which was hard enough for we Brits to understand, but the German crew, neither of whom could speak a word of English, had no clue to the drama that was about to unfold before their very eyes.

From an orange crate, Geordie pulled a grey and white rabbit that had clearly been purchased from a local pet shop. As he held it aloft for us all to inspect, the rabbit started to throw itself around as the camera crew closed in for a better shot.

'When ye tak yer boony oot o it's snare, it'll be in shoke and will chuck itsel' aboot like this!'

The camera crew got closer.

'If ye grab it like this wi yer three fingers aroon' its twa legs and hang it upside doon, it'll be much handier tae control, like!'

The boom mike hovered over Geordie's head.

'Tae stope it struggling lika bastar', jist gie it a wee stroke, like, an' it'll soon calm itsel' doon!'

Sure enough, as Geordie stroked the back of the rabbit's head, it started to settle and was soon quite calm as it responded to his touch.

'Noo, calm as ye like, it'll look up tae see whits goin' oan.' And with that the rabbit raised its head slowly and started to look around at the assembly of ravenous aircrew.

'It's then that ye tak a bloody big log frae behine yer back and smack it…' and with that he pulled a four-foot log from behind his back and hit the rabbit firmly on the back of its head. As its neck broke, blood spurted from its nostrils and covered the sound man's boots, who, having not understood a word that had been said, promptly fainted.

Gales of laughter ensued and the camera crew scuttled off to lick their metaphoric wounds.

Geordie broke us up into groups of four and then, as if a magician on a stage, pulled four more live rabbits from the crate and issued one to each group. Thankfully, Garth Gardner, a navigator from 2 Squadron, volunteered to introduce our rabbit to its maker! The four of us dined well that night on rabbit stew, but, conscious of the lesson on food management when surviving, held back the bones to make a nice broth the following evening.

The following afternoon we were trucked out into the forest to participate in a map-reading exercise as a prelude to our night Escape and Evasion phase that would bring the exercise to an end. Strangely, whilst searching for firewood in order to prepare our 'rabbit bone' broth, I found two small Tupperware containers that had been left by previous 'escapees' against a tree trunk and underneath the snow – one contained salt and the other curry powder, so we dined on rabbit curry that night and, despite my protestations of innocence, was doubted ever after as having brought 'contraband' with me on the exercise.

Soon we were released with a map and a Silva compass and directed to various checkpoints along a rough route that would take us to a friendly 'Resistance' RV and safety. On our way in the dark, the directing staff had recruited the assistance of a crack troop of German Mountain Troops to apprehend us. Priority was to escape, but evading capture was very much a part of that and we knew that anybody who failed would end up being interrogated by trained British interrogators from the School of Interrogation in Kent. First lesson of evasion – avoid the roads. Second lesson of evasion – avoid moonlight. Third lesson of evasion – stick together as best you are able. Fourth lesson of evasion – do not get caught!

Iain and I set off through the woods and made good progress initially. We detached ourselves from the main body of escapees and took ourselves off at a tangent and not in the most direct route to the first RV. We listened before we moved and we checked for headlights and other escapees or enemy forces before we stood from our crouch. Two hours passed, and by 2100hrs we were confidently progressing along our chosen route. At 2200hrs, as we came out of a forest and were walking along its edge, we heard that infamous call that threatened many of our wartime predecessors on the run in Nazi Germany. *'Halt! Hände Hoch!'* I froze and Iain grabbed my arm. Quickly we dropped to the snow and stayed there. Far in the distance we heard the recognisable sound of fellow airmen handing themselves in and realised that it had been a close call, we were still free. After a good forty minutes lying quietly in the snow we checked our surroundings and decided to move forward. It was deathly quiet and the snow crunched crisply under our steady pace.

Suddenly, as we rounded a copse, we were confronted by three mountain troopers and we very quickly realised the game was up. It was unfortunate that we had just stumbled upon them, but a quick assessment of our situation made us realise that there was little point in running. They grabbed us roughly by the collar and quickly moved us about half a kilometre to a snow hole where they left us in the charge of another who had already got about six escapees to hold whilst we awaited transportation to the interrogation centre. It was a long and cold wait. After about twenty minutes Iain started to undo one of the pockets on his cold weather jacket and extracted a rubberised waterproof packet from within.

'Halt!' said our concerned guard. *'Was macht sie? Was ist das?'*

'Schokolade,' said Iain quickly. *'Möchten Sie?'* Our German evening classes were beginning to pay dividends.

'*Ja,*' said Fritz, as he watched Iain begin to peel off the rubber wrapping.

He watched more intently as Iain extracted the miniflare gun from its holding and screwed a miniflare onto its firing pin. Fritz should by now have called a halt to the whole proceedings, but his curiosity was fully alert and his senses were completely shaken as Iain pulled the trigger and the flare shot past Fritz's left ear!

'Run,' shouted Iain as we all bolted for the exit of the snow hole and made off into the darkness and freedom. Unfortunately, we did not get too far, as the detonation had alerted Fritz's pals, and the flare had illuminated the night sky and made their task of re-arrest much easier. We tried.

As I queued up to be stripped, searched and issued with prisoner fatigues, I was engaged in conversation by the storeman. 'Had I enjoyed the skiing at Bad Kohlgrub?' 'Yes I had.' 'Was it bitterly cold out there tonight?' 'Yes it was.' 'How was I captured?' Etc, etc, etc, with me giving, at most, three word answers, but grateful to meet a friendly face after what had been a pretty tortuous journey in the back of a truck with a blindfold over my head.

I was taken from there into a holding area that seemed, as far as I could tell with my black hood still over my head, of circular construction. I, along with all the others in there I imagine, was placed in a stress position and told not to move. If I moved, dire consequences would follow. It seemed ages before anything else happened and I calculated that this was just part of the breaking process; so I thought that entertainment would help pass the time better. Blind with my hood on, I worked out when a guard was approaching and would, whilst still facing the wall in the stress position, move my head in an arc and follow his footsteps as he passed behind me. Each time he approached I followed him blindly. Eventually he worked out what I was up to and gave me a severe consequences warning; but I did not stop. What could he do? He could not kill me, he could not even really harm me. He might be able to rough me up a little or verbally abuse me, but I had heard all that sort of stuff before from Sergeant Barnes at AOTS, so nothing much could come of my disobedience.

After about two hours sat in the same stress position, I was dragged to my feet and taken for interrogation. It seemed to last forever and the very first guy I met was, most definitely, the hard man! He attacked me verbally, he attacked my family, of which he seemed to know quite a bit, and he attacked my role as a 'war monger'. He asked me what my mission had been and where I was based, and who my commanding officer was, but I stuck to my guns.

'David Herriot.' 'Flying Officer.' '8025055,' I responded continuously. He got nothing from me and soon dispatched me back to the circular barn and my guard-baiting antic.

Next I met the soft man. 'Would I care for a cup of tea?' 'Would my family be concerned, would I like to write them a letter?' and other such solicitous approaches. 'It would be easier for you if you would just tell us what type of aircraft you fly?' Nothing.

'David Herriot.' 'Flying Officer.' '8025055,' I robustly told him.

One more session with the hard guy and they got nothing out of me – I felt very pleased with myself as I was ushered into the commanding officer's office for a debrief.

'OK. The exercise is over for you now,' he said. I did not respond.

'No seriously, I am here to debrief you and hear what you thought of the Escape and Evasion phase.'

'No kidding?' I asked.

'No kidding,' he promised.

'You did very well on the interrogation,' he said, 'neither of the interrogators managed to get you to talk about anything, so you should be very pleased.'

'Thank you.' I did not quite trust him.

'This training will stand you in good stead should you ever find yourself behind enemy lines being interrogated by the Soviets, so I hope it's been valuable and you've learned from it.'

'I have.'

'Good, well you're clear to go. There's hot soup outside and coaches will be here shortly to take you back to Zur Post.'

'Thank you.'

'There's just one thing,' he said, 'did you realise that you let yourself down by speaking to the storeman who gave you your denims?'

'Storeman? Wasn't he just a storeman?' I asked, 'I didn't tell him anything, just pleasantries really.'

'No, there is no such thing as just a storeman after you have been captured. Everybody has a role to play in the interrogation chain and that chap was there to assess those who will likely crack and those who won't!'

'Thank you for that – a lesson well learned then, good night sir,' I said as I took my leave and headed for the hot soup and home to bed.

Our last day at Bad Kohlgrub was spent back on the slopes, and before long we were dining and tucking into our last pints of Hackerbrau with our new-found friends in Bavaria; our interrogators had joined us for our last night madness event!

Jennifer Haycock came to Laarbruch in the summer of 1973 and was amongst the last batch of schoolies to arrive before I left the unit in April 1974. She was stunningly pretty, had long dark hair, and all her curves were in proportion and in the right place! Compared to many of the rest of the schoolteachers, she had something about her that attracted me. When I eventually managed to introduce myself to her, we got on famously as we seemed to have the same interests and desires. Hard as I tried, however, she was a little hesitant to form a relationship, using the excuse that the close community of the officers' mess limited her in her thought of forming a relationship with anybody at Laarbruch. What I did not know was that other schoolies, who had been at Laarbruch a long time, were discouraging her from having anything to do with me as I was renowned as a bit of a party animal, and Jen was quite a shy and retiring individual. Nevertheless, I persevered until, eventually, she relented and agreed to a dinner date in one of the local restaurants, but distant enough so that we were unlikely to bump into anybody from Laarbruch. From that, although in secret initially, there formed a long-lasting and loving relationship that took us away for weekends together to Goslar, in the Hartz Mountains, and to the Mosel. As our time together grew and grew, I had fallen head over heels for Jen, and was delighted when

I was invited to meet her parents who lived in Huddersfield. I felt very at home in the Haycock household and thoroughly enjoyed being in the company of her parents, Jen and her younger sister Caroline. Jen and I talked about future plans, and whilst the subject of marriage was never addressed, the language indicated that that might be a possibility if the relationship bore the passing of time. I was in love. I quietened down my activities in and around the officers' mess, and although Jen enjoyed a party as much as the rest of us, I did my utmost to let her know that my previous alcoholic extravagances were just that and that I could be a responsible and willing partner in our relationship. Jen and I thoroughly enjoyed our time together at Laarbruch over those last months of my time in Germany – we were almost inseparable and people now knew it. Even the station commander, Group Captain Mike Knight, had worked it out when he invited me for drinks at Laarbruch House one evening. Both Jen and I received separate invitations for the same event and it was anticipated that we would arrive together. In the RAF, station commanders would invite wing commanders for dinner, squadron leaders for a buffet supper and flight lieutenants and flying officers for drinks from 1800–2000hrs. At 2000hrs, holding Jen's right hand, I approached the station commander, thanked him for inviting us both and informed him that it was time for us to take our leave!

'You're not going anywhere,' he retorted, 'just let me get rid of these boring buggers and we'll have a proper drinking session!'

Jen and I left Laarbruch House at about 0100hrs having drunk, with the rest of the non-boring buggers, most of the CO's whisky supply. I am eternally grateful to Mike Knight for his comment in my last F1369, Annual Confidential Report, which stated:

'Herriot will be good value – possibly very good value – for the Service as he matures. He will need some 'understanding' handling on his next tour; but I confidently expect him to be scoring well by the end of it. He is not ADC material (unless some senior officer is looking for a more than usually 'interesting' tour). However, I do not hold this against Herriot; and I do not think it detracts from his overall potential.'

Thanks to his comment I never became an Aide de Camp, nor a PSO to a very senior officer, which is somewhat ironic, as for the past twenty years, in my capacity as the Honorary Secretary, I have been acting as PSO to the President of the Buccaneer Aircrew Association, one Air Chief Marshal Sir Mike Knight! Since that night drinking his whisky, our paths crossed regularly throughout our years of service. Despite our difference in both age and rank, a strong bond has been formed, such that today I consider him to be one of my most valued friends and advisors.

As I reflect over my thirty-nine year RAF career, I thank my lucky stars that I had the opportunity to serve my first tour on XV Squadron. It was a steep learning curve for a first tourist, but with the support, guidance, encouragement and camaraderie that existed in the first years of the first RAF Germany Buccaneer squadron, the enjoyment of my flying career in the RAF was set. When XV Came to Laarbruch: What a Happy Day…

Chapter Nine

NATO Trouble Spots (1974–1978)

L ife on XV Squadron as a first tourist navigator cum flying officer had been pretty clear cut from the outset. The basic scenario had been: fly with Iain who will keep me out of trouble; drink with Wings who will get me into trouble; sit in QRA where I can relax from the former and recover from the latter; keep out of sight of the Boss both professionally and socially as best as I am able; and do not get myself noticed other than for things positive. Having got into trouble on innumerable occasions in and around the mess, but having survived the tour, now was the time to put all that behind me and build a career during my second tour.

So much for the plan! Needless to say, no plan survives first contact with the enemy! Of course, XV had no role to defend the southern flank of NATO, but it did have a requirement to introduce the unwary (ie 22-year-old navigators) to the 'trouble' spots of the Mediterranean and that, you will have realised, had already happened in Sardinia. Familiar as I was with some of NATO's more sun-soaked trouble spots, I had no idea just how familiar I was going to become, and with those on its northern flank, throughout my time on 12 Squadron. Especially when one's past evokes a preponderance to routinely and regularly draw attention to oneself because of your serious immaturity, coupled with a liking for the amber nectar and the influence of Mr Wings. So, it was no surprise really when I was eventually tourex, and tasked with defending the southern flank of NATO, that my arrival on 12 Squadron was not going to go unnoticed!

Picture the scene: April 1974; Honington, Suffolk; No 1 Hangar; top floor corridor; end of first week; youthful 24-year-old; still a flying officer navigator; sat in the crewroom with feet on table contemplating when I can reasonably escape to the bar and whether Happy Hour here will be as good as that tax-free haven across the Channel! Suddenly, door opens, a heavily-moustachioed flight commander sticks his head round the corner and makes it clear that it is time for my arrival interview. Aw, shit! I had hoped to sneak off to the bar and maybe avoid such a meeting at least for the first week. Never mind, better follow dutifully behind and think of something appropriate to say to ingratiate myself with him before I actually get to his office. 'Yes, Sir, I'm really looking forward to the next few years of being totally lost over the oceans of the world.' No, I decided, that is unlikely to be effective, he looks a bit serious! 'Yes, Sir, XV was OK, but I am really looking forward to doing what the Bucc was designed for.' Hang on, that might encourage him to ask deep and meaningful questions about just that! What, was it now? Some Soviet cruiser that could supposedly shoot you before you shot it if you weren't careful! What was it called? Damn! Can't think of its name and I am getting seriously close to his office now. Got it! 'Nice to meet you, Sir, and how is Mrs Crone?' Christ, we're here!

'Herriot, sit down and welcome to 12 Squadron, but before we start let me tell you that if you think that you can behave here like you did on XV, you are mistaken!'

Hell, how did he know about that? Best I sit tight and answer his questions straight!

'…there you are, work hard and play hard is the 12 Squadron motto, so welcome aboard!' intoned Henry Crone as the interview came to a close.

'Thank you, Sir, I won't let you down!' was all I managed in the end!

'Oh, by the way, you will be joining OC A Flt on the advance party for 'Dawn Patrol' next week; happy?'

'Sounds good, Sir!'

'Right, coming to Happy Hour?'

'Yes, Sir!' – do ducks pee in the lake?

And so we left together heading for the bar with me thinking that I must ask Wings what and where 'Dawn Patrol' is? Ah, I forgot to tell you, my social mentor on XV Squadron had arrived on 12 before me! Anyway, I need not have worried, a Honington Happy Hour in 1974 was no different to one at Laarbruch and, if the beer was more expensive, nobody noticed and certainly nobody complained! More importantly, the advice in his office relating to me, XV and 12 was of little significance once in the bar as it was self-apparent that the 12 Squadron Executives led the drinking and the merriment from the front!!!

So, now that you have the background, let me give you an insight into life on 12 Squadron where I will focus on some of our adventures in those 'trouble' spots.

Now Malta! What a jewel in the Mediterranean that is. The sun-baked and potholed roads, the sharp bends, a boat trip through the Blue Grotto and the hill climb to Medina were all regular pastimes for us at weekends. What possible trouble could a mellow group of Buccaneer aircrew bring to a nation that had endured so much that it had been awarded the George Cross in more difficult times? Well, none really! Most, of anything that I recall, happened around the RAF Luqa Officers' Mess. Typically it was watching Wings as he hurtled on a motorbike around the 'bullring' in front of the Mess before he attempted (and often succeeded) to mount the steep steps into the officers' mess and dashed through Reception and barrelled into the now exhaust fume-filled bar to a tumultuous round of applause. Then, ecstatic at his success on one particular occasion, he succumbed to the demands of a young and very drunk Vulcan co-pilot to instruct him to do likewise. The ensuing carnage when the young pilot failed to mount the steps, tumbled over the handlebars and crashed onto the steps and broke his wrists was, of course, not Wings' fault – we had no sympathy with the lad's 'self-inflicted wounds'! We had, however, much sympathy when we all sobered up and watched the poor young man being sent home, in plaster and in disgrace, by the OC of the Vulcan squadron to 'repent at his leisure!' After his departure, and back in the bar for another evening of drunken foolery, Wings was hailed by his Buccaneer brethren for breaking yet another Vulcan co-pilot! Where the motorbike had come from nobody knew; not even, I suspect, Wings himself!

Throughout history Malta has held significant strategic importance, situated as it is at the crossroads of the trading and warring routes of the Mediterranean Sea, halfway between North Africa and Sicily, and Gibraltar and Alexandria. When war broke out in September 1939, Malta very quickly became again the coveted strategic jewel that had dogged it throughout its history. From the Allies perspective, Malta was key to ensuring a staging post to Alexandria and access to the Middle East, whilst the Axis Powers viewed it as a threat to the resupply of Rommel's Africa Korps.

In 1974, Malta's strategic importance had not diminished, and Great Britain's involvement in it both politically and militarily had not been ignored by our NATO allies. Consequently, NATO maritime exercises were routinely and regularly launched from its Grand Harbour, or from its airfields at Hal Far and Luqa. It was to all intents and purposes a garrison island. Despite its proximity to Sicily, its barren limestone surface is more akin to North Africa. The national language, Maltese, too, is more Arabic than European, but because of its long association with the UK, most, if not all, of its inhabitants speak English well. At the time of this tale, the islanders were still eternally grateful for the support given by the British during the war and were, as a result, great Anglophiles. It was to this historical background that I and the BEngO[1] ventured out, led by OC A Flight, Len McKee, to visit the delights of the island's capital, Valletta, on our first night in town!

We thanked the taxi driver outside the double arches of the Victoria Gate that led into the narrow streets of Valletta and looked for our first bar. Then our second and finally, our third! The City Gem, which was somewhere to the left and behind the Victoria Gate, stood at the top of Strait Street and purported to hold in its stock every Scotch Whisky ever distilled! Certainly, if the array behind the bar was anything to go by, then it was not an idle boast. What The City Gem did sell, however, was one of the best steaks on Malta and with its location at the more refined end of Strait Street, or 'The Gut' as it was known to every sailor (or airman) who ventured ashore on Malta, it was an ideal venue to fortify oneself before venturing into the seamier side of Malta's nightlife.

Suitably refuelled, Len asked: 'Ever been down The Gut?'

Not only had the BEngO and I never been down The Gut, this was our very first night in Malta!

'No!' we chorused, 'what's it like?' Of course, we had heard of it. Who had not in the military? However nothing, other than quite a few bottles of Cisk and Hopleaf beer, had prepared us for what we were about to experience!

'Follow me,' uttered Len as we settled our bill at the restaurant and headed out into the sleazier side of Valletta. Thankfully, being late April, it was still daylight as we wandered down the narrow street with its tall, multi-level terrace of houses with an occasional balcony and washing lines spread amongst the telephone and electricity cables suspended above us. Crowded, smoke-filled bars lined the street on both sides, each one full of squaddies and matelots enjoying a bit of 'down time'. In almost every doorway, scantily-clad women made offers as we passed – but we declined

---

1. The engineering staff on the squadron were commanded by the SEngO (Senior Engineering Officer), who was a squadron leader and supported by the JEngO (Junior Engineering Officer), but, at the time, the RAF posted young first-tourist engineering officers, without portfolio, to squadrons to gain experience – they were nicknamed BEngO (Baby Engineering Officer).

their invitations! Bleached by the sun, paint peeled from the doors and woodwork of the bar entrances. Bars with such exotic names as 'The Lucky Wheel', 'The Silver Stallion' and 'The Egyptian Queen', or 'The Galvanised Donkey' and 'The Gypo Queen' as the latter two were referred to amongst the many. The occasional shop front perforated the haze of cigarette smoke that ushered forth from the bars and a cacophony of noise assailed our ears as we wandered past the open doors!

I have no idea now just how far we walked down Strait Street that night or, really, how many bars we did or did not enter, but I do recall that by about 11pm the BEngO and I had decided that we had had more than enough to drink and needed to head back to the Mess at Luqa, as although it was Saturday the following day, we had work to do to prepare for the Buccaneers' arrival on the Monday. Len was less persuaded that it was bedtime and despite a number of approaches to warn him that 'we're leaving now', he refused to join us! We found a 'Fast Black', as taxis were termed in the Buccaneer force, easily at Victoria Gate and were soon back at Luqa, teeth brushed and beds found! Not so, it seemed, for the luckless Len, who appeared at breakfast the following morning looking particularly sallow having discovered that his wallet had been stolen and, without hard cash in his pocket, had found it a particularly difficult walk back from Valletta at 3am!

Exercise Dawn Patrol got underway without a hitch and, even before I had understood the squadron role completely, I found myself airborne in a Buccaneer undertaking sortie profiles that were completely new to this young navigator who had, for just under six hundred hours on type, ground his operational teeth over the flat plains of West Germany at low-level. The primary task of a squadron assigned to SACLANT in the ASuW role in 1974 was to attack surface warships of the Warsaw Pact should the Cold War heat up and bullets start to fly! On 12 Squadron we had almost the exact same weapon inventory as we had had in Germany, but the delivery profiles to attack warships were significantly different to those used to attack static targets overland. In addition, there was a requirement to carry out night attacks at sea that required us to deliver Lepus flares, with their one million candela light source, from a Vari-Toss attack. From the benign environment of level laydown attacks in Germany, it came as something of a surprise to me to find myself conducting practice Lepus attacks, albeit in daylight, over the Mediterranean on my first trip on 12 Squadron on May Day 1974! Three days later, I was doing it in the dark against HMS *Lowestoft* somewhere off Corsica! This was topped some thirty minutes prior as I watched in amazement as, under a starlit sky, my pilot conducted 'dry prods' against the trailing refuelling basket of a Victor K2 tanker that we had stumbled upon as we moseyed north-west at high level towards our target. They would have been 'wet prods', had I completed the groundschool at Marham and, at the very least, done it once for real in daylight previously!

Of course, having arrived from Germany, been rushed to Malta and having not actually been allocated a dedicated pilot as my own, I was lucky to get any flying at all on the exercise. But my logbook tells me that I not only got some flying, I actually got eight sorties in eleven flying days; including one on each of the two Saturdays that were covered by the exercise programme. It was non-stop, full on and I loved it. None of the missions flown were anything like what had gone before in Germany. Leading a pair of Buccaneers low-level around Sicily before dropping MDSL[2] delivered PBs at Pachino Range on the south-east corner of the island was analogous to a sortie in 2 ATAF. But then, the following day, flying as Number 2 in a four-ship of Buccaneers for a coordinated attack against RFA *Sir Lancelot*, followed by twenty-degree dive bombing against the 'Splash' target that it towed one hundred yards behind it in its wake, was something else entirely. It was fantastic fun. Searching for and locating ships at sea was akin to searching for the inimitable needle in a haystack. If this was what life on 12 Squadron was going to be like it was certainly going to be a challenge, but I was definitely up for it, and could not wait to become Combat Ready and play a full part in the squadron's operational capability. What is more, there is no better way to join a squadron than when it is on detachment and the only place to gather after a hard day's flying is in the bar of an officers' mess on a remote sun-drenched island at the crossroads of the Mediterranean Sea. Nights at the Hilton Casino in Floriana, pizzas at Il Fortizza on Sliema front, steaks in The City Gem, and forays down The Gut were all part of Malta's attraction, and there would be many more visits for future maritime exercises throughout my, about to be, four years on 12 Squadron.

Back at Honington, the squadron was engaged in supporting a BBC documentary about the RAF entitled *Skywatch*. There were two parts to the filming for the documentary that involved, firstly, a live firepower demonstration on Salisbury Plain where 12 Squadron was tasked to provide four Buccaneers, each loaded with four full pods of HE 2-inch RP; a total of one hundred and forty-four rockets per aircraft. Secondly, a live broadcast from RAF Wittering, hosted by the BBC's Raymond Baxter, which involved synchronised flypasts of the RAF's hardware along the Wittering runway. I was tasked with participating in the Wittering piece and deployed in the second of two Buccaneers to Wittering on 18 June 1974 to rehearse and then fly during the live broadcast on the twenty-first. The whole thing was designed as a daisy chain of contemporary for 1974 RAF aircraft. We all formed up somewhere over East Anglia, probably overhead Marham – but the grey cells have dumped that unnecessary part of the tale – and wended our way in groups designated by role on a westerly heading towards Wittering and Raymond Baxter's dulcet tones. 12 Squadron, being of the maritime persuasion, were 'tied' to a Nimrod that was planned to fly at 240 knots to ensure that it did not overtake the transport aircraft up front. After a great deal of explanation about the ability of a Buccaneer to stick on a larger aircraft's wing at 240 knots, it was eventually agreed that we fast jets could, 'do our own thing', as long as we under-flew our 'mother ship' overhead the designated Wittering 'on-top' at the appointed hour! The most difficult thing for our pair was not flying the sorties to the on-top, which we were well capable of doing after a couple of practices with the Nimrod. No, that was the easy part. However, with a thick head after each of the previous two nights (and early mornings) of hard drinking in the Wittering officers' mess bar, where Raymond Baxter, an erstwhile RAF Spitfire pilot,

---

2. Weapons delivered manually (ie. on the pilot's trigger press) in a 20° dive attack at 450 knots; weapon release initiated at 2,150 feet (indicated).

was intent on spending all of the BBC's entertainment budget on us, our problem was being able to master the mathematical calculations required on the ground to ensure that it worked out for the cameras in the air!!

Routine training on the squadron was not, by any stretch of the imagination, mundane. By the time I arrived back at Honington in April 1974, the squadron had been operational in the Maritime Attack role for the best part of five years. It was fulfilling well its task of supporting the Royal Navy at sea and replacing the Buccaneer squadrons of the Fleet Air Arm, which had been withdrawn from service over the preceding six years. From an inventory of four aircraft carriers, one of which (HMS *Victorious*) had participated in Operation Pedestal in Malta in 1942, only one, HMS *Ark Royal*, remained by 1974. '*Ark*' was equipped with an air wing that consisted of: Buccaneer S2s in the ASuW role; F-4 Phantoms to provide air defence of the fleet; Fairey Gannets as the eyes of the fleet that provided over the horizon AEW; and a smattering of Whirlwind helicopters that provided both SAR and ASW roles. It was a tall order for 12 Squadron with just twelve aircraft and eighteen crews, and regular exercise tasking was only one of the routines that we aircrew and our ever supportive ground crew had to contend with. But ships at sea move and routinely deploy to distant seas and, therefore, are often found in foreign waters participating in maritime exercises with their NATO cousins. That was why we had been in Malta, to provide an attacking force for NATO's largest annual maritime exercise in the Mediterranean.

But back at base, as a new boy, I had to learn the ropes. Most of the tactics and weapon deliveries practised had been developed by our fellow Buccaneer aircrew in the Fleet Air Arm and had been adopted by the squadron aircrew, many of whom had, in those early days, learned their skills flying on exchange with the Royal Navy. Weather conditions in Germany, and the preponderance of surface-to-air threats that protected enemy airspace had we ever gone to war against the Warsaw Pact, invariably precluded anything other than a low-level penetration and recovery to and from the target area and a low-level delivery of a retarded weapon against mainly stationary targets such as airfields, military logistic sites, barracks and lines of communication (roads and railways); described as a Lo Lo mission. Here at Honington we had greater distances to cover just to get to the target, let alone find it amongst a sea of waves and not much else. Accordingly, our sortie profiles were usually high level to a position some one hundred and fifty nautical miles short of the anticipated target position before commencing what was termed an 'Under the Lobe Descent'[3] to avoid radar detection by the target or any of its supporting vessels. After an ultra-low-level attack against the primary target within a SAG, the formation would egress from the target at one hundred feet until it was deemed sufficiently safe to climb back to height and recover to base; described as a Hi Lo Hi mission. Operational

---

3. A means of descending to low-level outside the maximum known radar range of a target. The Buccaneer was equipped with an S/X-Band radar receiver, Wide Band Homer, that could detect the EW radar on WP ships. Once detected at high level, the navigator would instruct his pilot to descend until the detection signal disappeared. When the lobe was detected again a further descent would be initiated and so on and so forth, until the formation of Buccaneers were at 100 feet above the sea and closing with the target at 540 knots.

attack profiles would vary depending on the ordnance to be dropped. From laydown and dive-bombing attacks, with 'dumb' 1000lb HEMC bombs fitted with retard tails and fuses, to an 'over the shoulder' Medium Toss attack with the same bombs, but fitted with ballistic tails and either impact, delay or proximity fuses, we practised them all. We also had a capability to deliver 2-inch RP, mainly against high-speed manoeuvring targets such as FPBs. In its war fit, the Buccaneer would carry four each of either retard or ballistic bombs in its bomb bay and, with eight aircraft in a formation, it was essential that each aircraft attacked the same target in an attempt to ensure that at least one bomb from each of the eight sticks hit the capital ship in the group. There is neither space nor time here to provide a lecture on weapons effects. Save to say that unguided 'dumb' weapons with non-state of the art aiming systems, when used against a maritime target, necessitated the delivery of a stick of weapons in the full knowledge that most of them would miss their target. I take here, for example, Operation Black Buck in the 1982 conflict to regain the Falkland Islands following Argentinean aggression. That operation culminated in an attack against the runway at Port Stanley airport by one Vulcan bomber equipped with twenty-one 1000lb HEMC 'dumb' bombs delivered from a level profile. Its purpose was two-fold. First, it was designed to cut the runway and deny its use to the Argentinean Air Force, which it achieved with just one crater on the runway! Some would say it was unsuccessful, but such is the result with dumb bombs and it was planned to happen just like that. For to fly down the narrow runway from one end to the other, releasing the stick as you go, would likely have resulted in not one bomb striking the runway, such was the inaccuracy of the weapon and the weapon aiming systems available at the time. However, second and much more importantly, Operation Black Buck served as a message to the Junta leaders of Argentina that Britain meant business and if we could strike at Port Stanley then we could hit Buenos Aires! So, in weapon effort planning terms, for eight Buccaneers using dumb bombs to be successful against a Soviet capital warship, it required more than one bomb to detonate on the target and eight possible hits was the best (or worst) that we could muster.

Now where was I! Ah yes, learning the ropes!

The work-up continued apace with regular and routine sorties to the four local bombing ranges of: Holbeach and Wainfleet, both in The Wash; Theddlethorpe, near Skegness; and Cowden on the coast of the East Riding of Yorkshire and south of Flamborough Head. All were within twenty minutes flying time from our base at Honington, which allowed us to conduct a full thirty minute range detail and also undertake some low-level over land and sea before recovering to base after an hour and a half. If the weather was poor in the south, then the alternative plan was to head west to Wales or north at high level to descend to low-level in Scotland before weaponry at either Rosehearty or Tain Ranges; the latter, you will recall, being the name of my mother's hometown.

Like the squadron work-up in Germany, crews had to qualify and meet the NATO standards in weaponry. There was also a requirement to be proficient in ship recognition and many an hour was spent poring over Jane's *All the World's Fighting Ships* attempting to differentiate between NATO and WP warships. In fact, it was generally quite easy to pick out the Soviet equipment from that of the NATO nations as a clear giveaway was the astonishing superiority in available firepower for the enemy! So, in the end, the crewroom game was who could identify a Kashin cruiser over a Kotlin destroyer from just a black silhouette above the waterline – for that was all that we would be able to go on as we ran in against it at 540 knots and 100 feet!

Although we did not have a UK requirement to stand QRA as we had at Laarbruch, the UK did have its own nuclear strike option and the Buccaneers of 12 Squadron were assigned alongside their larger cousins in the V-Force to this role. Back in the vault, we had to study our allocated strike target, know and be able to describe the features on the IP to Tgt run and learn the procedures for launching aircraft that were nuclear loaded. These procedures were slightly different from those adopted by SACEUR and the launch was always announced by a deep, resonant prophet of doom voice over the HF radio that would start with the words: 'This is the Bomber Controller, This is the Bomber Controller'. After hours sitting at cockpit readiness waiting for a simulated launch on a routine exercise, those repeated five words certainly got the adrenaline pumping! Our target on 12 Squadron was significantly further east than those available to aircraft based in 2 ATAF who flew Lo Lo missions to avoid the enemy defences on the IGB. Happily, however, our mission from Honington was mainly over the less well-defended sea and took us out over the North Sea at high level to join up with an AAR tanker before we headed onwards towards Jutland and the Baltic Sea. Studying the route for the first time in 1974, I was intrigued by two significant directives printed on the high level chart. The first, outbound towards the target, was: 'Jettison Underwing Tanks'. This was a sensible offering to encourage you to get rid of excess and unnecessary drag once the tanks had served their purpose, and thereby improve the fuel consumption. The second, now inbound over the Baltic having survived the defences in the target area and the detonation of our own nuclear weapon, was much more disconcerting! There on the high level chart, just south of Sweden, and in bold type, were just two words: 'EJECT NOW'! The target was so far east that, even with AAR and jettisoned external fuel tanks, we did not have enough fuel to get home to the UK, or what might have been left of it, after Armageddon had taken place!

Although we were separated by some distance, Jen Haycock and I had managed to maintain our relationship after I had left Germany. We kept in touch and made plans to see each other whenever I could get to Laarbruch between detachments, or she could get across to the UK during school holidays. I was very optimistic, I knew I was in love with Jen and as my mother always said, absence makes the heart grow fonder.

Shortly after we got back from Malta, I was encouraged by a fellow bachelor navigator, Ray Morris, to relinquish my room in the officers' mess and share a rented farm bungalow near the village of Culford, some five miles south-west of Honington and close to Bury St Edmunds. I use the term 'share' quite loosely as Brickfields Bungalow had only three bedrooms and Ray was already sharing it with David Smith, a fellow RAF navigator serving on exchange with 809 NAS, and a chap by the name of Les Carlo, who was an Eastern Electricity Board electrical engineer. However, Ray sold it to me with his stories of wild parties, local girls, relaxed dress and pub crawls and so I moved from the comfort of a room in the officers' mess to a camp bed in the corner of the dining room in Culford! Not ideal, but never regretted as, when David Smith went to sea for six months, I used his allocated room, his allocated bed and paid his allocated share of the rent. It was a situation that suited us all both financially and socially. The hot bed routine was not an inconvenience in reality as, when 809 was at home, I was almost invariably on detachment for long periods and, when not, the camp bed was sufficient for a good night's sleep. Indeed, on one memorable occasion after a successful 'pick-up' on one of our regular visits to the Angel Hotel on a Saturday lunch time, it was big enough to share! The relationship did not last, however, as her wealthy parents, who lived in Thetford, were rather concerned at the age gap and had grown particularly concerned about the bad company their rather wayward 18-year-old daughter kept in Bury St Edmunds; I might add, of which I was not one, but they did not get the chance to get to know me to find that out. Eventually, David Smith married his girlfriend Jane, became David Cleland-Smith and bought the rather wonderful and listed Priory Cottage in Ixworth. With his departure to married life, the number two bedroom at Brickfields Bungalow became mine in my own right.

Not long after I had moved in and whilst Dave was at sea, I got a call from Jen telling me that she was on her way to spend a weekend with me! I was over the moon. The bedding was washed, ironed and reset. The kitchen was scrubbed. The lounge hoovered and arrangements made for dinner at Tuddenham Mill. It came as a shock when, over dinner on the Saturday night, she informed me that she had fallen for an engineering officer at Laarbruch and was getting engaged! It was more of a shock when she let it be known that her future husband was to be the very engineering officer who lived in the room opposite mine in Block 13A and who had watched and heard her comings and goings from my room whilst we were together at Laarbruch. I was devastated and, with heavy heart, waved her goodbye as she headed off in her Mini Countryman back to Felixstowe, the ferry for Zeebrugge and her new life as the wife of an engineering officer! My mother was wrong – absence clearly does not make the heart grow fonder when you are surrounded by testosterone driven males in an RAF officers' mess!

In early July 1974, I was sat in the crewroom when Henry Crone entered and told me that XV341 was ready for a full air test and, since I was doing nothing, could I join him. The aircraft had undergone major servicing and required to be put through its paces to check out all its systems before it was handed back to the squadron for routine flying. I was happy, any flying is good flying and I had not done many full air tests previously. Henry briefed the mission and handed me the Air Test Schedule, which spelt out each and every stage of what was required with directives, in plain speech, as to what action each of us had to take at a particular point in the test. Having successfully lit both engines and taxied to the Holding Point for Runway 27, we carried out the various required checks before seeking take-off clearance from ATC. After departure, we climbed to 35,000 feet and I began to read through the checklist whilst Henry responded to each of the instructions given. The first action at height was to shut down and relight each of the engines in turn, and ensure that light up occurred within a specific number of seconds, all the while monitoring that the HP RPM did not exceed the limits set. Whilst Henry monitored the instruments, I had to monitor times and prepare for the next step in the test. With both engines relit, we carried out high speed manoeuvring to check that all the flight controls worked normally and that the hydraulic pressure in the flying control system remained within limits. Then a 'loose article' check had to be done by turning the aircraft upside down. Inverted flight in a Buccaneer could only be held for ten seconds otherwise the fuel recuperators, designed to feed the engines under negative 'g' conditions, would fully empty and the engines would flame out! However, inverted flight is not the most comfortable experience and rest assured that ten seconds is quite enough to ascertain whether an aircraft technician had left a spanner on the floor under your ejection seat! With nothing other than dust floating around our heads, Henry righted the aircraft and, with full airbrake selected and the throttles closed, we carried out a plunge descent to 5,000 feet and steadied ourselves for the next phase of the test, a check of the hydraulic system, the undercarriage and the arrestor hook. The checklist fed us through the procedures required to set the aircraft in the approach configuration. Systematically, Henry followed my instructions.

'Below 300 knots,' I said. 'Autostabs to Approach and Aileron Gear Low Speed.'

'Below 280 knots, Flaps 15-10-10.'

'220 knots, Flaps 30-20-20 and undercarriage down.'

'Three Green Lights and 30-20-20,' responded Henry as I watched the flap and aileron 'cheeses' move evenly together and watched as the blow pressures increased, reassuring us that the boundary layer control system was functioning properly.

'Below 200, Flaps 45-25-25 and select hook.'

'Four greens and cheeses moving together,' responded Henry.

I checked the fuel load, calculated the AUW and offered Henry the appropriate Datum Speed[4].

Henry set the datum and we started to simulate an approach to the wave tops below us. Once happy we moved to the next phase of the air test, which was a low-level acceleration. The process now, according to the schedule, was to slam both throttles evenly to their end stop and time how long it took the aircraft to accelerate from Datum Speed to 580 knots. A figure of about forty seconds was anticipated, but it did depend on the weight of the aircraft and the datum speed flown. Henry talked about preparing ourselves and the need for me to be ready to 'hack' the stopwatch as soon as he called that he was slamming the throttles. I was ready.

'Five, four, three, two, one – hack,' called Henry over the intercom as he slammed the throttles to full power. I hit the stopwatch and watched as the seconds began to climb. Speed began to increase slowly and Henry called out the significant speeds as his ASI increased.

'200 knots.' I watched the stopwatch closely.

'300 knots.' The time continued to increase.

---

4. The Buccaneer was not flown with a decaying approach speed, but with a constant datum speed that was a throwback to its days as a carrier-borne aircraft.

'350 knots.' I began to be concerned, twenty-five seconds had passed and we were never going to get to 580 by forty seconds!

'There's a problem,' I told Henry, explaining what the 'problem' was.

'Keep an eye on it,' he replied. '450 knots.'

As we passed 480 knots there was an almighty bang and the aircraft lurched!

'What was that?' I asked as I called out fifty seconds.

'Oh shit!' cried Henry, 'We're still dirty! We had not raised the hook, the undercarriage, or the flaps, ailerons and tailplane flaps!

'Bollocks,' came Henry's next comment. 'How did that happen?'

By now I was frantically scouring the air test schedule in an effort to ascertain how I could have possibly missed the lines that would have instructed us to clean up the aircraft before the acceleration check. There was nothing there! Nothing to indicate that that should have been done. I informed Henry that that was the case and, whilst he took the news with some element of scepticism, he had more important issues to contend with other than whether his navigator had screwed up or not. That was for later; right now the undercarriage had been overstressed by over 200 knots and the flaps, etc, by even more. Thankfully the aircraft was still handling reasonably normally, although there was a distinct rumble coming from somewhere on the airframe. Henry managed to climb to 5,000 feet and, after a little effort on the squadron discrete frequency, raised another Buccaneer that was nearby whom he invited to join up and give us an airborne inspection!

The other Buccaneer eventually hove into sight and took up a position on our port side. After about thirty seconds he reported that the undercarriage was down and looked normal. The flying control surfaces on the port side were also normal and there appeared to be no holes or punctures on the surfaces. He slid backwards behind us and manoeuvred himself into the same position on the starboard side. The message was the same – no snags to report. He left with a cheery wave and recommended that we should undertake a precautionary straight in approach in the single-engine configuration to land at Honington. We had already decided that that was the most appropriate means of getting the jet back on the ground safely. We called Honington Approach as we made our way round to the LLEP and landed some fifteen minutes later after an uneventful approach. When we climbed out and inspected the airframe, we were astonished to see that whilst from each side the aircraft looked normal, the flying control surfaces on the port wing were in a completely different position to those on the starboard side. In fact the only damage was to the port flap hydraulic jack which, had been distorted and required changing. Such was the strength of the Buccaneer airframe!

Back in the crewroom Henry examined the air test schedule minutely, but, thankfully, discovered that my airborne scrutiny had been absolutely correct. The document that we were required to follow religiously in a challenge and response method was inaccurate in that one most critical aspect. We filled out an Incident Report. All Buccaneer Air Test Schedules were amended forthwith and nothing was said about the incident again.

By now I had been crewed up with Bill Petersen, a USAF exchange pilot on the squadron. Bill had flown F-4 Phantoms in the USAF previously, but a story prospered that he had never been an aircraft captain and as such, needed an experienced navigator to guide him through the work-up on the Buccaneer and together, achieve CR status. I had flown with Bill on two occasions during Dawn Patrol, but now, by mid-July, I was his designated navigator and together we got on with practising dive bombing, toss bombing, laydown bombing and rocketry. We spent many hours finding and attacking simulated targets over the North Sea and enjoyed flying at 250 feet in the low flying areas and corridors of England, Scotland and Wales. I thoroughly enjoyed flying with Bill, who was an able pilot if not an outstanding one – he was steady and that was important to me. However Bill, as an American, was not permitted by the MOU between our two air forces to go to war on behalf of the UK or in a British aircraft. Consequently, were the balloon to go up, Bill and his fellow countryman Bill Butler, a USN navigator on exchange also, were to stay behind and look after the families whilst we Brits fought the war in the air. On such an occasion it was planned that I would fly in the back seat of Bruce Chapple's aircraft.

On Saturday, 20 July 1974 the balloon went up! Turkey invaded Cyprus.

The following Monday, Bill and I had just joined the pattern at Holbeach Range to carry out the delivery of four 28lb PB on Target 5, the dive-bombing circle, when we were instructed by the RSO that he had instructions to tell us that we were recalled to base immediately. With all our weapon switches made safe, we departed the range and headed back towards Blakeney Point for a speedy RTB. Back on the ground and with the aircraft back in position on the ASP, Bill and I walked into the squadron operations room and were told to get ourselves up to the crewroom where the boss, Ian Henderson, was waiting to address all the aircrew.

Ian Henderson had a very stern face and we all sat agog as he told us to go home, pack a bag, say nothing to anyone and get back to the crewroom ASAP; a quaint military acronym that does not mean as soon as possible, but actually means PDQ[5]!

I raced back to Brickfields Bungalow where I found Ray already packing his aircrew holdall.

'Any idea what's going on?' I enquired, but he had no more information than me. I stuffed as much as I could into my holdall, threw it in the boot of my TR6 and headed back up the A134 and back to Honington where Ian Henderson still waited in the crewroom.

After very few words it became quite clear that we were being deployed to RAF Akrotiri in Cyprus to attack Turkish forces should the invasion of Aphrodite's island birthplace advance further across this sun-kissed sanctuary in the eastern Mediterranean. I was to fly with Bruce as planned and, after a number of intelligence briefings and planning a sortie that would take us to Cyprus via Malta, the advice was to head to the mess and relax or get some sleep as we awaited the decision from HQSTC to launch to the war zone.

Bruce was, and still is, a larger than life character and an excellent pilot. I knew that I would be safe in his hands, but, never having really given much thought to actually going to war, I was not prepared for him taking me into a quiet room where he explained to me just what he would do if we were intercepted by Turkish F-104 Starfighters at

---

5. Pretty Damn Quick.

high level as we entered Cypriot airspace! The thought had never crossed my mind! We shared a room in the officers' mess that night where he slept in the bed and I slept on the floor tossing and turning as I thought of the prospect of being in a lumbering Buccaneer at 30,000 feet with a Starfighter on my tail and Bruce rolling us over, airbrakes fully extended and the throttles fully closed, plunging for the deck!

When we turned into the squadron the following morning, we sat around for about two hours before we were stood down and told that the powers that be had decided that Phantoms from Wattisham would be sent instead! The Buccaneer, in the early 1970s, was the unwanted poor relation in the RAF!

So back to the work-up training syllabus it was and Bill and I busied ourselves learning the intricacies of the new weapon system that was coming into service for Buccaneers engaged in the maritime attack game. Hawker Siddeley Dynamics, based at Hatfield in Hertfordshire, had developed a missile system capable of being launched from a stand-off position against surface targets. It was available with either a TV or an AR seeker head and the MOD had bought plenty for 12 and 809 Squadrons based at Honington. It was universally known by its acronym MARTEL, which stood for Missile Anti-Radar Television. The AR version was launched at low-level at a distance of more than fifteen miles from the target. It was what is known in the trade as a fire and forget missile because, after it left the rails, it climbed to 19,000 feet and homed onto either a Topsail or a Headnet C radar on a WP vessel and detonated when its proximity fuse sensed the appropriate distance, thereby shattering the wire mesh radar array and closing down the enemy fleet's EW radars. The TV version, on the other hand, required the navigator to control the missile via a data-link pod fixed to one of the inboard pylons on the launch aircraft. It was launched at low-level at a range of ten miles from the target and, after launch, the missile climbed to 2,000 feet and tracked towards the target. A TV screen between the navigator's legs in the rear cockpit displayed a view of the ocean and was controlled by a joystick on the right-hand side of his cockpit. Camera panning and step-up, step-down or right and left manoeuvres could also be inserted to assist with target detection or to avoid a low cloud base. When the target eventually hove into sight, the navigator would select 'Terminal Phase' on his control panel and the weapon would then enter a pre-programmed dive towards the target with the navigator concentrating feverishly to ensure an impact on the DMPI. To allow us to train routinely, the squadron had a number of TVAT[6] pods that allowed us to detect targets by flying the missile profile after a simulated missile launch. It required considerable skill by the navigators to get the profile right as a low flier would result in a steep dive in TP and an early selection of TP would result in a shallow dive and the likelihood of the missile mushing into the sea short of the target. We had to work hard at it and more so when we discovered that the squadron had been allocated six missiles to fire on Aberporth Range later that year. Only the best crews would secure a missile on Exercise Mistico!

One of the squadron's regular haunts for maritime exercises was back at the Royal Navy's Buccaneer home. HMS *Fulmar*, as it was known in its Fleet Air Arm heyday,

---

6. Television Airborne Trainer fixed to Station 1 on the port wing, that allowed the aircraft to fly missile profiles against simulated targets at sea.

was now RAF Lossiemouth and, with its excellent weather factor, it was a great place to deploy to for a war with NATO navies. For 12 Squadron, Lossiemouth was a home from home. We would use it regularly for a lunchtime stop if we were tasked at Tain or Rosehearty because to refuel at Lossie meant that we could gain better low-level training value in the desolate landscape of the Western Highlands. Night stops were also a regular occurrence and a night in the bar at Lossie, with the possibility of repairing to 'The Bothy[7]' after the bar shut, was almost too attractive to waste.

In September each year, however, the squadron took part in NATO's annual and largest naval exercise in the eastern Atlantic. Variously called: Northern Merger (in 1974); Highwood (1975); Teamwork (1976); and Ocean Safari (1977), the squadron deployed away from Honington to participate as either Blue, in support of the fleet, or Orange, opposing the fleet, forces. In the first three of these years the deployment was to Lossiemouth and, in my final year, the exercise was held in the South-West Approaches and so our deployment then was to St Mawgan in Cornwall. The format was always the same and it was preferable to be Orange rather than Blue Forces! Orange tasks were preordained by date and time and allowed us to schedule a flying programme and allocate crews accordingly. Whereas Blue tasking was mostly 'On Call Tasking', which required all crews to be available twenty-four hours a day for the duration of the exercise. Orange equalled live in the officers' mess with access to the bar and the comfort of its facilities. Blue meant that our accommodation was in the remnants of the Lossiemouth Strike Force Dispersal with field catering, cabin sleeping, unreliable ablutions and no alcohol facilities whatsoever. The SFD had been built to provide facilities for the V-Force when Lossie acted as a Strike Launch FOB for Valiants, Vulcans and Victors in the 1960s. It was, to say the very least, basic in the extreme and in a cold wet Scottish autumn, not the most pleasant of locations on the northern edge of the airbase, with its only advantage being a short taxi to the threshold of Runway 23.

Once airborne on a mission, however, the flying was always fantastic. Six-ship and eight-ship formations conducting Alpha 3, Alpha 4 or Alpha 5 attacks against flotillas north of the Shetlands or out in the Atlantic. Wheels in the well and straight out to sea at 100 feet in battle formation and operating under radio silence with each aircraft flying in exactly the right position and at the right speed. Radars switched to standby until, closing with the last known target position, the monologue from the TacDi[8] or COVEC[9] aircraft reassuringly guided the attacking force towards its

---

7. A Scruffs' Bar where aircrew could get a beer without having to change out of uniform or flying kit. It was run on an honesty basis and was available twenty-four hours a day.
8. TacDi (Tactical Direction), the game of *Battleships* at 450 knots and 100 feet! The Tactical Navigator in a Shackleton AEW2, of 8 Squadron based at Lossiemouth, plotted the maritime surface picture and, by means of a coded message, transmitted actual warship positions within a 'battleship game' matrix to allow the attacking Buccaneer crews to form a surface picture and identify the HVA (High Value Asset) target within the SAG. A Canberra or Hawk aircraft was occasionally used on a LOPRO (Low Probe) mission to identify individual ships.
9. COVEC was similar to TacDi, but relied upon a means of transmitting vectors towards the target group and by coded message, fixing the HVA target in the centre of the designated box by latitude and longitude. It was provided by an MRR (Maritime Radar Reconnaissance) Vulcan B2 from 27 Squadron at RAF Scampton. A Canberra or Hawk aircraft was occasionally used on a LOPRO (Low Probe) mission to identify individual ships.

target. Ears pricked as the information began to paint a picture of the ships' latitude and longitude, their disposition and the location of the prime target within the SAG. Hearts beat faster as we ran towards the updated position. Then, depending upon the simulated weapon load fitted and thus the tactic to be flown, each navigator would watch for the telltale black smoke as the leader accelerated to attack speed. As his own pilot advanced the throttles to stay in position with the leader, each back-seater would bring his Blue Parrot radar out of standby and start sweeping ahead to identify contacts in a group as described by the monologist's voice. With his range and bearing marker set on the radar screen at 30nms ahead, each navigator waited until the leader called 'Bananas, Bananas', which designated the radar blip under the 30nm range and bearing cursor as the target that we would all attack in either a Medium Toss, or a laydown, or shallow bunted dive manoeuvre. The Alpha tactics required each of the six or eight Buccaneers to split apart at a predetermined range from the target to ensure safe separation of aircraft and weapon loads on the target whilst still achieving the required synergistic effect! All this took place at 580 knots and 100 feet customarily over a violent and turbulent sea! My command of English does not allow me to convey here on paper the exhilaration felt as we pulled 4G in a ninety degree bank turn with the wave tops screaming past the wing tip and the vortex generators whipping a fog of moisture over the wings. Fifty seconds later the turn was reversed with a further onset of 4G as we pulled back through 130° towards the target with the navigator's view now reversed over the other wing tip. Words cannot effectively describe the tension as the pilot looked ahead for the target, monitored the positions of the rest of the formation, and prepared to release the weapons on the capital ship in the group, and then effect a safe recovery and join up in the correct position within the formation. Whilst all that activity was going on in front of me, I had to: monitor the aircraft's height and speed; make ready the weapon system; check the radar range; contend with the high-pitched electronic screams in my headset from the RWR as the targets' warfare officers tried to bring their weapon systems to bear on the advancing and very low-level Buccaneers; and, if a missile lock was detected, direct my pilot to take any evasive action necessary. However, with less than ten miles to run to weapon release, it was now 'do or die' and if a missile found us, it would just be our unlucky day! This was an exercise, of course, and therefore the additional task of the lead navigator, amidst all this mayhem, was to make the mandatory radio call to the Fleet's Safety Cell to gain approval for the attack!

With the addition of MARTEL, tactics were developed to allow a war load of both missiles and iron bombs on various aircraft in a formation. These, known as Alpha 1 and Alpha 2, involved an initial salvo of AR MARTELs to neutralise the fleet's search radars followed by salvoes of TV missiles released at ten miles and well out of range of the fleet's defences against a Buccaneer below 100 feet! The only problem was that, with no missiles fired for real, the fleet often never knew we were there and that they had been targeted. From our perspective, apart from practising a TV MARTEL post-launch recovery, we gained no training value whatsoever from the mission. So to boost the value for both, and after simulated missile launch, the launch aircraft would all climb to 2,000 feet, reduce speed to 420 knots and cruise toward the target making like a MARTEL missile. This allowed the navigators to practise their target acquisition skills and experience the TP tracking required against realistic DMPIs before the pilots pulled out of the attack at 500 feet. It also allowed the warfare officers to track the 'missile', although the radar cross-section of a Buccaneer was somewhat larger than that of a fourteen-foot-long missile!

We were, without doubt, a well-oiled and very professional team and recognised across the NATO maritime forces as a formidable maritime attack force. The Royal Navy respected our skill, but was often dumbfounded by the fact that we were able to sneak through their defence system and attack almost with impunity. Of course, these were exercises, no bullets were fired in anger and pride meant that neither they nor we were going to admit too much in public. Without the modern computer systems available today that can determine 'kills' and order combatants out of the fight, it was often far too difficult to assess who had killed who and when or how! The Royal Navy, however, would always claim kills against the Buccaneers after our simulated weapons were in the air and heading towards them. When challenged they would always come back with the rejoinder that, 'there's no air threat at sea'! In the mid-1970s this was a difficult riposte to argue against – there was indeed no Soviet air threat at sea, but the pigeons came home to roost for the Royal Navy when, within ten years, they found themselves fighting a war in the South Atlantic against a very potent and capable Argentinian Air Force that managed to sink a number of ships that we had routinely trained against in my time on 12 Squadron.

On Northern Merger we were tasked as Orange Forces and, consequently, had a pre-ordained tasking schedule that allowed us to be accommodated in the officers' mess with regular access to the bar! The mess was once a Royal Naval Wardroom and was a vast 1960s structure with three floors across a U-shape with plenty of accommodation for a host of visitors and regular station personnel alike. The dining room was a vast cavern, and the food, cooked by RAF chefs, was to a very high standard. When we were not night flying, the mess was great to relax in, but with more than just 12 Squadron lodged there for the duration of the exercise, the bar was a good place to meet old friends and acquaintances from across the RAF. When its shutters came down at 2300hrs, The Bothy Bar was always available to repair to if you were not on the first wave in the morning; or even if you were for the hardened drinkers with whom I seemed to have fallen in! 'The Bothy' was run on an honesty basis and so end of detachment bar bills would always come as a bit of a surprise when the actual number of bar chits for beers bought in The Bothy were totted up and added to your expenses over the fortnight in Scotland.

Northern Merger was Ian Henderson's last detachment as OC 12 Squadron. It had gone very well and he was especially pleased as the aircraft taxied onto the SFD apron from the last exercise sortie and shut down their engines. All the aircrew were assembled in and around the Ops Room to find out if the exercise was actually over or whether we would be required to fly again on what had already been declared as the last day of the exercise. The duty authoriser was in regular communication with our tasking authority, but was receiving little or no information that would allow us to get back to the mess for the traditional last night booze up! Eventually, the Boss rang and spoke to 'higher authority' and, as he put down the telephone receiver, we all stood directly facing him awaiting his words with anticipation.

'That's it, chaps. ENDEX!' he said with a smile on his face. 'Everybody get to the bar. I've got a few things to tidy up here, but when I get there the first Morangies are on me!'

The rush for the exits was quite undignified, but the bar had been open and at least ten minutes of drinking time had been lost! About an hour later the Boss arrived and, as promised, cracked open the Glenmorangie[10] vault. As we drew back the pale amber nectar, he explained that he had left the navigation leader at the squadron to tidy up some of the outstanding business and answer any calls that might come in. As he was saying this, he was forced to stop as the mess tannoy system blared into life.

'Wing Commander Henderson to reception please. Telephone call for OC 12 Squadron at reception.'

He left midsentence, but was back within about ninety seconds.

'OK chaps,' he said with a studied expression on his face. 'We have just been tasked with a night four-ship against targets in the Norwegian Sea! I need four volunteer pilots and navigators who have had nothing to drink yet.'

There was a deathly hush across the assembled company. I had already had three pints of the bar's best '80 Shilling' beer and had, without any hesitation, drained my Morangie glass dry! Nobody spoke other than to question why the Nav Ldr had not told the taskers that they had already stood us down and that we were all in the bar.

A rumble of side conversations began and eventually people started to consider whether they were sober enough based on the amount of alcohol consumed! Given that the RAF had an edict of 'Eight Hours Bottle to Throttle' it seemed slightly foolhardy that some were beginning to consider going flying after a pint of beer and a glass of whisky. But a four-ship of the most sober individuals was soon organised and off they departed back to the SFD and out over the North Sea at 400 feet! My Brickfields Bungalow partner, Ray Morris, volunteered to be one of the navigators. They took off at about 2000hrs and were back in The Bothy before midnight! The mission did not go well. The tasking authority had failed to provide support to assist with target location and, after stumbling around in the dark for thirty minutes looking for the ships, they decided to abort the mission and head back to the bar. It was on the journey home that the impact of the two pints of '80 Shilling' started to concentrate Ray's mind! As they cleared Runway 23 and taxied back in the dark to the SFD, Ray, with his ejection seat made safe and now fully unstrapped, asked Tim Cockerell in his front seat to open the canopy so that he could stand on the seat and pee over the side of the aircraft! Such was the pressure that the first pint cleared the wing! And with that baptism of the starboard Rolls Royce Spey, Northern Merger was officially closed!

I spent only my first twelve months on 12 Squadron crewed with Bill Petersen. When Henry Crone moved on he was replaced as OC B Flight by Martin Engwell

---

10. A malt whisky distilled in Tain, which had been accepted universally across the Force as the Buccaneer aircrews' 'go to' favourite malt.

whom I had known on XV Squadron and now, on promotion, was to be my first reporting officer and my pilot. With Martin, I quickly accelerated my position on the squadron from wingman to six-ship and eight-ship lead navigator and also became an airborne flight supervisor and authoriser. I was also an AAR instructor and spent a significant amount of my time taking new pilots to Towline 5 off Flamborough Head to introduce them to the delights of refuelling from a Victor K2. Two weeks after our return from Lossiemouth, I found myself doing just that with a quite senior flight lieutenant – in the dark! He was a relatively recent arrival on 12 Squadron and had been having trouble with night tanking. I was briefed to take him to the tanker on Towline 5 to conduct AAR in the dark before then descending to Tain Range for Medium Toss bombing. As a QFI on Jet Provosts at one of the RAF's BFTSs, he had not seen much operational flying in the previous twenty years. He did not lack skill, just confidence, when faced with the unnatural practice of closing with another aircraft with an overtake of four knots! Tanking in any aircraft is difficult and the Buccaneer was no exception. In daylight there was a tendency to focus on the trailed basket which would always result in a 'miss', for to do so would guarantee that a pilot would 'chase the basket' and, just before penetration, the airflow over the refuelling probe on the starboard side of the nose of the Buccaneer would disturb the stable basket and result in the probe passing under the basket in its seven o'clock position. The trick was to focus on the refuelling pod and close with it from a constant position, tracking from its seven to one o'clock and ignoring the basket all together – difficult and akin to not staring at a golf ball in a bunker when the best method of getting it out of the sand first time is to aim two inches behind it!

At night it was even more difficult as the references were more difficult to see and disorientation under a starlit sky could be a killer. The basket was highlighted with luminous beads around its circumference whilst the pod itself was illuminated externally. My man this night was a basket focuser. Under the control of Staxton Wold Radar, we climbed to join the Victor at 35,000 feet and, once in visual contact, followed our leader into position alongside its port side and abeam the cockpit window such that the captain of the Victor could see his newly arrived 'chicks'. Once in position and talking to the Victor, our leader was cleared behind the starboard hose and, when settled, we were cleared behind the port hose.

'Clear contact Starboard,' called the Victor's Nav Rad over the discrete UHF radio frequency.

'Clear Starboard,' replied our leader as he moved his Buccaneer forward and very quickly informed those who were on frequency, 'Contact Starboard.'

As the traffic lights on the pod changed from amber to green, the conversation followed naturally from both key players.

'Fuel Flowing,' called the Nav Rad. Whilst almost at the same time our leader responded, 'Fuel Flows.'

All very slick, and so competently executed by these professional airmen that SOPs existed that permitted the whole procedure to be undertaken in the dark under complete radio silence!

'Clear contact Port,' came the reassuring voice from the Victor and with that my man eased the throttles forward and closed with the Victor.

'Rim,' I declared as we slid under the basket – just touching it as we did so. The Nav Rad knew that we had missed as his aircraft was fitted with a downward-pointing periscope that allowed him to monitor what was going on behind him.

Now, back stabilised behind the hose again, came the call, 'Clear contact Port,' and again we slid forward, but with no luck. I could feel the tension building in the front cockpit as we continued in a north-easterly direction up the towline and all the way down heading south-west again without any success. Turning again at the bottom, we continued to chase the tanker and the basket without any triumph. We missed, rimmed, or soft contacted[11]. My pilot was bunched and had started to introduce a sinusoidal wave into our flight path as we turned again onto a north-easterly.

'Don't try and engage the basket in the turn, you'll just set up a PIO that will make your life more difficult as we roll out,' I instructed from the rear seat. He was grateful for my advice and settled behind the Victor as the three aircraft banked into the turn. On roll out I recommended that he compose himself and reassured him that, with one final attempt, I was sure that he would do it this time. When cleared he eased the throttles forward and slid effortlessly into the basket, the nozzle engaged and the comforting words 'Fuel Flowing' reassured us that all was well and we had succeeded – for a nanosecond!

Suddenly, and with no warning, the Buccaneer lurched forward in a downward trajectory, disengaged itself from the basket and fell out of the sky. I instantly checked our altitude and began calling out key heights every 5,000 feet as I attempted to find out if my pilot was alright and what had gone wrong! The aircraft was falling in the dark quite rapidly such that the Victor and our leader were almost invisible to us, but for the regular flash of their red anti-collision lights now well above us in the dark night sky. I had made my decision that if we were still falling as we passed 10,000 feet I would resort to what is quaintly known as a Martin Baker Letdown. I had no desire to end up in the North Sea on a dark October night, but the prospects of surviving in the water were much brighter than staying in the aircraft if my man had been incapacitated or failed to recover us to level flight. We levelled off just after we passed through 20,000 feet and I reassured myself, with his agreement, that staying put had been better than a wet landing in a rough sea.

Once we had composed ourselves we agreed that the prospect of transiting to Tain for a few practice bomb deliveries no longer had the appeal that it had had before take-off so, bidding our leader goodnight, we headed back to Honington and a few post night flying beers. On the way he explained to me that as the probe locked in the basket, and with his right hand gripping the joystick tightly, his thumb had inadvertently hit the trim button on the top of the stick, which had resulted in him selecting full nose down trim. The consequent result of his inadvertent action

---

11. A soft contact occurs when the nozzle on the receiver's probe engages with the basket, but does not lock into position. It is easily identified by the fine spray of aviation fuel that escapes and covers the receiver's cockpit!

could have been catastrophic and ended this memoir here! Unfortunately, he never did overcome his angst about AAR and was soon removed from the squadron and returned to the more comfortable pastime of teaching ab initio pilots to fly.

By the time we headed north again the next year, Martin Engwell and I were very much at the front of the squadron in terms of leading and executing missions. Graham Smart had taken over from Ian Henderson as Boss and the squadron was gaining in experience in the maritime game and had developed the embryo tactics of the previous 'campaign' against the NATO navies and become a formidable force at sea. However, on this occasion we were tasked mainly as 'Blue' air assets and so were consigned to live within the SFD for the duration of the exercise rather than in the officers' mess! Picture a windswept and remote corner of a northern airfield cut off from the rest of humanity, and penned behind an iron curtain, and you have just about got a picture in your mind's eye of the SFD! Now add to it prefabricated buildings with poorly fitting iron-framed windows, remote toilet and ablution blocks devoid of heating and a prepared surface to reach them from the poorly maintained buildings and you are just about at one with the misery of its 12 Squadron occupants. Think of the worst 2-Star accommodation that you have ever slept in and add to it the equivalent of a condemned Victorian 3rd Class Sleeper train, but without any clear view window, no heating and pale green walls – no room to swing a cat or store your belongings – and your transformation is complete! Welcome to Exercise Highwood 1975!

The initial sorties on the exercise this time were described as 'harassment' sorties against the fleet. I love that word harassment in a military context. It conjures up all sorts of images, but, on exercise, it was a licence to beat up ships as fast and as low as possible before then joining a bombing pattern to conduct weaponry against the Splash Target! Sheer unadulterated hooliganism and all within the rules too! Sometimes, however, we had to be cautious as all maritime exercises were shadowed by the Soviet Navy and it was quite common to find more than one AGI lurking close by ready to listen to our radio transmissions or send our tactics back to Moscow! To the unwary eye it was also possible to think that the little boat in amongst a group of British or Icelandic trawlers was just another fisherman, but it was often not – it had a far more sinister intent!

Occasionally, if we were not flying or on standby, we were released to the officers' mess so that we could relax in comfort. But these were very rare occurrences and in the main, we spent our time in the air, briefing or debriefing a mission, waiting for tasking, or sleeping in our 'compartments'. Boredom was overcome by unending games of Uckers or dreaming up other ways to pass the time. Eventually, in inimitable RAF style, an 'Escape Committee' was formed amongst rumours of escape tunnels being dug and the occasional sight of one of the navigators, Ratty Adams, wandering the wire emptying trails of earth down his trouser leg. The passing of surreptitious notes and whispers became the norm, and in an odd way, lifted our morale as we played out our fantasy and honoured the history of our forebears held in captivity by the Germans only some thirty-odd years before! No alcohol passed anybody's lips during the ten days of Highwood other than on the only middle Sunday when we were stood down and given a day's R&R.

The Escape Committee had it all planned out! A team of about a dozen escapees, of which I was one, assembled in the SFD ready to make a run for it. Lunch had been booked at the Gordon Arms Hotel in Fochabers, which was to be followed by a tour of the Glenfiddich whisky distillery in Dufftown. Vehicles were arranged and whilst the 'guards' were not looking we sauntered out, climbed in and drove off! Lunch in Fochabers was a raucous affair with much beer and wine consumed over an excellent Sunday lunch in very posh surroundings. By three o'clock, which was about on cue for our departure for Dufftown anyway, we were asked to leave before the gentile ladies of Fochabers arrived to partake of afternoon tea! Having paid the bill, we stumbled outside, climbed aboard our 'escape' minibuses and headed south down Speyside to that river's junction with the River Fiddich, from which the whisky takes its main ingredient and its name! A tour of the distillery that culminated in their 'Tasting Room' completed an excellent day out in The Highlands and so, just before 1800hrs, we staggered back into the officers' mess at Lossiemouth to recover before heading back to captivity and more excellent flying the following week.

'Hey, Chaps!' someone called out. 'Let's have a quick beer in the bar!'

The bar in the officers' mess at Lossiemouth was just on the right as you entered by the main door. It was not easy to miss and even more difficult to avoid! So without any hesitation, and rather than head upstairs to the anteroom to read the Sunday papers, we all turned right and headed into the bar! The shutters were firmly closed. We had forgotten that the bar did not open until 6pm on a Sunday and we were five minutes early. Then one of Lossiemouth's greatest 'old retainers' was spotted in the stockroom at the end of the bar. 'Mr Mac', a locally employed civilian, had been a stalwart of Lossiemouth for many years and a friend to every officer to whom he had ever served a drink.

'Mr Mac, any chance of a beer please?' we chorused almost in unison – well it would have been had we been sober!

His response should live forever in the annals of officers' mess barmen's responses.

'Ach nae, sirs, ye cannae hae a beer cuz the bar's nae open yet!' And after a short pause to gauge our reaction. 'Mind, ye can hae a whisky whilst yer waitin'.'

God bless, Mr Mac!

In November 1975 we were back at Lossiemouth for Exercise Ocean Safari and back to being 'Orange' and the luxury that that brought of no OCT and life in the officers' mess. The flying was still fantastic, but the fixed flying programme allowed us a little more flexibility with our social programme in the bar. A huge fleet had been assembled north of Scotland and our role, once again, was to present them with an air threat. As well as HMS *Ark Royal*, with its complement of aircraft that included our sister Buccaneer squadron, 809 NAS, the fleet included a number of USN ships including two aircraft carriers, the *Nimitz* and the *Independence*. Such a formidable array of airpower, that included the air defence Phantoms from the Royal Navy's 892 Squadron, heightened the odds against our missions being a success. An unrealistic scenario it may have been, as the Royal Navy had insisted previously with regard to the lack of an air threat at sea, but we took the threat very seriously indeed and determined to get through to our targets unimpeded, and more often than not, we did.

On the very last exercise sortie, Martin and I were flying as Number 2 in a six-ship formation that required us to refuel east of the Shetlands before descending to our targets in the Norwegian Sea. As we plugged into the basket behind the Victor tanker and the fuel began to flow, our leader, sucking fuel from the starboard hose, informed us that a very thin fuel spray was discharging from the spine of our aircraft. I checked the fuel gauges in the back whilst Martin checked all his indications in the front. There was no apparent malfunction and all seemed well with the world! We stuck with it until, after about five minutes, it became obvious that the fuel tanks were not filling – the gauges were not increasing. There was no way we could continue and, as we broke away from the refuelling hose, the fuel spray from the aircraft's spine did not abate! We determined that with insufficient fuel and an apparent fuel leak, there was nothing left for it but to beat a hasty retreat back to Lossiemouth. As we set ourselves up for a straight in landing on Runway 23 I looked in the mirror and noted that as we had descended, and the air pressure had increased, the fuel seemed to be flowing even more freely from behind my head along the fuselage! It was at that point that a most disturbing call came over the radio!

'Aircraft on short finals at Lossiemouth – EJECT, EJECT, EJECT!'

Thankfully both Martin and I realised that whoever had made the call had misidentified the fuel spray as smoke, thought the aircraft was on fire and reacted accordingly. We stuck with it, landed on at Lossiemouth and walked away rather than put our trust in Sir James Martin's most magnificent invention!

Twelve months on we were back at Lossiemouth for my last detachment there with 12 Squadron and Exercise Teamwork. The bar staff had become predominantly service men and 'Mr Mac' had a new role as a receptionist on the late/night shift. Living again in the officers' mess we were unrestrained in our antics, the most memorable of which involved me, Les Whatling and the officer commanding the RAF Police Flight.

It is customary for a squadron on detachment to let the local RAF population know of their presence on the airbase! The 12 Squadron ground crew, suitably armed with cut-outs of the squadron badge, a fox's mask, in sticky-back dayglo, had made themselves known by placing these 'zaps' on various signs and road signs around the base. There were, perhaps, rather more than would have been appreciated by a tolerant station commander, but the enormous one on the front of the airmens' mess that was visible from the main gate about eight hundred yards away was, I suppose, a little over the top! It resulted in a stern warning, typed on an index card and placed on a lectern just inside the entrance to the officers' mess and outside the bar door. It read:

*'TO ALL OFFICERS IN CHARGE OF AIRMEN DETACHED TO
ROYAL AIR FORCE STATION LOSSIEMOUTH*
*All officers in charge of airmen on detachment at RAF Lossiemouth are to make
sure that squadron Zaps are not to be placed on buildings and signs around the
station.*
Signed
OC Police Flt'

This was a red rag to a bull for Les who took out his wallet, extracted a Zap and smacked it straight on the notice before wandering into the bar and buying me a beer! On our return from the squadron the next evening the notice had been replaced:

*'Would the officer who placed a Zap on the notice that referred to the placing of
Zaps on notices at RAF Lossiemouth report to OC Police Flt immediately.*
Signed
OC Police Flt'

ZAP! This new game had bags of potential and could certainly keep us and our fellows highly amused as the days of the detachment progressed. Next evening:

*'Would the officer who insists on placing Zaps on the notices that refer to the placing
of Zaps on notices at RAF Lossiemouth report to OC Police Flt immediately.*
Signed
OC Police Flt'

War had been declared. We stole that notice and popped into Reception and with the ever trusting Mr Mac's permission, typed a new notice on a piece of index card that he found in a drawer. It read:

*'Would the officer who has removed the notice about the zapping of notices that
referred to the placing of Zaps on buildings and signs at RAF Lossiemouth report to
OC Police Flt immediately.*
Signed
OC Police Flt'

Needless to tell you, a new notice had been placed on the lectern by the time we returned from flying on D-Day +4. Its tone suggested that OC Police Flt was getting particularly angry about people fiddling with his notices and undermining his authority! So we decided to inflame it even more with our *coup de grace*!

Once again with Mr Mac's permission, and his provision of a necessary ball of string and a paperclip, we went to work! Once complete, I stole the lectern and ran with it up three flights of stairs and along various corridors to find the remotest toilets in the mess. There, in Trap 1, I left it, pulling the door behind me as carefully as possible to avoid its too early detection. Meanwhile, Les set about positioning the notice we had created before meeting up with me for a beer in the bar. When OC Police Flt arrived in the mess that evening he was confronted with a piece of paper suspended by string and a paper clip from a central heating pipe above his head. It read:

> *'Would the officer who has removed the lectern that held the notice about the zapping of notices that referred to the placing of Zaps on buildings and signs at RAF Lossiemouth report to OC Police Flt immediately.*
> *Signed*
> *OC Police Flt'*

We never reported to OC Police Flt and he never ever discovered who had been pulling his wire for the previous five days! He was, however, clearly less than amused and we took great delight in eavesdropping his irate conversation with his fellows from Handbrake House[12] in the bar that evening!

Sadly, by the time the RAF Buccaneer Force redeployed to Lossiemouth permanently in the early 1980s, I was based on 16 Squadron in Germany and serving my last tour on the type. I would have loved to have served in Scotland, and particularly at Lossiemouth, but I was only ever a casual visitor.

As well as the sunny climes of the Mediterranean and the north of Scotland, as part of its operational commitment to SACLANT, a tour on 12 Squadron offered the opportunity to explore also the north-eastern corners of the NATO region. On my four-year tour on the squadron, I was fortunate to visit almost every airbase in Norway and Denmark, sometimes just for a weekend on an overseas Ranger flight, or on exercise for up to two weeks at a time. When I arrived on 12 Squadron I had never been to Scandinavia. Despite its proximity to Scotland, links to Europe in the 1960s were nowhere as good as they are today and it was only the discovery of oil and gas in the North Sea in the late 1960s and the subsequent oil and gas boom of the early 1970s that formed the economical bond that aligns Scotland (Aberdeen) and Norway (Stavanger) today. Anyway, as I have already explained, holidays in the Herriot household were idyllic if frugal and a continental holiday was quite beyond the means of my hard-working parents who were stretched as it was to educate the four of us to a standard suitable to carry us forward into later life. Moreover, in the 1960s, Brits did not take Continental holidays quite as much as they do now.

My first trip to Norway was to Bardufoss Airbase, which sits some 69° north of the equator and, thus, some 180 nautical miles inside the Arctic Circle. It was November 1974 and the squadron had been there on exercise for about a week, operating in the twilight hours of the Arctic winter and operating off an icepack runway. It was an exercise in extreme flying and I and my novice USAF exchange pilot had been deemed too inexperienced to participate fully. However, our reward for our forbearance was that we were to fly to Bardufoss on the last Friday of the detachment to join the team for the final party and a weekend in north Norway. We departed Honington on a

---

12. Station Headquarters, the administrative hub of a station, was known as Handbrake House by aircrew because any service that you requested from them was usually met with a negative response.

cold 8 November, and, having climbed to cruising altitude, crossed the North Sea towards Stavanger and picked up the airway that paralleled the coast of Norway. The sky was beautifully clear as we flew on a north-easterly heading tracking the coastline visually past Trondheim and Bodø before reaching the top of drop for our descent into Bardufoss. The planned flight time from Honington to Bardufoss was three hours and with the sun well established over the southern hemisphere in November, there were only ninety minutes of useable daylight at Bardufoss. Timing was thus critical at our destination to ensure a daylight landing. We touched down after three hours and five minutes on a hard-pack, snow-covered runway and slid gracefully to a halt as the sun finally dipped below the horizon for another twenty-two hours. Within thirty minutes of landing it was pitch dark and, with nothing else to do, we dumped our bags in our on-base rooms and joined the rest of the 12 Squadron team at Happy Hour; it was about 1430! After about four hours of drinking, ten Kroner were extracted from my hand and I, and a large handful of the 12 Squadron throng, was encouraged away from the bar with cans of beer to a laundry room in the bowels of the officers' mess. There, a RNoAF conscript was running a movie show that, as far as I could make out from my lofty perch on an airing rack, involved pigs, donkeys and naked women doing unspeakable things to each other. At a very early age, I discovered what it was that kept Norwegians occupied during the long dark nights of the Arctic winter.

The following morning started about 1130hrs when the sun eventually appeared above the horizon. I joined a motley crew that had assembled, in full Nanook of the North kit, to brave an expedition to a local beauty spot where we could walk on (ice-covered) water and admire the beauty of the frozen north. As a youthful 25-year-old, I was not normally entranced by nature's wonder, but I have to say that the scenery was outstanding and the sight of the two-inch long, ice-formed fern leaf patterns took my breath away – as did the bloody temperature! With the sun in decline at 1330hrs, we headed back to the officers' mess for a cold but inviting beer, stopping on the way to purchase a full reindeer skin to adorn my room in the mess at Honington. Back at Bardufoss a party was already in full swing and it did not take us, who had braved the cold, long to get into the mood of it.

I am not quite sure why I decided to draw a face on the back of the reindeer skin, wrap it in a blanket and present myself to the assembled throng of drunks as a ventriloquist, but that is exactly what I did! I can only imagine that, in drink, my passion for entertaining people had risen to the fore once again! Anyway, probably because of the copious amounts of alcohol that had also been consumed by the audience, it went down a treat and 'Wally' subsequently became a regular feature – 'on demand' – at many a 12 Squadron party both back at Honington and on detachment. Such was Wally's popularity that I eventually replaced the reindeer skin (it was getting tiresome re-nailing it to my bedroom wall after every performance) with a proper ventriloquist's dummy that I purchased from a junk shop in Bury St Edmunds. That dummy travelled everywhere with me on detachment and even became popular with the children of squadron members. Sadly for me, but happily for Wally, he eventually went into a happy and well-earned retirement with the Chowns, whose daughter Melanie had taken a shine to him.

By about 2000hrs on that Saturday night at Bardufoss, two of my usual partners in crime decided that it would be a bloody good idea to go into the local town, Andselv, and scout out the night club there. Drawn into their plan, I pointed out a number of facts that they had clearly overlooked in their attempt to locate an alternative hostelry to continue the night's revelry. First and foremost, it was pitch dark outside and about minus 20°C. Moreover, whilst it was a crystal-clear night and I was qualified in astronavigation, I was not keen to put it into practice whilst shivering from both the cold and an overindulgence of alcohol. Critically, Andselv is about four kilometres from the main gate at Bardufoss along a narrow road that skirts a forest and in the prevailing weather conditions and without a vehicle, it was likely that we would freeze to death before we arrived at our planned destination.

'Aah Hah!' said Wings. 'But we have a vehicle!'

'Yeth!' slurred Art Legg, 'we have got bikes!'

'Bikes!' I echoed, 'We'll freeze even quicker on bikes or die under the wheels of a car as we skate across the icy road out of control! Anyway, you may have bikes, but I don't!'

'Yeth you do,' from Art, 'we've done a recce and the command spare is leaning against the mess wall, go and get it.'

So I did, more out of curiosity as to how the evening might develop rather than for the devilment of the events unfolding before me.

Soon I was joined by Wings and Art on their 'acquired' transports and the unlawful three-ship departed the main gate of Bardufoss heading out for the delights of Ands Inn! It was, frankly, a ludicrous adventure. It was almost impossible to stay upright on two wheels on the icy road surface and with that much alcohol inside you. Three drunken RAF officers in a foreign land, on stolen bikes in a frozen waste, under a starlit sky convinced that their crime would go undetected! I guess I must have been the least drunk as I soon found myself some three hundred yards ahead of the other two who were constantly giggling and falling off with much clatter. Then tragedy struck! An almighty crash followed by a hollow moan that pierced the night air!

'Herriot! Herriot! Get back here quick!'

'What's happened?' I called out to Wings.

'Get back here quick, it's Uncle Arthur, he's broken his leg!'

I turned my bike around and pedalled back along the road as quickly as I could on the ice. When I got back to the point on the road where the voices had come from there was nobody there, only pitch blackness and the still night air.

'Dave, for fuck's sake! We need help, Uncle Arthur's fallen off his bike in a ditch and he's broken his leg!'

I searched around in the gloom for Wings and Art and by following Art's quiet moans, I located them both with the bikes on top of them in a ditch on the edge of the forest. As I approached they started to giggle and it was then that I noticed the open bottle of Teacher's whisky and the top, brimming with the amber liquid, being supped by the pair of them.

'Shit, Dave, it's fucking cold,' said Art, 'do you want a wee nip to keep you warm?'

As we sat in the freezing ditch drinking the whisky and laughing about our adventure, we saw headlights approaching from the direction of Bardufoss.

'Get down,' said Wings, 'it might be the cops.'

As we peered out of our hideaway, we saw the distinctive markings of a military police jeep travelling northwards to Andselv!

It is at this point, as I relate this story some forty years on, that I ponder the thought of why did we not turn south and sneak back onto base and return the bikes from whence they came. But we did not. We climbed back onto the bikes and followed the disappearing lights of the police car towards Andselv, where we hid the bikes behind a bus shelter and entered Ands Inn. It was not long before the police arrived in the club and very quickly we realised that the individual with them was the owner of the bike that I had been riding. I owned up immediately and offered my abject apologies to the young Norwegian officer, who had just popped out to the officers' mess to get some beer only to discover that some drunk had pinched his bike whilst he was doing so. As is the way with military personnel and the camaraderie that they share, he fully accepted my apology and the beers that we bought him in Ands Inn that night. The police were content that it was but a merry jape and departed, taking the three bikes with them back to camp and left the four of us to enjoy the rest of the evening together. We shared a taxi back to Bardufoss at the end of the night and no word was ever spoken of the event – until now!

I had many more adventures in Norway at both Sola Airbase, near Stavanger, and at Bodø, which sits just above the Arctic Circle. There is not much that one can say about a weekend in Stavanger other than that it served to inform just how expensive it was to live on the Norwegian economy in the 1970s! No wonder Her Majesty gave us such wonderful allowances whenever we visited Norway or Denmark, which was not much better. It became standard practice, wherever we went in Scandinavia, that each of us would take a bottle of Scotch as currency to buy favour or assistance from the most influential person that you met on your travels; or just to drink if the need became pressing! Routinely, this would turn out to be the first woman that you stumbled across who was invariably the receptionist in the SAS Royal Hotel – as a rule a stunningly beautiful blonde – so the motive was perhaps not always honourable! Now this does seem like a very fickle response to the situation that we found ourselves in, but I can assure you that it was not! You see, by using our aircrew guile, we ensured that we were able to chat up someone who was employed to provide us with local information, whilst at the same time, perhaps, we might just inveigle her into joining us in our evening plans as a personal guide and all for a bottle of cheap duty-free booze! I cannot ever recall this being a successful tactic for me, but it was always fun trying. The second and perhaps more important lesson learned was to make sure that you had enough Kroner in your wallet as, now being devoid of your personal ration, the price of booze in bars in Scandinavia was astronomically high and one was never going to enjoy oneself if the 'Kroner Gun'[13] ran out of ammo halfway through the weekend.

---

13. An aircrew colloquialism - From many a foray into the expensive bars in Norway and Denmark, the 12 Squadron guys coined the expression 'Kroner Gun' for your wallet and hence evolved 'Kroner Gun in fast ripple' when they were describing just how much money they had unwittingly managed to get through on an evening out in these lands of the Vikings!

In early 1975, Ray, Les and I decided that the time was right to go our separate ways and move into the property market. Much as we had enjoyed our wild bachelorhood in Culford, with Dave's departure for married life in December 1974, we began to look to our futures too! So Brickfields Bungalow was handed back to our landlady and I purchased a new-build semi-detached three-bedroomed house in Fordham's Close in Stanton, which I moved into in the late summer of 1975. It cost me £9000 and the mortgage almost broke me! It was something of a home from home as in that road, as well as a smattering of locals, there also lived a number of RAF aircrew. Martin Wistow lived almost exactly opposite me, with Pete New, an erstwhile Lightning pilot and now a simulator instructor, next door to him and further down the street were Ray Lomas, a former Canberra navigator also working at the simulator, and Mike Rudd. Mike, previously a 'creamed-off'[14] QFI, was on exchange with 809 NAS based at Honington, but was often at sea serving on HMS *Ark Royal*. So the party spirit that existed at Brickfields Bungalow continued in Fordham's Close, albeit at, perhaps, a slightly subdued pace given that some of the RAF residents were married with kids. I moved into 33 Fordham's Close with my bare but essential possessions: my large Pioneer stereo system, purchased in the NAAFI at Rheindahlen when I had been based at Laarbruch, and capable of keeping the street well entertained if I had been inconsiderate enough to leave the windows open when I played it at full volume – always; a Hotpoint twin-tub washing machine, bought for the move; an ironing board, essential to eat off and retain my military bearing; a double bed, just in case; and, on hire from Radio Rentals, the largest television available at the time, which came in a large wooden cabinet with fold open doors. Number 33 soon became known as the 'Fordham's Close Odeon'! I managed to find a second-hand settee at a house clearance dealer in Bardwell and, with my TR6 parked on the drive, I was ready to receive callers.

With Graham Smart at the helm of 12 Squadron, detachments to foreign shores to repel marauding NATO navies continued with considerable regularity and some gusto. We were always well hosted by the local military both socially and with the minimum of fuss when it came to our logistical needs. Accordingly, it became practice to organise a cocktail party wherever we went, to thank our hosts and entertain local dignitaries who had a key part to play in welcoming us and our ground crew in the local towns – there was many an airman released on bail thanks to the free-flowing whisky at a cocktail party. However, to lay on such largesse it was necessary to ensure that there was always sufficient alcohol available on the night, which would have been difficult for the squadron personnel to support even with temporary Local Overseas Allowances were it to be purchased at the invariably exorbitant local market prices. Accordingly, it was common to take a supply of duty-free alcohol with us and once, on a deployment to Bodo, I had the discomfort of deploying in a C-130 that was filled, floor to ceiling, against the forward bulkhead, with crates of beer and cases of spirits that certainly ensured that that detachment's 'Cockers P' was an outstanding success!

---

14. A colloquialism for a pilot taken straight from training to become a QFI without first undertaking an operational flying tour.

By now I was crewed permanently with Martin Engwell. Martin, a respected QFI, and I became firm friends throughout our years on 12 Squadron together, and he and his lovely wife, Ann, became the most faithful and caring godparents to my daughter Sarah when she was born in 1979. At the end of the month we deployed with the rest of the squadron to Aalborg, a Danish Air Force base in the north of Jutland, to take part in Exercise Bold Game. Aalborg was Denmark's second city and it had a distinct party atmosphere about it. We, however, were professional aircrew and we were there to provide a vital role as an anti-FPB maritime attack force. What sport! FPBs, by their very nature, are extremely manoeuvrable, and have an ability to get themselves into nooks and crannies that even the most eagle-eyed and determined Buccaneer aircrew cannot locate. It was going to be a testing two weeks, but, as we were about to find out, not only in the air!

Our arrival in Aalborg had been welcomed by a beer call in the officers' mess hosted by the resident F-104 squadron. The Danes preponderance for drinking is renowned and as hosts they threw down the gauntlet at a very early stage in our fortnight with them. The pilots of 726 Squadron drank a particularly evil concoction, a 'depth bomb', which was simply a pint of strong lager with a 'depth bomb' of aquavit submerged in a glass in the lager. It had a devastating effect and I do not think I lasted much after about ten o'clock on our first night in Denmark. Not so, other more experienced Buccaneer aircrew! Quite a few took themselves off into Aalborg to sample the delights of this ancient Danish port, promising to report back on their 'recce' mission the following morning at the mandatory in-theatre flying briefing in Aalborg Ops, given by our host ATC and Station Operations staff. The whole squadron seemed to be assembled at the appointed hour and the briefing was just underway when there was an almighty crash at the back of the room and two slightly dishevelled members of our elite management team stumbled into the room professing abject apology for their late arrival. It would seem that the unavailability of Danish taxis at 0700hrs from town to airbase had been their downfall! Additionally, their attempts to scale the perimeter fence to make the briefing time had been thwarted by an RDAF policeman and his trusty hound who had accosted them. It was only the alcohol on their breath, their exceedingly hung-over demeanour, and lack of Danish that convinced the policeman to call his dog off and allow them to proceed to their destination – their story of the police dog responding to their thrown stick, and they then fleeing into the briefing, was at the time very funny, but frankly quite implausible. Anyway, the standard for the detachment had been set and the next two weeks proved to be some of the best weeks spent on 12 Squadron of the four years that I survived there.

The Ambassador Night Club in Aalborg was a vast building on three floors with two dance floors and far too many bars for poor aircrew to work out which one he should be drinking at. I recall a regular promenade of intoxicated 12 Squadron aircrew wandering aimlessly from bar to bar in the Ambassador in the vain hope of finding whoever it was that they had not seen for, as far as could be ascertained under the inebriated conditions, virtually all of their life! Nevertheless, it became the home of the more youthful members of the squadron throughout our time in Aalborg, so much so that the bouncers became our agents, giving freely of door passes to allow us to come and go as we pleased. The Ambassador had one distinct advantage over most other ports of call in the town in that it opened about 2100hrs and remained so until 0600hrs during the week, but 0800hrs at weekends.

The deployment to Aalborg was marked also by the hospitality of our hosts who went considerably further out of their way than was the norm to make us feel welcome. Nothing was too much trouble for them and although they were the 'enemy' in the air on Bold Game sorties, they were anything but on the ground. Any excuse for a party and the Danes were up for it. Even the international aircrew football match was supported by strong drink and, when it became clear that Chunky Lewer had a pretty good pair of hands in the 12 Squadron goal, the Danes sent a Viking raiding party to tie him to the goalpost – considerately, they ensured that he was regularly refreshed with bottles of Carlsberg until the game was abandoned in favour of the Barbecue and more alcohol!

It was party, party, party at Aalborg and the stories are too many to mention and thankfully, I do not think I was involved at the forefront of every one of them, but that might just be my selective memory kicking in. Certainly, I do have absolute recall of the events of the middle weekend when my good friend Kyle Morrow and I got up rather more 'flying speed'[15] than we required at the Friday Happy Hour; if you recall, that's the Scandinavian one that starts at 1430hrs and ends about 2000hrs! After a skinful we headed off into town to sample the bars on the *Jomfru Ane Gade*[16] before heading to the Ambassador for the rest of the night. We did not return to the airbase until about 1600hrs on the following Sunday and before you get any fancy ideas about what might have gone on in between, let me assure you that we did not get into any bed in the intervening forty-four hours, nor did we sleep other than the occasional nap in the top bar of the night club. When the Ambassador closed on the Saturday morning, we were starving hungry and decided that a breakfast search was in order. We soon found a small café that was providing a service for those early risers who were looking for sustenance on their way to work. It was ideal and the bacon and eggs were just what we needed to set us up for the rest of the day. I am not sure that the bottle of Jagermeister that washed it down was such a good plan! Nevertheless, the whole feast did certainly establish our mood for the rest of our mammoth session and we set off from the café determined to stay out for as long as we were able. After a fruitless and hungover/drunken attempt at shopping, we eventually decided to scout out a few of the bars and locate other members of the 12 Squadron team. Before very long we bumped into Wings, Art, Chunky and a few others who were already enjoying a quiet Carlsberg in one of the medieval beer kellars in Aalborg. By the time we left this bar, we had consumed even more beer and I had managed to convince a drunken Wings that the pink lozenge that cleanses the Gent's urinal was actually a

15. An aircrew expression for a few quiet drinks with friends before having a few more slightly louder drinks with friends!
16. 'Virgin Anne's Street' is possibly Denmark's most famous street. It is popular with both locals and tourists for its lively atmosphere. It is said to be the street with the longest continuous stretch of restaurants and bars in Denmark.

large fruit polo! I know! I am not proud of it, but he has to take some of the blame as he was as foolishly drunk as I was and everybody else around the table knew exactly what it was that I had in my hand – anyway, I had washed it first!

Day drifted into night, and Kyle and I were soon back in the Ambassador where the rest of the aircrew had assembled for an evening of dancing and drinking with the local girls. However, by about 2300hrs I was really beginning to flag and took myself off to the top bar with the resolve to catch a few ZZZZZs and get myself back up to speed. I came to at about 0100hrs to find myself surrounded by some of the faithful who had also decided to repair a few brain cells in the quiet of this lofty retreat. Famished, we were resolving how to overcome such an affair when a local Dane, who seemed even more drunk than we were, arrived and ordered a hamburger and chips! We did not know that at the time, as none of us spoke Danish, but that is what was delivered so one must assume that that is what he wanted to eat. Sadly, by the time his food did arrive, the alcohol in his brain had sent him to sleep, but, undeterred, the waitress placed it before him and completed her part of the deal. He was solid gone! Not even the smell of the greasy repast awoke him.

I definitely heard one of our group say, 'Shame to let it go cold!' and before you could say 'scoff' it was dissected and gone – chips an' all! Whilst that was a crime in itself recoverable by offering to pay for it, the next action of the group was highly amusing, but as it turned out, disastrous for the dead to the world Dane. Slumped with both his hands on the table in front of him, one of our brethren placed the man's knife and fork in his cupped hands as if he had just consumed the meal that had been on the now empty plate before him. He stirred not one muscle whilst the gibbering Brits completed this part of their act. He stirred not one muscle for a further fifteen minutes afterwards either. He did not stir until the waitress returned seeking payment for his meal. None of us spoke Danish and none of us were quick enough to intervene even if we had been able to communicate our remorse. Still, hungry or not, he should not really have lost his rag and he should not really have unwittingly waved the knife, that he did not realise he was holding, in the waitress's face. The outcome was inevitable! Before you could say 'you're nicked', two burly bouncers arrived on the scene, grabbed the now extremely agitated drunken Dane and threw him at a door behind the bar that thankfully gave way to allow him to fall down the first flight of stairs that would eventually lead him to the street below and an ignominious exit from the night club. There seemed little point at that stage in confessing and, I think, for the first time in my tour on 12 Squadron, I was not actually a participant, but a mere observer of the proceedings, so I quietly took my leave.

I flew a total of twelve day sorties on Bold Game, which included a farewell flypast of Aalborg in Diamond Nine on route back home to Honington, and the highlight of my time at Aalborg, my first, and last, ever flight in a Danish Air Force TF-104 Lockheed Starfighter of 726 Squadron. If you have been paying attention you will recall that as a young man I had spent Saturday afternoons sneaking around the black hangars of Scottish Aviation at Prestwick Airport admiring these sleek machines of the RCAF that were there on routine maintenance. Now, some ten years later, because of the camaraderie that NATO forces have and nurture most often in the officers' mess bar, I was to fly in the back of one with Lieutenant Hansen at the controls on May Day 1975 to explore the envelope of the Starfighter and conduct a few PIs. What I remember of the hour-long mission was the uninhibited view[17] from the cockpit in all directions and the immense power from the Pratt & Whitney J79-11A engine. After we completed the PIs we turned west over the North Sea and Hansen engaged the afterburner. The acceleration was almost imperceptible, but as I monitored the gauges in the back seat it was clear that the Mach number was increasing rapidly. Suddenly everything went quiet as the aircraft broke the sound barrier, eventually stabilising at Mach 1.25 before Hansen closed the throttle and decelerated back onto an easterly heading to take us back to Aalborg. It was my first ever Mach One encounter and Hansen had, unwittingly, fulfilled my teenage dream to feel what it was actually like to be a fighter pilot!

The following weekend it seemed like a very good idea to take a trip to the Tivoli Gardens in Aalborg. The world-renowned Tivoli are actually in Copenhagen, but Aalborg's smaller version was on our doorstep and it seemed like an opportunity for some fun on the various fairground rides and activities therein as well as an opportunity for a few team beers. The afternoon was quite uneventful and we were all thoroughly enjoying ourselves when we headed towards the Ghost Train! Once again, I was with Wings, Art and Chunky, and although we had not over indulged, we were quite happy and mellowed by the beer already consumed. We stood watching as the Ghost Train came and went with its happy band of Danish children and young adults out for a pleasant afternoon in the spring sunshine. A small band of 12 Squadron aircrew began to assemble around us and some took themselves onto the cars and disappeared into the haunted hollows of the ride. Eventually, Wings and Art stepped forward, jumped into a car and Chunky and I followed.

The swing doors of the ride crashed open as our car followed the one in front into the dark bowels of the chamber. Ghouls and spectres filled the air, accompanied by ghostly music and plaintive wails, as we crashed through and around each blind corner. Suddenly, as we rounded a bend in the pitch black, I felt hands tighten around my throat. I looked left towards Chunky and smiled at him as we both realised just how realistic the Danes had made their Ghost Train. However, the hands stayed firmly locked to my neck as we careered around the track as more paper phantoms billowed before us and pumped smoke filled the air. The noises and wailing were becoming hysterical when suddenly we crashed back into the daylight only to see Art standing on the back of our car laughing his head off! We all dismounted and made off before we could be accosted by the management.

After we had been on a number of other rides, and consumed a few more beers, we were making our way towards the exit when Chunky declared that he fancied one last ride on the Ghost Train. It was about 1630hrs and we were keen to get back to Aalborg to refresh before we hit the Ambassador that night. Nevertheless, we

---

17. The Spey intakes on the Buccaneer prevented the navigator from having any view downwards without the pilot banking one way or the other.

relented and told him to RV outside the Ghost Train at 1700hrs after we had been for another couple of goes on the dodgems!

At the appointed hour there was no sign of Chunky. We asked passing squadron members whether they had seen him, but nobody had. We began to despair as time was marching on and we were now encroaching into our evening's entertainment plans. Suddenly, after we had been stood there for a good ten minutes, the doors of the Ghost Train crashed open and a beaming Chunky appeared sitting in the left-hand seat of a car that also carried a young ashen-faced Danish teenager! In his inebriated state, Chunky had decided to emulate Art by stepping out of his car to await the next and unsuspecting customer to travel through the ride! Unfortunately for Chunky, and, as it happened, the young Dane, nobody had taken a ride on the Ghost Train for about fifteen minutes, leaving Chunky stood in the dark with no idea of which way to walk to get out – until, that is, the unsuspecting youth had arrived in the dark and been confronted by his unwelcome travelling companion!

Twelve months later, Graham Smart and Tim Cockerell, with me and David Cleland-Smith respectively in their rear seats, took two Buccaneers for a weekend Ranger to Bodø. However, unlike my first introduction to Norway, mid-May is 'Land of the Midnight Sun' time in Norway and the weekend that encompasses the seventeenth has the happy excuse for being Norwegian Independence Day! Until my arrival at the SAS Royal Hotel on 14 May 1976, I had no idea that Norway had won its independence from anyone, but on handing over my bottle of gin to the blonde goddess behind the reception desk all became clear. Norway obtained its independence from Sweden on 17 May 1814 when the Constitution of Norway was signed in Eidsvoll, some thirty-five miles north-east of Oslo. However, such was the mood of the King of Sweden that Norway was returned to Swedish control in November of that year when the constitution was amended and the two countries were reunited again in a personal union under a single (Swedish) monarch. The country remained in such a state of suspended animation until Norway's parliament dissolved the union on 7 June 1905. However, with the rise of Nazism in the 1930s and the subsequent occupation of Norway by Hitler's Reich, many Norwegians believe that true independence was not reached until the Second World War ended in Norway on 8 May 1945. So, complex as history always is, that is the nub of it and if you are a Norwegian, then any day for a celebration in the summer sun is as good a day as any and 17 May was the one that was chosen! More importantly for us was the fact that, unwittingly, we had stumbled into Norway on a bank holiday weekend only to discover that we could not leave until the airbase at Bodø reopened for business on the Tuesday! Consequently, we were there for three nights rather than the planned two and, if we were to survive, our 'Kroner Guns' needed to be on 'Single Shot' rather than 'Fast Ripple'.

On the Saturday evening, the beauty behind the hotel's reception desk recommended that we take a taxi to the mountain top restaurant that sat high above the town with the most amazing view over the Lofoten Islands. It seemed irresistible, and an ideal venue for four gentlemen aircrew desirous of participating in the local culture and the fine cuisine of this northern metropolis. The taxi ride was expensive.

Most things are in Norway, but inconsequential when four people are splitting the bill and Her Majesty has lined your pockets and there is a fine dining establishment in sight! The thirty Kroner entry charge to the restaurant seemed a little steep and was quite unexpected, but hey, we were not in the mood to jump back in the taxi just for the sake of £3 each! We walked through the entrance hall of the restaurant past a Viking longboat that must have been at least five metres long and which was stuffed to the gunwales with king prawns.

'Christ, look at that lot!' said one of the merry throng!

'Jesus, Kroner Guns on fast ripple!' said another, as we climbed the stairs to the panorama restaurant above.

The maître d' found us an ideal table by the window where we were able to watch the sun drifting over the Lofotens on what was a crystal clear summer's evening. Eventually, the menus appeared and we settled down to make our choices.

'A bit pricey,' said the Boss with typical understatement.

'Fucking Hell!' said Tim, adopting a more direct approach, 'have you seen the price of the wine?'

The evening began to collapse around us as we searched, in vain, for something that would not run us out of ammo before we had even ventured to a downtown bar!

Without any warning, the wine waiter appeared at our table. Perhaps it was the revolving floor that brought him so silently to us, or perhaps we had just been too engrossed in the volume that made up the extremely expensive list of choices. Nobody thought for a second that it might just have been his absolute professionalism – posh places do tend to have well-trained, unobtrusive staff working for them. Anyway, save to say that his arrival came as a shock to us all and I for one just hoped that he had not heard Tim's outburst but a few moments earlier.

'Can I get you a drink, gentlemen?' he asked in sonorous but clear English.

Taken aback, and not prepared to lose face any further, I asked if I might possibly have a beer.

'Yes, Carlsberg would be fine.' I had not looked at the wine list but I was bloody sure that after Tim's earlier comment beer must be cheaper than wine – even this far north!

'I'll have a beer too,' echoed three English voices, and yes, they too would be happy with Carlsberg.

The wine waiter departed and left us in our financial misery. It was at that point that we agreed that the whole place was a scandalous rip-off and that we had definitely been seen off by the beauty behind the reception desk! I reckoned she either had shares in the place or her father was being held to ransom by the owner!

Eventually, we had just started to pick from the cheaper end of the menu when our wine waiter arrived with the Carlsbergs!

'Gentlemen, if I can be of any help with the menu, please let me know.'

'Well actually, you could assist.'

'Sir, was it explained to you at the door?'

'Was what explained to us at the door?'

'The cover charge. The thirty Kroner.'

'No – we paid thirty Kroner, but nothing was "explained" to us.'

'Gentlemen, the thirty Kroner allows you to help yourself to as many king prawns in the Viking longboat that you can fit onto your dinner plate.'

Things were beginning to look up and, as we took our first sip of our beers, things got even better.

'You can go back to the longboat as many times as you like,' he finished.

'I see,' we chorused as one voice, realising that the safety catches could be put back on the Kroner Guns for at least the next couple of hours.

We spent a marvellous three hours in the restaurant, eating our prawns until we could eat no more, whilst watching the sun dip below the Lofotens before returning above the horizon some thirty minutes later – the sky did not darken and no longer did our mood. We left the restaurant much happier beings than when we entered and full of at least three bottles of their finest red wine. After all, it was one of the cheapest places to eat in Bodø; and Kroner were designed to be spent on booze. Kroner Guns to fast ripple!

On our way to the hotel's cellar disco the following night, Dave and I noticed that every house in the town was patriotically flying the Norwegian flag in celebration of the weekend's festival. These were no small flags! Each house was adorned with a piece of red, white and blue cloth that would have covered a good-sized family table. We agreed there and then, and without the Boss overhearing, that our next challenge was to each steal a Norwegian flag from a flagpole to take home to adorn our dining rooms. It was a great plan and well thought through too. After the disco closed about 0300hrs, we would sneak from the hotel in the dead of the night and shimmy up the closest and shortest poles to retrieve our individual prizes. Dave would support my climb and I would support his. We would be back in the hotel and in our rooms before anybody knew what had happened.

When the disco closed, the Boss and Tim headed up the stairs to their rooms whilst Dave and I lingered in the entrance admiring the receptionist (not the same one, but they are all beautiful and blonde, you understand). When the coast was clear we ducked through the doors of the hotel to be confronted by – broad daylight! We were, of course, in the Land of the Midnight Sun and the flags stayed firmly on their flagpoles as a result!

By now I had fallen in love and, I hoped, this time it was for keeps. It all came about after I had been chatting to Mike Rudd in the bar at a Honington Happy Hour when, out of the blue, he had said: 'You ought to meet my sister! Why don't you come round for dinner tomorrow night?'

I had heard about his sister, but had never met or seen her. If the rumours were to be believed she was attractive and blonde; I was doing nothing on the Saturday night so accepted Mike's invitation gladly. A relatively short period of courting followed, and, by late 1975, we were engaged, with our wedding date set for 25 September 1976.

Pace on the squadron did not diminish throughout the period of our courtship, and I found myself under considerable pressure to ensure that my relationship held and my career progressed, but I have to confess that being in a relationship with a woman once described as having the body and looks of Olivia Newton-John meant that it was the career that took to the sidelines, as I was determined to ensure that I did not lose this one. Sure, I flew as often as I could and I deployed on exercise when the task demanded, but I spent more time wooing than I did studying to pass the C Promotion Exam and took little or no interest in the first step on the Individual Staff Studies programme, which was designed to groom young officers for future stardom! Life was too short for that nonsense. I had a good woman at home and I had a lust for operational flying, so bugger the consequences! Of course, I did not advertise that view, but it must have been self-evident to those tasked with managing my career. What is more, despite my desire to settle down with Sue, I still behaved like a fool when I had a drink inside of me. I was, I know, a thorn in the flesh of Graham Smart and whilst he admired me for my professional ability, he must have despised me for the case load of flak that I often brought to the squadron on a Monday morning after a particularly good Friday night in the bar!

I know that I upset him on a number of occasions with my brash exterior and my Glaswegian sense of humour. Not least on a squadron detachment to Bodø when, at the end of a particularly good evening of cocktails, etc, with our hosts, he was obliged to give a speech in response to his counterpart's gracious thanks for the function that we had just given, and in which he mentioned our professionalism, our party spirit and the strong bond between our two nations. The whole speech was given in Norwegian, with a young RNoAF captain providing a simultaneous translation into English. It was met with resounding applause from the gathered aircrew, station personnel and local dignitaries, and had come, I am sure, as a great surprise to Graham Smart, who, undeterred, rose to his feet to respond. Off he set, ad-libbing his speech in perfect English and broadly smiling to the assembled company. The smile soon left his face, however, as I sidled up beside him and began to provide simultaneous translation in Norwegian. OK, I have never had a Norwegian lesson in my life, but I had seen the Swedish Chef on *The Muppet Show* and, inebriated as I was, it just seemed a reasonable thing to do with a bit of inflection here and there, and the occasional '*Pho de hädo*' and '*hönda shæda*' thrown in. The place erupted in laughter, but the Boss was not impressed.

I also upset him significantly after he led an abortive Lossie-based six-ship mission to attack a SAG in The Minch. After landing he conducted a particularly speedy debrief and concluded by asking for any points from the floor. Mine was the only hand raised! I challenged him as to why he had tried to lead six Buccaneers down to low-level under a blanket of cloud that was clearly too thick and too low to be safe to do so. I know I should not have been so direct in my approach and I know I should not have used profane language, but I respected him so much as an aviator and a leader that I was carried away by the moment and my own, I suspect now, self-importance.

He closed the debrief immediately and left the room asking me to follow. Outside the room he said: 'Don't you ever do that to me again!'

I apologised.

'What I did today was dangerous and you were right to tell me so,' he responded, 'but, don't ever do that again in public!'

He was livid, but was man enough to admit his mistake and I respected him for it. He too respected me for my professionalism, if not for my tactless outburst in front of the ten other aircrew! The thing that we all knew and respected in the Buccaneer Force was that we flew this aircraft at the extreme edge of its envelope and in some of the most hostile conditions. It was not a role, an aircraft, or a mission to be toyed with. Consequently, debriefs were honest affairs and often quite cut-throat, but they had to be, lives depended upon it! However, they were not that cut-throat that the Boss should be humiliated by a junior officer even if he was a potential QWI! As we always did, especially after a particularly hostile debrief, we repaired to the bar at Lossie and the whole issue was forgotten and mutual respect maintained.

Graham Smart had appointed me Squadron Standard Bearer in time for the squadron's 60th Anniversary celebrations on 21 February 1975. A lot of preparation went into organising the parade and I had a key role to play as the squadron was to be presented with a new standard on the occasion. Research was conducted to identify a suitable past squadron commander to present the new standard to me, and the troops took to the ASP to practise their drill so that the standard could be protected by two flights of airmen and officers as it was paraded before the assembled guests. Bruce Chapple and Chris Donovan, who had a particularly steady and neat hand, were tasked with sorting out the guest list and invitations. Others were tasked with roles within the marching body whilst I was taken aside to practise marching with the standard and kneeling and standing before the drum alter upon which the new standard would be blessed. All went swimmingly well, and those tasked identified a First World War ace and former 12 Squadron commanding officer in 1929, Air Vice-Marshal F.H.M. Maynard, as a suitable individual to present the new standard. Helpfully, the AVM's son was then the current Commander-in-Chief of RAF Germany and a likely candidate to ensure that the invitation fell into the right hands.

The response from Air Marshal Sir Nigel Maynard was informative, but terse. His father, who was to die less than a year later, was too infirm to attend let alone present a standard, but that he, as C-in-C, would be more than happy to oblige on his behalf. The squadron was over a barrel. Sir Nigel had absolutely no connection with the squadron and was not even remotely close to being on a reserve list to present the standard, but, with his renowned belligerence, nobody was prepared to tell him that he was not welcome. It was decided, nonetheless, that whilst the son would present the standard, the father would be invited along to observe.

The planning continued. When they were not flying, Chapple and Donovan hid themselves away in an office upstairs and busied themselves designing the guest list and preparing invitations. Chris, in his best calligraphy, prepared a practice invitation in order to scale the task and on it he wrote Air Vice-Marshal Sir Nigel Maynard CB, AFC. And to explain that further for this story: that was father's rank; son's title and forename; father's awards! He then got on with writing the invitations, leaving the practice invitation on the desk before him as his sample. Suddenly, the door swung open and Chapple and Donovan were hauled out to airtest an aircraft that had just become available from servicing. Whilst they were airborne, the Boss ordered two junior officers up to the office to start putting invitation cards into envelopes.

Unbeknown to the two replacements, in his haste to respond to the flying task, Chris Donovan had swept the practice invitation onto the floor and stood on its reverse side as he exited the office!

When Sir Nigel Maynard received his invitation in Germany, he was appalled to see that it had his father's rank, his title and name, but his father's post-nominals. Moreover, when he flipped it over and found the imprint of a size 9 flying boot on its reverse, he was incandescent with rage, and our poor squadron commander found himself strapped to a Buccaneer heading for Laarbruch with his best uniform in the bomb bay and an interview with the C-in-C that required him to wear a hat, but was not accompanied with a cup of coffee!

Sir Nigel was in no better humour when he presented me with the new standard and, as I knelt before him at attention, he rammed the base of the standard into the receiving 'box', which was sitting at the end of my Standard Bearer's Cross Belt and just above my groin! I winced and then grabbed as I realised that he had not 'slowly released the standard as the Standard Bearer slowly and sedately raised his hands to take responsibility for it', as he had been required to do from the briefing provided by his PSO. I just managed to catch it before it passed through forty-five degrees, when gravity would have won the battle with my right bicep to recover it to the vertical!

As part of our ASuW role, it was common practice for squadron aircrew to take to the high seas with the Royal Navy to witness our tactics from the target's perspective. Routinely this would require a Sunday afternoon train ride to Portsmouth Dockyard and a leisurely sail up the North Sea on a Leander or Rothesay Class Frigate to Rosyth, all the while being attacked by Buccaneers for the five days of the working week and then an express train journey back to Peterborough, and thence, at a sedate pace, onwards to Bury St Edmunds just as the bar closed after Happy Hour on the Friday. Reports were strong of the value of the experience both from a tactical and a social point of view!

'Dave, a quick word if you will.' It was Len McKee who was tasked with arranging 'Navy Weeks'.

I followed him along to his office and sat down opposite him.

'It's your turn for "Navy Week" this coming week. Up for it?'

'Yes, sir!' I replied. I was up for anything and had heard good reports from those who had been before.

'OK! But yours is not the standard,' said Len.

My heart sank a little as I wondered just which short straw I had just been selected for.

'You have to report to HMS *Fife* in Chatham dockyard on Tuesday, 27 May.'

I was speechless with delight. HMS *Fife* was a County Class destroyer and was far more potent than a frigate and considerably larger too. But Len had not finished.

'The ship will sail on Tuesday evening and head through the Channel into the Bay of Biscay and on Friday, it will park up in Bordeaux for a three-day trade fair where it will be used as a cocktail party platform for the British Consul. It will then return to Portsmouth. You will be away for ten days total. Is that OK?'

'OK, Sir? It's fantastic! Thanks very much.'

It was a truly fantastic experience. As the only Crab[18] on-board, I was a bit of an oddity and it took some of the ship's officers a little time to get used to my presence. However, there were only thirty-three of them and it did not take me long to win them over. As the ship made passage through the Channel, we were regularly attacked by marauding Buccaneers from 12 Squadron and, as the ship was put through its paces, I watched with a clinical eye as to how the ship reacted to the air threat. Heated discussions in the bar afterwards became routine as the ship's warfare officers tried to counter the points I raised about the effectiveness of our tactics. They never did take the point that our weapons would have been released long before the aircraft overflew the deck and that all our weapons were targeted against just one ship in any convoy. Their final words were, as always, 'Well, there's no air threat at sea!' As previously stated, that might have been fine when talking about the Soviet Navy in 1975, but in 1982, when the Argentinian Air Force and Navy caught numerous British warships holed up in the Falkland Islands, things were very much different and a significant number of British warships were lost as a result of air attack.

When we were not under attack, asleep, or drinking in the bar in the evenings, I was given guided tours of the ship or went flying in the ASW Wessex Mark 3 with Lieutenant Brian Hodge at the controls. I flew twice with him. On the first sortie, I was winched off the deck into the helicopter and on the second, after lift-off, the ship turned and sailed immediately into a fog bank, which necessitated us having to do a CCA to get back onboard! Unlike a GCA at a military airfield, which uses radar height and azimuth to determine the aircraft's position relative to the glideslope, a warship's CCA overcomes azimuth issues by the chucking of smoke floats off the stern of the ship, thereby assisting the crew with locating the ship in the fog! It could only be of any use to helicopters, I hope!

As *Fife* made its way slowly inland up the River Garonne and towards Bordeaux, the ship's company were tallied off to perform Procedure Alpha[19]. I had decided to stay below and out of the way, but after three days at sea, and fully integrated and indoctrinated, was informed that I had earned my place and so, if you look very closely at the photograph, just above and left of the ship's pennant number, you will see a Crab participating in Procedure Alpha!

In order to keep the ship's company out of mischief in Bordeaux, a full entertainment programme had been organised. As soon as we had tied up alongside and customs formalities had been undertaken, three large coaches pulled up and we disembarked for a visit to a wine cave. Further tours over the three days in Bordeaux included one to the Ricard factory and one to the village of Cognac, where half the ship's company visited the Martell distillery whilst my half went to the Hennessy distillery. Each

---

18. Derogatory term used by the Royal Navy when referring to the RAF. The blue RAF uniform is similar in colour to the grease (known as 'crabfat') used on Navy gun breeches. The grease was so called because it in turn resembled the colour of the ointment used to treat sailors for 'crabs' (genital lice!).

19. A procedure for entering port. Other than essential crew to man the ship, the lower decks are cleared of all non-essential personnel who then take up pre-determined positions along the rail on the upper decks dressed in best blue uniform and SD hats.

evening, dressed in our best uniforms, the officers of HMS *Fife* and I entertained the British Consul, a number of sales teams from British Defence industries and various local dignitaries, to a traditional Royal Navy Cockers P fully supported by a band from the Royal Marines.

The Royal Navy do these things so well, but then you cannot beat a warship if you want to impress! It was quite a fantastic three days and the effort that had been made to keep the troops entertained and out of trouble was quite monumental. There must be nothing worse for a host city than the prospect of hundreds of drunken matelots roaming the streets as one bar after another ejected them and they sought refuge in another. The Shore Patrol was routinely deployed to collect waifs and strays, and, where necessary, drag serious miscreants back to the 'chain locker' to cool off! So whilst the entertainments programme worked well during the daylight hours, it was not completely watertight. It was quite common to see packs of roving, drunken sailors as they meandered through the alleyways of Bordeaux, their legs unable to carry them forward in a straight line or even support their weight reliably. Most were at least able to navigate their way back towards the dock; however, many were drunkenly elated if and when they bumped into the Shore Patrol, which was always happy to take them home for a night in the cells.

On the Saturday night, after a particularly lively Cockers P, I went ashore with Hodge and the Medical Officer. We had already got a bit of 'flying speed' up with the unrelenting flow of cocktails and enjoyed a few more bars and beers amongst the happy throng that were enjoying the delights of Bordeaux that night. By 2300hrs, however, we decided to knock the partying on the head and wend our way back to *Fife*. She was not difficult to spot as her superstructure towered above the rooftops of the buildings surrounding the port and she was illuminated from stem to stern with bright party-like illuminations. Slightly inebriated, we climbed the gangplank, stopped, saluted the quarter-deck and headed off to the bar for a nightcap. Not, however, the medic, who was accosted by the Officer of the Watch at the top of the gangplank and invited below to deal with a number of drunken sailors, two of whom were suffering from stab wounds. I doubt that they received the neatest sutures ever stitched, but I suspect that they awoke the following morning completely unaware that they had received them!

With the trade fair over it was back to sea and home via Portsmouth. Having not had the privilege of flying Buccaneers off the deck, my introduction to the Royal Navy and HMS *Fife*, in particular, was a valuable one.

By mid-June 1975 the squadron was back in Malta for yet another Exercise Dawn Patrol. Again, and not unexpectedly, it was a lively affair, with the now regular consumption of beer and forays downtown to Valetta and Sliema for a change of scene after a hard day's flying at 100 feet and 500 knots over the Med. Martin and I had found ourselves pretty heavily involved in the initial tasking on this Dawn Patrol. So, after four days of early starts to fly two missions a day, plus a night sortie to regain currency, we were feeling a little punch drunk. Happily, after a discussion with the following morning's programmed flight authoriser, it was agreed that we had earned a lie in. We would not be called for the dawn patrol the following morning. Now a nod is as good as a wink to a blind man! A lie-in in Malta in any aircrew language normally means a few Hopleafs or Cisks the night before. In Buccaneer language it equated to: a few Cisks; soaked up by a pizza at Il Fortizza in Sliema and chased by copious amounts of Marsovin Special Reserve; before a few Hopleafs at the Hilton Casino; a drunken cavort with any passing tourist (or yourself) on the minute Hilton dance floor and racing back to catch the bar at Luqa before it closed for the night at about 0200hrs. A perfect evening for a young 12 Squadron officer who has been guaranteed a lie-in! Assuming, of course, that the authoriser was true to his word; but then you would trust him to be honest wouldn't you? It came at 0400hrs, after just two hours of unconsciousness!

'You two, out of there! Transport's outside to take you to the squadron!'

'Christ!' we each thought as we came to in our twin-bedded room, 'there must have been a complete change to the attack plan if we are being called as well!'

We struggled awake and attempted to dress in our flying suits. To be fair Martin was more sober than I was, but it was very early and neither of us had had much sleep! After about ten minutes we were booted and spurred and in the wagon.

'Christ! This must be for real, nobody else here!' I thought out loud.

I wondered what time the rest of them had been called if this was a lie-in! There was nobody else there when we got to the squadron, just the authoriser! We were to probe the Messina Straits for the morning wave that was still tucked up in bed; take-off was to be 0600hrs! No ifs or buts were listened to and so we set to the task of planning, marshalling our brains and getting airborne into the gloom on another dawn patrol. With the wheels in the well and Malta in our quite dark rear-view mirrors, Martin settled XN976 at 600 feet and 420 knots as we headed into the Mediterranean pre-morning sky. Messina was not far, just east of north a bit, and keep on trucking until you get Sicily and Etna on your left-hand side. Anyway, this was what the old Blue Parrot was designed for. Pick out a few ships, see a coastline, navigate your way between the lumpy bits, and when the sun comes up, transfer a few pennant numbers to a DISPORT[20] matrix and start bleating to the attacking force. OK! I overdid the grape and grain mixture last night, but I knew I could hack this, and anyway, I could now see on my radar screen clearly a long line of warships congregating in single file to the north of the Messina Straits ready to penetrate the gap between Sicily and Italy's famous toe. So we set to our task. There was no point in progressing too far north as it was still dark and we would not be able to see the numbers on the sides of the ships, so a racetrack to the south seemed appropriate whilst we awaited their arrival from the Tyrrhenian Sea. On the northbound leg, using my Blue Parrot radar, I watched and assessed their movement through the gap, whilst on the five minute southbound leg of our racetrack Martin and I made sure that our cockpit housekeeping was in order and discussed just how we would proceed once the ships were through and back in a hostile formation. Up and down, up and down we flew at

---

20. A method of locating and identifying warships on an alpha–numeric grid square for subsequent transmission to an attacking force; akin to the game 'Battleships'.

300 feet and 420 knots, with the sun, all the while, making its slow and post-slumber journey above the horizon. It was going to be another very hot day in Malta.

I was very happy with our position. I could see quite clearly the coastlines of Sicily and Calabria on my radar and I knew that we were positioned well out to sea and clear of any of the hard lumpy stuff that can ruin the day for an unwary airman. The weatherman had told us that there would be no cloud below 1500 feet and that the wind would be calm, and although I could not see any cloud in the dark, I had no reason to doubt him. In addition, the radio altimeter warning was set at 200 feet and with us not cleared below 300 feet in the dark I was happy that I could leave the flying to Martin whilst I concentrated on the task in hand. Slowly but surely the ships ventured south. Slowly, but surely, the sun rose in the east. Slowly but surely the darkness of night formed the glow of Morning Civil Twilight[21]. Suddenly the mountains of Sicily and Calabria began to appear dimly out of our cockpit. As the sun rose further above the horizon, the glow of its warming rays illuminated more of the steep slopes of Etna and the beaches that proliferate the eastern shores of the island. More importantly, however, the arrival of the day proved just how wrong a weather man can be and how dangerous it was to fly in the area south of the Messina Straits where high tension electricity cables traverse the straits to provide Sicily with the electricity it needs to sustain its population and industry! The cloud was lapping our cockpit in places and the cables were no more than 1000 feet above the sea at their lowest point. It had never occurred to either of us in our mind-fuddled state at 0400hrs that any such hazard was worthy of consideration over the sea. We survived! We grabbed as many pennant numbers as we could and identified which was the capital ship and therefore the primary target in the group. I transferred the detail to my DISPORT card and began to transmit on our exercise frequency to anybody who was willing to listen. After two hours and forty-five minutes we landed back at RAF Luqa somewhat chastened by our experience, but much wiser aircrew for it.

Although Bill Petersen and I had been selected to fire a MARTEL missile at Aberporth Range in October 1974, circumstance contrived against us. We had been allocated missile six; the last of those allocated. Fully trained and prepared, we flew our mission perfectly until, at the 'minus thirty seconds to launch point', the missile indicated that it was unserviceable. With much disappointment, and in accordance with the Misfire SOP, we diverted to STCAAME at RAF Valley in Anglesey where the missile was downloaded and sent back to the manufacturer for analysis. However, 1975 brought another allocation of six missiles and now, crewed with Martin Engwell, my name was pretty much at the top of the list to fire one.

On Monday, 6 October, with our missile firmly attached to the port wing of XT281, we set off for the range in Cardigan Bay supported ably by our wingman, who, similarly loaded, would act as the reserve firer if anything were to go amiss with our systems. We had to be in the descent to low-level overhead Harlech and on range frequency with clearance to proceed. Harlech was just ten minutes flying time from

---

21. The period when the geometric centre of the sun is 6° below the horizon (civil dawn) and the sun rises fully above the horizon. Length varies dependent upon latitude.

the firing point and whilst Martin checked in with the range and advised them of the missile's number, I had to carry out a number of checks that included ensuring that the Mode Selector was in 'Nav', Terminal Phase was switched 'Off', Fuse Mode was set to '2', Breakaway was selected 'Port', and Aperture set to 'Wide'. On a heading of 296° magnetic, we continued our descent until we were two minutes and ten seconds beyond the Llyn Peninsula when we commenced our turn onto the attack heading of 160°. Halfway round the turn, at the five minutes to launch point, whilst Martin made his weapon selections in the front cockpit and ensured that we were stable at 2,000 feet, I turned on the cockpit voice recorder, ensured that the 'Lock' light was out and checked that we were tracking towards our designated target. Continuing our descent, we established ourselves at 200 feet and 420 knots with thirty seconds to go. I had checked that I had a 'Present' lamp, had turned on the Weapon System Performance Recorder, checked over and over again that Terminal Phase was 'OFF' and tried desperately to steady both my breathing and my nerves. This was a very expensive missile and there would be no acceptable excuses if I were to screw things up at this point! With just fifteen seconds left, Martin checked that the firing trigger was set to 'Live' and I confirmed that the 'Ready' light for the missile was lit. Now holding our heading constant and maintaining the wings level within five degrees, Martin made sure that we were in the best possible position to launch the missile. My only role at that point was to ensure, once again, that Terminal Phase was 'OFF'. As we passed 'Zero Hour' the range controller, whose telemetry systems would track the missile in flight, called 'Clear to Fire' and without a moment's hesitation Martin squeezed the trigger to send our twelve-hundred-pound and fourteen-foot-long missile on its way to a watery grave.

For an almost imperceptible moment nothing happened. Then, with a roar and a sudden marked yaw to starboard, I watched in amazement as the telegraph pole that had been our companion in flight for the last forty-five minutes or so took its leave! It flew clear of the aircraft and entered a climb to establish itself at, or about, 2,000 feet and 420 knots, heading directly towards our allocated target. I did not have long to watch it as almost instantly I felt the g-force come on as Martin banked and pulled XT281 into the required escape manoeuvre. With the wave tops flashing by just 200 feet below, I quickly regathered my composure in time to see that the data link had been established with the missile and a very fuzzy picture of the wave tops was beginning to appear on the TV screen situated between my legs! The missile performed perfectly and, before I knew it, its 10 nm flight was nearly over as the target, a triangular construct with three vertical sides, each of which sported a black diamond on a white background, hove into sight on my TV. I selected Terminal Phase and with the joystick on my right-hand side, flew the missile as best as I was able into the target. It is not the most comfortable of experiences to view the end game of a missile travelling at over 480 mph whilst, apparently, sitting in its front seat! Thankfully, we were now comfortably at 2,000 feet and heading for RAF Valley and lunch. My missile, I was subsequently informed, struck the target on the edge of a diamond in the ten o'clock position – not bad for a first attempt! I was luckier than my wingman that day. The following day he and his pilot flew exactly the same profile, but when he selected Terminal Phase his missile decided that it preferred the sky to the sea and entered a vertical climb. There was nothing he could do to stop it. The last he saw of it was when it entered cloud at about 3,000 feet heading for outer space. The range had to destroy it, but not before the missile had flashed past the nose of an RAF Phantom tasked, as part of the trial, with seeing if he could catch the missile in flight on his CW radar and obtain a firing solution for his Skyflash missile. He had not anticipated the MARTEL missile taking exception to this and he went off back to Leuchars with his tail between his legs and probably to seek a change of underwear!

Exercises in Gibraltar were just as much fun as were our regular trips to Malta. The 'Rock' was, and is, very pro-Brit and, as history explains, Gibraltar has been dutifully faithful to Great Britain ever since it was ceded in perpetuity by the Treaty of Utrecht in 1713; almost as if it were, like Scotland and Wales, part of the UK mainland. The only disadvantage that Gib had over Malta was that in the 1970s it was constrained by having a sealed border with its Spanish neighbours, who remain as disgruntled about the 'Rock's' history today as they were in 1713.

We usually and regularly deployed there for an exercise called Open Gate. However, little was 12 Squadron prepared for the adventure that unfolded and the trouble that ensued the day the Boss declared, on a windswept morning at Honington in April 1976, that 'Gib may close because the wind is from the south, but we are going anyway!' And with that he left to lead the first of three pairs to the tanker and onward to the sunspot at RAF North Front. His last words to the now agog remnants of the deploying aircrew were, 'Listen out on HF, any probs and we'll divert to Lisbon!'

OK, that'll be fine then! Best we follow at the planned fifteen-minute interval! Martin Engwell and I led the second pair whilst Norman Crow and Ken MacKenzie, they of the errant MARTEL missile, brought up the rear, which was by now a three-ship, as the Boss's wingman had gone unserviceable on start, but had made it to the spare in time to join on as back marker. So all plain (excuse the pun) sailing then! All six airborne, all gassed up from the tanker over Land's End and onwards to Gibraltar until…

'Mike Charlie Romeo Oscar Alpha (the Boss) to all chicks inbound Gibraltar,' (on HF), 'transmitting blind; Gibraltar closed, diverting Lisbon.'

Now is that Lisbon International Airport buried deep in the urban heart of the city, or the military base at Montijo that sits happily in rural tranquillity across the estuary of the River Tagus? Well, whatever, it was going to be one of them and a navigational steer might be apparent when we speak to someone on the other end of a radio!

Aahhah! It's International, then!

'Right, Engwelly, how are we going to set ourselves up for this one?' I asked from the comfort of the backseat of XV340.

'Straight in pairs?' It was a rhetorical question from my professional and responsible pilot.

'Seems good to me.' was the only appropriate reply as I delved deep into my Nav Bag for the appropriate TAPs, which had been quickly stuffed in there following the Boss's parting shot at Honington.

In we came, a 'Pairs ILS' to land! Nothing simpler, weather gin clear, saw the runway from miles out nestled amongst the rooftops of the city and landed on with our wingman tucked neatly on our starboard side. We rolled to a slow pace behind the 'Follow Me' truck and taxied to the Portuguese Navy dispersal where the Boss was already practising his language skills. We climbed out, met our unsuspecting hosts and started to put the Buccaneers to bed; we were there for the night. Well Lisbon had to be a different run ashore, but nothing would deter us from the plan. Gib/Lisbon; Lisbon/Gib, interchangeable really! Then the first spot of trouble loomed! Norman Crow and his two wingmen had seen the runway from a long way off too and had decided to dispense with the TAP, ILS and any other ground-mandated arrival procedure; they had been cleared for a 'pitch'[22] and pitch they were going to… at 580 knots and 50 feet off the ground… at an International Airport!

'Ahh Shit!' Said a new voice behind us that subsequently introduced itself as Commander Johnny Johnston, the Naval and Air Attaché from the British Embassy in Lisbon! 'I wish he hadn't done that. This place is really very sensitive right now and it would have been better if you had not come here at all!'

Now I have been unwelcome in many places across the Globe, but usually upon departure as the result of events undertaken, but never upon arrival when no alcohol-induced actions have yet taken place. This was a new one on me!

'So what's the problem?' said a now very relaxed Graham Smart, who having spent a while with the Navy in a previous incarnation, was at ease with his opposite number the attaché.

'Elections! First free election for twenty-five years and the Communist Party is riding on a wave of popularity!' he replied, 'I have booked you chaps rooms in the Penta Hotel and have a bottle of Scotch and two hundred fags[23] for each of you; eat and drink in the hotel and do not under any circumstances go on a run ashore tonight!' He watched our shocked expressions. 'I need you guys as low profile as possible and out of here in the morning when Gib will reopen!'

Fair enough then! Penta Hotel – bar, restaurant, bottle of whisky, cigs and a bed – what more could hungry, tired aircrew need? Nothing actually, until they have emptied the bar and bottle, filled their stomachs and are ready for some action!

'Fast Black's outside!' I recall were the last words I heard before I found myself with Mike Perry (our RN exchange pilot), Martin Engwell and a few others inside just another bar in another town in another country in NATO. That was when the trouble really started! Having been at the forefront of the call for a run ashore, we next saw our navy pilot atop the Communist Bandwagon with a Soviet Red Flag in his hand whilst careering around the streets of the Portuguese capital cheering for a revolution! Thankfully no arrests followed, but we did notice the rather unfortunate

---

22. Run and break in RAF speak. A procedure used by high-performance aircraft to join an airfield traffic pattern without requiring the aircraft to spend a long time flying at low speed. As such, it is a procedure normally used by military aircraft at military airfields and is designed to reduce the aircraft's exposure time to hostile enemy action.

23. If you are reading this book following an American education, I can assure you quite categorically that we were not each supplied with 200 'fags' in Lisbon – fag in my language refers to cigarettes!

headline on the Communist Broadsheet on election morning as we merry souls departed for Gib: 'BRITISH AIR FORCE JETS IN LISBON TO SUPPORT CAPITALIST CAUSE!' Oh well! We did not mean to get involved and if the Boss had not insisted that we launched to a doubtful Gib, things would have turned out very differently.

Not long after our return from Gibraltar I was detached from 12 Squadron, with Dave Ray as my pilot, to undertake No. 5 QWI Course. An intense course that lasted three months and would entitle me forever after to hold the title Qualified Weapon Instructor and take no prisoners when it came to weaponry debriefs on the squadron after a sortie. It was an arduous three months both in the classroom and in the air, where every mistake, every idiosyncrasy and even every personal habit was scrutinised and commented on at a very personal and candid debrief in front of your peers! The detail of the course will, for reasons that will become apparent, be covered in the next chapter.

No sooner was the course over and the QWI tick awarded than it was back to my fiancée, back to the squadron and back on exercise to Lossiemouth for Exercise Teamwork that would last until 23 September. I had arranged my Stag Night for the night of the twenty-fourth! The following afternoon Sue and I were married in All Saints Parish Church, Stanton. I felt rough!

Although the wedding took place in the afternoon, the excesses of the night before had taken their toll by the time Mike Hall and I rolled up outside the church. Given the lack of time between the end of the Lossiemouth exercise and the actual wedding, the Stag Night had been done in the traditional style. No long, and unnecessary, weekends in Krakow or Hamburg in the 1970s, just a night in a pub with my mates and, as was the norm, on the last possible night of 'freedom' too! The Dun Cow in Bardwell was the chosen location and a strong team of ne'er do wells assembled there to ensure that my life of bachelorhood ended with true ceremony! We drank long, we drank fast and we drank hard! By the time the bar closed, I was not the only one the worse for wear! But no matter, nobody cried, 'Not for me, Boss' when Graham Smart called us all to reassemble at his house just a mere ten minutes' stagger from the pub. Loathe to leave, but encouraged by Mike to do so, he and I took up the rear of the conga that meandered through the night to be served 'eggy bakes' by the Boss's faithful and quite unsuspecting wife, Jane! Mike and I arrived at their cottage last and by some margin too! The others were all assembled in the living room and we could hear the welcoming chatter through the open lounge window; it was a balmy late-September night. I do not quite know why, but it seemed a good idea at the time to enter the house via the lounge window rather than by the front door! Jane was, by now, in the kitchen frying eggs and grilling bacon and so the only witnesses to this escapade were my fellow drunks and the Boss who, by now knowing me for a drunken fool, was not at all amazed or disturbed by my entrance. However, my fellows, realising that I was the worse for wear, took pity upon me and shepherded me to a chair by the fireside and sat me down before I could get into any more trouble. Somebody put a beer in my hand and, eventually, Jane entered the room, gave me a welcoming smile and some words of marital encouragement, whilst at the same time she stuffed an 'eggy bake' into my other hand. Boy! Was that sandwich welcome! The warmth of the food healed my worried soul and the beer quenched my raging thirst. I was at one with my fellow aircrew and ready for the day ahead and my future life as a family man.

It was then that I noticed a couple of rather attractive African Violets in their pots in the hearth. Beer sunk and 'sarnie' consumed, that little devil who rather too often appeared on my shoulder pressed me into action. He had got me into trouble many times in the past in the search of a laugh and he was about to do so again! I picked up the first pot, soaked up the aroma of the flora sufficiently energetically to attract the attention of my chums and then, with everybody watching, bit off the flowers of the *Saintpaulia* and chewed them sufficiently to allow me to wash them down with my second beer. Undeterred by the gasps from my audience, I picked up the second and did likewise! After a pause of two seconds, loud guffaws filled the room. The Boss was not amongst those amused by my trick and when his wife re-entered the room I could tell that she was definitely not amused!

What I had not known, and would probably have ignored anyway in my drunken state, was that Jane Smart was especially delighted with her *Saintpaulia* 'breeding programme'. She had quite an array of African Violets around the house and the two that I had consumed were some of her best and proudest blooms!

I have no idea what time Mike Hall ushered me into a taxi and took me back to the officers' mess to sleep off both the alcohol and my guilt. It was late and the head that welcomed me on the morning of my wedding day was not a very happy or clear one. However, it was clear enough to allow me to realise that I needed to right a wrong, and so, on my wedding day, the first task that I set to was to repair as best I could the damage I had caused Chez Smart. Off to the florists I drove, purchased the biggest bundle of flowers I could find and headed off to Bardwell to convey my sincerest apologies to my hostess for consuming her prized flowers. Jane, I am pleased to say, accepted my apologies with good grace and wished me well for the rest of the day.

By now detachments on 12 Squadron were becoming the routine. We seemed to be spending more time away from home than at base. Certainly, in February 1977, and again in May, we spent much of our time in a fogbound Denmark waiting to participate in a JMC, or on Exercise Bright Horizon and Bold Game. Each of these was planned to exercise our tactics against NATO navies in and around Jutland, but most of our time was spent watching the fog clear to just below flying limits or checking the bottom of empty beer glasses in the officers' mess bars at RDAF bases Skrydstrup and Karup respectively. It was tedious and morale on the squadron had dropped, partly because of the constant time away from home, but also because the weather was precluding the thrill of getting the wheels in the well and heading off into the blue to scout out ships to bash! There is only so much beer you can consume and there are not too many delights in the towns of Vojens and Viborg for homesick aircrew! We had crept into Skrydstrup under a lifting fog on 17 February 1977 and not a wheel had turned for the rest of that week. By the time Saturday morning came, the decision had already been made to get out of the place and head off to Copenhagen to view the Little Mermaid and other such delights, not least of which was the Vin & Ølgod bierkeller! We set off from Haderslev railway station early in the morning, and hoped to arrive in the Danish capital with sufficient time to get two good sightseeing and drinking days in the city. We were booked into the Savoy Hotel and were very much looking forward to a team run ashore. Unfortunately for the other passengers, we had decided to get up some 'flying speed' on the journey, and before the train puffed into the hold of the ship that would carry us across the Great Belt and onwards across Zealand to Copenhagen. I had probably drunk more than I should have at that early stage of the weekend, but was undeterred as I led a team of equally drunken officers through a door on the upper deck that found us inside the funnel! All great fun, but not quite so when the dope at the back of the conga closed the door and we found ourselves traipsing about in the dark looking for a way out! We escaped sanction by the captain, who failed to notice that this motley crew of passengers had penetrated the innards of his ship and so we returned to our seats and quickly blended in with the crowd before we were reported by a crew member and made to walk the plank!

Upon arrival in Copenhagen we made for the Savoy, which was nothing like its namesake in London! The hotel, which is situated at Vesterbrogade 34 in the city centre, was built in 1905 and, in 1977, was a relic of a past luxury age. Its décor was dark and the drapes were positively archaic. The reception desk was inside and on the left, and just before it was an ancient elevator that would carry us to our rooms where we could dump our bags before heading out for our first beer of the afternoon! Having checked in, we crammed six people into the tight box with its concertina metal door that formed the lift cage and, once on-board, stuffed our bags into a corner. The lift struggled to move, but slowly and surely it ascended while all the while sparks flew from the electrical contacts on the door jamb! After each salvo of sparks the lift juddered to a halt until one of our number, who knew and understood these matters, jammed his foot firmly against the door whilst it rose another few feet amidst a myriad of sparks and the occasional audible crack! Somebody had the audacity to point to a sign on the side wall that indicated '3 Personnen Max'. Undaunted, we carried on regardless and, after chucking our bags in our rooms, were surprised to discover that the lift had been declared unserviceable by the management, which forced us to descend by the stairs to get on with our sightseeing. It was, perhaps, a clever ploy by the manager who happened to be awaiting our arrival at the bottom. Our defence of being unable to read Danish was pretty woeful and the two chaps who offered Mickey Mouse and Donald Duck in response to being asked for their names did not help matters! Nor did the manager's letter to our squadron commander when it arrived in his in-tray some three weeks after our Copenhagen adventure! A 'hats on without tea' meeting in the Boss's office followed for all! I cannot be sure, but I am bloody convinced that he was smiling to himself after we all trooped out suitably chastened! Thank God nobody had seen Graham Seaward leaping from the roof of one bus shelter to the next as the rest of the gang moseyed drunkenly along a Copenhagen thoroughfare looking for the next bar to set the Kroner Gun to fast ripple in!

By the time Martin Engwell and I led a four-ship of Buccaneers to Karup on Friday, 20 May 1977 for our next deployment, the weather had improved markedly. After a quiet weekend bedding in and sampling the delights of Viborg, we were quite ready to get involved in Bright Horizon on the Monday morning, leading a six-ship against targets in the Kattegat. We did the same the next day. Exciting stuff! It was difficult enough to find them in and amongst the many inlets that form the east coast of Jutland. But actually achieving a successful weapon-firing solution against agile FPBs was nigh impossible, but great sport. It was the perfect cure for a hangover. Thursday of our first week at Karup was my twenty-eighth birthday and the weather forecast for that day was particularly poor. It seemed right, therefore, to celebrate my birthday a day early as there was no first wave scheduled. That night we stayed rather too long in the officers' mess keller bar where, following its Nazi construction in 1940 as Einsatzhafen[24] Grove, a Swastika formed the centrepiece in its mosaic floor. However, with flying not programmed until noon, there was plenty of time for the birthday boy to recover!

One of the things I learned on my twenty-eighth birthday was never to believe the Met Man! 26 May 1977 dawned without the promised mist and poor visibility, with the only hazard for unprepared aircrew being a patchy low cloud base and a very bad headache for yours truly. The odds were in my favour. There were eighteen crews on the squadron and only a third would be required should a six-ship be tasked! Damn! There I am! Toted to lead a four-ship with Engwelly for a 'Baltic Recce'! So, just a trog around the Baltic keeping an eye out for any NATO warships. Nothing really operational, more an exercise in getting the squadron's flying hours target up to date.

We climbed out of Karup to 1000 feet and headed in a generally south-easterly direction past Aarhus and across Zealand towards the entry to the Baltic Sea. When we coasted out we bid farewell to Danish air traffic control. They who had been monitoring our progress and keeping us clear of airliners heading for Copenhagen. We changed frequency to 'Icecap', the callsign for the GCI station situated on Bornholm Island that guards the entrance to the more easterly extent of the vast sea.

'Icecap this is Red Section, good morning, on handover from Copenhagen,' I called over the radio whilst also monitoring our height in the descent to 100ft over the sea.

'Red Section, good morning, this is Icecap, you are clear as per Flight Plan,' came the reply from the Danish controller on the island.

Our plan was to descend to low-level and fly a very simple route in Battle Formation[25] around Bornholm, to then skirt the Polish Bight at the 12nm territorial limit, before we exited through the 40nm gap between Sweden to our north and East Germany to the south. It was the height of the Cold War, Sweden was a neutral country and the Soviet controlled East Germans were very much hostile to our very existence. The Blue Parrot was my friend. It would be very easy to avoid both territories if I stuck to our plan and used the radar to identify coastlines as and when they appeared. Nothing could go wrong and, having selected one hundred per cent oxygen shortly after take-off, my headache was beginning to clear.

---

24. Operational base.
25. A defensive formation flown at 2000 yards lateral separation. It allows each element to keep a check on the 6 o'clock of the other, making the formation less vulnerable to an unannounced rear sector fighter attack.

'Good morning, Royal Air Force!' said a very heavily accented voice over the Icecap frequency as we established ourselves at low-level. I did not reply.

'Vood you like to see a nice Russi…an varship?' It continued.

'Bloody hell!' said Engwelly, 'who is that?'

'I have no idea, but I'm going to ignore him!' I replied.

'Kom right thirty degrees for nice Russi…an varship,' said the inanimate tone.

'What shall we do?' Engwelly again.

'OK, come right thirty degrees and let's see what happens.' I responded.

Martin eased us right onto a heading of 150° and the three other aircraft in our formation followed suit.

'Keep coming, Royal Air Force,' said the voice, and so we did. We were now pointing straight at East Germany and the hairs on the back of my neck were beginning to stand on end. I was also sobering up very quickly!

'That's right, Royal Air Force, nice Russi…an varship dead ahead now!'

There, about 5nm ahead and sat at anchor, was a Soviet Navy Polnochny LST. We flew directly overhead it and, as we did so the voice spoke again.

'Good morning, Royal Air Force!'

'Christ!' I called on the intercom. 'Come left ninety degrees and let's get back to what we are supposed to be doing!'

Martin cranked the aircraft round onto 060° and, without a word of command, the three wingmen executed a perfect Battle Turn and took up their defensive stations with numbers three and four 2000 yards abeam on our right-hand side and Number 2 in Arrow on our left wing. I was, frankly, bloody glad to be heading back to track and mightily relieved that Red Section had not just turned the Cold War hot! After a further five minutes at low-level, whilst Martin and I were pondering just how the Soviets had been able to pull such a stunt, I heard the voice again and this time in much less threatening tones.

'Good Morning, Royal Air Force!'

We had just flown underneath a West German Navy Atlantic MPA! The buggers! The Atlantic crew had seen us coming in more ways than one!

We turned onto a southerly heading around the back of Bornholm and headed towards the Polish Bight, content that with judicious use of the radar, I could maintain the formation outside Polish waters and, thereby, avoid any further international incidents. Despite our earlier detour our fuel was more than sufficient to complete the task and get back to Karup in time for a bit of Egyptian PT[26] before the rigours of the night and the inevitable supplementary birthday celebrations.

'Red Section, Icecap, you have two bogeys heading north at speed at 10,000 ft!'

Two! Heading north! Anything heading north towards us must be over Poland, my throbbing brain computed.

'Roger, Icecap, acknowledged,' I responded.

'Red Section, bogeys now at 30nms closing.'

'Roger.'

---

26. Aircrew slang for an afternoon nap.

'Dave, are you sure we are outside Poland's territorial waters?' asked my man in the front seat.

'Absolutely, we are definitely well outside the 12nm limit and will soon be turning north-west and back towards Karup,' was my reply.

'20nms, Red Section.'

'Acknowledged.' And with that I watched in amazement as our Number 4 peeled off south and headed towards the two, probably Polish Air Force MiG-21 Fishbed, interceptors.

'Oh bloody hell!' over the intercom. 'Prissick has just declared UDI and gone off to see what he can find!'

We did not need to worry, Mal was not that stupid to risk causing an incident or, for that matter, mad enough to think he could take on two fighters in a Buccaneer. He was very quickly back in formation and at the debrief let us know that he just wanted to see how they would react if challenged. By the debrief we knew exactly how they had reacted because Icecap had informed us thirty seconds after Mal had stabilised on a southerly heading.

'Bogeys have turned onto south and are heading back into Poland,' came the call. Chickens!

The rest of the trip was uneventful, no international incidents occurred or were reported and the four-ship landed back at Karup after an hour and thirty-five minutes and I was very soon horizontal and preparing for the night ahead!

The squadron returned to a fogbound Denmark one last time in March 1978 and, apart from flying to Stavanger for a weekend Ranger, I flew only one sortie throughout our twelve-day deployment. The other weekend was spent in Hamburg where we drank in the world-famous, 1200-seat capacity Zillertal Bier Halle on the Reeperbahn. We ventured, out of curiosity, to Herbertstrasse, a short cobbled street with a three-metre chicane-type barrier at either end. A sign at the entrance, in both German and English read: 'Entry for Men under 18 and Women Prohibited'. An inquisitive peek around the barrier explained why. Each of the terraced houses in the street had a large plate-glass window and behind each sat an attractive but naked woman unashamedly advertising her wares. Of course, we knew that such an occupation could be found all over the St Pauli area of Hamburg, but I, for one, had never realised just how blatant the activity was. We chose to view Herbertstrasse, the Palais D'Amour and the like from a distance.

Dick Back and I were programmed as Number 2 in a four-ship to undertake a laydown bombing exercise on Römö Range on Monday the thirteenth! The range is located on the north shore of the island of Römö just to the west of Jutland. Because aircraft were not allowed to overfly the island, the laydown bombing pattern had to be flown around the island to the south. The sortie was going according to plan until we approached the target for our second pass. At 200 feet and 500 knots we hit a massive flock of seagulls. The aircraft juddered violently and the smell of burning flesh pervaded the cockpit as two or three of them were sucked into the engines. The aircraft started to climb slowly, but the juddering did not stop. I called to Dick to regain communications and got no reply. I called again as the aircraft began to roll slowly to starboard. We were passing about 800 feet and things were now getting serious. Still no reply. In a split second I had made my decision, if the aircraft were to turn upside down any chance of survival from an ejection at low-level would be lost. I placed my right hand on the lower ejection seat handle and placed my left hand firmly around my right wrist and prepared to pull. Dick suddenly called over the intercom, 'I've got it, Dave!' Although the aircraft was still juddering, Dick slowly regained its equilibrium and levelled us off at 2,000 feet. I relaxed my grip on the handle and quickly transmitted a PAN[27] call on the international emergency Guard frequency. We organised a visual inspection from one of our wingmen, and with the aircraft still shaking violently, prepared for a straight in approach to Karup with a very flat-fronted and a not at all aerodynamic nose to our aircraft. We had lost the complete radome! We landed back uneventfully at Skrydstrup and started the business of writing up an Incident Report.

The summer of 1977 was a wonderful one and during it Her Majesty the Queen celebrated her Silver Jubilee. In the Herriot household the anticipation and excitement of a newborn boy or girl due in late August kept our emotions high. Life on the squadron became more stable, with no detachments other than a four-day sojourn at Lossiemouth in July for Exercise Highwood, a jaunt to Decimomannu in September for our annual APC and, for a change, a major maritime exercise in the south-west approaches flying out of St Mawgan in October. Moreover, by the time winter arrived, I had in my hand a posting notice to the OCU in April 1978, which would allow our new family to bond without the hassle of having to up sticks and move elsewhere.

On 13 June, Engwelly and I were invited over to the station's secure vault for a briefing with the Stn Int O. With the squadron EWI, Dave Wilby, present, we were informed that a Soviet fleet that had sailed from Murmansk, and been shadowed by Norwegian MPA around North Cape and down the Norwegian Sea, had been lost after the shadow task had been handed over to an RAF Nimrod MR2. Our task, using two AR MARTEL war stock seeker heads fitted to training missile bodies, was to find them! 'Them' were two Krivak 2 frigates, one Kresta 2 cruiser and a Boris Chilikin AOR. They had been last seen to the east of the Shetland Islands on a south-westerly track and were predicted to be heading for Cuba.

Not an easy task! It was akin to looking for a needle in a haystack. Every time I had been tasked to find warships at sea previously their last position was known and somebody was keeping a beady eye on them! This was a completely different ball game, but the S and X-band war seeker heads would undoubtedly be of some assistance; but I for one had no idea by how much!

Back at the squadron, Dave Wilby briefed us in a closed room about the MARTEL technique to be used after we had left the Victor tanker, with which we were to rendezvous over Tain Range at 36,000 feet. He was explicit that I was not to switch the missile heads on until we were abeam John O'Groats and in the descent from

---

27. A step down from a MAYDAY call. It is used to signify that there is an emergency on board, but that for the time being at least, there is no immediate danger to anyone's life or the aircraft.

high level. That way he was convinced they would do what they do best; identify the Topsail surveillance and the Headnet C acquisition radars on the three warships. Suitably briefed and duly authorised we walked to XV349 on the ASP, confident that we could complete the task off the north coast of Scotland, land at Lossiemouth then refuel and recover to Honington before the sun went down.

As we filled our tanks at 36,000 feet, I decided that I was going to ignore the EWI's brief and so turned both missiles on. Routinely, if I recall correctly, they took about five minutes to warm up, but within less than two minutes one of the seeker heads indicated a pretty solid lock about ten degrees left of the nose! I informed Martin in the front seat and we agreed that despite the gypsy's warning of doing so too early we should stick with it and leave the missiles switched on. Leaving the tanker and entering a descent to low-level I switched the Blue Parrot from 'Standby' to 'On'. Given our height at that stage, I had to tilt the scanner downwards to improve the picture. Nothing! Absolutely nothing! In desperation I tilted the scanner further down to ensure that I could get a view of the coastline below us and, sure enough, there they were in all their glory, Cape Wrath to the west and John O'Groats almost immediately on the nose. I tilted the scanner back up, pleased that the radar was at least working, even if nothing was visible in the sea ahead. Then I saw it. A very faint blip just left of the nose and about 200nm ahead. I checked the steer information being offered by the MARTEL and informed Martin that I had a radar response two hundred miles ahead and exactly on the bearing that the MARTEL indicated. We came left five degrees and continued our descent until we were 100 feet above the sea. The MARTEL missile was now very positively and solidly locked onto a Topsail radar! Pushing the speed up to 480 knots we closed on the bearing until suddenly, on my radar, I saw quite clearly four radar returns that appeared to be in a tight huddle and just 30nm ahead. On receiving this information from the back seat Martin pushed the throttles up and we very soon settled at 540 knots[28]. At the twenty miles to go point, Martin declared that he had four warships on the nose and pushed the height down even lower. Just over two minutes later we shot in front of the bow of one of the Krivaks and pulled up to 1000 feet to survey the scene below us. There they were, just as briefed at Honington. The Kresta 2 was standing off the starboard beam of the Boris Chilikin at about 1000 yards, the recently accosted Krivak was behind by about double that distance and the other frigate was quietly minding its own business latched onto the refuelling pipe of the tanker whilst it undertook RAS operations. They were doing no more than ten knots and were sitting ducks… for a bit of fun? With our planned landing at Lossiemouth and almost no fuel used during our not very lengthy search of the ocean, we had bags of gas to hang about and watch proceedings unfold. Slowly the ships made their way to the north of Scotland and about 150nms off the coastline. It was time for a few beat ups! But beat ups within the rules! NATO military aircraft were not allowed to fly over WP warships lower than 500 feet and no closer than 500 yards. Anything outside that bubble was fair game. So off we went to show these Soviet sailors just what the Buccaneer was capable of.

---

28. 620 mph, 9nms/minute or 304 yards/second!

Down on the deck and at 580 knots, we thrashed around between and past the four ships. I had been given a camera to take appropriate photographs to be analysed later. So occasionally we would pop up and slow down to allow me to snap our enemy. We were there for forty-five minutes putting the Buccaneer through its paces when, all of a sudden, the captain of the Krivak that was now no longer attached to the AOR, decided to let us see just what he could do. Its bow rose out of the water and, from almost a standing start, the frigate shot forward with such force that the wake very quickly grew and grew behind it. My TR6 could accelerate from 0–60 in 8.2 seconds; the Krivak was the Soviet Navy's TR6 equivalent. Within a minute he must have been doing in excess of 30 knots! We landed at Lossiemouth slightly chastened by our experience, refuelled our jet and set off back to Honington through the Highlands at 250 feet and a sedate 420 knots. It had been some day with the Soviet Navy.

Later that month a substantial flotilla of warships was assembled in the Solent as part of the Silver Jubilee celebrations. A Spithead Review by the Queen was scheduled for 28 June 1977 and in and amongst a host of nearly one hundred and fifty Royal Navy vessels of various sizes were a number of warships from far and near neighbours. Significantly amongst these was USN *CARGRU 6* led by the nuclear-powered cruiser USS *California*.

Nine days after our success against the Soviet Navy, Engwelly and I were tasked to lead a pair of Buccaneers to provide simulated attacks against the US fleet, which was, by the twenty-second of the month, in passage to the south and west of Ireland. We found the targets easily, and, having completed our attack, were invited to undertake a 'flyby'. In 1977, the bow section of the *California* was exceedingly 'clean'. Its SSMs were housed in silos set into the deck and there were no obstructions to impede our progress at very low-level! The rules were also different for NATO ships, there was no 500 foot and 500 yard bubble around the ships like there was with the Soviets. As low as you can and as fast as you can was fine with clearance from the ships concerned. It was not, however, a sensible tactic to fly across the stern of any ship as that was where the gulls concentrated, and a gull and a jet engine do not usually make for a very happy congregation. Martin told our wingman to follow us through and set himself up to pass in front of *California's* prow; well that is what it looked like to me from my slightly elevated and off-set right position in the back seat, and at about 5nms out from the target. As the ship got closer and closer, and as we settled at 580 knots, it became self-evident that we were not going to fly in front of the ship! We flew just above the SSM launchers and at no more than thirty feet over them! As we did so I looked left and up at the bridge and straight into the eyes of the captain, who was smiling down at us as we creamed across his ship's bow. Gathering ourselves together with our wingman, we saluted the ships goodbye with a low pass from stem to stern and headed back to St Mawgan to prepare ourselves to do it all again later that day and again the following morning.

My son Christopher was born in late August 1977 and, without the luxury of Paternity Leave then, I soon found myself back on detachment and separated from my family once again. By mid-October, 12 Squadron found itself at RAF St Mawgan attacking many of the ships that had participated in the Spithead Review. The routine for Exercise Ocean Safari was very much the norm and one with which we were all well practised. Fly, drink, sleep, fly, drink, sleep, fly, drink… etc, etc. We deployed to the south-west on 16 October 1977, a Sunday, and set to the task on the very next day. For the next twelve days we flew continuously and often twice a day. Out from St Mawgan straight to low-level over the sea, onto operational frequency and, once found, attack the ships and RTB. As the ships progressed further into the Atlantic, we often had to extend our range by taking fuel on board from a Victor tanker. Many of the missions were over two hours in length and on one, with tanking outbound and in, Martin Engwell and I clocked up three hours and thirty-five minutes in the air on a singleton probe mission into the Bay of Biscay. On the second last day of the exercise I received an early morning call and was surprised when I arrived at the squadron to discover that Martin Engwell was still in bed. My task on this morning was to fly a probe mission with the Boss, and despite my rather immature and inappropriate treatment of him in the past, we held mutual respect for each other as professional aviators and had flown a number of times together.

We took off in the dark and headed off into the South-West Approaches, looking for one ship that had slipped the convoy and needed to be located and attacked. This was a different affair from my past adventure in the Messina Straits. For a start I had not got bladdered the night before and although still dark, the weather was gin clear, with visibility beyond the curvature of the earth. We had been allocated a square box, an area of 2,500 square miles, to search for the ships. Its centre was some 150nm to the west of St Mawgan. A tanker had been allocated to support us and would stay on station whilst we climbed to suck fuel and then descended back to the task in hand before returning for another top up. There were no ships at sea that morning. Certainly none that were remotely close to the search box and none in and around it either. We searched in vain and, when necessary, climbed to 27,000 feet to suck some gas. We were beginning to despair when I suddenly noticed a radar contact well removed from the box and just to the south of Ireland. I told Graham that I had a contact, but was inclined to ignore it because of its location. He, equally desperate, suggested otherwise, as there was little else inviting our interest. I gave him a heading of 285° and he pushed the throttles forward to cover the sixty miles or so quicker in case it was of no interest and we had to get back to the box and resume our fruitless task.

By now the sun was rising in the east and a faint glow was reflected in the rear-view mirrors in the cockpit. It took just less than nine minutes to cover the distance and before too long the structure of a large vessel began to appear on the horizon, assisted by the glow from the morning sun. There was a definite white glint off its superstructure and, having quickly identified it as a civvy, I called Graham back onto a south-easterly heading to return to our search.

'Hang on a minute,' he said. 'Let's take a closer look.'

He pushed the throttles up until we were cruising at 580 knots, and with the sun now just above the horizon, dropped our height down to somewhere in the region of 100 feet! We shot past the *QE2* at deck-line height and, as we got abeam her stern, Graham pulled the nose up and rolled the aircraft rapidly right before straightening the wings and continuing our climb.

'That'll wake the buggers up!' It was 8.30am and breakfast was probably just being served!

We never found the ships and returned to St Mawgan after three hours and thirty minutes, deflated by our disappointment, but with a secret smirk hidden behind our lips! No complaint was ever raised and why should it have been? We were going about our business, doing what we were tasked with and attempting to find a needle in a haystack! Of all the needles that I found in the maritime haystacks on 12 Squadron, none shone so crisply as Cunard's flagship, the *QE2*! It was to be one of Graham Smart's last acts as squadron commander, as he left on a pre-planned posting upon our return to Honington and was succeeded by Wing Commander Peter Harding.

The Christmas break provided small respite from the rigours of life on the squadron and with 1978 there came an early year deployment to Gibraltar and Malta for Exercise Springtrain and Exercise Sardinia 78 respectively. Peter Harding had not completed his Combat Ready training and so a small detachment of four aircraft was deployed under the leadership of Squadron Leader Phil Leckenby; Leckers to his mates!

With my impending departure for the OCU and the need for Martin Engwell to establish himself with a new navigator, I was crewed with Bill Graham for this deployment. Our task in Gib was to attack ships in passage through the Straits of Gibraltar and we were supported by a Nimrod MR2 that provided us with TacDi to allow us to locate, track, identify and attack the capital ships in the SAG. However, on one sortie, when we had under-flown the Nimrod at 100 feet following his direction to the target, the captain of the MPA took the odd decision to file an AIRMISS[29] report against the four-ship of Buccaneers. Odd in that we were talking to him on the radio, he knew where we were at all times and we were at least nine hundred feet beneath him. The end result was that Leckers was summoned to see the Gibraltar Air Commander, an air commodore well versed in the workings of the RAF's MPA fleet, who tore him off a strip and made it quite clear that, in his view, Nimrods had priority over every other aircraft that had ever taken to the skies – that probably included Wilbur and Orville Wright!

Leckers was still steaming when he arrived in the officers' mess bar at RAF North Front later that evening and determined, after a couple of beers, to respond to the air commodore once we were out of arm's length and firmly based in Malta the following day. His signal to the Maritime HQ in Gibraltar read:

> *'Buccaneers now deployed to Central Mediterranean area, trust this now gives Nimrod sufficient airspace to operate!'*

The eight of us piled into the officers' mess at RAF Luqa in Malta and immediately clocked a large poster on an easel beside the reception desk. It declared: 'Valentine's Party, Friday, 10 February 1978, Officers' Mess RAF Luqa, All Welcome'. Perfect!

---

29. An instance of two or more aircraft in flight on different routes being less than a prescribed safe distance apart.

Sardinia '78 was scheduled for just two days and would end mid-afternoon on the tenth. A few beers at Happy Hour, a Valentine's Party, a late night and a quiet weekend patrolling Sliema's City Gem and other haunts, and a sedate high level transit back to Honington on the Monday morning would complete a very pleasant week in the Mediterranean. Bags installed, we headed to the bar where we bumped into the aircrew of 29(F) Squadron who were in town to complete an air defence APC, flying and firing against a banner which was pulled through the sky by a target-towing Canberra. They were a lively bunch and we soon fell in with thieves!

After our early morning sortie against the ships off Sardinia, Bill and I and the rest of our four-ship headed back to the mess for lunch and were astounded to see that, since breakfast, the party poster had been emblazoned with a banner that now declared that the party was for RAF Luqa permanent mess members only! Disheartened, we started to come up with other plans for our Friday night after Happy Hour ended.

29 Squadron were not down-hearted, however, not even as a result of the fact that it was their doing that caused our, and their, misfortune! Apparently, earlier in the week and before we fell out with the air commander in Gib, one of their number had meandered his very intoxicated way to the toilet to offload some of the many Hopleafs that he had consumed in the bar. Staggering backwards in front of the urinals, he had steadied his sinking ship by grabbing hold of the copper piping that ran their length. 'Twas to no avail! The whole shooting match separated from the tiles (that's Maltese workmanship for you) and he came to with the piping across his chest and the flood waters growing around him! Result! A rather draconian decision taken by the PMC, a Wing Commander Greenhalgh I recall, to ban all visitors from the weekend's festivities!

In the bar on the Thursday night, 29 Squadron declared that it would make no difference to them as they were now planning a 'black tie' pizza extravaganza at the Il Fortizza restaurant in Sliema! The whole squadron was going to head down there after Happy Hour! We had still no plan and arrived at Happy Hour quite disappointed that we had failed to come up with any plan, let alone anything that would get us another drink after 1900hrs when the bar was scheduled to close. We need not have worried. As the shutters came down on the bar, and out of embarrassment for the decision that had been taken by the PMC, members of the resident Canberra squadron appeared at the bar door carrying crates of Hopleaf and Cisk that they left with us for the evening whilst they went off to get into their DJs for the Valentine's Party. We tucked into the free beer just as a tuxedo-clad 29 Squadron hailed taxis to take them into town for a pizza!

Just after 2230hrs we heard a loud clamour of voices in the bar entrance as 29 Squadron returned fully inebriated and stuffed with pizza. They were intent on having a party and had come up with the idea of holding an 'alternative' party in the Ladies' Room. One of their number, sporting dark glasses and carrying a white stick, was tasked with dispensing tickets from a roll of toilet paper. Just one sheet was required to gain entrance. Meanwhile, the rest of their team carried crate after crate of beer into the designated 'alternative' spot! We, of course, were all invited, and by the time we had finished the last of our donated beers and got to the Ladies' Room the far wall was completely covered in crates of beer from floor to ceiling! It was going to be a good and long night!

As more and more of the beer wall emptied, things began to get out of hand. 29 Squadron formed up in single file and each man, in turn, assumed the role of a brass player and made the appropriate sound and hand movements of his chosen instrument. With the 'band' assembled, they fell to their knees and waddled off into the main party blasting out, 'Hi Ho, Hi Ho, it's off to work we go' on their imaginary instruments. They shuffled their conga down the corridor and through the dining room, where the mess members were enjoying their private party to the absolute bewilderment of the station hierarchy, the delight of the junior revellers and the fury of the PMC. They were soon back shuffling into the 'alternative' venue with most, if not all, of the mess members who realised that our party was far better than theirs! The PMC was incandescent with rage and stormed from the mess whilst the now combined revellers cheered with delight! Our four Buccaneers landed back at Honington having left two senior officers in the Mediterranean reeling from the hammer blow cheek of Buccaneer and Phantom aircrew!

Ah! Malta! What a jewel in the Mediterranean! A Second World War fortress so brave it was awarded the George Cross. An island of people so beloved of, and by, the British. An island of potholes and churches. An island where the drivers of ancient buses sat on the edge of their seats to allow the good Lord to settle beside them. An island where the sun never stopped shining. An island that provided the Royal Navy with one of the best deep water harbours in the world and an airfield for the RAF to mount operations in and around the Mediterranean, North Africa and onwards to the Middle and Far East for many a decade. An island that, under Dom Mintoff, aligned itself with Libya and Muammar Gaddafi and, despite previous bon accord, threw Britain and its Armed Forces out of the country!

An island that was, most definitely, one of 12 Squadron's best playgrounds in the 1970s. What a shame, no more runs ashore to Sliema, no more meals in the City Gem, no more pizzas at Il Fortizza, no more Blackjack at the Hilton Casino and, most thankfully, no more adventures down The Gut!

I flew my last sortie on 12 Squadron with Peter Harding on 14 April 1978, packed my professional belongings into a holdall and carried them two hangars east to take up my post as an instructor on 237 Operational Conversion Unit. As I wandered those two hundred yards, I pondered the thought that I doubted that any 12 Squadron navigator could deny that at some stage in their maritime tour over the salty wastes that they were never temporarily unsure of their position!

Chapter Ten

Training, Trapping and Trouble

The Buccaneer was not an easy aircraft for pilots to master. The lack of a trainer variant exacerbated this problem and it fell to us luckless staff navigators on the OCU to step into the back seat on a student pilot's second ever sortie in a Buccaneer. Of course, the student would have undertaken ten simulator sorties and been checked out on the OCU's fleet of four Hunter T7As or T8Bs, but none of these were equal to actually putting the aircraft through its paces for real. Their first sortie, with a QFI in the navigator's seat, was sufficient to iron out basic handling and circuit work, but after that it was up to the staff navigators to ensure that student pilots were competent and in control.

To help in our survival, a staff pilot took new navigator instructors airborne to show them just how quickly a student pilot could get into trouble. After just three days as an OCU instructor, I was airborne with John Redford to be shown just how crazy some pilots could be. There are two flying terms that pilots know only too well and which are explained and demonstrated during flying training. The first is a 'UP', or Unusual Position, and the second is a 'PIO', which stands for Pilot Induced Oscillation. A PIO is easily identifiable and I had experienced them previously when tanking on 12 Squadron with pilots who attempted to 'chase the basket' during AAR. I was not, however, prepared for quite the 'showtime' that John introduced me to as we 'bashed the circuit' at the end of our seventy-minute sortie. Too low on the approach! Too fast on the approach! Too high on the approach! Too slow on the approach! The Buccaneer was fitted with a very effective ADD[1], primarily for use in the circuit, but equally valuable during high g manoeuvring. As John put XV338 into various UPs on the approach at Honington on 19 April 1978, the noises in my headphones, which varied from deep resonating burbles, to the high penetrating shriek of the high notes, were etched on my brain and stored for future reference. The Buccaneer was a dream to fly at high speed and low-level, but to the unwary in the circuit it could be an absolute bitch and many a pilot learned that to their cost throughout its career.

My indoctrination to the OCU and its C to I Course continued throughout the month of April, but by early May 1978 I was cleared to fly with my first students. Initially, I flew with pilots who were halfway through their course, but on 15 May I was out-briefed to fly a Fam 3 with Ken Alley, a USAF exchange pilot, who was eventually destined to join the staff of the OCU. Ken was an experienced F-111

---

1. Airstream Direction Detector provided both audio and, by means of a traffic light system, visual indications of Angle of Attack (AOA), thereby allowing the crew to maintain visual contact with the runway threshold during an approach, or with other aircraft and the ground during high g manoeuvring.

pilot who had seen service in Vietnam, but this was to be only his third sortie in a Buccaneer. For me, however, it was my first venture to the circuit with a student pilot! I need not have worried. I had flown with Bill Petersen on 12 Squadron previously and I was well aware, and Ken proved it, that the USAF only sent their very best on exchange tours to the UK. May continued with a varied selection of sorties, both day and night, with both staff and student pilots alike. I settled in neatly to my new instructor role.

237 OCU in the mid-1970s had something of a reputation, however, throughout the RAF. It was renowned as a 'tough school' and there was definitely an element of 'if your face doesn't fit' around the place. To be fair on the Boss and his staff, the Buccaneer was not an easy aircraft and it was operated by both the RAF and the RN at the extreme end of its flight envelope. Consequently, you had to be as robust as the airframe itself if you were going to fit into the Buccaneer brotherhood. Nevertheless, there were a number of characters on the OCU staff when I joined who seemed to delight in adopting an overly aggressive posture towards students who were not matching the standard required. It was not uncommon to see course photographs in the staff room with '*Green Shield*' stamps stuck above the heads of university graduates[2] and bloodied axes drawn above those who were struggling to get through the course. Those who failed had their heads cut from the photograph and placed within a bloody red circle at their feet! This was a less politically correct age than now and little or no thought was given to the fact that it might cause offence to those who fell by the wayside. It is a known philosophy in flying training circles that students who are struggling find it difficult to admit to their failings, but most are relieved when the pressure is removed and they find themselves flying in a more benign environment well removed from the FJ world. The Buccaneer was most definitely not a benign environment, and students, in the main, appreciated the necessary pressure that life on the OCU brought; not all did, however!

By July 1976 I found myself selected as the QWI to return to 12 Squadron as a member of the HQ 1 Gp Inspection Team to assess the squadron's compliance with SOPs and regulations – the Trappers' Visit! I had routinely been subjected to similar annual scrutiny on XV and 12 Squadrons, but now had to prepare to return to my very recent crewroom and put my pals through the various assessments required by headquarters. The team included QFIs, IREs, QWIs, and included the CI who would lead us two hangars west and liaise directly with OC 12 Squadron throughout our four-day visit to the squadron. I flew four sorties with the squadron and found nothing to criticise. I monitored QWI debriefings and assisted in the checking of all documentation and scrutiny of procedures. The squadron, I knew, would excel, and did not disappoint. There was only one 'blip' as far as I was concerned and it happened on the first of the four sorties that I flew. Andy Marrs, who was a QWI pilot on the squadron, and I, were tasked as Number 3 in a four-ship to undertake

---

2. Officers who, in the 1970s, had entered the RAF under the 'Graduate Entry Scheme' which gave them accelerated promotion to flight lieutenant, were known as Green Shielders after the dividend stamps issued by some stores in the UK in the 1960s and 1970s.

an FRA and Academic Bunt Retard at Donna Nook Range on the Lincolnshire coast and then head out into the North Sea to practise some of the Alpha tactics that I had been so familiar with over the previous four years on the squadron. Everything had gone according to plan on the range and we had dropped four reasonable bombs on the target. We were both very comfortable with each other and were laughing and joking about my new-found position having only just left the squadron a few months previous. We settled into the first attack against a maritime radar contact heading in a NW direction through the relatively calm waves of a summer in the North Sea. We had split ten degrees starboard at the appropriate point and, with the target now drifting off to our left, Andy dragged the Buccaneer back as I called forty seconds from the split point. Now, with the target dead ahead under the cursor on my Blue Parrot CRT, I looked left to reassure myself that our leader was in the anticipated spot of sky and deconflicted for the pull-up and simulated Medium Toss manoeuvre – we were at 520 kts and 100 ft. I was back in my element.

At three miles from the target, Andy pressed the Accept Bar[3] on his port throttle and entered a 4G pull-up, which allowed the simulated bombs to leave the aircraft at a pre-determined point and 'fly' towards their simulated target. As he did so – as was common practice – he flicked the bomb bay to 'OPEN' to allow the simulated four 1000lb weapons to leave the bomb bay! There was an instant and disturbing rumble throughout the airframe, and the more the nose came up and the speed dropped off the greater the vibrations became! We aborted the attack and recovered to level flight whilst we contemplated what had happened! Andy closed the bomb bay – the vibration ceased! Tentatively he reopened it – the vibration started! That simplified matters, and without further ado, with the aircraft functioning normally, we agreed to continue the sortie with the bomb bay firmly closed, all the while monitoring instruments and warning panels for any misadventure. Nothing untoward occurred again and we made an uneventful recovery and landing back at Honington. As we taxied to a stop in dispersal, Andy rolled the bomb bay open for a last time and shut down the engines! At the foot of the ladders we turned to peer under the aircraft and saw to our dismay the cause of the rumble. The aircraft had recently returned from a weekend ranger and there at the front of the bomb bay was a 'cakestand'[4]. On it, firmly secured, were two main wheels and a nose wheel! They should have been removed before our flight and, if not, a red-line entry in the F700 should have alerted us to the fact that the bomb bay was not to be rotated in flight. It had been an oversight by the ground crew, but one from which we all learned a lesson and in the end no harm was done apart from a few frayed nerves!

Life was certainly more settled on the OCU than on the squadron. There were few if any detachments, but any sortie flown with a student required not only a full brief and debrief of the syllabus exercise flown, but also the completion of the

---

3. Pressing the Accept Bar increased gyro sensitivity at the appropriate stage of a DSL attack and started the automatic sequence according to the attack mode selected on the Attack Selector.
4. A contraption similar to an afternoon tea cake stand. It had three levels, each capable of carrying either a main wheel or a nose wheel complete with inflated tyres. It was used on deployments to ensure spare wheels were available immediately should one need to be changed.

student's written report. If you were appointed a course commander, you then had to collect and collate all the reports of those navigators in your charge and prepare their F5000 folder before the staff progress meeting, which was held every Friday afternoon before the bar opened at 1700hrs. Staff meetings could be torrid affairs and not every staff member was as conscientious in report writing as they might be! On one memorable occasion, I was sat at the back of the room when the senior navigation instructor was having a tirade about 'poor writing' on post-sortie F5000C forms. He was in full flow when he suddenly said: 'And here's a prime example of what I'm talking about! This is a post sortie report for a student navigator who has just failed the Hi-Lo-Hi sortie for a French low-level mission. Listen to this – "Nav Fucking Spastic!" That's all! No explanation of why the nav might have been fucking spastic! Just those three words.'

We all cringed in our seats, and before we knew it the student's folder was scything across the room at head height towards the desk at which the author was sat.

'Not good enough! Get that back to me before five!'

I have to say, we were mildly amused sat at the back of the room. Everybody knew that the navigator in question was 'fucking spastic', but I suppose his efforts at low-level in France merited a few more than those three choice words, which whilst accurate, did not quite tell the whole story. The navigator in question did not last much longer in the FJ world. He had flown Vulcans previously and, I think, returned to the heavy brigade after he failed the Buccaneer OCU, and completed a number of successful tours on the Nimrod.

That summer I was approached by Barrie Chown, who had been my instructor when I had completed the QWI Course in 1976, who informed me that he had proposed my name as his successor in running the 1978 QWI Course. I was delighted and thrilled to have been considered, but worried that I could never live up to his example. Nevertheless, despite strong lobbying by a fellow navigator QWI, I was chosen by the Boss to be the staff navigator on that year's course with Ivor Evans, who would be the staff pilot.

In the RAF, the term Qualified Weapon Instructor evolved during the 1970s/80s as those trained in the finer points of weaponry and the instruction thereof sought to gain recognition alongside Qualified Flying Instructors within the Service. In the RN in the 1960s, weapons instructors were known as Pilot Attack Instructors and with the arrival of the two-seat Buccaneers, this was changed in the RAF to Buccaneer Attack Instructor to recognise that the task of the BAI could be undertaken by either a pilot or a navigator. The first RAF BAI course was held on 237 OCU in 1973. Three student crews left their respective squadrons, usually as constituted crews for the duration of the three-month long course, and returned having completed an intensive period of training where no quarter was given to those who were unprofessional or slapdash. Every day started early and finished late, whether it involved classroom lectures, phase brief preparation by the students, or flying. Indeed, when the flying phase started the days became even longer. As soon as one student-led sortie had been debriefed, the next day's lead crew would commence preparation for their mission. Sortie briefings had to be presented on the blackboard (yep, chalk and duster!) with all writing legible, evenly spaced and straight. QWIs became masters of flat-bottomed blackboard lettering as most chose to use a straight edge to ensure neatness of the finished product. Remember, this was in the days when PCs did not exist, or at very best, were no further advanced than the Sinclair Spectrum! It was not uncommon to see QWI students burning the midnight oil with chalk, ruler and duster in hand attempting to correct the final points of their briefing before the 0700hrs met brief the next day. Students quickly learned that an uneven curve on the depiction of the base-leg turn at Wainfleet Range was enough to raise comment by the staff before the sortie was even flown. No wonder the BAI course was referred to (by those who were not selected) as the Bullshit And Ignorance course. However, the efforts of the staff to ensure the very highest of standards were deliberate, and although some students failed to make the grade as QWIs, none failed to respond or appreciate the need to be pressurised as a weapons instructor. Dropping live bombs is not an arcade game and accuracy and the utmost professionalism are required by all, but even more so by those who instruct.

Following an initial mathematics revision period, the academic phase of the course included instruction in the calculation of sight settings and the necessary processes required to work out different sight settings for varying wind conditions, delivery profiles and release heights and dive angles. Knowledge of the Buccaneer weapon aiming system was, of course, essential, and understanding the necessary calculations to ensure safe separation between aircraft and weapon detonation and aircraft and the ground during dive attacks was imperative. The theory of 'Flight Path' weapons (bombs) and 'Non-flight Path' weapons (rockets/guns) was also taught. Terms like ballistics, muzzle velocity, gravity drop[5], forward throw, time of flight, dip[6], and many more, became routine to the QWI. A new lexicon had to be known and understood. The majority of this instruction was given by members of the 237 OCU QWI cadre, but weapon delivery Phase Briefs were researched and conducted by individual students prior to each phase of live training on the local East Anglian bombing ranges. In the 1970s, when the Buccaneer was new to most in the RAF and new crews were joining the force almost every month, the role of the QWI was to work up these crews on their weaponry skills in preparation for them being declared LCR and then CR. Consequently, in these early days, QWI students learned the finer points of each weapon delivery practised by the Buccaneer force to allow them to instruct effectively when they returned to their squadrons. In my years as a Buccaneer QWI, crews practised the following attacks regularly:

Visual Laydown. A visual low-level bombing attack flown at 200 feet and 500 kts TAS for delivery of retarded conventional 1000lb HE bombs or nuclear weapons. The attack was very much dependent on the pilot being straight and level at release, as 1° Nose Up at release could throw the bomb 217 feet short.

---

5. The effect of gravity on a weapon in flight.
6. The vertical distance between the pilot's eye and the weapon on the aircraft pylon.

Bunt Retard. An 8° visual dive bombing attack at 500 kts TAS and an indicated release height of 570 feet for delivery of retarded conventional 1000lb HE bombs. With this attack, as with all dive attacks in the Buccaneer, the pilot was dependent upon the rate at which the navigator called out briefed heights in the dive in order to assess the correct dive angle; an error of 1° steep or shallow would result in a 70 feet error long or short respectively.

Medium Toss. A radar-laid lofted delivery of ballistic conventional 1000lb HE bombs at 520 kts IAS and flown at 200 feet ATL. This could be a very accurate attack for the delivery of sticks of weapons if the Buccaneer weapon system was harmonised well. However, compounding errors in varying aircraft systems across the Alliance resulted in the 'acceptable' NATO standard for this attack being 300 feet radius from the target. The huge advantage of this attack was that it provided an IMC attack capability against Russian capital ships, which is exactly what the Buccaneer was built to do.

Vari-Toss. A visual-laid, timed release, lofted delivery of ballistic conventional 1000lb HE bombs, LEPUS flares, or nuclear weapons at 550 kts TAS from a 100 feet (visual) run in. Following a nine second, timed pull-up, the bomb was released at 65° Nose Up and 4000 feet ATL. Because wind speed changes with height, this attack could be quite inaccurate; 10 kt wind error equalled 700 feet error in the fall of shot. Consequently, Vari-Toss was generally restricted operationally to the delivery of flares to illuminate target areas by night, or to nuclear weapons that required less accuracy to gain the required effect from its damage mechanism against the target.

Radar Laydown. A radar-laid low-level bombing attack at 500 kts TAS developed by the RAF's overland squadrons to permit the IMC delivery of nuclear weapons.

Low-level Auto Depressed Sight Line. A low-level attack with pop-up to deliver ballistic conventional 1000lb HE bombs. The run in was at 400 feet and 460 kts IAS, until, at 3.5nm from the target, a pull to 10° Nose Up was executed. At 900 feet in the climb, a bunt over manoeuvre was started, topping out at 1500 feet ATL. The pilot then tracked the target in the dive until the weapons were automatically released at 1050 feet ATL at 450 kts IAS. In order to escape the weapon fragment envelope on detonation, the pilot executed a 4G 30° Nose Up escape manoeuvre to at least 2000 feet. This was a highly accurate attack and it was not unknown for an expert to gain six DHs from six passes on the range.

All the above events were conducted for training on Strike Command bombing ranges using practice bombs to simulate the real thing. However, in addition to these events, QWI students conducted operational deliveries of rockets and live 1000lb HE bombs whilst undergoing training. Most sorties to and from the bombing range would include field targets for Simulated Attack Profiles, whilst all the while being harassed by 'bounce' aircraft; the Fleet Air Arm had christened this latter activity – which was in modern parlance 'evasion' – Strike Progression and thus it remained throughout the life of the Buccaneer. In order to service the needs of the Buccaneer Maritime Attack squadrons, QWI students were also trained in the art of Splash Bombing. All QWI course sorties were flown as constituted four-ships with a staff crew flying in the Number 2 position to assess the lead crew's performance. The debriefs were conducted immediately after landing and were never complete until the Strike Sight[7] film had been fully analysed and the learning points and critical points assessed in minute detail. Subsequently all, apart from the next day's lead crew, would retire to the bar to wash away any metaphoric bruising from the day's activities! In more recent years, and as a consequence of failings during the war in Iraq in 1991, QWI training has focussed more on the operational art and a requirement for more in-depth knowledge of an aircraft's operational capability.

The operational phase of every QWI Course run on 237 OCU prior to 1978 had taken place in the low flying areas in Scotland, with turn-rounds at either RAF Lossiemouth or RAF Leuchars in Fife. Not so, for the course that Ivor and I were to run in 1978! That year's course, it had been decided, was to participate with 208 Squadron on Exercise Red Flag 79/1 at Nellis AFB in Nevada.

In 1975, following analysis of combat losses during the Vietnam War when US Air Force F-4 Phantom crews struggled in combat against nimble enemy MiGs, the USAF developed an intensive combat air training exercise – Red Flag. The exercise was designed to give inexperienced – in combat – aircrew a taste of battle so that when they went to war for real it would not be a baptism of fire. The RAF was the first foreign air force invited to participate alongside their USAF cousins and in 1978, exercise RF79-1 was the second such participation by the RAF. Buccaneers had participated in the exercise in 1976 and their prowess at low-level over the salt flat desert areas of Nevada had become something of a legend amongst the USAF. Not many Buccaneers had been 'shot down' by USAF aggressor[8] aircraft on that exercise and the word was out around the USAF that a Buccaneer 'kill' was the star prize on RF79-1! The exercise took place in the last weeks of October 1978.

Before we deployed 'Across the Pond' however, there was the small matter of completing the work-up programme. Although the Buccaneer was well established in the ranks of the RAF, and in the FAA, and the South African Air Force, as the ultimate low-level weapon delivery platform, we all needed to complete a training syllabus that involved flying at 100 feet in specifically cleared LFAs in Scotland. The QWI students, along with Ivor and me, formed a strong constituted four-ship formation. The staff crew always flew in their usual Number 2 position so that we could monitor more closely the lead student crew. Unfortunately, one of the navigators had already been suspended from the course for his lack of a credible image during briefings and debriefings – whilst he was a high performer in the air, he was too much of a polite

---

7. Head Up Display.
8. Red Flag opposition forces included a squadron of F-5 Freedom Fighters marked up in Soviet camouflage and red stars. The crews were trained in Soviet Air Force tactics and flew accordingly.

gentleman to make a worthy QWI! So to complete the constituted four-ship for both the work up and Red Flag itself, we co-opted David Cleland-Smith, my 'flatmate' from Culford days, and now an OCU staff navigator, into our 'gang'. Thus, with Ivor Evans and me as the instructors, our four-ship included Nigel 'Rip' Kirby and Chris Finn from XV Squadron, Mal Prissick and Graham Seaward from 12 Squadron and Brian 'Boots' Mahaffey from 208 Squadron, who, after his navigator had been suspended from training, was flying with David Cleland-Smith. Each student crew lead the missions in turn, whilst Ivor and I rode shotgun. After four work-up sorties flying complex missions at ultra low-level over the North-West Highlands of Scotland, with turn-rounds at Lossiemouth, we deployed by RAF VC10 to Nellis AFB to acclimatise for a week before flying started in earnest on Red Flag.

Nellis AFB in 1978 was the tactical fighter hub of the USAF! It was the USAF's equivalent of the USN's Top Gun and, indeed, one of the units on base was the renowned USAF Fighter Weapons School – the RAF's QWI equivalent. Also on base resided the USAF Air Demonstration Squadron 'Thunderbirds', plus a host of other units hiding under the clandestine guise of *Research and Development* and veiled to the prying eyes of aliens from a foreign land.

The base was jam-packed with military hardware of all types, and whilst Red Flag aircraft filled the majority of the vast dispersal, its headquarters and operations facility occupied just one very large building in which were sufficient offices and planning rooms to house all the visiting participants. It also included a vast amphitheatre wherein were held a daily mass briefing and a mass debriefing before and after each day's exercise activity. Two parallel runways, each over 10,000 feet in length, ensured that there was ample space for the large numbers of aircraft participating to launch and recover from the Nellis Ranges situated to the north.

On this, my first taste of Red Flag, we were accommodated on base in BOQs. These comprised a suite of rooms within which were provided all modern conveniences including a large TV and an enormous beer fridge! Catering and bar facilities were readily accessible in the Officers' Club and there was a host of typically American fast food joints spread liberally across the base. With Red Flag in full force, the bar was always well subscribed to, and Happy Hours were held twice a week on Wednesday and Friday nights at 1700hrs – strippers performed on a stage in the centre of the bar from 1730hrs onwards! As Happy Hour progressed, there was never any shortage of aircrew willing to assist the girls on stage and vast numbers of dollar bills would be pressed into knicker elastic as many a young man felt the urge to 'secure' his prize. However, Nevada State Law did not permit the removal of bikini bottoms and, certainly, touching the dancers was likely to get you thrown out on your ear – well, apart from squeezing dollar bills onto their person of course! It was a riotous assembly and many a very happy night was spent in the Nellis bar on RF79-1.

We, on the OCU, were quite fortunate in that we were allocated the afternoon wave to fly on each day. This meant that our 'eight hour bottle to throttle[9]' regime allowed

---

9. In the 1970s the RAF rules stipulated that aircrew were not allowed to imbibe alcohol within eight hours of flying.

us to drink relatively late into the night and still remain within our flying regulations the following day. Consequently, after each mass debrief, we would repair to the bar to discuss the day over a beer before rising the next morning, slightly hungover occasionally, to prepare for our afternoon mission.

What we lacked, however, was transport! The twinkling lights of the Las Vegas Strip were no more than ten miles south-west, but without 'wheels' we felt somewhat stranded on base. However, the one thing that an O Club benefits from, that a Royal Air Force Officers' Mess lacks, is a significant number of veterans amongst its active membership. It was after one such Happy Hour that Dave C-S announced to our small group that he had managed to 'strangle' a couple of vehicles for us. Lord knows how he had done it, but considerable training in overseas ports during his tour with the FAA on 809 Squadron undoubtedly helped. No questions had been asked by the owners. Insurance was taken for granted and no compensation was required by us other than to respond to requests to 'keep talkin' to me, ah just love your Limey accents!' We were now the proud 'owners' of a Chevy pick-up truck and a VW Rabbit[10]! Vegas was now within reach and Caesar's Palace was about to get a visit.

Las Vegas is tacky and is best viewed after the sun has gone down and the lights have come on. The licencing laws, however, when associated with its gaming laws, are something of a benefit to thirsty aircrew. If you are sat at a gaming table and parting with your money, then all drinks are free. I suspect that their G&Ts were much diluted and that there was much more T than G, but to a 29-year-old brought up in an alcohol free zone, surrounded by like-minded aircrew, mild gambling whilst drinking was akin to the best night out ever! We never stayed long in any casino as, most often, our small gambling pot was depleted quite quickly. There were other establishments to explore, including The Jolly Trolley, which just happened to be a suitable last port of call on our way home. It was a small casino, tucked into the corner of a group of shops on the corner of the Strip at the junction of South Las Vegas Boulevard and West Sahara Avenue and opposite the Sahara Hotel. Its attraction was not so much its slot machines, but more its so-called Burlesque Show in the back room behind a red velvet curtain!

The flying was demanding and it required absolute concentration. Each sortie would start with a fairly benign departure from Nellis and a climb out and cruise at about 15,000 feet through a designated corridor into the Nellis Range complex. Once clear of the corridor, the formation would descend to low-level to be at 500 kts and 100 feet as we approached the 'gate', or start point of the exercise, which on Red Flag was known as Student Gap. All missions were deconflicted by space and time at Student Gap, so it was critical that you hit your allocated time slot. Routinely a five minute 'trombone[11]' would be built in to allow either a slow down or a catch up in case of a problem with the departure from Nellis.

---

10. American derivation of the VW Golf.
11. A low-level leg, shaped like the extending tube of a trombone, would be built into each mission. It was usually five minutes outbound and similarly inbound and marked with one minute marks. This allowed the lead navigator to adjust his timing early or late in order to depart the 'gate' exactly on time.

From Student Gap it was eyes out, ears open and hard aggressive flying. At such speed and flying so low, pilots had to focus ahead and rely on their navigators to: warn them of any hazards such as HT or telephone cables, for example; advise them of EW alarms on the RWR; keep them updated on other aircraft positions in the formation; monitor the rear quadrant from two o'clock round to ten o'clock for opposing fighters; describe navigational features; give clear and precise directions with regard to the route to be flown; and scream for evasive action to be taken if intercepted or if locked up by one of the many Soviet SAM systems that were spread strategically across the desert floor. It was hard work! It was made easier by the light years visibility in the prevailing weather conditions, which meant that navigation was ordained mainly by flying at ULL to the next mountain ridge where the pilot would turn onto the next heading by 'ridge rolling'[12] to reduce as much as possible the time that the aircraft was skylined! Contact with the 'enemy' would result in a call of 'Buster'[13] and probably a call of 'Counter' or 'Break'[14] either to port or starboard, but always towards the threat in an effort to reduce his firing options.

Whilst all this was going on, the navigator was also responsible for: ensuring the safe navigation of the aircraft; avoiding restricted areas, of which there was an abundance; not overflying farms; locating the target area; setting the switches for a live weapon release; and making sure that we did not crash! In addition, a particularly sensitive area, known as Dreamland or Area 51[15], within the range complex and always very close to our prescribed flow routing, was a must avoid! To infringe Dreamland would result in a very one-sided interview with a very senior USAF officer, a grounding and a very early departure back home for any crew that even slightly strayed into the 1600 nm^2 area; and that included any US military personnel too!

With one orientation mission, the QWI Course flew five missions on RF79-1 between 23/27 October 1978 and dropped sixteen 1000lb HE bombs between us from both Vari-Toss and Laydown deliveries. It was an outstanding success and although we saw a number of the aggressor units ranged against us whilst we were airborne, none were bold enough to gain a confirmed kill. We struck all our targets successfully and fared better than many of our contemporaries in the USAF and USMC.

The daily mass debrief was nowhere to hide if you had screwed up on the ranges. Each mission commander held court and each flight leader had to account for his formation's performance, explain their tactics, admit their faults and announce

---

12. At the crest of the ridge the pilot rolled the aircraft almost inverted and pulled the stick back to allow the aircraft to dive towards the ground before rolling the wings level and continuing at ULL. To do otherwise (a pull up and push over) would mean that the aircraft would balloon above the ridge line, making it vulnerable to both ground and air defences.

13. Internal radio call by any crew member in the formation to alert others to the fact that a fighter was on our tail. On hearing the call, all pilots 'bustered' to max speed, usually 580 kts.

14. 'Counter': a max rate turn towards the threat. Break: a max permissible 'g' turn towards the threat.

15. The primary purpose of Area 51 is publicly unknown; however, as an adjunct of the US DoD's Test and Evaluation unit at Edwards AFB, it is commonly regarded as the location for flight testing of most, if not all, of the USA's 'Black Programmes'.

their kills or simulated losses! Honesty was the best policy and came naturally to the Buccaneer Force, which had always known that a hard and honest debrief, even if brutal at times, was the only way to survive and operate an aircraft at the extremes of its operational capability. It came as something of a surprise, therefore, when the USAF brigadier general appointed to manage the day's proceedings on one particular day took to the stage at the end of the debrief. His comments went something like this:

'Gentlemen, I thank you for an honest and upfront debrief. The mission seems to have gone well and the kill rate against Blue Forces by the aggressors was not particularly high. We have suffered no casualties and the recovery plan back at Nellis, whilst complicated, worked extremely well. I will see you all in the bar in about thirty minutes. However, before I leave you I would like the leader of the F-4 formation from Moody Air Force Base to meet me in my office in ten minutes. And so that you can get your story straight, you might like to wonder why the mailman on the dirt road west of Belted Peak is in Tonopah Hospital with burst eardrums!'

And with that he left the room!

It transpired that the Moody formation, a flight of eight Phantoms, had had extreme difficulty finding their 'convoy' target on the desert floor and, after a short square search, had elected to drop their Mk82 bombs on the only 'convoy' in the area – the mail van with a cloud of dust behind as it streaked across the desert floor! Here lives the age old military adage – 'Don't Assume! Check!'

We planned our final sortie on the Thursday evening before we repaired to the bar. It was a conscious decision by the lead crew because of the usual complexity on the last Red Flag mission flown on each exercise. As is usual, missions had started relatively simply and become more complex as the days of the exercise had passed. The USAF Mission Commander for the very last wave of RF79-1 had introduced a really complex scenario and it had been a unanimous decision to get ahead of the game rather than wait to the following morning.

Ivor and I were also aware that our old Laarbruch station commander, Mike Knight, was due to arrive at Nellis that evening in his capacity now as SASO HQSTC, in the rank of air vice-marshal. He was on his way back from visiting the Harrier detachment on ops in Belize and wanted to witness Red Flag at first hand. We were busy ploughing through the ATO[16] and SPINS. Navigators were drawing lines on maps whilst pilots prepared IP to Tgt maps when Mike walked through the door. I had not seen him in four years and nor had Ivor; we had been lowly flying officers when he had last seen us. He walked straight over, clapped us both on the back, addressed us by our first names and asked how we were doing and how the exercise

---

16. The Air Tasking Order is a means by which the Air Commander controls air forces within a joint operations environment. The ATO is a large document that lists all pre-planned air sorties for a fixed 24-hour period, with individual call signs, aircraft types, and mission types (i.e. close air support or air refuelling).

had gone. I was mightily impressed. After a brief discussion he circulated around the rest of the QWIs before excusing himself as he needed to make his number with OC 208 Squadron. As he was about to disappear I called after him and let him know that we would be heading for the O Club bar shortly if he wanted to join us. He smiled and nodded as he left the room.

One hour later we were all sat on bar stools around a large round table when in he walked.

'What are you drinking, chaps?' he queried.

'Eight Buds and one for yourself!' we responded as he passed by and headed for the bar. As he disappeared into the crush at the bar I shouted, 'It's cheaper by the pitcher, Sir!'

Five minutes later he was back with eight pitchers of Budweiser! It was going to be a good night. We chatted and drank together for about twenty minutes before he once again excused himself to circulate. As he left he acknowledged that we planned to head into Vegas later and, without agreeing outright, he once again smiled and nodded.

He joined a group of 208 Squadron executives who were standing close by and I overheard him being asked by the squadron boss if he would care to join them for a quiet dinner in the Club so that they could brief him on Red Flag and 208 Squadron's performance. He declined.

'I'm afraid not, Phil,' he said, 'I've been invited downtown with the QWI Course!' The look on the CO's face had to be seen to be believed!

A little later, and by the time we had supped the pitchers, he was back and ready for the off! Ivor and Dave C-S had drunk the least and opted to drive. I climbed into the back of the Rabbit and Mike Knight joined me, throwing his 'scrambled egg' hat onto the parcel shelf. Mal Prissick climbed in with Dave in the front. Ivor drove the Chevy with Rip Kirby and Boots alongside him on the bench seat. With no room for Graham Seaward in any of the vehicles, he grabbed an easy chair from the O Club, threw it onto the pick-up and climbed onto the open rear and sat down to relax. The race into Vegas was hysterical. With the fresh air now mixing with the alcohol in Seaward's brain, we were very lucky not to be arrested because of his antics. Mike Knight was staying at the Desert Inn and needed to go to his room to change before we sallied any further forth. He insisted that we join him and partake of the contents of his beer fridge whilst he changed. We did! Once booted and spurred we hot-footed it through the lobby of his hotel and across the road to The Stardust to consume some, if not all, of their all you can eat buffet for $1.95[17]. We were starving!

The Stardust was renowned, despite the price, for the quality of its cuisine. It was also renowned for its central feature at the buffet of a 'constant refills' champagne fountain! We filled our stomachs with king prawns and caviar, smoked meats and cheeses and plenty of other culinary delights. We downed glass after glass of

---

17. Another by-product of the gaming scene in Las Vegas was that every casino hotel provided very palatable buffets at rock-bottom prices. From Caesar's Palace and Circus Circus, to The Dunes, Flamingo and Tropicana all provided food for its punters to keep them within their gaming walls!

champagne and kept going back for refills even after we were replete and could eat no more! Suddenly a rather large Afro-American approached our table, and all the while patting his pistol in a holster under his left armpit, advised us that to continue to use the champagne faucet whilst no longer dining was against the establishment's rules! 'In fact, gentlemen, it's probably best if you leave now!' was the best advice that we had had since our arrival – I for one had no intention of finding out whether it was a Smith & Wesson or a Beretta that he was packing!

We left quickly and turned left to contemplate what opportunities now presented themselves and how, for the first time in our lives, we had been thrown out of a hostelry with a Two-Star officer!

The Jolly Trolley hove into view. We knew it well. Mike Knight had never heard of it. It was now past 11pm and so we pushed through the small group of gamblers huddled around its slot machines and headed for the red curtain. After a few knowing hellos from the girls, who acted as waitresses when not divesting and writhing, we settled at the stage and waited for the next performer to appear. Our first Bud arrived about the same time as the next dancer. Mike was enthralled! We stayed long enough to see our favourite girl gyrate in her Stars and Stripes bikini to Exile's '*Kiss You All Over*' – it was now 3am and Mike Knight was settled for the night! We left him. He had just a short walk back to the Desert Inn and did not have to fly the next morning. The following morning we barely made the Mass Brief and we all felt bloody awful, and, I suspect, looked it. Just before the briefing commenced Mike Knight appeared looking every bit as fresh as if he had gone to bed at 8pm and hadn't touched a drop of alcohol in the previous twenty-four hours! God knows what time he went to bed, but it is better that a flight lieutenant does not ask such questions of an air vice-marshal!

The OCU was, at the time, in a slight doldrum. A squadron leader pilot, who had been suspended from training on the Buccaneer previously, had appealed the decision with AOC HQ 1 Gp and had been reinstated on the course. He had been OC General Duties Flight at Honington when the AOC had been the station commander and had used that connection to sway the AOC in his favour. The decision upset those OCU staff members who were on the staff when he was suspended and, more so, when they were informed by HQ that they were precluded from flying with him at his second attempt to succeed on the course. Since I had not been on the staff at the time I was one of the few navigators nominated to fly with him. An erstwhile Vulcan pilot, he was very much set in the ways of a pilot in command of a large crew. However, I was quite taken aback when he established inter-cockpit communication with me with the words: 'Captain to Navigator, do you read, over?' when I first flew with him in early February 1979 on a STRIPRO 3 sortie. It was common in the Buccaneer cockpit to refer to each other by first name unless the significant other happened to be a senior officer, but never so formally by role. It surprised me because, by this stage of the course, he must have been told beforehand that it was inappropriate and he had already partially completed the OCU before he had been 'chopped' previously! I got the distinct impression right there and then that he was not prepared to change his ways to fit into our force model! Nevertheless, I pointed out in no uncertain terms that

I would not respond to him if he continued to refer to me in such a way throughout the sortie! He apologised and the sortie continued, but he was not a natural aviator in the two-seat environment. One of the problems that the OCU staff had with him was that, on his previous course, he had kept a 'little black book' within which he kept notes, comments and criticisms of staff members. He had used it in providing his evidence to the AOC. We were all well aware that he was doing so again!

My next encounter with him came just one month later on 6 March. Having failed the sortie with me, he was re-flying STRIPRO 3 but, to be fair-handed and because of his history, it had been decided that he should undertake the retest with a different staff navigator in the back seat. John Broadbent was the man chosen for the task. STRIPRO 3 was designed as a Lo Lo sortie from Honington over the North Sea to LFA 11 in Yorkshire, eventually coasting out south of Flamborough Head and turning south-east back to the Honington Visual Entry Point at Blakeney Point on the Norfolk coast. The whole thing was planned to last about seventy-five minutes and, with Frank Waddington in my front seat, I was programmed as the lead navigator of a four-ship formation that included one Buccaneer tasked to act as Bounce. He and John were flying as Number 3.

The sortie was fairly uneventful from the outset, although I found myself mainly engaged in jotting down Frank's comments about the aforementioned pilot's poor formation positioning to assist with the debrief back at Honington. A number of contact calls were made when the Bounce hove into sight and appropriate actions were taken to counter his attacks. He was doing reasonably well under John's guidance and was neatly in position 2000 yards abreast when we coasted out and began our turn onto 150° and home. As we rolled out on heading there was no sign of his aircraft! We searched the horizon for what seemed like ages, but there was nothing! We looked to both sides of our aircraft as far as the eye could see, but – nothing! Eventually, Frank called on the radio asking them where they were. John Broadbent replied, 'With you shortly!' There was impatience in his voice. We set up an orbit at 500 feet to the east of Flamborough Head, advised them of our location, asked the Bounce to hold off while we reformed and waited. We waited, we waited and we waited. All the while Frank was fuming in the front cockpit and giving me a running commentary for the debrief that I jotted down on my plastic kneepads. My head was bent forward as I scribbled and I took little heed of what was happening outside the cockpit, relying on Frank's ability in the air, his common sense and his regular interruptions in his diatribe to provide height checks, fuel checks and system checks.

Suddenly, and without any warning whatsoever, Frank exploded with an, 'Oh for fuck's sake!' as he snapped 4G and pulled the aircraft hard round into the face of a Buccaneer coming from the north with a Lightning fighter hard on its tail! It was a quite natural reaction, but one that I was quite unprepared for. And with my body relaxed whilst writing copious notes I was unprepared and not braced for the onset of 'g'. My forehead hit my right knee and I felt an excruciating pain in my back. Frank quickly levelled the wings when he heard my painful yell and once we regained control of the formation and our wayward crew, we headed back to base where we carried out a straight in approach to land. Medical assistance was called for and I was evacuated from the rear cockpit under the supervision of the Station Medical Officer. Subsequent analysis at the SMC suggested that an x-ray was necessary and so I was despatched forthwith to the RAF Hospital at Ely for further examination.

The diagnosis was not good! I had crushed the T4 vertebra in my spine. It was an injury commonly associated with aircrew that have ejected and the usual routine was a four-week stay in hospital lying flat on one's back and without any movement whatsoever! That is exactly what the consultant was demanding. I knew it was impossible. I had a number of tasks planned for the next few weeks, none of which I could put off to while away my time in Ely Hospital. These included the C Promotion Exam, which I had continued to fail to apply myself to, but more important than that, the birth of my second child was imminent. I was getting nowhere fast with my attempts to convince the consultant that I should be allowed home. He kept quoting rules at me that, in the main, revolved around the fact that every ejectee was obliged to be admitted to hospital and spend four weeks flat out! That was it, of course! I wasn't an ejectee! The rules didn't apply to me!

It worked! I convinced him and he agreed that I could go home, but he insisted that I must go straight to bed and stay there for the next three weeks and lie horizontally throughout my period of incarceration! I agreed! However, I had no intention of spending the period isolated upstairs away from my wife and son whilst they busied themselves downstairs awaiting our new arrival.

My first action when I got back home, therefore, was to dismantle our double bed and, with my wife's assistance, carry it downstairs and into the dining room where I could at least engage with my family. I arranged the revision books for the C Exam by my bedside in a positive effort to convince myself that I needed to study. Yet, with the sure knowledge that the exam day would be come and gone by the time my three weeks horizontal was up, I rarely looked at them.

Damn! The forward thinking Education Officer decided to send an invigilator to my home to allow me to take the exam in my sick bed! I failed! Again!!

Two weeks into my prostration I leapt from my bed and drove Sue to hospital where Sarah was born, on 24 March 1979, to complete our family.

Before I was permitted to fly again I had to undertake two weeks medical rehabilitation at RAF Headley Court[18] in Surrey before I was signed off by the medics as fit to do so. The facility provided medical rehabilitation for RAF personnel injured in everything from sports injuries to aircraft crashes. Dependent upon your injury decided your grouping. There were groups entitled for example: 'Early Legs', 'Late Legs', 'Early Arms' and 'Late Arms'. I was allocated to 'Early Backs'! Every patient paraded at 0800hrs for 'warm-ups' and again at 1330hrs for similar torture! However, 'Early Backs', by their very nature, have to be careful even if their injury is unlikely to cause paralysis – because you cannot be too careful, can you!

---

18. Now the Defence Medical Rehabilitation Centre Headley Court, made famous for its work in rehabilitating armed forces personnel injured and maimed in the wars in Iraq and Afghanistan. In 1979, however, it was a relatively small RAF medical unit with limited resources, but a very effective rehabilitation regime.

'Early Backs' was a breeze! We spent most of our time lying on rubber mats on the floor doing mild leg raises or hip rolls. If we were not doing that we were lying on rubber mats playing Scrabble, lying on rubber mats in the sunshine on the lawn, or taking a quiet stroll through the walled garden of the former Victorian pile. It was a most enjoyable two weeks. We even had a dining in night where one of the after dinner games was to traverse the oak-panelled drawing room without touching the floor. For those in 'Early Backs' it was simple! However, it was hilarious to watch aircrew in full mess kit, but on two crutches or with securing bolts protruding from their legs negotiating a thin oak dado rail some four feet above the ground! Amazingly, many of them succeeded.

I returned to flying in late June and was quickly thrown back into the routine of student syllabus sorties. However, on 12 July 1979, XW526 suffered a catastrophic structural failure in one of its wings and crashed in Germany, killing the crew. The whole Buccaneer fleet was grounded and my return to flying was short-lived. The grounding required each and every Buccaneer to be inspected in the area of the wing fold joint. Early analysis of the wreckage had proved that fatigue in the wing fold mechanism had allowed the massive titanium bolt, which locked the wings in the down position, to fall out in flight, which had resulted in the wing folding and breaking off. From that position, at low-level, there was no recovery and absolutely no possibility of a successful ejection. Morale was low amongst the aircrew in the Buccaneer force. However, in less than two weeks, some of the aircraft on the OCU had been inspected and cleared to fly, and by the end of the month I was flying with student QWIs again, although my time spent away from flying with my broken back had precluded me being considered for the running of the course this time round.

On the morning of 10 August, a Friday, Les Whatling and I, along with Norman Crow and David Cleland-Smith, headed south, via Yeovilton, for a weekend Ranger in Gibraltar. As instructors on the OCU, it was an irregular opportunity to get away for the weekend with two aircraft and practise our deployment skills, which included putting the aircraft to bed and waking it up again the following Monday when it came time to leave. It was a most marvellous weekend, but come the Monday morning, XT274, the aircraft that Norman and Dave had flown south in, was unserviceable. A quick call back to base resulted in us being informed that Les and Dave had to get back to fulfil their responsibility as course commanders for the latest intake of students; they were ordered to take our aircraft and we were instructed to await the serviceability of theirs! Norman and I were stranded in Gibraltar, and with a now identified inability of the local RAF engineers to fix the problem; we were not sure for how long. Ground crew from the OCU had to be assembled. Repair kit, spare parts and transportation had to be organised, and flights from Heathrow to Gibraltar flown before any work could start to repair the problem. Norman and I repaired to the bar to await further instructions. The ground crew arrived late on the Monday night and the following morning began work to repair the snag. Meanwhile, Norman and I took further advantage of our extended stay on the Rock. However, all good things must end and XT274 came back to life late morning on Wednesday, 15 August. The temperature at Gib had, by 1100hrs, reached plus 30°C. Norman and I, being professional aviators you understand, had already decided that it was too late to attempt a take-off at that temperature from Gib's 'wet at both ends' 6000 feet of tarmac with only a rather ancient CHAG to arrest any forward momentum should we realise too late that Algeciras Bay was approaching faster than V_R[19]! Unfortunately, whilst assessing how long we would have to wait until the Officers' Mess bar opened at lunchtime, we were called to the telephone to take a call 'from the CFI'; Tom Eeles. All our protestations about high OAT and lack of Buccaneer performance in these conditions were to no avail and we were ordered back home that very day!

Norman and I extracted the ODM[20] from the bomb bay and began to construct our flight plan. XT274 was equipped with two ARAM[21] training missiles on the outer pylons and a full complement of fuel. In short, its All Up Weight was 52,000lbs. The Buccaneer is fortunate in that one of its design features was the inclusion of BLC or 'Blow'. This meant that different configurations could be set for take-off or landing to match the prevailing conditions (either weather or airfield or both). At Gibraltar on that day in August 1979, we were left with two calculations to make to work out the TOD[22] required; whether 15-10-10 Unblown, or 30-20-20 Blown? The ODM was explicit: for 6000 feet of tarmac and plus 30°C, the TODs were either 6100 feet Unblown or 5900 feet Blown. With only 6000 feet available there was only one choice – 30-20-20 Blown it had to be. Norman spoke personally to the ATC local controller prior to getting into the cockpit and informed him that we would need every inch of the runway on take-off. He also informed him that we would require the latest OAT before brakes off and a guarantee that the overshoot was clear of any boats. We taxied out and almost reversed onto the orange and black chequers that mark the 'round down' on the easterly end of Gib's runway. When all was ready, Norman set the throttles in the top left-hand corner and advised ATC that he was ready to roll, but would be grateful for the OAT and his 'guarantee' before he released the brakes.

'Plus 32 and clear,' came the reply.

'What difference will two degrees hotter make, Dave?' he asked.

'Sorry, Mate, don't know,' I replied, 'ODM's in the bomb bay.'

'Clear for take-off,' chimed ATC and we were rolling!

Well we were moving. Acceleration did not seem to happen, although very imperceptibly the speed was increasing. As we crossed the Spanish Road I know that I was having second thoughts about our decision not to go to the bar, I assumed Norman was doing likewise! However, as the Buccaneer got to the 100 foot distance to go board, 5900 feet gone, the aircraft leapt into the air and steadied at about 15 feet

---

19. V_R is the speed at which a pilot 'rotates' - lifts the nosewheel from the runway to start a climb away from the airfield.

20. Operating Data Manual – provides performance data for the aircraft in various configurations and stages of flight.

21. Anti-Radar Acquisition Martel – training round that simulated the operational missile in everything except warhead and launch capability.

22. Take Off Distance – The distance needed for the ground run of an aircraft including an appropriate safety margin when all engines continue to operate normally and when one engine fails at the decision point.

above the runway. At this moment Norman called out, 'Oh Shit', which, under some circumstances, can sound like 'Eject!', but on this occasion it was quickly followed up with, 'Look behind you', which ensured that I remained firmly connected to my aircraft. As Norman banked our lumbering Buccaneer onto a southerly track to avoid Spanish Airspace, I did as I was bid and to my surprise saw three Spanish fishermen swimming feverishly back towards their upturned rowing boat. Jet wash at very, very low-level can have a most devastating effect on the unwary! The rest of the sortie back to Honington was uneventful and the CFI was very pleased to have his aircraft home. As for the Spanish fishermen? I can only guess they were poaching within Gibraltar territorial waters as we never heard another word on the subject!

I failed to knuckle down to the C Promotion Exam and although I did eventually pass it whilst on the OCU, I did so at the expense of the ISS[23] course that I had enrolled in and which, like the C Exam, was a necessary evil that had to be overcome to progress through the officer ranks. I failed Phase One of ISS and was back-coursed. Mike Heath, who was also taking the course, failed it too. We were in the same boat and were no help to each other when it came to checking each other's work prior to submission. Our progress was slow and I still had not completed the course by the time I left the OCU staff in 1981. Mike, on the other hand, took the bull by the horns and, after struggling with the course and its demanding deadlines for several months, marched into the Boss's office and informed him in the politest possible way that he could stick ISS where the sun didn't shine! Phil Wilkinson, who had recently taken command of the OCU, advised him of the career-limiting consequences of such an action, but Mike was adamant! He resigned from ISS and rose, eventually, to the rank of air vice-marshal – I wish I had taken his advice and followed suit!

On 7 February 1980, the Buccaneer Force was devastated by the crash of XV345 whilst on a Red Flag mission in Nevada. Circumstance seemed to be identical to the crash of XW526 just seven months previously and the fleet was, once again, grounded instantly. Analysis of the wreckage this time, however, indicated that whilst the result had been the same – a wing had broken off in flight – the reason was not due to the loss of the titanium bolt that locked the wings in place. The accident to XV345 was caused primarily by fatigue cracks in the titanium 'spectacle' frame, which was the strongest part of the airframe. However, many of the RAF's fleet of aircraft, ex-RN in this case, had surpassed the fatigue specimen[24] at Brough, which at the time had not been realised was programmed for the benign over-the-water role for which the aircraft was originally designed – tragic consequences that resulted in many aircraft being chucked on the scrap heap and even more tragically, resulted in the loss of another crew!

23. The first phase of staff training; the Individual Staff Studies course was a distance learning course, of some eighteen months duration, that introduced junior officers to the vagaries of service writing and staff work.

24. During the construction programme one aircraft is held at the factory and used as a fatigue model. Mounted on hydraulic jacks, the aircraft is constantly placed under pressures that simulate its planned operational profile. It is normal practice to 'fatigue' the aircraft ahead of its operational cousins such that fatigue cracks, etc, can be realised before they happen for real in the air.

The grounding lasted six months whilst each and every aircraft was stripped down and inspected thoroughly. Some were found to be irretrievable and had to be scrapped, whilst others were deemed recoverable if the cracks were polished out and the structure retained its previous strength. Limitations were placed on those airframes that came back into service that limited the amount of 'g' available. All-in-all it was a disaster for the fleet. When flying eventually recommenced, there were only sufficient airframes left to provide for four squadrons and an OCU, rather than five operational units; 216 Squadron, the last to form, was disbanded.

The dilemma for the RAF from the outset was what to do with the aircrew who would now have to kick their heels and lose flying currency until the aircraft returned. Single-seat Hawker Hunters were resurrected and delivered to Honington and Laarbruch to allow the pilots to 'keep their hand' in. However, other than the occasional ride in a two-seat trainer variant of the Hunter, navigators were left to consider their options. For the OCU the task was equally difficult, but at least the sensible decision was taken to turn off the student flow and redirect those destined for Buccaneers elsewhere.

As I contemplated my options, my boyhood dream of becoming a Lightning pilot streamed into my brain. In 1980 the RAF still operated the English Electric Lightning at RAF Binbrook and, although numbers were small, there was still a training unit that operated two-seat trainers, which were perfectly adequate from a navigator's perspective. A scheme was already in place for navigators to choose a temporary posting, on an aircraft of their choice, during the grounding. I approached the SNI and applied for a temporary move to the Lightning Training Flight at Binbrook! It was approved at HQ and I readied myself for a short sojourn in Lincolnshire and the opportunity to fly at Mach 2 in a Lightning.

I was due to arrive at Binbrook on a Monday morning in March 1980 when I received a telephone call whilst sat in the crewroom on the Friday before waiting for the bar to open. The squadron leader on the end of the phone announced himself as being from LTF and wanted to welcome me to Binbrook and let me know that they were expecting me at 0800hrs on the Monday. I thought 'how considerate' to ring me on the Friday and introduce himself. I was delighted and told him I was really looking forward to coming to Binbrook, and to, eventually, get some hours in the Lightning. His mood, which had been pleasant up until then, suddenly changed!

'You are not flying in the Lightning, lad!' he exploded, 'we've got some jobs that need doing and you are tasked with doing them!'

I tried to explain to him that the whole purpose of my coming, as agreed between HQ 1 Gp and HQ 11 Gp, was that I would get some flying to keep me current and interested whilst the Buccaneers were grounded. He was having none of it. The conversation ended badly with me telling him that if that was the case, then I was definitely not coming to Binbrook. He slammed the phone down. I went straight to the SNI's office and explained the predicament to him. He agreed and asked me to go and see the Boss and explain to him just what had gone on. Phil Wilkinson too was sympathetic and got straight on the phone to HQ 1 Gp and cancelled my 'vacation'. I never did get to fly in a Lightning, but I had flown in a Starfighter, which I imagine was just as good. I stayed at Honington and flew as often as I could in the two-seat Hunters. Life was good, and it allowed me some time to crack on with tasks at home and spend more time with my family.

The Buccaneers came back in late July and I was back in harness on the thirtieth and tasked to attack HMS *Cardiff* in the North Sea just one day later; both sorties flown with Captain Ken Alley, the OCU's tame USAF exchange pilot. Ken and I flew again on 1 August 1980 and then, on the fourth, he caught me napping in the staff room and asked me if I wanted to join him in a Hunter for a quick bit of GH. The aircraft was sitting idly on the pan and we had an hour on our hands. I jumped at the opportunity. Airborne on a low-level departure from Honington, we were soon over Norfolk and heading towards the coast at Cromer. As we coasted out at about 5,000 feet, Ken asked me if I fancied taking control to do some aerobatics. I looked left towards him and raised my eyebrows! He encouraged me to have a go.

'Do a loop,' he said. I queried what was required. He said, 'Just pull back on the stick!'

I pulled back on the stick and the aircraft entered a very gentle climb at a rate of about 1000 feet per minute.

'No!' he said. 'Pull hard back on the stick!'

With that I yanked the control column hard into my stomach and the aircraft snapped about 6g! Ken very quickly rammed both his hands on the stick to prevent me pulling it any further back such that, as he pushed, the g-meter indicated –1g! Ken quickly took control of the aircraft and recovered us to level flight.

'Ah shit!' were his next words, quickly followed by, 'I think we've overstressed it!'

Overstressing an aircraft is not a good idea! It causes unnecessary fatigue on the airframe and requires the ground crew to do a full stress check after landing! Ken turned the Hunter for home and we both prepared to face the music, which we knew would not be long in coming. Phil Wilkinson was not impressed, but he understood the circumstances and was not too harsh in the words he used towards me – I have no idea what he said to Ken after I had been dismissed, but I am sure he was pretty sympathetic to our friendly Yank. If I had not done so before, I realised then exactly why the RAF had decided that I would make a better navigator than a pilot!

It wasn't difficult really; you could see it coming a mile off. The Akrotiri Officers' Mess bar had been the pivot point for similar 'my Dad's bigger than your Dad' discussions for many an evening previously, so why should this night have been any exception. During the day, the Phantom mob were there to ensure that the bar always opened on time and we were there because we hadn't had a kebab for a while and there was a rumour going around that the Tombs of the Kings at Paphos were worth a look. In reality, and although it never seemed to stop the Lufwaffe from having a go forty years before, the weather in the UK in November was notoriously appalling. Thus it was, for a training unit tasked with 'maintaining the line', that alternative plans needed to be in place to ensure that clear blue skies were available to ensure that we stayed at least 'on the line'. God knows why the Phantom mob were really there, as

I have always discovered that once the grey mist and 8/8[ths25] had been breached, there was always ample blue above to have a bit of a punch up!

This was 237 Operational Conversion Unit's annual Exercise Winter Watcher and we were getting back to the 'line' at the request of a very considerate staff at HQ 1 Gp. Two weeks in Cyprus in November 1980 with not many students, if I recall, and a bunch of instructors who were in the habit of not getting many overseas perks routinely. Our near neighbours from Wattisham, 56 (Fighter) Squadron, under the command of Brian Johnson, were there to shoot the banner and protect the Sovereign Base Areas[26] if the bad guys in the littoral states at the eastern end of the Med kicked off. We were led by the spirited Phil Wilkinson and had a number of irrepressible and renowned members of the Buccaneer brotherhood in our midst.

The Keo had been flowing for nearly two weeks and the Brandy Sour Lake had been drained on more than one occasion. Banter levels were high in the bar and, with that rather annoying air of arrogance that a group of Flashhearts bring to any party, the schoolies had fallen for the rather doubtful and outspoken charms of the 56 Squadron aircrew! We, of course, were not troubled by this air of superiority that pervaded the atmosphere and, as mud-movers[27], had a natural understanding of our own value! We knew that revenge would be ours!

So it flowed across the bar! 'My Dad's bigger than your Dad!' 'No he's not!' 'Yes he is!' You know the sort of mature conversation that aircrew have when they are happily sitting outside the contents of a rather large brewery, or when their skin has taken on that rather soft puffy appearance as a result of basking in a lake for rather more time than is reasonably sensible. We were, of course, past masters of both, and a few idle words from a bunch of prima donnas would be rewarded in due time.

'You guys do airfield attacks, don't you?' (My Dad's bigger than your Dad, incoming!)

'Might!'

'Nah!' in an inebriated slang, 'You do, don't you!?' 'Bet, you can't get through to this one while we defend it!'

'Oh yeah!' 'How much?'

'One Brandy Sour Lake!'

'Yer, on!'

'Right, we'll set up a CAP[28], and you attack Akrotiri!'

'OK!'

---

25. Cloud cover is described in meteorology in eighths. 8/8[ths] describes a full overcast whereas a smattering of light fluffy cumulus cloud might be described as 1/8[ths]; no cloud would be described as SKY CLEAR.

26. The Sovereign Base Areas of Akrotiri and Dhekelia are British Overseas Territories on the island of Cyprus. The SBAs, which include military bases and other land, were retained by the British, under the 1960 treaty of independence, agreed and signed by the United Kingdom, Greece, Turkey and representatives from the Greek and Turkish Cypriot communities, which granted independence to the Crown Colony of Cyprus.

27. Aircraft that deliver air-to-surface weapons.

28. Combat Air Patrol.

'When then?'

'Whatdya mean, when? You guard it, we'll attack it; winner takes all, or one Brandy Sour Lake for internal consumption as appropriate!'

'No! We need to know when, we can't guard it forever!'

'What! Thought you were fighters! Isn't that what you're supposed to do? Defend the SBA!'

'Yeh, but! We've got the banner[29] as well you know! We need to know when?'

'OK! Thursday!'

'What time on Thursday?'

'Give us a break! You're Air Defenders, use your GCI mates at Olympus and defend the SBA on Thursday!'

'OK! But we need to know the time!'

'No way! You said you'd defend Akrotiri, so get on with it! See you Thursday!'

So the scene was set. There were twenty-four hours in Thursday, 20 November 1980, and we had the upper hand already! Needless to say, there were not many Phantom guys in the bar on the night of the nineteenth, as QRA had been mounted by midnight for the first time at Akrotiri since the Turks had invaded Cyprus six years before.

The dissimilar Air Combat Training rules of the day stated that any such activity should, at the very least, be preceded by a telephone briefing. However, with both outfits sitting at opposing ends of the same airfield, our new SNI had been despatched earlier in the week to thrash out the Rules of Engagement for the mission, but with strict instructions to give nothing away of our plan. Thus, everybody would play by the rules, and injury to anything other than pride would be kept to an absolute minimum. He returned pleased as punch that he had 'secured a good deal'. He had agreed an attack corridor 'anywhere north of the 270° radial' and fixed that we would SQUAWK[30] the required code when under radar control from Olympus. He had failed! A quick look at the map and knowledge of the local 'no over-flight of Cyprus' rule would have made it obvious to a blind man, with or without a white stick, that this was a huge constraint for any attacking force. The poor chap lost any goodwill he had had and was pilloried unmercifully for days – he had just handed all the advantage back to the enemy! Undeterred, and with the Boss's blessing, we vowed to cheat, but remain within the rules set, in principle, whilst at the same time ensuring that we regained the advantage!

Ivor Evans was given the lead with Geoff Coop in his back seat; I was matched with Norman Crow who, despite his rather laid-back attitude to life generally, had one or two masterful strokes up his sleeve ready for when they were required; we were to be No 4! The others in this tale were: the Boss with Norman Roberson; and Pete Atkins with Ron Pegrum.

---

29. 56 Squadron were in Akrotiri to conduct air-to-air gunnery practice against a banner towed by a Canberra tug.

30. IFF transmissions are described as squawks.

Before our time on 237 OCU, Norman Crow and I had served on 12 Squadron together and I remember many facets of his character that epitomised the charm that he brought to the Buccaneer Force. Apart from our earlier exciting departure from Gibraltar together, two other moments stick firmly in my mind whenever I think of Norman Crow. It was he who was the pilot on Trial Mistico 2 whose TV MARTEL decided to take to the sky, vertically, rather than to the sea when Ken MacKenzie selected Terminal Phase! The other was his habit, more famous amongst the Junta than the squadron executives, of dutifully applying for the RAF C Promotion Exam each year, but never ever turning up to take it! Once, when I was having particular difficulty applying myself to my studies in preparation for the exam, I challenged him as to why he never took the exam. He explained in the way that only Norman could, that by applying he was always able to answer honestly the Boss's question regarding his application, and by not turning up on the day, he managed to secure a day off without anybody knowing or, for that matter, worrying where he might be!

Not a Phantom wheel turned that morning as Flashheart and his chaps wrestled with the tricky problem of identifying when they might be required to defend the hallowed Akrotiri soil. They were, of course, at the Eastern end of the airfield and we occupied the Western sunspots, so they did not have easy visual contact with us on our dispersal and relied on scouts to do their spotting for them. Without any warning to our brethren in QRA, we slipped our mooring at about 1130hrs and managed to get airborne on a westerly heading with little or no fuss, but with a positive ID from the 'enemy'. Our departure was uneventful as we climbed to high altitude squawking as required and under radar control from Olympus. They clearly thought that with us held tightly in their grasp, their Flashheart mates were up for a 'Turkey Shoot' – not if we had anything to do with it, they weren't!

At Top of Climb, around 35,000 feet, we levelled off, and proceeded as planned through West Point and onwards towards the Maros and Toska air traffic reporting points, making like airliners whilst the 'enemy' gathered themselves and their mighty weapon systems into the air. The incessant height and heading confidence-boosting chatter from Olympus began to wear us down, but, like the true professionals that we were, we responded and assisted them in their preparations to provide a top-notch GCI service to 56 Squadron. We were, of course, lulling them into a false sense of security as we had no intention of playing absolutely by the rules! Beyond Maros we turned starboard as if to intercept the 270° radial from Akrotiri, and once established inbound, formed loose arrow formation, throttled back, rolled, opened the airbrake and switched off the IFF!!! We were about to cheat! We would soon be below Olympus radar cover and out of radar control, so there was little point in providing them with height updates during our VFR descent. The Buccaneer Flight Reference Cards quote 16,000ft/min for a Max Rate Descent at 0.85Mach/400kts. However, my memory tells me that it seemed much less than two minutes on that day in 1980 before we were at low-level over the Med, where the Bucc was happiest; 100ft (give or take) above the 'oggin! Echoing in the ether behind us were the plaintive cries of Olympus, asking us politely to check our Squawk and our altitude. We changed to

'Exercise Mistico' – Flying over damaged targets with a clean missile pylon on Station 3: 6 October 1975. (*Author*)

'Wannabe QWIs' – No 5 QWI Course, 237 OCU, RAF Honington. L to R: Lou Kemp, Dick Harden, David Ray, Ray Morris, Author, Nick Berryman: 2 June 1976. (*Crown/RAF Honington*)

'Maritime Sortie Brief' – SFD Briefing Room, RAF Lossiemouth. L to R: Norman Crow, Derek Heathcote, Howard Lusher and Ken MacKenzie are briefed by Mick Whybro for a mission on Exercise Teamwork: 12 September 1976. (*Crown / RAF Lossiemouth*)

'12 Squadron on Parade'. (*Crown / RAF Lossiemouth*)

'Taxying for Kodak' – Rob Williams with the Author in the back taxi out at RAF Honington for a company MARTEL photoshoot: 29 March 1977. (*Hawker Siddeley Dynamics Ltd*)

'Maritime Warload' – XX895 with ARM, DLP and 2xTVM: 29 March 1977. (*Hawker Siddeley Dynamics Ltd*)

'Found – The Soviet Navy!' – The newly replenished KRIVAK II at speed: 13 June 1977. (*Author*)

'Watchout! BIRDS!' – The result of a multiple gull strike at 100 feet and 540 kts, Römö Range: 13 March 1978. (*Crown/RDAF Skrydstrup*)

'Beating the Yanks!' – Author on Red Flag 79-1: 20 October 1978. (*Crown / HQ STC*)

'Instructors and Crew' – 237 OCU staff and groundcrew. Author is sat on the canopy and the 'spirited' Phil Wilkinson is reclining on the aircraft's nose. (*Crown / RAF Honington*)

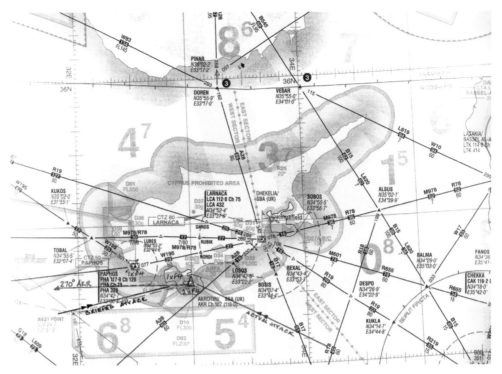

'The Attack Plan' – What we briefed and what we did: Akrotiri, 20 November 1980. (*No 1 AIDU*)

'To the Victors the Spoils' – 237 OCU aircrew and groundcrew relish the moment (Author crouching 3rd from left wearing 'aviators'): 20 November 1980. (*Crown / RAF Akrotiri*)

'Enemy Territory!' – 100ft over Nevada on Red Flag 82-1: 5 November 1981. (*16 Squadron Album*)

'We're Behind You!' – Leading the Flypast of four Buccaneers and four Jaguars at JHQ Rheindahlen for HM Queen's Birthday Flypast: 11 June 1982. (*Crown/JHQ Rheindahlen*)

'2000Hrs Buccaneer' – With Peter Norriss. Warhawk Beers upon arrival at Spangdahlem; Cluster J Hartley III holding the beer crate: 12 July 1982. (*Author's Collection*)

'Before its Loss' – XV160, in 208 Squadron colours, before it crashed on Frasca Range on 20 September 1982. (*Via Key Publishing*)

'Sorry Sight!' – XV 160's tailplane floats in the Mediterranean: 20 September 1982. (*16 Squadron Album*)

'Swan' – The Black Saints: 25 September 1982. (*Crown / RAF Laarbruch*)

'Exercise Maple Flag' – A mixed XV and 16 Squadron team at RAF Lossiemouth on 'work-up' (Author on extreme left): 26 April 1983. (*Crown/RAF Lossiemouth*)

'Glen Tilt on a Tilt!' – Navigator's view at low level in The Highlands. (*Glenn Mason*)

'Where it's Most Comfortable!' – A Fleet Air Arm Buccaneer S2A over Loch Borralan near the Altnacealgach Hotel in the Western Highlands. (*Clive Morrell*)

'Lossiemouth Maritime Wing' – 12 & 208 Squadrons. (*FlyPast Magazine*)

'Killer Punch' – Some of the Buccaneer Aircrew Association's Weapons Collection at Yorkshire Air Museum: 540lb Bomb, 1000lb Bomb, WE177 Nuclear Weapon, TV MARTEL Missile, Sea Eagle Missile. (*Graham Pitchfork*)

'Maritime Attack Weapons' – 12 Squadron RAF Lossiemouth: 1993. (*FlyPast Magazine*)

'Down and Dirty!' – Buccaneer with Westinghouse jamming pod, two CBLS and a Pavespike pod. (*FlyPast Magazine*)

'And so to Tornado!' – XV Squadron Tornado GR1 leads a XV Squadron Buccaneer S2B during handover celebrations at RAF Laarbruch: June 1983. (*Richard Somers-Cocks*)

'Saved from the Breaker's Yard!' – XX901, owned by the Buccaneer Aircrew Association, on display at Yorkshire Air Museum. (*Yorkshire Air Museum/Ian Finch*)

'The Assembled Company' – SAAF Memorial, Bays Hill, Pretoria: 9 November 2008. (*SAAF Swartkop*)

'Happy Author' – Last flight in a Buccaneer, Thunder City, Cape Town: 14 November 2008. (*Author*)

'Thanks, Ian!' – Thanking Ian Pringle for my last ever flight in a Buccaneer (XW986/ZU–NIP), Thunder City, Cape Town: 14 November 2008. (*Author*)

'Personalised Plate' – The Author's Saab in the shadow of XX889 at Bruntingthorpe: 25 August 2013. (*Author*)

our squadron discrete frequency, as frankly their pathetic wailings were beginning to get on our nerves!

Meanwhile, our temporarily grounded students at Akrotiri were noting the antics of our adversary and reported later their deeds to the attacking force. The valiant four-ball from 56 Squadron had got airborne in reasonably short order after our departure and three CAPs were soon established; one Phantom on the 270° radial south of Paphos; one orbiting in Episkopi Bay; and two capping over the airfield itself; all at about Ten Grand! They surely must have believed that we would be easy meat and that we lacked cunning or any intent to deceive – little did they know!

Upon reaching our new 'cruising' height, we bustered[31] and turned south-south-east to fly the route of the airways that circumnavigate Cyprus to the south, but far below them and far below any possibility of radar control or contact! Our intent was to confuse Olympus and our foe before they could establish any Mental Air Picture (MAP) or catch a glimpse of us at low-level – we needn't have worried as reports subsequently told that the volume and confusion of the calls on GCI were proof enough that any Radar Air Picture or MAP had gone out the window!! When we ran out of Cypriot airspace at the Egyptian FIR, we turned north-east and flew parallel to the FIR boundary, still at low-level, aiming for an IP seventy nautical miles south-east of Akrotiri and on an attack heading of approximately 310°, which was some 140° different to that briefed to our adversaries. OK, we were cheating now, but we satisfied ourselves that the Russians would have done so also, and anyway, the fighter jocks needed the practice! The noise and accusations on GCI were evidently something to be heard as both Olympus and the 56 Squadron formation scoured the skies for our four-ball to the west of Akrotiri.

Once at the IP we pushed back up to 580 kts IAS and pushed down to an appropriate attack height! As we ran from Israel towards Akrotiri, the approach controller rumbled us, but only when we called for attack clearance. She had no reason to be faithful to us or to 56 Squadron, but there was absolutely no reason for her to tell the chap from Olympus where we were; she could only have been seeing him at the weekends, we were in the bar all week! The game was up, but far too late for the defending force to gather itself suitably to repel an attack from the south-east. Our Goofers on the ground reported afterwards that, once the confusion of, 'They're where?!' had been resolved and the overhead CAP had been despatched for the intercept, they were disturbed by a thunderous roar as the Episkopi Bay CAP passed through the overhead at about Ten Grand heading in a south-easterly direction; quickly followed some two minutes later by a blue haze and the 'close to the Mach' shadow of a Phantom from Paphos Bay heading towards Israel!

It was all too late! Yes, they saw us one hundred and eighty degrees out, but we were far too low and they were far too disorganised (subsequent confession) for them to get a reasonable Fox-1[32] shot off and by then our front pair were crossing the beach and Norman and I were in touch with our leader with about forty seconds

---

31. Accelerated to maximum speed (580kts at sea level).
32. Head-on missile firing solution.

to run. Just as we hit the beach I looked out and called a Phantom turning in our four o'clock in an attempt to gain a shot on us. Norman took immediate straight line evasive action; slammed the throttle closed and popped the airbrake full out. XT274 stopped on a tanner and the Phantom overshot and failed to get his shot off (admitted)! We didn't. But of course we didn't ever have a gun and in 1980 there were no Sidewinders available for the Buccaneer Force!

The team assembled at opening time with a buoyant Phil Wilkinson and his mob, staff and students, gathered to receive their prize. The boys of 56, of course, were noble in defeat as they ate rather generous helpings of humble pie. The lake was declared open and a bloody good night was once again had by all! Norman had got his kill and I am sure to this day that the back-seater of that Phantom has still got the imprint of his radar screen firmly embossed on his face from the deceleration as his pilot realised that his firing solution would never come and the game was up – he had been about to 'die'!

'Hey, you guys ever done gunnery against the banner?' My Dad's bigger than your Dad, incoming!

Pass me another Brandy Sour, there's a good chap!

There were plenty more alcohol-driven antics on that Winter Watcher and plenty of good flying too, but none to match the day we defeated 56 Squadron and got through their defensive screen to attack Akrotiri.

It would not salve my conscience if I did not apprise you, dear reader, of the infamous 'ever so slightly miffed' party and the resultant 'broken toilet' event in the Akrotiri Officers' Mess during that exercise! It will be a necessary and cathartic act to recount it here, although I am unsure if the statute of limitations will have any bearing after so many years! I suspect I am OK, as the events unfolded over thirty years ago and none of the participants were sober enough to recall events the day after, let alone now that we are mostly in our mid-60s!

For some unknown reason the mess decided to close the bar to us one Friday night whilst they held a private function. They were good enough to lay on an honesty bar in the Ladies' Room for us, but that did not quite have the same cachet as a Happy Hour in the bar with all the usual high jinks that accompanied such an event!

Heaven forfend that we had set out to cause damage. Nothing could have been further from our minds. It just happened! It was just one of those unintended consequences that often leave one temporarily unsure of one's position in life!

The evening had started off quietly in the Ladies' Room with a well-stocked bar and polite conversation. Of course, we started drinking long before the party goers arrived for the function to which we were rightly excluded. It was a private affair, not a mess organised event, and so quite rightly we, as temporary interlopers, were skipped from the invitation list. Soon, from the confines of our exclusion zone, we watched like children at a sweetie shop window as the guests started to arrive. The men were all wearing dinner jackets whilst their ladies ventured into the mess in silky flowing evening gowns. It looked like they were going to have a great time and so would we, if only we had stuck to our limited space.

After about two more hours of drinking, someone came up with a cunning plan – I think it was Norman Crow! He had been prompted by one of our number who had just returned from de-tanking in the Gents' loo! He reported that the dinner party guests were now in a similar 'off-load' state and that he had seen quite a queue forming outside the Ladies' toilets! That was enough for Norman.

'Let's lock the door and remove the key!'

Well! I and a few others had now had sufficient beer to concur with Norman that that was a 'spiffing idea' and that it would raise a laugh, and our morale, if we held onto the key for a short period of time. So, during a quiet spell in their need, we quickly sallied forth, locked the Ladies' Loo and scurried back to our enclosure with the key grasped firmly in our hand! About ten minutes later we heard a kerfuffle in the corridor as black-suited man after black-suited man attempted to work out just why the loo door seemed to be jammed! Shoulder barges were to no avail and multiple twistings of the handle proved absolutely useless. We sniggered as quietly as we could as we watched from a short and hidden distance. The girls were now desperate as their hopping on one leg now clearly indicated.

'Nothing for it!' said one black-suited man, 'Into the Gents', girls, whilst I stand guard on the door!'

Damn! We had been foiled by a lateral thinker!

Undeterred, however, Norman and I came up with another cunning plan! And this, dear reader, is where the wheels came off our runaway wagon! With the Ladies' Loo key now hidden within the Ladies' Room, and during yet another lull in the party-goers' 'need', Norman and I strode off to the Gents' and began to lock each of the cubicles from the inside! Well, in truth! Norman stood guard whilst I locked the first, climbed onto the seat then the cistern and down into the next cubicle by the reverse means. It worked a treat. One after the other, each of the cubicles was locked from the inside to deny the ladies any means at all of completing their most natural function!

Then that unintended consequence reared its ugly head! With five cubicles locked, I climbed onto the seat and then onto the cistern to make my way into cubicle six. I was not to know that the cistern in cubicle six was not securely fixed to the wall, and that is my defence, m'lud! The whole bloody thing came adrift from its surroundings and crashed onto the loo seat and thence to the floor! There were shards of porcelain everywhere, but, and much more importantly, cold water was gushing from a severed pipe! I quickly joined Norman outside the row of cubicles and surveyed the crash site! It did not look good! The shards of porcelain were not the main problem as they could be cleared up easily even in our drunken state. However, finding the stop cock and recovering the whole situation back to where it had been five minutes before was a bit more of a tall order! We did our best, but failed miserably, and soon found ourselves at the Reception Desk trying to explain just how it was that the cistern just 'fell off the wall!' The water was soon stopped and an admission of fault soon saw clear to releasing us from our ignominy if not our guilt! Amends were made and a contribution to the cost of repair soon resolved the whole issue. Of course, it spoilt our evening completely, because, with the Gents' Loo now out of commission, we were forced to relinquish the key to the Ladies' so that everybody in the mess that night, including us, could carry on drinking in the sure knowledge that at least the Ladies' Loo was available for us all to de-tank in!

But it did not always require alcohol to stimulate we aircrews' sense of fun or the bizarre! Sunday, 23 November was to be our last night in Akrotiri. We decided that a quiet night at the cinema was in order before we packed up and headed for home, via Sigonella in Sicily, on the Monday morning. The film being shown at the Astra Cinema that Sunday evening was a horror movie entitled '*Friday the 13th!*' It was a stirring tale about a group of young American post-High School students who were attending a summer camp for a bit of hunting, fishing, shooting, backwoodsman-ship and shagging! Unfortunately, a silent killer was on the loose who was systematically killing people with a large sword which would suddenly appear from under the bed and through the bodies of the copulating couples! Just the kind of movie that broad-minded aircrew need to watch after three weeks away from home and the night before we all returned to our loved ones! After dinner we sauntered along to the Astra mob-handed, parted with our Cypriot loose change and took up our seats in rows near the back. The movie was quite tense and we sat there in the dark drinking in the horrible scenes that unfolded before our eyes. Childish pranks against each other tried to ease the tension, but it would be fair to say that we were all gripped by the film, and a huge sigh of relief rose from the whole cinema as the young hero and his heroine managed to escape in a rowing boat into the middle of the lake at the end of the film! The feeling of relief was tangible until, suddenly, and just as we anticipated the credits rolling up the screen, a morbid shell of humanity rose from the depths and pulled the happy couple under the water and to their deaths! The whole audience rose vertically as one from their seats in shock!

As we left the cinema we tried to laugh it off, but it was apparent that the film had had an effect on us all – there was nothing for it, we needed a nightcap!

'Who's coming to the bar?' Paul Dandeker[33] asked. Only the Boss declined, informing us that he had some paperwork to catch up on before he started packing. After just a couple of beers we wandered back to our beds in the block still alive with thoughts of the film and its outcome. The transit blocks at Akrotiri were single storey with a long veranda to the front that provided a covered walkway to the ablutions in the centre of the building. Front and centre of the block were two single rooms that were not in a terrace like the rest, but stood alone and isolated from the main building itself. Phil Wilkinson had been allocated one of these and it was clear from the light shining through his curtains that he was still awake and working on his papers.

'Let's wind up the Boss,' some joker suggested, and with that the posse of OCU instructors dispersed around the outside of his room and started making low haunting noises, hollow screams and sexual moans. It had little effect! There was no reaction. Then somebody found the circuit breakers for the whole building! That started it! The lights went off! They came back on! The lights went off! They came back on again! It emulated beautifully, in our eyes, a perfect scene from the film. God knows

---

33. Known throughout the RAF as D².

what Phil thought of it, but still he did not react. I assume, like all sensible senior officers, he knew we would grow tired of it and eventually go to bed.

He clearly did not know us as well as he thought – a cunning plan was developed that was bound to get a reaction and, again, it would echo a scene from the film. One man was tasked with quietly and surreptitiously unlatching his window from the outside. Another was posted at the circuit breakers whilst two more picked up a large dustbin and stood poised and ready!

The lights flickered but did not go off! They flickered again. And again. And again. And then, as the block was plunged into darkness, the window was flung open and the dustbin hurled through the curtains exactly like the dead body had been thrown into the dorm in the film! The Boss's scream could be heard across the camp! We fell about laughing and he came out of his room, and with a huge smile on his face ordered us all to bed!

Norman and I had an uneventful journey home in XV355, made all the better for our lunch stop in Sicily!

As 1981 dawned I decided to speak to my desk officer[34] at RAF Barnwood near Gloucester. I got a very pleasant surprise. He told me that I had been short-listed for an exchange tour at Mountain Home AFB near Boise, Idaho, in the USA. The USAF Bomber Wing at Mountain Home operated F-111 swing wing bombers. More importantly, I was number one on the list and nothing could knock me off that spot if my family and I wanted to spend three years in the USA, he informed me as we closed the conversation. I agreed to think about it and let him know my response before the end of March. I was mightily excited. The prospect of flying the F-111 was sufficient, but the prospect of three years in the USA could not have come at a better time for our young family. Certainly, although schooling might eventually become an issue for Christopher, it would only have been towards the end of our tour. Sue agreed! Neither of us could stop talking about the prospect. Whilst she admitted that she was not overly keen on the idea of a hunting, shooting, fishing existence in Idaho, she knew that it was a career-enhancing move for me and the notion of a different life Stateside was not one to be turned down. Unable to wait until the end of March, I rang my desk officer back in the middle of the month to let him know that we were up for it and to go ahead and finalise details and dates!

I was not prepared for his response. In fact, I did not recognise the voice on the end of the phone. My desk officer had been reassigned and his replacement was altogether singing from a different hymn sheet. He let me know unreservedly that I was no longer number one on the list, but had dropped to number two. When I asked him why, he explained that my efforts on the C Exam and my lack of application to ISS indicated that I was not career-minded and that in itself had resulted in him reversing the decision taken by his predecessor. I knew both the guys who were on

---

34. The Personnel Management Centre at RAF Barnwood was responsible for the management of officers' careers in the RAF. Each officer, dependent upon rank and branch, would be looked after by an officer one rank above who was responsible for grading his officers for promotion and for organising postings best suited to specialisation and performance. In the aircrew world these 'desk officers' were broken down further into aircraft type; I was looked after by the FJ Nav Desk Officer.

the list with me and I knew only too well that the chap now at number one had had similar, if not equal, difficulties with both of the speed bumps that had just cost me a wonderful tour in the USA. Try as I might to persuade him of this he was not to be swayed! The decision had been taken and he was not a man to change his mind.

I was incensed and try as Phil Wilkinson might to go above my desk officer's head at Barnwood, it was to no avail. Graham Seaward and his wife Helen had a most wonderful tour in Idaho, and I was left pondering what might have been.

In that same month my old Boss from 12 Squadron, Graham Smart, arrived on the OCU for a refresher course. He had been promoted to group captain and was about to take command of RAF Laarbruch in Germany. I was appointed his navigator for the duration of his short course and flew all his 'non-QFI' syllabus sorties with him before he was cleared to depart the OCU to take up his new command appointment. Following my unnecessary outburst against Graham Smart after he had tried to lead the six-ship formation into dense low cloud in The Minch, we held a mutual respect for each other's professionalism. Indeed, when he was my Boss on 12 Squadron, I would have had no hesitation in climbing into the back seat of a Buccaneer to go to war with him. He was an outstanding pilot and a very good and safe pair of hands. After he had completed a couple of trips with the CFI to re-familiarise himself with the aircraft, he was handed over to me. We flew our first sortie on 11 March 1981 and were tasked to take the jet for a bit of low flying to allow him to reacquaint himself at low-level. We had plenty of gas on board and so we planned to undertake a hi-lo-lo into the Highlands. It was as if he had never been away from a Buccaneer cockpit. The checks flowed smoothly. He flew it with ease and I had absolutely no concerns or negative comments throughout the mission. Having completed the overland low-level portion of the mission we coasted out at Arbroath to practise low flying over the sea; we had been authorised to fly there at 100 feet. Shortly after we stabilised at our authorised height, Graham asked me if I minded if he took it down a bit lower. I was not concerned and very comfortable with his ability. I knew that the Radio Altimeter would 'lock-out' below fifty feet and become unreliable – if it gave any reading at all. We were soon settled at about thirty feet above the sea and we screamed along happily at 480 knots as we wended our way back to the Norfolk coastline and recovery back to Honington. Our next three sorties together completed the weapon delivery phase of his course and, after just three weeks in our midst, he was off.

Also refreshing about the same time, prior to taking up command of 16 Squadron at Laarbruch, was Peter Norriss, who had been a good friend on XV Squadron on my first tour. Whilst they were both in the crewroom one day, I took another call from my desk officer who was offering me a posting to be the first QWI navigator on the first squadron, 9 Squadron, to operate the Tornado GR1 that was about to come into service. I was not too sure about the prospects of going to a brand-new squadron and both Graham and Peter were aware of my lost posting to the USA. When I put the phone down, Peter asked me what they were offering me. I explained the offer to move across the airfield again to 9 Squadron, but they could both see that I was less than enthusiastic about the whole affair. Reading this, you might think me mad to even pause for a second when such an offer was made. But I was still smarting after my shoddy treatment over Mountain Home and I really did not fancy setting up yet another squadron's chinagraph boards or crewroom. When a new squadron forms, particularly with a new type of aircraft, there are often more problems to be ironed out than not – my heart wasn't in it!

'You know,' said Peter, '16 Squadron are going to be really short of middle management experienced aircrew.' Graham Smart concurred with that view and clearly knew what was coming next.

'Why don't you come to 16?' he continued, 'I could really do with someone with experience like yours on the squadron.'

'Great idea,' said Graham, 'Peter and I would look after you and then you could go to Tornado after that.'

I have to admit it had plenty of appeal, but I knew that first I would have to run the idea past Sue; there is a huge difference between three years in the USA and three years in Nord Rhein Westfalen! I knew I could assume nothing.

In and around the OCU, Peter and Graham kept telling me of all the advantages there would be by going back to Germany and how they would 'look after me'. I knew it made sense and, as an aside, it would allow me to be one of the first to achieve over 2000 hours in a Buccaneer.

Sue was very much up for the challenge of a new life in Germany and agreed instantly to accept the offer being made. I had to take no action with Barnwood myself. As soon as I informed them both that we would be happy to go to Laarbruch, Graham Smart picked up the phone and squared it all away with my desk officer.

April, May and June passed in a flash and before long, with the house packed into a removal lorry, we headed over to Sue's parents in Norfolk and, after a short weekend with them, set sail from Felixstowe to Zeebrugge and another tour in 2 ATAF.

There is a twist in this tale, however. I left the OCU under a cloud. A cloud that was not of my making, but one brought about from interpretation by, frankly, somebody who should have known better. I had had an outstandingly successful tour as an instructor and my last Aircrew Assessment was glowing:

'Flight Lieutenant Herriot is one of my most experienced instructors and is highly respected by both staff and students. He is a very capable navigator in all aspects of Buccaneer operations, and as a QWI is amongst the very best. His weaponry briefings are detailed and precise, and his post flight analysis is searching and accurate. He is responsible for a large proportion of weaponry phase briefs, and his excellent instructional technique ensures they are well presented. He has continued to take responsibility for an element of staff training associated with the maritime aspects of the unit's war role. Flight Lieutenant Herriot's experience and professionalism continue to be an asset to the OCU. Above the Average as a Navigator and Instructor.'

So said the Boss on 31 May 1981. However, not so the SNI, when he debriefed me on my ACR the same month and prior to my departure. His report covered everything that I expected it to and reflected mostly what the Boss had said above, but his last paragraph, and his spoken comments regarding it, floored me:

'Whilst I am very impressed by Flight Lieutenant Herriot's professionalism in his squadron duties, he has not been totally convincing in his determination to progress within the service. In 1980, through lack of personal effort, he failed the C Exam and withdrew from ISS after failing two phase exercises when all were clearly within his grasp. However, to his credit he has retaken the C examination and has re-enrolled for ISS starting in June 81. He has chosen what I believe is the soft option of an overseas tour remaining within the Buccaneer force, in preference to a more demanding and challenging Tornado posting. Whilst I think he is ambitious he has not fully appreciated the importance of consistently demonstrating his suitability for higher rank, and has not produced enough evidence, apart from his competency as a navigator and a QWI to support a strong recommendation for promotion.'

In 1981 there was no open reporting system and the SNI was not obliged to, nor did he, read me exactly what he had written. Only a decision taken in 2001 to release all one's reports to individuals has allowed me to actually read his words. What appalled me at the time was that he informed me, to my face during that ACR debrief, that he had marked me down because I wanted to go to Germany so that I 'could buy another duty-free car'! He had given no thought or consideration that I had had to study for the C Exam whilst lying prone with a broken back. No heed was taken of the fact that I had been encouraged to opt for 16 Squadron by two senior officers who were desperate to have that 'experience' so well trumpeted in my Aircrew Assessment. By reducing my overall promotion assessment to 'Recommended', he broke a chain of previous 'Highly Recommended' assessments that were essential to maintain in order to even feature at the top of the desk officer's pile when he did the pre-boarding for each year's promotion board. He had, in one fell swoop, dashed my promotion prospects for a considerable number of years and, whilst I do not think he did it out of any malice, he should at least have understood some of the difficulties that I had had and the reasons why I was off to Germany.

So incensed was I that after his debrief my next port of call was to Phil Wilkinson. He was sympathetic and had attempted to ameliorate some of the damage in his own assessment, but he had stopped short of raising my promotion recommendation. I was going to have to put in a supreme effort on 16 Squadron if I was ever to recover from this career crash!

Chapter Eleven

This Is The Life For You And Me

Was it the right decision? Probably not! Did it enhance my career prospects? Definitely not! Was it worth it? Well yes it was, but with a caveat or two thrown in for good measure!

Life on the two Buccaneer squadrons in Germany had not changed much since I had left XV Squadron in 1974. We still stood QRA. We still dropped bombs at Nordhorn Range. We still stooged around 2 ATAF at 250 feet. We still went to Decimomannu annually. We still flew very little in January and February because of the low cloud and appalling visibility over the North German Plain. And we still drank copious amounts of Heineken and Carlsberg in the officers' mess bar, where we still had Rolf, Gunther and Franco to tend to our every need. But for me it was different. I was now a married man and a father of two children and one Cavalier King Charles Spaniel. I was now an experienced hand and a third tour QWI. I was a flight authoriser and supervisor. And I was the Boss's navigator! I had much more responsibility than I had had on my first tour in Germany and I was going to be given even more before my tour was up.

We moved as a family to Germany in mid-summer 1981 and were allocated a married quarter at 6 Gocherstrasse in Weeze. The house was situated in a terraced row on the northern outskirts of the town, which gave me something of a three-mile drive to the main gate every morning. Thankfully, although the house was within the German community, few of whom spoke English, our neighbours in Gocherstrasse were all RAF officers and some of the husbands had been recent students of mine on the OCU. Consequently, Sue settled in well to her new surroundings and was content with an easy walk into town to enjoy '*kaffee und küchen*' or a 'fried egg' ice cream at the Eis Parlour with other wives. Before long, however, we were reallocated a quarter on base and we moved to 12 Cochrane Way on the officers' married patch. It was a happy time for the family. Christopher, who was four that August, was enrolled in the nursery school and Sarah blossomed in our new home's large back garden. Meanwhile, I concentrated on completing the Combat Ready work-up programme so that I could quickly take my place in QRA and, with the Boss, take the lead of the more complex missions that we were required to fly should the WP hordes invade. It was still the Cold War and the ever-present threat of the Soviet 3rd Shock Army was still our main concern in the west. For the immediate present, however, the squadron was planned to participate in Exercise Red Flag in Nevada in October 1981, where Peter Norriss and I would be expected to lead large formations, and so that became our main focus during my initial months on the squadron.

In late September 1981 the squadron deployed to Lossiemouth to complete the Red Flag Work Up syllabus. It was essential to work up crews who were routinely unaccustomed to flying at ULL and the North-West Highlands of Scotland provided the ideal opportunity to do so. Unlike the ULL syllabus on the OCU for my first visit to Red Flag, this was a comprehensive affair involving nine sorties in all. The missions started off gently with selected crews flying singleton sorties at 100 feet to familiarise themselves with flying the aircraft in the low flying area. This then built up to two-ship formations and then four-ships with a Bounce thrown in for good measure! The final sorties were designed to allow the 'key players' on the squadron to lead bounced eight-ship formations and Peter Norriss and I were fully involved in these, at the front, towards the end of the work-up.

There was time, however, for fun and frolic, and the Lossiemouth bar was as good a place to start – and finish! Well, until the Bothy Bar opened after the main bar shut that is! Unfortunately, after one particularly overly-indulgent night, I, and a few others, decided that it would be a good idea to do a bit of 'fishing' in the main bar before we retired to the Bothy for a nightcap. All we needed was a snooker cue and a ball of string to effect the necessary tools that would penetrate the shutters of the bar and give us access to the optics and glasses behind the bar. A cue was soon produced from the Snooker Room on the first floor and, from an unlocked drawer in Mr Mac's desk in Reception, a small ball of string provided sufficient length to manufacture the necessary noose and pull cord!

The Mess Manager was not at all impressed the following morning when he discovered that there had been a raid on the bar. He was very quickly on the phone to the PMC who, in turn, was quickly on the phone to Peter Norriss. We were summoned, hats on, to his office to explain ourselves. Maybe the Boss was not too enamoured when, as the ring leader, I started my response to his first prompt for an explanation with the words, 'Well, Sir, it was like this…'! But there was no denying who was responsible and so we took our bollocking manfully and left his office to consider our future and even whether we might be barred from Red Flag, which was unlikely, given that we had just completed the compulsory work-up and there were only two weeks to get back to base and prepare the aircraft and ourselves for our deployment.

We were banned from the bar for the remaining few days of the detachment. After the initial furore, the Mess Manager, along with the Bar Officer, realised that we had written bar chits for more alcohol than had actually been taken and, since there was no damage to the bar structure, he was happy to let matters drop with no financial penalty to the miscreants! The Boss, however, did not change his tune and so Tim Partington and I were reduced to sitting in the corridor outside The Bothy for the next two nights whilst the rest of our team provided cans of beer from the fridge inside.

Our return to Laarbruch found the squadron thrown into a station MINEVAL[1] and the disruption of our preparations to deploy to the USA. Nevertheless, such is the way of the military, the squadron cracked on with exercise flying whilst at the

---

1. A station organised exercise that usually lasted about 3 days. It was designed to work up the whole station in preparation for the RAFG MAXEVAL exercise that would precede the annual NATO TACEVAL.

same time preparing maps, charts, flight plans and aircraft for the deployment, which was scheduled to take place over four days the following week. Buccaneer squadrons in Germany did not undertake AAR routinely. Indeed, the crews were not trained in AAR because it was not practical to fly at high level to attack our Soviet enemy and so all war missions were planned as Lo Lo – this, of course, to avoid the sizeable threat presented by WP AD forces on the IGB and within East Germany. They were both prolific and potent, so the only route in and out of the Soviet Sector was to fly as low and as fast as possible. Consequently, RAF Buccaneers based in Germany had long had their AAR probes removed.

Thus, to deploy our Buccaneers to Nevada required us to fly them across the Atlantic Ocean without the aid of Victor tankers. The route planned staged the aircraft through St Mawgan, Cornwall; Lajes AFB in The Azores; CFB Gander in Newfoundland; Seymour Johnson AFB in North Carolina; and Bergstrom AFB near Austin, Texas, before we reached Nellis. In order to get all nine aircraft to Nellis, the plan was to fly three three-ship formations at thirty-minute spacing. The Boss and I were to lead the last two legs and, up to Seymour Johnson, our formation included my old mate Iain Ross, who was now back on XV Squadron as a flight commander, with Dick Cullingworth in his back seat. Their purpose of coming with 16 Squadron was to provide some sort of cross-fertilisation of tactics between the two squadrons. It was a very sensible decision to enhance operational capability across the Laarbruch Wing.

With Paul Croasdale and Terry Cook leading, and with us flying in the Number 3 position, we launched bright and early from Laarbruch on 15 October 1981 and headed south-west towards St Mawgan. We climbed across Holland to be at the London FIR boundary at reporting point Mike Charlie 6 at FL280 and, with clearance, continued overhead Brize Norton and Yeovilton to land in Cornwall in time for lunch. A Royal Air Force C-130, acting as 'sweeper'[2], was on the ground ahead of us and had already disgorged our ground crew and necessary equipment to effect the aircraft turn-round whilst we headed off to the mess for lunch. It had been an easy transit and a routine one for us, as we often trogged across Holland and into the UK for low flying exercises when Germany was fogged out. Arriving at St Mawgan in the middle of their TACEVAL was not part of the script, but, with our own ground crew available, we did our best not to get in their way!

Not so the next leg of our adventure. None of us had ever taken part in quite such a mammoth trek in a Buccaneer before, and most of the navigators had had to refresh themselves on how to calculate the Point of No Return[3] and Critical Point[4] necessary

---

2. Sweeper aircraft accompanied every such deployment. Their purpose was to provide servicing cover on route and 'sweep up' any aircraft that might fall by the wayside mechanically at every stopover.
3. A technical term in air navigation to refer to the point on a flight at which, due to fuel consumption, a plane is no longer capable of returning to the airfield from which it took off.
4. The point in the flight where it would take the same time to continue to the destination as it would to track back to the departure airfield. The CP is not dependent on fuel available, but the actual wind, as it affects the groundspeed out from, or back to, the airfield of departure. In nil wind conditions, the CP is located halfway between the two airfields, however, in reality it shifts, dependent upon the windspeed and direction.

on the next two legs when flying over the ocean and miles from land and a diversion airfield. Any miscalculation could prove fatal and any malfunction or fuel problem would, almost inevitably, find us putting into practice those sea survival drills that I had so detested from my earliest days of navigator training. It did not matter now whether my Y Category swimming certificate was nailed into my logbook or not – we were about to cross an ocean in a two–seat, two–engined warplane that was designed and built, and in which we were more accustomed, to fly over land and sea at 250 feet – not over an ocean, from one coast to another, at 30,000 feet.

The Azores is an autonomous region of Portugal and the archipelago sits in mid-Atlantic some eight hundred and fifty nautical miles due west of Lisbon. The region consists of nine volcanic islands and Terceira, one of the largest, is home to the large USAF base at Lajes, which operates twenty-four hours a day to support trans-Atlantic military routing to and from Europe and Africa to the USA. Our plan was to night-stop in Lajes before heading north-west the following morning for lunch in Canada. Lajes is some twelve hundred nautical miles from St Mawgan and thirteen hundred further to Gander in a north-westerly direction.

Now the more astute amongst you, if you are not educated in the mysteries of air navigation, will be asking yourselves the question: 'Why the hell fly SW to the Azores and then NW to Newfoundland when the direct route would be to fly just north of west directly from St Mawgan to Gander?' Certainly, if you take a look at Google Earth it would seem that that is a much shorter line than the one to Gander via Lajes! However, if you actually draw the line you will see that it is a distance of some nineteen hundred nautical miles and at some stretch for a Buccaneer into a prevailing westerly jetstream. Also the distance, when drawn on a globe, is deceiving, and the deception is what we navigators call the difference between a Great Circle[5] and a Rhumb Line[6] route.

The flight to Lajes was uneventful, if a little stressful for me as one of the three navigators in our formation. Once clear of Cornwall and at 30,000 feet over the Atlantic, I had little navigation equipment available to me in the rear cockpit. The Blue Parrot radar was useless and would only come into its own when and if we were close enough to the Azores, in azimuth, for it to pick out the islands when we started our descent. There were no TACAN beacons out at sea and the Blue Jacket, with its preponderance for diving off in the wrong direction straight after take-off, was but a mere guide to where we might be over the ocean at any one point in time. The Met Man had provided us with a forecast wind for the height we were flying and

---

5. The great-circle is the shortest distance between two points on the surface of a sphere, measured along the surface of the sphere (as opposed to a straight line through the sphere's interior) where there are no straight lines. Flying a great circle route involves a constant, albeit small, heading change to maintain track.

6. A line on a chart that intersects all meridians at the same angle. On a plain flat surface this would be the shortest distance between two points. Over the Earth's surface at low latitudes or over short distances it can be used for plotting the course of a vehicle, aircraft or ship. Over longer distances and/or at higher latitudes the great circle route is significantly shorter than the rhumb line between the same two points.

the Blue Jacket seemed to concur, give or take, with his prediction of a very strong westerly. However, there was always doubt in my mind as to whether our combined skills would take us to Lajes or to a watery grave! The reassuring silence from the other two navigators in the formation suggested that their Blue Jackets agreed with my Blue Jacket and was of some comfort, but it was all a bit by guess and by God until, with about two hundred miles to go, the Lajes TACAN beacon indicated a strong lock and a distance and track to fly to the overhead.

About fifty miles from the Top of Descent I switched the Blue Parrot from Standby, rotated the scanner to its optimum angle for the height we were flying and was amazed to see a group of islands ahead and at the correct range. Paul called us into arrow formation and we continued in the descent to Lajes where, again, more of our ground crew awaited to put the aircraft to bed for the night whilst we headed for the O Club, a beer and a good night's rest before the next day's planned two legs into North America.

The following morning we moved up the formation from Number 3 to 2 whilst Tim Partington and Roger Barker, who had flown the first two legs in the 'comfort' of a C-130, took the lead in XW546 and responsibility for our safe passage to Newfoundland. At the briefing we discussed again the importance of the PNR and CP, and the need to ensure that all the fuel tanks fed properly whilst we were in the climb out of Lajes. The Boss emphasised that any fuel problems at that stage must be called and that all three aircraft would return to Lajes so that rectification could be carried out if any one of us had a problem. The one thing we were not going to do was send an aircraft across the Atlantic on its own!

The Buccaneer had a slightly strange fuel system in that its main tanks and its UWTs and BBT were gravity fed, whilst the BDT was electrically pumped. Thus the procedure briefed for the trans-Atlantic sorties was that, once established in the climb, the navigator was to switch on the feed from each of the overload tanks in turn to ensure that each fed properly, and then sequence the tanks in the order UWTs, BBT and BDT.

Take-off from Lajes was uneventful with all the tanks in our aircraft checked and feeding properly by the time we reached the Top of Climb at FL260. With the Under Wing Tanks now feeding the main fuel tanks, I sat back and relaxed whilst Roger and Tim took the strain. Peter and I conducted our routine safety checks as we continued on our way and I made sure that my Blue Jacket position was where I expected it to be based upon the morning's forecast. Generally we just chatted about life, the universe and the next three weeks on Red Flag to pass the time. We were well past the PNR and CP when we received a radio call from Iain now flying in the Number 3 position.

'Two from Three, my bomb bay tank is refusing to feed!'

'Roger!' replied Peter. 'What will that mean, Dave?' he asked me through the intercom.

After a moment's pause I replied. 'He'll probably crash about a hundred miles east of Newfoundland!'

'You're joking, right!'

'Nope! Without fuel from his bomb bay he will not make it,' I confirmed. 'However, it will probably feed again when he starts his descent and the air pressure increases, but that is not guaranteed!'

'Standby, Three.' Peter called over the radio, and to me he said, 'Can you calculate how far they can continue before they run out of fuel please, and then call our sweeper on the HF and ask him to warn the Canadian SAR that they may well be ditching off Newfoundland.'

'Three from Two, we reckon that your fuel will probably feed in the descent, but if it does not, prepare to eject about a hundred miles east of Newfoundland! Delta Hotel is contacting Ascot 4792 to ask them to relay that information to Canadian SAR.'

A large 'thinks bubble' appeared above their cockpit and a curt 'Roger' came out over the radio.

I had been maintaining a listening watch on the briefed HF frequency and so quickly called the sweeper Hercules, captained by Group Captain Joe Hardstaff, who was the RAF Lyneham station commander. His aircraft was well ahead of us and already within UHF contact with Gander; I briefed him on our predicament. He showed no hint of anxiety on receiving our grim news and confirmed that he would radio ahead immediately to alert SAR. He was slightly more perplexed when we asked him to inform Oceanic that we were climbing to FL300 to reduce fuel consumption which would, hopefully, get them a bit closer to land before they had to eject.

As predicted, in the descent into Gander their BBT began to feed and all three aircraft landed safely onto a very cold and wintry Newfoundland; it was a stark change from the sunny morning that we had left behind in Lajes. The debrief was an interesting one and took place over a sandwich lunch in the terminal building at Gander International. Apparently, Dick had completed all the necessary checks in the climb and the bomb bay had fed properly at that stage. However, when it came to the point when it was actually needed, it had stubbornly refused to do so. It was a fraught ninety minutes that they, and we, had spent at 30,000 feet over the Atlantic, but in the end, the Buccaneer had done what it was supposed to do and delivered them to their destination safely.

After lunch we headed south across Nova Scotia, the US border, and along the New England coast southwards past New York and overhead Washington DC before we turned south and onwards into North Carolina, where, after three hours and thirty minutes strapped to our bang seats, we headed for the Seymour Johnson Happy Hour. It was Friday night! Needless to say, we fell in with thieves and were royally hosted by our American cousins who flew the F-4 Phantom. Saturday was designated as R&R and found many of us venturing into the local town of Goldsboro to find out just what does go on in the USA's 'Bible Belt' on a Saturday afternoon! Not much, we quickly discovered, and getting a beer without having a meal was a particularly difficult task!

The Yanks had invited us for a BBQ at the squadron and so there was little point in hanging about searching for a beer in town when there was beer aplenty back on base. We were treated like kings by the Americans and had a great party on the airfield at Seymour Johnson that Saturday night. But we had to be back in the saddle the following morning and onwards through Texas to be on the ground in Nevada before sundown on the Sunday evening.

Bergstrom lies to the south of Austin, Texas, and was two hours and forty-five minutes flying time from Seymour Johnson. Navigationally it was one of the easiest legs on our journey as there were plenty of TACAN beacons available to keep me on track as Peter and I led the other two aircraft across the southern states of South Carolina, Georgia, Alabama, Mississippi and Louisiana. After about an hour and a half, the huge swathe of the Mississippi River became clearly visible ahead of us and, as we crossed it, Peter and I marvelled at its beauty and the vastness of the land over which we were now flying. Soon, however, we were on the ground at Bergstrom and preparing for the next and final leg of our journey. The base was home to an RF-4 Wing, but the aircrew were on detachment in Europe and so there was not much activity around the base. However, we busied ourselves with our preparations for the next leg whilst we sent a couple of scouts out to find out where we could get lunch. They were gone less than sixty seconds before they bounced back through the doors with a bevy of American beauties in their trail. Each beauty was carrying a tray or a basket within which was hidden the most magnificent fayre that they had prepared for our lunch! It turned out that, with their husbands away overseas and no 'men' to care for, the squadron wives had taken it upon themselves to show the passing 'Brits' some southern hospitality! As the preparations continued over a most magnificent spread, somebody happened to remark that we had rather more fuel than we needed to get to Nellis at high-level. Another remarked that we had more than enough to get there at low-level! It was a beautiful Sunday in Texas and the forecast for the route ahead was CAVOK[7].

'What are the rules for low flying?' someone proffered.

'No idea!' said another voice.

'Why don't we?' said another and so on and so forth until 'going low-level' began to formulate as the priority in the plan!

The duty sergeant in the USAF Base Ops was slightly taken aback by our quick question and seemed incredulous that anyone would want to go low-level the whole way, but that was probably because not many fast jets could do over a 1000 miles at low-level. Nevertheless he confirmed that the whole area between Bergstrom and Nellis was cleared for low flying, but that the minimum height on a Sunday was 1,000 feet AGL. It was a no-brainer and Peter Norriss was quickly convinced that it was doable, and, more importantly, permissible. I, and the two other lead navigators, quickly planned a low-level route north-west out of Bergstrom that would take us past Albuquerque in New Mexico along the rim of the Grand Canyon in Arizona, across the State border north of the Hoover Dam and into Nevada. The only warnings we were given were that we must avoid the White Sands Missile Test Range in New

---

7. Ceiling and Visibility are OK. Specifically, there are no clouds below 5,000 feet and no cumulonimbus or towering cumulus. Visibility is at least 10kms and there is no current or forecast significant weather such as precipitation, thunderstorms, shallow fog, or low drifting snow.

Mexico and that the minimum height to be flown down the Grand Canyon was fifteen hundred feet above the rim. We lodged our VFR Flight Plan with the duty sergeant and, noticing our slight hesitation and sceptical looks, he said, 'If the Flight Plan is accepted, Sir, there is no problem.' It was and there wasn't.

We departed Bergstrom with a nominal ten minutes spacing between each three-ship and were soon at our new cruising altitude of 1,000 feet. The view was fantastic as we passed north of San Angelo and south of Lubbock across vast swathes of emptiness or neat ranches with well-maintained crops. 'Cowboy' named towns passed on either side and after fifty minutes we were over New Mexico, and soon the sparkling adobe houses that proliferated the Albuquerque area hove into sight. With hardly a change in our north-westerly heading, we continued past Albuquerque and onwards to Arizona and the Grand Canyon.

On our way back from 'Work-up' at Lossiemouth, most of those present had flown a Diamond Nine formation overhead Laarbruch to signal our successful return to our wives and families. So, whilst over Texas, a short conversation ensued on our squadron discrete frequency promoting the notion to do so again as we flew down the Grand Canyon. The Boss, in my front seat, was less than taken with the idea. It had taken some small persuasion to reassure him that flying low-level to Nellis was not breaking the rules and so his initial internal cockpit thought of a nine-ship was a step too far. After all he was right; it should have been briefed formally at Bergstrom before take-off. However, with the assistance of a few encouraging words from the aircraft behind, I persuaded him to do it and to take five minutes now to brief it in the air. He did, but, for safety reasons and probably his own neck, he emphasised that we should 'keep it loose'!

After another forty minutes the first signs of the Colorado River appeared below us and, as they did so, the Boss called all nine aircraft into Diamond Nine formation. Once established, it must have been a fantastic sight for the thousands of visitors to the canyon that day to look up at the sound of military jets and see nine of them in a diamond formation above their heads, and just fifteen hundred feet above the gorge rim. I wonder how many of them realised that they were British! At one point Number 9, who had borrowed my cine camera, detached from the formation to film our adventure. At about the same time John Sheen, in the back of Dick Johnston's aircraft, removed his flying helmet and donned a Stetson, recently purchased, as he roared down the Grand Canyon at 450 kts. There are not many people in the world, alive or dead, who can write in their memoir that they flew down the Grand Canyon in a fast jet in Diamond Nine formation!

Just a further eighteen more minutes and we were north of the Hoover Dam and in radio contact with Nellis Approach. There was some confusion as to our whereabouts and altitude as, I suspect, they had anticipated us arriving from high-level, with a formal handover from Los Angeles Centre, and that we would conduct a simple instrument approach using one of their TAPs to get us all on the ground in good order. They had either not received or not read our F2919[8]. We had ascertained

8. RAF F2919/UK CA48 – ICAO Flight Plan form.

from listening to the base's constantly transmitted and updated 'Information[9]' that Runway 21 was in use, which facilitated the next stage of our un-briefed plan. At Apex[10] and still in Diamond Nine, Peter Norriss asked permission for a flyby over the airfield in a majestic display that would signal the Buccaneer's return to Red Flag. Permission was granted, but just as we were setting ourselves up on the runway heading we were advised that the runway had been changed, and with that we were passed across to the Tower frequency. Confusion reigned in nine cockpits. As we changed frequency the Boss, with eight aircraft hanging in on his wing, gently eased the heading to the north of the airfield and headed west on a long base leg to position the formation ready for a run-in for Runway 03. Another lazy turn now onto north-east brought the Nellis runways into our twelve o'clock and the nine aircraft settled on the approach at 1000 feet to fly overhead the airfield before turning downwind to split into three separate formations again for our final arrival.

We were beautifully lined up and in our diamond over the airfield when, unexpectedly, the local controller ordered us to 'Pitch Now!' There was no way that that was going to happen. Nobody in their right mind would pitch from a diamond formation! Clearly the message translated by us to the Approach Controller had not been transmitted clearly, if at all, to the Local Controller. We carried on regardless, all the while hearing his ignored pleas to Black Formation to 'Pitch Now!' whilst Peter Norriss kept trying to explain in his best English accent that pitching was not an option!

Suitably unimpressed with our welcome at Nellis, we carefully broke the diamond up into three arrow formations and ran in again at thirty-second spacing to pitch and land on the left-hand of the two 10,000 foot runways. As we turned off at the end of the runway, a 'Follow Me' car indicated that he had the lead and our nine Buccaneers, with hoods now firmly wound back, taxied the length of the ASP past row upon row of military hardware to our parking spots at the SW corner of the dispersal. On the Boss's command all nine aircraft folded their wings simultaneously. The Buccaneer Boys had arrived at Nellis in style and, with the aircraft heading to bed, we headed to the bar to meet our adversaries!

Unlike my prior visit to 'Flag' we were not accommodated in BOQs this time, nor were we to enjoy the delights of living at Nellis AFB. The whole squadron was accommodated in hotels in Las Vegas with all the promise that that brought of a high rolling life amongst the Blackjack and Roulette tables! Whilst our ground crew and support staffs were allocated rooms in a reasonable hostelry some way off The Strip, we aircrew found ourselves in a very pleasant, if small, hotel just off The Strip and within an easy stroll of most of the main attractions.

We had a full week to acclimatise to the heat and the time shift before we started the exercise flying at one hundred feet, so we had plenty of time from the outset to

9. Automatic Terminal Information Service, or ATIS, is a continuous broadcast of recorded non-control aeronautical information in busier terminal (i.e. airport) areas. ATIS broadcasts contain essential information, such as weather, active runways, available approaches, and any other information required by the pilots, such as important NOTAMs.
10. Nellis AFB's Visual Reporting Point from the east.

explore the city and its casinos. It was on this detachment that I fell in with Paul Dandeker and Mike Gault. Paul, who was an ex-Lightning pilot, had gone through the Buccaneer OCU when I was on the staff and we had become firm friends. Mike Gault was one of the Laarbruch medical officers and, like-minded as he was to our aircrew ways, he had been nominated as the 16 Squadron doctor and, for Red Flag, our detachment UMO. Paul was the squadron entertainments officer back at Laarbruch and although Tim Partington had been given the role for Red Flag, Paul had persuaded us all before departure to pack our DJs. He had a plan, and a plan that he was determined to implement.

After a considerable amount of research, which included Mike and me being dragged to see a performance by Eddie Rabbitt[11], Paul set about organising a squadron dinner party at Benihana's Japanese Restaurant in the Hilton Hotel. The restaurant is very popular even today and requires its clients to bring with them a party spirit and a game for a laugh attitude. The aircrew of 16 Squadron had absolutely no difficulty providing either! The food was prepared on a Hibachi Grill in front of us and there were usually nine people at each table; that included the chef, who was a master craftsman and an accomplished entertainer. Japanese Saki flowed freely and the twenty or so officers from 16 Squadron were soon off to a flying start dressed as we all were in our dinner jackets. Heads turned in the Hilton that night as we participated fully in the culinary administrations of our chefs! At the end of the meal, and with the bill paid, Paul gathered us all together and asked us each to give him ten dollars. We then congregated at the front of the Hilton whilst the concierges pulled taxis over and, with us all piled on board, we headed off to The Tropicana to see the 2200hrs show at the Folies Bergere!

Paul was very busy and once he had got us all assembled and warned us not to move for fear of death, he wandered off towards the theatre. He was back within ten minutes and with a strict order to 'follow me and don't get lost' we stepped forward into the vast arena and, with a maître d' leading us forward, took our places at a table that was situated right up against the stage – so that was what the ten dollars each was for! Paul had back-handed the maître d' and got us seats in the best position in the house. The evening was a fantastic success. Our presence at the edge of the stage, our dress, and our gentlemanly behaviour was a master stroke. At one point we were introduced to the assembled arena as a convention of maître d's to much applause from the audience. More importantly, however, we managed to psyche out one of the topless dancers in the chorus line with our winks and charm. Every time she appeared on stage she was drawn to our group and she could not stop smiling at us to the extent that we nearly put her off her rhythm. Some of the dancers sent a message forward at the end of the show asking if we would like to go backstage for a drink, but we were by now full of beer and well past socialising and so were forced to decline. As we wended our weary way past all the slot machines and tables in The Tropicana, some bright spark suggested that, as a last gesture before bed, we should put the whole of the squadron kitty on 'Black' on the roulette table. It was a bad

---

11. An American singer-songwriter and musician.

decision not to as we would have doubled our stake, but, in truth, we would probably have continued gambling with it well into the night and lost the lot – so no harm done in the end!

There were many more hilarious episodes on that Red Flag, and we even managed to venture as far afield as Los Angeles and San Diego at weekends. Water skiing on Lake Mead was also popular, as was visiting the Hoover Dam, which sits astride the Nevada/Arizona border, impounds Lake Mead and converts the raw power of the Colorado River into energy.

After shakedown sorties around Nevada at low-level on the twentieth to iron out any unserviceability in the jets after the Atlantic crossing, flying started in earnest on the twenty-sixth with a 'range recce' of the Red Flag target and low flying areas. Three days later the Boss and I found ourselves at the front of a six-ship formation and in the thick of the exercise dropping 1000lb bombs on Mount Helen Airfield[12] and the following day, as Number 2 in a six-ship doing the same thing on Kawich Airfield. Just as in 1978, all the sorties started benignly with a climb to medium altitude to transit the narrow corridor that divided the Nellis Ranges and hopefully to leave Student Gap on time. Of course, with sometimes fifty to sixty aircraft taking part in the exercise on any one launch, it was hard enough to get airborne on your planned time even with all the pre-planning and deconfliction discussions and negotiations that took place during the planning stages and with all other participants, including the bad guys! So leaving Student Gap on time was a test and the previously described timing trombone was every lead navigator's best friend and a vital addition to every mission planned.

By 1981 the USAF had invested heavily in Red Flag and unlike my visit three years earlier, we now had to contend with Smokey SAMs[13] and actual WP AD radars, rather than simulators, either mounted remotely or 'as purchased' and fitted to their original mother vehicle bodies, such as the SA-8 'Gecko'. Such sites had to be avoided at all costs as a 'kill' by a radar site would be transmitted back to Red Flag HQ and relayed to the crew involved before the mass debrief. In the early years of Red Flag an ACMI[14] system was used to monitor missions operating within the ranges, but by 1981 this had been improved with the installation of the Red Flag Measurement and Debriefing System, which allowed for increased radar operating range and a more thorough debrief. To facilitate the scoring system, every aircraft

---

12. These Red Flag airfields were ploughed out of the rough desert and formed exactly like WP airfields that we would go against if we ever went to war. Occasionally, derelict WP aircraft captured in Middle East wars would be left on the airfield as pinpoint targets.

13. The Smokey Sam simulator includes single- and four-rail launching pads, an AN/VPQ-1 radar set and GTR-18A smoke-generating rockets themselves. When launched, the GTR-18's rocket motor produces a distinctive white plume, providing a realistic simulation of the launch of a surface-to-air missile.

14. Air Combat Manoeuvring Instrumentation. The ACMI system involves state of the art sensors on the aircraft that allow the ground controllers of the air war to 'see' a 3-D picture of the simulated air combat, including air-air engagements, air-ground strikes, etc. in real time. The data can be recorded and played back during the pilot debrief for training purposes.

operating within the ranges had to be equipped with an AIS pod[15], for without one there was no access to the range. Thankfully for the Buccaneer force our aircraft had recently been equipped with AIM-9G Sidewinder air-to-air missiles and so the wiring looms required for the AIS pod were available.

Thus equipped, we went to war on Red Flag 82-1. Stripped of our overload fuel tanks and with an AIS pod, a Westinghouse AN/ALQ-101-10 ECM jamming pod, one AIM-9G and a bundle of chaff[16] strapped in our airbrakes, we were ready to take on all comers! Live or Inert 1000lb bombs were loaded in our bomb bay and a CBLS[17] was carried on the last remaining wing pylon should the ATO require us to deliver PBs rather than heavy weapons on a particular mission. We had, of course, no intention of getting into a dogfight with an AD fighter or two! For us to engage with the enemy in that way would only have had one result and not a good one for us at that. However, flying at ULL over the Nevada desert in a four-ship 'Card' formation allowed each aircraft an element of autonomous manoeuvrability and flexibility, whilst at the same time, it provided mutual security and lookout protection should a fighter drop into the six o'clock of any of the aircraft in a formation. 'Card' could be flown in any size of formation and indeed was when we flew eight-ships towards the end of the exercise.

Our tactics were relatively simple but well-practised. The first indication of any contact by either ground-based or airborne radars would be indicated both visually and audibly on our RWR. A radar lock would initiate a turn towards the threat and if an indication of a firing solution from the threat was identified, the formation would take appropriate avoiding action by bustering[18] to maximum speed and getting as low to the authorised height (or lower) as possible in an attempt to outrun or outmanoeuvre the threat. We used terrain masking as much as possible to negate SAM threats and hoped that our ECM pod, for which we had no cockpit indicator, was jamming the threats as they appeared. Without a gun in the Buccaneer, the AIM-9G gave us the option of firing on any fighter daft enough to drop into the middle of the formation, and provided an element of surprise for a fighter who thought that we were as unarmed as we were when the Buccaneer first came into military service. The chaff strapped in the airbrake served to confuse enemy radars but was only really ever used whenever we were in the pull-up for a Toss attack to confuse radars on the

---

15. Airborne Instrumentation Subsystem pods contain sophisticated electronics that are electronically 'interrogated' by equipment at receiver stations within the range area. The raw information is then passed back to a computer at the Range Control Centre that translates it into height, speed, range, etc. The computer then analyses all the returns received and calculates relative information and decides on 'kill' or 'no kill' status.

16. Chaff, originally called Window by the British, is a radar countermeasure in which aircraft or other targets spread a cloud of small, thin pieces of aluminium, metallized glass fibre, or plastic, which either appears as a cluster of primary targets on radar screens or swamps the screen with multiple returns.

17. The CBLS enables military aircraft to carry up to four practice bombs on each weapon station. The use of practice bombs in place of operational weapons significantly reduces the costs and risks during aircrew weapons training.

18. Full power, throttles to the top left-hand corner and get away from the threat as fast as possible!

target itself. If you had not got rid of it before the target then that was where it went! Having spoken to many fighter pilots over various exercises, the Buccaneer Force had discovered that the one thing a fighter pilot feared the most was being caught in the blast and fragments of a live weapon close to a target. Consequently, they never followed bombers through the target area if, indeed, they knew what the target was likely to be. So, on route to the target, we also used our offensive weapons as a defensive weapon should a fighter be lucky enough to drop into the close six o'clock of one of our aircraft. With one of the live bomb stations selected by the navigator on the 8-way bomb distributor in the back seat, it was ready to be dropped full in the face of any fighter that wandered into 'Knickers'[19] range during a sortie.

Through Student Gap at 500kts and 100 feet in four or eight-ship 'Card', we would invariably head north-east to find sanctuary behind the Worthington Mountains and the Reveille Range, before popping across the Kawich Range and into the 'Badlands'. There were plenty of rocky valleys to hide in, but these mountain ranges were often some three minute's flying time apart, which left the formation exposed over the desert floor. We knew that our size and speed would make us difficult to spot by a fighter at 15,000 feet, but they routinely had AWACS[20] to assist with target location and identification. Additionally, the flash of an aircraft wing during a turn, or a speeding shadow over the desert floor, was always a good give-away. We designed our navigational route to minimise such eventualities.

Once past Kawich Range, the RWR would light up with multiple SAM threats, and the white plumes of Smokey SAMs littered the horizon as these fireworks shot from their rails and headed in our general direction. As each crew identified a threat or took evasive action, aircraft would start to scatter across the broad plains and often become completely detached and lose visual contact on the others. However, everybody within the formation had their own designated TOT, plus an alternative, and each knew exactly what was required of them to complete the mission successfully. As the result of intercepts or SAM engagements, we were often in complete disarray approaching the IP, but more often than not a quick glance over the shoulder whilst running towards the target would reassure the lead crew that everybody was in position and ready to strike as briefed.

Of course, getting everybody back together after the target was as important as getting people over the target at the right point in space and time. The fragments from the detonation of a 1000lb HE bomb can take up to thirty seconds to fall to earth and are a threat to any following aircraft. Consequently, the individual aircraft split over the target for an eight-ship could last as long as four minutes! To gather those aircraft back into 'Card' could take even longer as the imperative after the target was to get out of hostile territory as quickly as possible. The last man through had the easiest task as he would usually have the shortest leg to fly to get back into

---

19. The code word used on the Buccaneer Force for a BIF (Bomb in the Face) defensive action.
20. An airborne early warning and control system is an airborne radar picket system designed to detect aircraft, ships and vehicles at long ranges and perform command and control of the battlespace in an air engagement by directing fighter and attack aircraft strikes.

formation. However, he had had the longest fanned out route to get the required spacing before the target and so, out of all the aircraft, had spent the most time in hostile territory. Also, with his leader going balls to the wall to clear the target area, it was never an easy task to get Tail End Charlie and others back on board whilst all the time SAMs were engaging you and fighter pilots were still determined to get their Buccaneer kill. So determined were USAF pilots to get themselves a Buccaneer that on one particular sortie on this Red Flag I heard a radio call to a flight of two USAF Reserve F-102 Delta Daggers, who were already heading south to clear the ranges, that advised them that, 'there are still Buccaneers in the area'! Quickly realising their luck, the two aircraft turned on their heels and headed back into the area, and so determined were they to 'kill a Bucc' that they pushed their throttles rather too far through the gate and inadvertently broke the sound barrier! They never did find us at 100 feet and 580 kts! However, they had a one-sided interview on their return to Nellis and we transited back through the corridor unscathed!

All too soon, however, RF82-1 was nearly over. We had spent up, drunk up and gambled almost our last dollars. We were tired and ready for home, but first, on 6 November 1981, Peter Norriss and I were to lead an eight-ship of Buccaneers on the very last sortie as part of a thirty-six-ship mixed formation attacking force! I was appointed Mission Commander for the whole of the attack force; which brought with it responsibility for liaising with every formation leader and ensuring that there was absolute deconfliction at Student Gap and in the range area. I was also responsible for managing and running the Mass Briefing and the Mass Debriefing and for planning the lead of my own formation. I had mountains of support from my team and together we led one of the most successful sorties that I have ever had the joy to participate in. Yes, we 'lost' a few along the way and we had our difficulties, but leading a mass formation on Red Flag has to have been one of my greatest and most enjoyable achievements in my RAF flying career.

And so Red Flag for me in a Buccaneer came to a close. I did not know then that I would do it all again in a Tornado, but for now, there was just enough time to tidy my room, pack my bags and buy the last few presents for the kids – Fisher Price toys were an absolute snip with the dollar exchange rate at the time! The VC10 was due to arrive that evening, bringing with it the XV Squadron aircrew who were going to participate in Phase 2 of RF82-1. For us, however, there was time for one last night out in Las Vegas before we had to report at the crack of dawn on the Saturday morning to climb aboard XR806 to travel home in luxury, albeit facing backwards, and once again via Gander.

It was a good last night and it seemed to last forever. We frequented a number of casinos, played a number of tables, never won a penny, but drank free as we did so, ate our last $2 buffet and were about to head back to the hotel when the Boss and Roger Carr declared that they fancied just one more punt at the tables in the MGM Grand. We were out and about in an eight-seater minibus and so it seemed churlish to refuse their request as a few of us had identified an opportunity for one last visit to the 'gentlemen's club', which had been a popular nightcap location throughout the detachment! As they stepped out of the vehicle, we agreed a final RV at the front entrance of the hotel at 0100hrs; sufficient time for them to have an hour on the tables and for the rest of us to have a couple of beers in the 'Crazy Horse Too'. Ron Trinder was driving with D², Mike Gault and I, plus a few others slumped somewhere in the back of the truck as we drove past the MGM's gigantic golden lion and pulled up to the grand entrance of the hotel. It was 0055hrs! There was no sign of the Boss or Roger! We waited! The entrance of the casino was still alive with people coming and going even at that time of the night, but there was no sign of our two passengers!

One o'clock came and went and the assembled passengers began to get restless. It was about a twenty-minute drive back to our hotel and the three beers consumed in the 'club' were beginning to press against our bladders! Still no sign!

'C'mon! Let's go!' said I.

'Yep!' echoed Paul, 'times up!'

'We can't leave the Boss,' said a conciliatory voice.

'Sure we can,' said another. I looked at Paul and he looked at me and that decided it!

'C'mon! Let's go! Hard school! He knows the rules!' we shouted from our repose on the rear seat.

And, with that, Ron put the vehicle into 'Drive' and we shot off back down the ramp and to bed! It was 0105hrs and they had missed their TOT! We managed to avoid the Boss and Roger during the check-in for the VC10 the following morning, but overheard something along the lines of the fact that it was rather an expensive taxi ride back to the hotel – we laid low, but 'rules is rules' as the saying goes!

After some time off with our families, with jets still over in the USA, the squadron did not start flying again until 19 November. It was soon back to the old routine however. Preparations for, or taking part in MINEVALs, were very much to the fore and for a pleasant break we undertook a Ranger to Gibraltar to carry out reconnaissance[21] of the Soviet anchorage at Hammamet off the Tunisian coast. MAXEVAL was successfully undertaken in April before TACEVAL then hit us in May. It was pressured work, but routine for an RAFG Strike/Attack squadron, which all the while was manning two of four aircraft that were sat on Strike QRA in case the Soviets launched a surprise assault on the west with nuclear weapons. The Cold War was anything but cold!

June 1982 brought with it a requirement for the Laarbruch Wing to provide an eight-ship formation to participate in a parade to celebrate Her Majesty's official birthday. The formation was made up of a 'Box' of four Buccaneers from 16 Squadron leading a 'Box' of four Jaguars from 2 Squadron. Peter Norriss and I led the formation and flew four practice missions before a dress rehearsal was held two days before the event itself on 11 June. The most important task for the lead navigator was to ensure that we ended up 'on top' of the dais on the parade square at JHQ Rheindahlen at exactly 1100hrs and exactly as the parade commander executed his 'General Salute'.

---

21. This was a mid-week deployment to Gibraltar (Wed to Fri) rather than a weekend ranger. I have no recall as to why an overland squadron was tasked with undertaking a maritime task, but clearly we did because we flew against the anchorage three times on Thursday, 18 February 1982.

Bread and butter to every navigator on the squadron, but made more complex by the fact that any delays on the ground would cause a stir in the air as we jostled to match the ever-changing timeline being transmitted to us by radio as we circled some ten miles north of the parade! It all worked out as anticipated and we overflew the parade ground right on cue.

In July 1982 I achieved two thousand flying hours in a Buccaneer. It had taken me just under eleven years to achieve the milestone, which would have happened quicker had the aircraft not suffered two periods of grounding in my time. The sortie that took me past the two thousand was simple enough. It was as lead of a four-ship on Exercise Argus, which I recall was designed to test the air defence systems of the NATO Alliance. Accordingly, after a transit east towards the ADIZ[22], aircraft would turn before the Buffer Zone[23] and 'penetrate' 2 ATAF and 4 ATAF and fly against area and localised AD systems. Although we took off from Laarbruch on 12 July for Exercise Argus, our destination was to be the USAF base at Spangdahlem in the Eifel area of Germany, where we were heading for a week-long squadron exchange with the 480th TFS. The Warhawks operated the F-4E Phantom and were very much like-minded with The Saints!

As we rolled to a stop in dispersal it was clear that there was a welcoming committee to greet the Boss. The Base Commander had turned up as well as the OC of the Spangdahlem Wing, both 'bird colonels'. The commander of the 480th was present also, along with a clutch of his aircrew. The welcoming committee was not, however, for the Boss, but for me. The word had got out that I would celebrate my 2000 hours on this flight and so, as aircrew do, this mass of humanity were not only present to greet me, but they had brought with them suitable libation to celebrate the event. Amongst them was a chap by the name of Lieutenant 'Cluster' J. Hartley the Third – what a fantastic tag to be given! Cluster!

Cluster and I got on like a house on fire for the whole week. He enjoyed his beer, he liked a good laugh, he did not mind getting in the shit (and regularly did so) and we fell together like lost souls searching out the best way to make sure that The Saints and The Warhawks would never forget each other! It started over a crate of beer in dispersal on that Monday and it continued for a full seven days, which included a most uproarious weekend on the Mosel, until we departed on the nineteenth. Such 'blood brothers' were we by the end of the week that we swapped our flying suit name tags! Cluster Hartley – what a guy!

Despite all the fun, games and Cluster of that detachment, my most memorable moment came on the fifteenth when I flew in an F-4E with a Captain Hansen on a Lo Lo mission to 4 ATAF. The Phantom had nowhere near the range of a Buccaneer so the sortie was relatively short, but most enjoyable. The rear cockpit was a completely different environment to that of a Buccaneer. It was a mass of black boxes and, unlike

---

22. Air Defence Identification Zone. A 3-D expanse of airspace abutting the Buffer Zone set up to prevent unintentional incursions of Allied aircraft into Eastern Europe. Whilst it was possible to fly under the ADIZ at low-level, its top height was 'unlimited'.

23. A 3-D expanse of airspace behind the ADIZ that abutted the IGB from ground level to infinity. No military aircraft were permitted to fly within the Buffer Zone.

us, had a relatively sophisticated navigation system known as 'Arnie'[24]. What I did not like about the F-4 back cockpit was the poor visibility forward and the limited rearwards view! Certainly nothing compared to the Buccaneer and, with no bomb bay and a lack of range, it was a poor substitute in my opinion! However, the USAF, the RAF and NATO had hundreds of them and so, to all intents and purposes, and along with the Starfighter, the Phantom was the workhorse of NATO.

Following a number of changes in the higher echelons of the squadron, I found myself filling the position of Squadron Weapons Leader, but still as a flight lieutenant. I had passed the C Promotion Examination in 1981, but was still struggling to complete the eighteen months of ISS. Promotion was yet a long way off, but the responsibility that came with my new role was some comfort and an acceptance by the chain of command that I had considerable experience as a Buccaneer navigator and QWI. On the squadron, I spent most of the summer months of 1982 planning and preparing for our annual APC at Decimomannu. We deployed on 1 September 1982 and the very next day I was on Frasca Range with the Boss, leading a three-ship undertaking laydown bombing. I had designed a pretty intensive programme of flying that included LIMAC[25] weaponry on all three events that the squadron had to qualify in, which were Laydown, 5° Dive Bombing and Visual Toss. I had also included one sortie that allowed each crew to deliver 1000lb inert weapons on the strike target at Frasca. It was hard work ensuring that the programme was achieved and that the results were recorded. With my fellow QWI, Ron Trinder, at my side and with Nick Berryman, the erstwhile Weapons Leader, but now flight commander, to assist us with Telford Camera debriefs, we had most eventualities covered. I even managed to build weekend Rangers into the programme to allow some crews to get away from Sardinia for the weekend. One four-ship had a weekend in Naples and Peter Norriss and I were part of a four-ship that spent the middle weekend in a sunny Cyprus. It was a rest from the regular evenings spent in the Pig and Tapeworm and drinking Flaming Sambucas in the Spaghetti Palachi!

Socially, Deci was no different to any of my previous visits. We were, of course, no longer welcome at Fortes Village after Barrie Chown's escapade with the golf buggy and the swimming pool! But there were plenty more beaches available for barbecues and some people took time out to play golf at Is Molas. D² had brought his guitar and many happy nights were spent on the veranda of the Pig and Tapeworm carousing drunkenly long into the night. One evening, Paul and I began to construct a squadron song[26] based on some of the more amusing activities or errors that happened in the preceding days. We entitled it 'We're Sixteen Squadron!' and it included a chorus that was alternately sung in English and then in French! I have no explanation why, but

---

24. F-4Es were retrofitted with a Lear Siegler AN/ARN-101(V) to improve navigation and accuracy of weapons delivery.
25. 'Limited Academic': 'Dry' passes initially, but once a bomb had been released all subsequent deliveries had to be 'hot'!
26. Music and lyrics are original so don't attempt to sing it to anything that might be buzzing through your head right now; (Full Lyrics available in 'The Buccaneer Songbook' by David Herriot).

it was one of those things that just happened and it definitely worked! It opened like this:

> *'We're 16 Squadron*
> *We're on detachment*
> *And we're having lots of fun,*
> *Drinking beer and playing hard*
> *And bronzing in the sun,*
> *But we've gorra lorra work to do*
> *And I'm sure you'll all agree*
> *Tha-a-t this is the life for you and me.'*

One of my favourite restaurants in Sardinia is Sa Cardiga e Su Schironi. We first stumbled upon it when I was on XV Squadron in 1972 and we were wending our way back from Fortes Village to Decimomannu. Then it was a corrugated iron shack by the beach on the coast road from Pula to Cagliari. When we walked in – in 1972 – there was plenty of beer, but no menu. When we asked what we could eat, David Cousins and I were ushered into the kitchen and shown a huge fridge that was stacked from floor to ceiling with King Prawns! We gorged ourselves on King Prawns and Ichnusa beer that night and, I recall, paid just a few thousand lira[27] each for the privilege. Ten years later, the restaurant had grown into a sparkling edifice and was one of the most popular restaurants amongst the Cagliari cognoscenti and the bill came to much, much more than a few thousand lira each!

The finale to the detachment in Sardinia was a bombing competition with a suitable trophy available to be presented to the winning crew. However, to ensure that everybody was ready for such a task, two weapons consolidation sorties were flown on the range beforehand. These included deliveries in each of the three modes previously practised, but required quick thinking in the cockpit to make sure that the weapons switches were changed to match the weapon and delivery mode required.

Pete Branthwaite, an ex-Vulcan captain, had only recently arrived on the squadron and was a late addition to the nominal roll of pilots on the detachment. He had produced consistently good weapons results from the outset and had been rushed through the weapons aspects of his CR training programme. On Monday, 20 September, after Peter Norriss and I had completed our competition sortie, I was detailed to be the flight authoriser in the Squadron Ops Room for the afternoon wave. After lunch at Enrico's I took over from the morning's authoriser in sufficient time to allow him to prepare to fly on the late afternoon wave. I spoke to the weather man, checked the airfield details, familiarised myself with the latest Hot Poop and, with the help of the flight sergeant running the engineering shift, I allocated crews and aircraft to the afternoon wave. Pete Branthwaite and Dave Major were allocated XV160 in a four-ship – Bristol Formation. The RAF's callsigns at Decimomannu were traditionally the names of British cities such as London, Bristol and Oxford.

---

27. In 1972 there were approximately 1500 lira to the British pound.

With Bristol Formation successfully out-briefed and walking for their aircraft I settled down to start drafting the following morning's flying programme. I was unprepared for the telephone call I received about forty minutes later informing me that XV160 had crashed on the range!

In his attempt to recover from the weapon delivery manoeuvre, Pete had lost control of the aircraft which entered a flat spin. The Range Controller called the crew to eject, which thankfully they responded to before the aircraft crashed on the side of the cliff. Both crew members were rescued by the Italian Air Force and recovered to Deci where Pete, although suffering from a sore back, was soon back in the bar. His navigator was less lucky and was quite badly injured. When he landed, Dave Major fell down the cliff side at Frasca, and had grit and rubbish pushed up underneath his helmet visor and into his eyes! He spent some time in hospital recovering and was CASEVAC'd back to Germany by C-130. The Board of Inquiry concluded that Branthwaite's post release egress was too steep, which resulted in a greater than anticipated loss of airspeed and a correspondingly higher than anticipated Angle of Attack. With a small margin of error in a Vari-Toss attack, the Board also concluded that, having heard the stall warning, the pilot overcompensated for the impending stall, which precipitated the resulting autorotation and loss of control. Thankfully, and most importantly, the crew had survived and, from a personal perspective, the Board of Inquiry placed no blame upon the flight authoriser, the squadron and my chain of command.

In true RAF style, another verse was added to '*We're Sixteen Squadron*' in the Pig and Tapeworm that night.

Graham Smart, then the station commander of Laarbruch, had asked Peter Norriss to work up a display team that could perform at the open days scheduled for RAF Wildenrath and RAF Laarbruch on the first Saturday after we got home. So, with the detachment drawing to a close, Peter Norriss decided to take advantage of the fine Mediterranean weather to practise close formation flying with a five-ship in order to get ahead of the game. Peter had worked out a routine that involved five aircraft which would fly as a five-ship for part of the time and then break up into a four-ship and a singleton. The two elements would then perform a sort of 'opposition' arrangement with each other in front of the crowd. The four-ship carried out continuous clockwise turns, changing formation from box to swan et al when furthest from the crowd, so that they could witness the changes. The singleton did the usual Buccaneer thing and passed in front of the crowd in different configurations: high speed and clean; low speed with gear, hook, flaps down and rotating the bomb-door etc – a bit like the Red Arrows,[28] but on a grander scale with regard to aircraft size and magnitude. Plenty of practice was required before the display day came and so the first practice at medium level at Deci provided an ideal opportunity for us to hone our close formation skills. We recovered to Laarbruch on the Wednesday and flew three practice formations on the Thursday and Friday before the performance at the two bases on Saturday,

---

28. The Red Arrows were also at the Laarbruch air show and, on seeing our display, said that if they had known it would be so good they would have videoed it!

25 September. We worked hard at getting the display to look right from the ground and were ably assisted by the squadron driver, a German civilian and the only man who had a video camera, who shot all the rehearsals from the control tower, which allowed us to make adjustments after each sortie debrief.

We called the team the Black Saints – 16 Squadron had always been known as 'The Saints' since its formation at St Omer in France in 1916 and sported the Simon Templar matchstick 'Saint' motif on the aircraft fins. The various sectors on the airfield at Laarbruch were colour-coded for ease of reference during exercises, and the 16 Squadron sector was known as 'Black'.

The make-up of the team for the first display was:

Peter Norriss/David Herriot – Leader
Jerry Witts/Colin Buxton
Dick Johnston/Geoff Tompson
Paul Dandeker/Roger Carr
Ron Trinder/Ray Horwood – No 5 and singleton

On the display day there was a strong on-crowd wind blowing, which led to a particularly sporting display, and Jerry Witts subsequently admitted that when the Boss called 'tightening', he thought he already had 90° of bank on!

We flew a number of other displays in the latter half of 1982 and, following some crew changes and postings at the end of 1982, some positions were formally changed, with Ed Whitaker joining the Boss whilst I moved to Paul Dandeker's rear seat and together we took up the No 5/singleton duties.

Our social life at Laarbruch was full on, both in the officers' mess and the squadron. However, now with young children to care for and a shortage of suitable and available babysitters, we began a round of dinner parties with the Dandekers and the Gaults. It seems now as if we were never out of one or others' houses at weekends. And although the Dandekers were quartered in Goch, some eight miles north of base, it was no hardship to drive if one of us was prepared to abstain from an over indulgence in alcohol for the evening. With children in tow, each of the three couples would turn up at the hosts' front door and bundle kids, sleeping bags and cuddly toys upstairs, whilst beer was being poured and tables were set downstairs for the evening's frolic. Then, normally about 0200hrs, children were hoicked from their slumbers, bundled into the back seat of the car and driven home, whereupon they would be bundled back upstairs and back into bed, where we hoped and prayed they would stay until the hangover was at least on the mend the following morning. We all became lifelong friends.

Shortly after our return from Decimomannu I was invited for a chat with the Boss. He explained to me that he was concerned about the development of a young crew that had recently arrived from the OCU and that he was about to make a proposal that, at first, I might seem disinclined to agree with. He wanted me to re-crew with the pilot whilst the navigator was to fly with Ron Trinder, the QWI pilot. It was felt that our experience would serve to bring both these youngsters on and improve both their professional ability and their airmanship. There was a suggestion that the navigator in question was not strong enough to curb the pilot's youthful exuberance which could have a disastrous outcome.

I was not particularly happy with the idea of not flying with the Boss anymore, but accepted the decision for the good of the squadron and for the development and wellbeing of the two individuals concerned. I had flown with the pilot, a young and flamboyant Australian, once before on a dive-bombing sortie on Frasca Range and he had been capable enough, if a little flashy in his approach. I did not doubt that I could curb his liveliness in the air and he seemed like he would be great fun to have around on the ground! We got airborne on our first crewed sortie together on the October 1982 MINEVAL. It was a simple singleton sortie to Nordhorn Range for a Radar Laydown FRA and once I got used to his Australian twang, it went very well indeed. He was confident, proficient and personable in the cockpit and I looked forward to more.

As 1983 dawned, talk around the squadron began to focus on the end of the Buccaneer's life in RAFG. The aircraft was to be replaced by the Tornado GR1 on XV Squadron later that year and, in early 1984, on 16 Squadron too. The Buccaneer was to be phased out over the latter months of 1983 and the two squadrons were to amalgamate for the last six months operating from the 16 Squadron sector on base and under that badge. I began to consider my options for my next appointment. Having turned down Tornado previously, it was now a sensible time to make the move to a more modern aircraft than the Buccaneer. What is more, with over two thousand hours on the Buccaneer and four tours under my belt, I needed a new challenge. I began to sound out a few options and discussed the matter with Sue, who had enjoyed her time in Germany, but agreed that it was probably now about time to go home. With both XV and 16 Squadrons reforming, there were plenty of Tornado slots available and more in the UK where some QWIs were already coming towards the end of their first tour. I was, therefore, hopeful and moderately confident that it would be a Tornado slot for me.

In mid-January, whilst contemplating my future, I was seconded to the NATO TACEVAL Team as an airborne evaluator for a TACEVAL at Liege/Bierset AB in Belgium. The two Belgian Air Force squadrons at Liege operated the Mirage V in the air-to-ground role and I very much looked forward to getting into the backseat of their two-seat trainers to see just what this aircraft could do. My task as an evaluator was a simple one. Loiter around the squadron and monitor the flight planning and planned tactics for the formations as tasked. Familiarise myself with the ATO and each ATM[29] to ensure that the squadron crews were responding to the allocated tasks appropriately and with the correct weapon systems. When allocated a formation to fly with, attend the briefing, fly the sortie and attend the debrief. Once airborne,

---

29. The Air Tasking Message is an expansion of the ATO and relates to an individual tasked mission. It details: Aircraft type; Number of aircraft; Base; Weapon load; Callsign; Target; Category of Damage and TOT required, etc, etc.

I had to monitor the sortie in the air and, whilst displaying strong airmanship, only speak with regard to the mission if things became dangerous.

Unfortunately the weather in Belgium in January 1983 was anything but fit for low flying! More importantly, the Belgian squadron's flying supervisors thought it a good idea to crew me for the duration of the exercise with Second Lieutenant van den Berghe, who was very inexperienced and held only a White Card[30] instrument rating! As a result, every time the traffic lights on the Hardened Aircraft Shelter flashed 'Green' to open the doors and launch our mission, we were prevented by the cloud base and visibility from ever leaving the HAS! It was a clever ploy by the Belgians to stop me flying and improve their TACEVAL scores! The weather that week in January was typically dull on the Continent.

However, I did fly on the afternoon of 11 January 1983 and with van den Berghe! The weather had improved sufficiently to allow us to get airborne on a two-ship BAI mission into Germany. Unfortunately, shortly after take-off, we discovered that the cloud was on top of the hills in the Eifel, which prevented any further progress at low-level, forcing us to complete a weather abort by climbing rapidly to height to avoid the hills now in cloud! The mission, as far as the TACEVAL was concerned, was a failure, or, as described in military terms, a Duty Not Carried Out. Nonetheless, we had enough fuel on board to allow us to carry out a bit of Air Combat Training against each other and so the next hour was spent overhead the Ardennes in a dogfight. I had never flown in a Delta-winged aircraft before and was unprepared for the difficulty I had in identifying which way up our opponent was as we chased each other through the sky attempting to get onto our leader's tail to get a missile or guns shot off! My problem was exacerbated by the fact that the BAF had cleverly camouflaged the underside of the airframe similarly to the topside – it was a nightmare, but I very much enjoyed the ride in the Mirage, which was a pretty potent aircraft, if basic in its cockpit design.

Inopportunely for the Belgians, the weather cleared the following morning to allow van den Berghe to taxi out and get airborne as Number 3 in a four-ship of Mirages tasked to attack a military barracks in Low Flying Area 3 in Germany. The sortie planning had gone reasonably well, but I had had a quiet concern that the leader had planned a one hundred and eighty degree turn directly onto the IP. The one thing that you never do is turn onto an IP by anything other than about ten degrees and only then if the IP is a 'dog's balls' feature that can be seen from some way off. The Belgians had chosen a bridge in a deep valley as their IP, so I was concerned from the outset that we would never see it, even if we were on top of it, but the chance of that being the case was extremely remote from a hard turn onto west!

As we crossed the German border, the four aircraft descended to the minimum permitted height of 500 feet and headed across the mountains of the Eifel and on

---

30. A White Instrument Rating is awarded to pilots who have passed the appropriate flying and ground tests in instrument flying, but lack currency or experience on the aircraft type. For a White-rated pilot, an Instrument Rating Allowance of 200 feet will be added to the Procedure Minima when calculating Decision Height when recovering to an airfield.

towards the Rhine, which we planned to cross just south of Frankfurt. The area over which we were flying was heavily forested and the clouds were, in places, touching the hilltops. As we soldiered on I became aware that we were slowly descending below 500 feet. Familiar as I was with low flying in Germany, I was conscious that we were down to about 300 feet and the radio altimeter in front of me confirmed this fact. I said nothing. It was illegal, but it was not yet dangerous! Very soon we started to 'letterbox'[31] over the hilltops and a quick look at the radio altimeter showed us to be well below 250 feet and closer to one hundred and fifty. I was unsure how accurate the Mirage radio altimeter was and so said nothing. It would have served no purpose because, as the weather became a bit trickier and the four aircraft got even lower, the rear cockpit radio altimeter suddenly indicated zero and the 'OFF' flag appeared! My young pilot in the front seat had clearly decided that switching the radio altimeter off was a fair tactic to allow him to remain with the other three aircraft as we all headed further into Germany skimming the hilltops and avoiding the low cloud!

We missed the IP! We missed the IP by a country mile, but took up the required attack heading without any further and apparent consideration by the lead pilot, a man by the name of Witte, in an attempt to regain track. The target was in a deep valley! We missed it! We would never have seen it anyway and I doubt their chosen laydown delivery would have allowed any bombs, simulated or otherwise, to strike the barrack buildings in such a deep valley had we even seen the DMPIs! We should have been doing dive bombing to stand any chance of hitting the target, but the weather had precluded any form of dive bombing at the planning stage, so laydown had been selected instead! We cleared the target area, but, I assumed now in deep panic about what I might say at the debrief, the leader failed to turn north on to the escape heading! I said nothing, I was there to monitor!

After about ten minutes I became aware that we were heading straight towards Cologne/Bonn Airport and that within five minutes we would infringe its perimeter fence and its runway. Things were about to become dangerous! Thankfully Captain Witte realised his error at about the same time and called harshly over the radio for the formation to turn rapidly on to three five zero degrees! The formation banked sharply and, as we straightened on our new heading, I looked down and saw the perimeter fence of the airport flash past our left wing. Thankfully, there were no aircraft in the circuit or on the approach and a disaster had been averted, albeit just in time. As I looked forward again the twin spires of Cologne Cathedral raced past on the left-hand side. It had been an eventful mission and one where the errors were fully admitted by Witte at the debrief. I thanked the pilots for the 'experience', acknowledged their honest debrief and the learning points they had raised and reported my findings to an aghast TACEVAL Team at the evening's hot wash-up!

In March, my young pilot and I headed off to Akrotiri for an extended Cyprus Ranger. This time, however, it was to be a 'working holiday' with planned bombing sorties on the targets in Episkopi Bay on the Thursday and Friday before we were allowed to relax over the weekend. Since Dom Mintoff had thrown us out of Malta, we

---

31. Passing between hilltops and low cloud, which appears as a letterbox ahead of the aircraft.

refuelled at Brindisi in Italy on route to and from the RAF base in Cyprus. With just two aircraft we were left very much to our own devices, but achieved four sorties to the range on the two days and also conducted reconnaissance of the Soviet anchorages in the Eastern Mediterranean. After a successful weekend, Monday morning came too soon and we were soon briefing for our recovery back to Laarbruch. Our leader had sought and been given clearance to do a 'beat up' of Akrotiri on departure and we had been asked to do a flyby at the RAF Hospital, which sits on Cape Gata at the most south-westerly point of the Akrotiri SBA. The hospital staff had asked us specifically to give them fifteen minutes warning so that they could get their patients out on to the veranda to watch us go by.

Akrotiri was on its westerly runway that Monday morning and so our beat up and flyby required us to form up to the south of Cyprus before we ran in at 580kts and 100 feet along the runway from the east. I authorised the sortie and briefed my pilot personally that he was to keep it loose on the lead aircraft and to not, under any circumstances, fly below the leader at any point during the beat up! He let me down, he let me down badly! He was well below the leader as we flashed down the runway at Akrotiri and he had breached a direct order and broken the confidence that he and I had so painstakingly sought to build over the previous six months! He had shown himself to be a bit of a rip-shit when the opportunity had presented itself.

When we landed back at Laarbruch, I took him aside and informed him just how I felt about his performance at Akrotiri. I advised him that it was inappropriate of him to breach the authorised height and it had been an irresponsible act that jeopardised my authorisation responsibilities on the squadron. He told me that he was sorry and that it would never happen again – I told him that, this once, it would go no further, but that if it ever happened again I would have no alternative but to inform the squadron executives. He humbly accepted my dressing down.

The following month the squadron were tasked to participate in Exercise Maple Flag[32] at Cold Lake AB in Alberta, Canada. And, just like Red Flag, a work-up programme had to be undertaken by all participating crews before deployment. So back we went to Lossiemouth in mid–April for more ULL in Low Flying Area 14T. It was the usual mix of 'Flag' preparation sorties and my Australian and I flew eight ULL missions out of Lossiemouth. Being one of the most inexperienced pilots, we flew predominantly as Number 2 in formations with the simple responsibilities given to Number 2s throughout aviation's short history to 'stick, search and report'! Everything went well for us until the very last sortie of the work-up when we flew as Number 4 in a six-ship tasked with an airfield attack at Wick Airport. The ULL portion of the sortie had been a good workout and we had now been cleared, as briefed, to overfly Wick at 100 feet, but with specific instruction to avoid the hangars and domestic site to the south of the runway. There was little room for manoeuvre

---

32. Maple Flag was established in 1978 and is one of the largest of such exercises in the world. The exercise occurs annually over a four-week period, which is split into two, two-week 'phases.' Maple Flag provides realistic training for aircrew from the RCAF, as well as select allied air forces from around the world and can be considered a Canadian version of the USAF Red Flag.

around the airfield and so a simple, non-tactical attack was planned that would result in three pairs flying in arrow at thirty-second spacing along the length of Runway 31. As we ran towards the coastline, and whilst out over the sea, I reiterated the words that I had shared with him as we had walked towards XV864 on the line at Lossie.

'Remember, not over the hangars and not below our leader at any stage.'

'Copied that!' he responded with his Aussie lilt.

As we crossed the threshold of Runway 31 our leader pressed down to 100 feet and held it there. We did not! As we got lower and lower, I found myself looking obliquely up at the underside of our leader's port wing and we remained there despite my demands from the back that he was to get back to the same height as our leader. It was a very frosty recovery back to Lossiemouth where I took him to task as soon as we were safely on the ground and taxying back to dispersal. He had no excuse for breaching the minimum height once again and against my explicit instruction. He had no reason either, he confessed – just a 'red mist' moment! Walking back into the squadron I talked the matter over with him further and explained to him that, as I had promised out of Akrotiri, a second offence left me no alternative but to inform the Boss that he had breached his authorisation again and that he could not be trusted when the red mist took over. He accepted my decision – he had no alternative! I made him well aware that I had been placed in his back cockpit in an attempt to moderate his behaviour in the air and my sole responsibility now was to protect the Boss and his squadron.

He was grounded, and although he was allowed to travel to Maple Flag as an Ops Officer, he did not fly any missions on the exercise. That, of course, had a knock-on effect on me, because the crews that had worked-up together were to fly together, but I, whilst qualified, now no longer had a pilot! I was devastated, but I knew that I had done the right thing by my conscience and by the squadron executives who would have been hung out to dry had we had a serious accident because of his 'gung ho' attitude to flying.

Upon our return to Laarbruch on Friday, 29 April 1983, we were informed that the deployment plan that would give us seven days acclimatisation in Alberta prior to the exercise had been altered. The plan had been that we would fly by RAF VC10 direct to Edmonton on 8 May, which was the following Sunday. We were informed, however, that no VC10 was available to take us to Canada until Sunday, 15 May, which meant there would be neither acclimatisation nor time to prepare ourselves for flying at ULL the following day unless an alternative could be found.

Peter Norriss spent most of the following week in discussion with staff at HQ RAFG in an attempt to negotiate a solution which did not compromise the acclimatisation schedule. HQ 38 Gp, who controlled the transport fleet from RAF Upavon in Wiltshire, was as intransigent as we had come to expect. There was no give and no take! Options considered varied between resurrecting the VC10 to depart Laarbruch no later than Sunday, 8 May, to providing civilian air tickets for the twenty-six aircrew involved. That was not a favoured option as it would segregate aircrew and ground crew, officers and airmen. But it was one that had to be considered as, although the ground crew would perhaps not be at their best for a few days whilst their bodies adjusted to the eight-hour time zone shift, for the squadron to authorise aircrew to fly at 100 feet under operational conditions in that state would have been a definite hazard to Flight Safety. Eventually, with HQ 38 Gp unable to provide an aircraft and Peter Norriss stating that his squadron would withdraw from the exercise if no acclimatisation was possible, HQ RAFG capitulated and agreed to fund airline passage to Edmonton for all the aircrew.

We left Laarbruch by 32-seater MT coach at 0630hrs on Monday, 9 May 1983 and headed for Dusseldorf airport to catch a mid-morning flight to London Heathrow. All the officers, bar one, were dressed smartly for the occasion in the hope that an upgrade might be on hand for any one of them. One of the squadron navigators, however, was dressed more smartly than all of us; Davie Paton had decided to travel in full 'Bonnie Prince Charlie' Highland Dress complete with Skean Dhu tucked tightly in his right-hand sock! He had not, however, bargained for the fact that it and his sporran would set off all the alarms as he passed through security with the concomitant result that he had to undergo a full tap down search by a rather larger than life Brunhilda!

At Dusseldorf we were shepherded together by a Royal Air Force movements officer who handed each of us a ticket and boarding card for the eleven o'clock departure. A quick and necessary check of the boarding card confirmed what we had been told by the 'mover' upon our arrival – we were travelling Club Class and, he had told us, that was the case for each of the three legs to get us to Edmonton! Seventh Heaven didn't feature in our thoughts – we were over the moon! In 1983, the only means of getting free alcohol on board an airliner was to fly in Club Class or above. The poor plebs who travelled in Economy Class had to buy their alcohol at the extortionate price charged on board!

As the wheels folded into their recesses under the Boeing 737, we tucked into our first G&T of the day and pondered just how many we could consume before they stretched themselves to take us onto the Heathrow tarmac. Three, I recall, was all that we received, but at least we had not had to pay for them. As we slowed to a stop at Terminal Three, we prepared to disembark to meet the next 'mover' who had the pleasant task of issuing us with our 'Club Passes' for the next leg of our journey across the Atlantic. It was just past eleven o'clock in the UK and we had three hours to kill before an eight-hour flog across the Atlantic to Canada on a British Airways Jumbo. Three hours to freshen up, gather our thoughts and have a couple of beers in the lounge before departure.

True to his associate's words at Dusseldorf, the UK-based mover was awaiting our arrival in the terminal building and handed each one of us a boarding card for our BA flight to Toronto. A wail of despair followed our group through the terminal building as we made our way to the duty-free bar on the 'Departures' level. They were Economy Class tickets! Quickly a decision was made; we needed a few sharpeners at a reasonable price before we got on-board and were stung by BA for a beer, let alone a G&T. Three tax-free G&Ts later we were ready to board!

Again, as the wheels lifted off the tarmac, we settled into our journey and readied for the first movie to be shown on the incredibly small screens some six feet away and above our heads.

'Bing Bong! "Ladies and Gentlemen, welcome aboard this British Airways Boeing 747 flight to Toronto, Canada, this afternoon. Travelling on this flight with us today are members of the British Airways Canada Club and, because of their esteemed presence on-board, all drinks on this flight will be served courtesy of British Airways!"'

What a coup! Free alcohol all the way to Toronto! We settled back in our seats at the back of the jet and awaited the arrival of the hostess and her wonderful array of beverages. Booze flowed freely, meals came frequently and the movies were not bad. D² and I were sat together and we entertained ourselves with cards and laughter whilst we plotted how we were going to entertain ourselves in Canada. Neither of us had been to Toronto and before long we had hatched a plan to squeeze a couple of nights there before we moved on further west. You will recall that we had flown the Atlantic previously in less comfortable surroundings and on the leg to Canada from the Azores one of our number had almost run out of fuel. There would be no running out of fuel on this behemoth of the skies!

'Bing Bong "Ladies and gentlemen, I'm sorry to tell you that we have run out of alcohol. Well that's not strictly true – we do actually have Tia Maria left. If anybody would like a Tia Maria please press…"'

Down the back twenty-six aircrew hands instantly hit their call buttons and twenty-six Tia Marias were duly dispensed! We still had an hour to run to our destination and the aircraft had run out of 'fuel'!

As we rolled through Canadian immigration, D² and I formulated our 'escape' plan as we stood in line to be cleared. We spied the Boss at the baggage carousel and, after a short explanation, he agreed with our plan to stopover in Toronto as long as we could rebook our flights to Edmonton where we were to arrive no later than Thursday. Off we scuttled to the Air Canada desk and within a blink of an eye our tickets were changed. It was five in the evening, we had no bed, no wheels and no idea how far the city was from the airport, but after some helpful advice and a few telephone calls we had secured the first and were soon in a taxi heading to our hotel. Bags dumped, we were on Yonge Street ninety minutes later and tucking into our first Molson.

Yonge is Toronto's main street and it is the place to be and be seen in the city. It regularly hosts parades, street performances and demonstrations and was named by Ontario's first colonial administrator, John Graves Simcoe, for his friend Sir George Yonge, an expert on ancient Roman roads. A clever distinction given that Yonge Street has been routinely described in the *Guinness Book of Records*[33] as the longest street in the world. But D² and I were not there to study the cultural history of

---

33. Until 1999, the *Guinness Book of Records* repeated the popular misconception that Yonge Street was 1,896km long, and thus the longest street in the world; this was due to a mistaken conflation of Yonge Street with the rest of Ontario's Highway 11. Yonge Street is actually only 56 kilometres long.

the place, we were looking to relax over a few beers and enjoy Yonge Street's other cultural activities in the eponymous and famous 'Downtown Yonge' shopping and entertainment district.

The following morning the sun was shining brightly over Lake Ontario as we took delivery of a hire car and set off in a westerly direction with no real plan of where we were going or what we might see on route. Our stopover whim had precluded any forward planning and we had little idea of what the geographical layout of the area was. We knew that if we headed west with the water on our left and the land on our right we couldn't go far wrong and, eventually, a suitable watering hole would present itself for a relaxing lunch, hopefully with a terrace overlooking the lake. We drove for about two hours keeping the water on our left-hand side. Through Hamilton and St Catherine's we drove until we came to a sign that read 'Niagara-on-the-Lake'! It was approaching lunchtime and we were ready for our first beer.

'What do you reckon?' said Paul. 'This place looks like it might have somewhere.'

'Worth a look,' I responded. So we turned off the highway and started to look for a suitable hostelry.

As we entered the town another sign caught our eye. 'Niagara Falls 20 Kms'. I looked at Paul, Paul looked at me and there was no decision to make. We swung right and followed the signs which took us away from the lake shore and south towards the USA border. Some eight miles later, with the windows wound down to let in the fresh May air, we began to hear a loud rumble! As we drove further the rumble turned into an enormous roar until suddenly we could hardly hear ourselves speak. We drove into the car park at Niagara Falls having been completely unaware that the falls were within driving distance of our unplanned stopover!

The sight was magnificent and the noise of the half a million litres per second cascading over the Horseshoe Falls was deafening. So much for our navigational prowess! So much for our pre-route study! To be fair, we were rather too heavily hungover from our excesses over the Atlantic the previous day to have realised anything of what we might encounter on route. Over a cold Molson, we both admitted that neither of us had realised that Niagara was on Toronto's doorstep. Photos secured and with the sound of the cascade diminishing in our ears, we headed west and back to Toronto, this time keeping Lake Ontario on our right-hand side. Three hours later we were back in a bar on Yonge Street.

We spent the Wednesday relaxing and in and out of the shops in the vast Eaton Centre shopping mall. The mall stretches two full blocks along Yonge Street and its vaulted glass ceiling covers six storeys of shops under which 'fly' a sculptural representation of sixty Canada Geese. It was at least a morning's work to travel the length of the shopping mall and buy gifts for our families, but soon we were complete and ready for our first Molson of the day. Day done, we were packed and ready for our onward flight to Edmonton the following morning with Air Canada.

As the Boeing 727 lifted from Pearson International, D² and I settled into our first G&T of the day courtesy of Air Canada's Connoisseur Class. Canada is vast and, in many areas, is a hostile wasteland. An estimated seventy-five per cent of its population live within one hundred miles of its border with the United States. Our flight hugged the American border, initially crossing two of the Great Lakes, Huron and Superior, before we passed over the southern tip of the Canadian Shield and onwards across Ontario, Manitoba and Saskatchewan until, as we crossed the Alberta boundary, we began our descent into Edmonton. In the grand scheme of the total distance covered since we left Laarbruch, this was a short hop of just over three hours, but we were refreshed after our exertions in Toronto and ready to join the rest of the team on 'acclimatisation' in the Sheraton Hotel before we moved north to Cold Lake at the weekend. Bags in our rooms, we headed for the bar and fell in with the usual bunch of rogues who were all too ready to regale us with the continuing story of their Trans-Atlantic 'drinkathon'!

They too had been delighted to discover that they were to travel in comfort in Connoisseur Class, but were disappointed when they discovered that the chief steward on board had decided that he would have to close the bar when they were only halfway across Canada because 'some passengers were getting a bit rowdy'! Hardly surprising really, they had been drinking since Dusseldorf and it was well past their bedtime by the time their Air Canada 727 was sat happily at 30,000 feet just north of Winnipeg.

The few days in Edmonton were well spent 'acclimatising'. Unfortunately, every hooker in Alberta had heard that there was a British squadron in town and that we were staying in the Sheraton. So the hotel bar was a place to be avoided at all costs, although we did have to run their gauntlet going in and out through reception! The Four Seasons hotel bar, situated on 101 St NW, just north of Jasper Avenue, and the Warehouse District on 104 Street, were much more central than the Sheraton and far more inviting than a bar where girls were on the make. More importantly for RAF aircrew, both were within Edmonton's 'Downtown' area and were close to the nightlife.

Come the Saturday we had to pack our bags and leave the highlife. A Canadian Air Force coach took us north of the city to CFB Namao for a thirty minute hop to Cold Lake on the pre-planned VC10 that had just arrived from Laarbruch with our ground crew on board. Bedded in, we began to prepare our operations room whilst the airmen readied the aircraft already on site for the Monday morning first wave. Sunday was spent with in-briefings from the Maple Flag staff and further mission planning.

Without my own pilot to fly with on the exercise, I had anticipated that I would spend much of my time on the Ops Desk authorising sorties and ensuring that the flying programme ran smoothly. I certainly did not expect to get much flying – if any. Work spent on reconnaissance, however, is seldom wasted and, after a few beers at the 'Meet and Greet' hosted by the Canadians, I found myself being invited to fly in the NATO E-3A Sentry on the very first day of the exercise. It was a fascinating insight into the coordination, deconfliction and Command & Control issues that the AWACS has provided to NATO and Allied forces since it achieved its Initial Operating Capability with the USAF in 1978. The commanding bird's-eye view of the battlespace provided me with a whole new aspect from on high and allowed me to monitor the tactics employed by the Buccaneers in evading their enemy in the air and recommend tactical changes during debriefs back on the ground. Later in the two weeks I managed to secure a seat on board a Huey[34] that was taking personnel into the ranges to man the radar sites. This too provided a further opportunity to assess our tactics and terrain masking techniques that I was able to feed back to the aircrew upon my return to Cold Lake that evening. Both missions were exhilarating and tactically informative, and both assisted greatly with the development of the squadron's operational procedures. Most enlivening from the helicopter, however, was being able to see beaver lodges and dams and watch Grizzly Bears fishing in the fast-flowing rivers as we flashed over their heads at about thirty feet. Not so invigorating, but definitely adrenaline-charging, was the sound of bears crashing through the trees no more than four hundred yards from the radar cabins; a very good reason to get back indoors if the noise started to head your way! I did manage to spend some time outdoors and did capture some fantastic images of Buccaneers at ULL on my cine camera which, some years later, I transferred to DVD[35].

Of course, it wasn't all flying and exercise, flying and exercise! There was inevitability about such gatherings within NATO that socialising formed part of the agenda. Every night the exercise participants would congregate in the bar to sing songs, drink beer, exchange stories, and argue triumphs and disasters over the battlefield that day. Many a pair of 'flying hands' would be caught circling over a pint of Molsons as yet one more fighter pilot tried to explain just how he'd managed to get on another fighter pilot's tail! Occasionally, some would head down town into Cold Lake town to see if there was any action there. There was not, and it was a somewhat intimidating place with inebriated Red Indians and drunken trappers keen to find someone who wanted a fight. I only ventured into the local town once; finding more comfort amongst like-minded aircrew in the officers' mess rather than the ne'er-do-wells of Cold Lake. However, on that occasion, I and the four other passengers in the Boss's limousine nearly never made it.

After a couple of hours in the mess we had managed to persuade Peter Norriss to drive 'the team' into town – I don't know why he agreed, but agree he did and, with him tucked in behind the wheel, five of us crammed onto the two bench seats and set off down the long straight road that led off base! Ahead, in the dark, stood the main exit to the air base and the final barrier to our getaway.

'Don't stop, Boss!' one voice said. But the Boss, being a sensible chap, slowed to a halt before the RCMP officer who was waving his hand in the air indicating that he should do just that.

Formalities over, the same voice from the back called, 'Gun it, Boss!' On that command and now emboldened by our escape, Peter Norriss slammed his foot on the accelerator and the car, with its tyres squeeling on the road surface, shot off and away from the RCMP officer, his car, and the guard post. Or so we thought! There in the

---

34. The UH-1 Iroquois (unofficially *Huey*) is a military helicopter, developed by Bell Helicopter to meet the United States Army's requirement for a medical evacuation and utility helicopter in 1952; it first flew on 20 October 1956.

35. The results were included in a tribute DVD that I produced in 2008 for the Buccaneer Aircrew Association that marked the 50th Anniversary of the Buccaneer's First Flight.

rear-view mirror were the undisputed flashing lights of a RCMP patrol car and they were heading in our direction fast! The Boss slowed to a stop and awaited his fate. The RCMP vehicle pulled in behind us and, as the officer approached our car, Peter rolled down his window. The police officer could hardly get a word out in between Peter's pleas of abject apology.

'Sir, just stop talking a minute and get out of the car please!' Peter did as he was bid and as he took his foot off the brake and vacated the vehicle, it began to slowly gain speed and move off down the road without him at the wheel. The two drunks in the front, thankfully, did not panic, but slipped the vehicle out of 'Drive' into 'Neutral' and applied gentle pressure to the brake. Peter, like the rest of us, was unaccustomed to driving an automatic and so, once again, his abject apologies began to flow from his lips. The policeman saw the funny side of the whole affair, realised we were Brits, made allowances for our stupidity and sent us on our way! We stayed in Cold Lake no longer than an hour – it was a dump!

Having spent so little time in Edmonton, D^2 and I had vowed that we would head back there at the weekend. It was about a two hundred mile drive, but we planned to hire a car and set off as early as we could on the Friday for two nights 'in town'. Once again fate stepped in. During an evening of carousing in the bar, we were commiserating with a Canadian C-130 pilot who had broken his leg and was in a plaster cast from knee to toe. He was bemoaning the fact that he was not allowed to fly tactically on the exercise, but was delighted that his Boss had agreed to allow him to take a C-130 to Namao for the weekend. When he heard of our 'drive there' plan he insisted that we come along with him for the ride! So, with his co-pilot responsible for the rudder pedals and the plan to rent a car discarded, we set off back to Edmonton by air on the Friday afternoon for two nights in the Four Seasons. We had recruited another half-dozen like-minded souls for the journey and an excellent weekend was had by all in and around the Sushi Bar in the hotel and in the various pubs on Bourbon Street in the West Edmonton Mall!

Despite my lack of a dedicated pilot, I did actually get airborne four times on Maple Flag with four different pilots! The sorties were invigorating, but very much akin to those that I had already flown on Red Flag twice before. Although the terrain was considerably different, the tactics and learning points were very much the same. The exercise closed on the day after my thirty-fourth birthday and I was grateful not to be involved in flying on that day. It had been a good thrash in the bar and with a number of aircraft departing back to the USA on the Friday night there were plenty of people to share my birthday with in 1983.

My hangover had diminished considerably when the Boss called me into a corner for a quiet chat. My wife, he told me, was having problems coping on her own at Laarbruch and had been round to his married quarter demanding that I be returned to base immediately. I was surprised by this turn of events as Sue had been perfectly happy when I had departed three weeks prior. We discussed the options available, but none would have got me home any quicker than the planned redeployment, which was scheduled to get me back to base within three days and at no extra expense to HMG. The message was relayed back via the Boss's wife and I knuckled down in assisting with wrapping up the deployment and preparing for the recovery back across the Atlantic by Buccaneer.

Following a day of aircraft preparation the squadron sallied forth from Cold Lake to CFB Trenton, near Toronto, on Sunday, 29 May 1983 – D² and I flew that leg in the back of the sweeper Hercules! At Trenton, however, after a light bite we climbed into XV161 and led a three-ship across Quebec following, predominantly, the line of the St Lawrence Seaway on the 900nm leg to Goose Bay in Newfoundland. After just over two hours flying we landed, handed the aircraft over to the ground crew and headed to the officers' mess for a beer and a night's rest before we took on the two legs the following day that would take us back to Laarbruch via Keflavik AFB in Iceland.

Back home at 12 Cochrane Way, I tried to fathom out just what had been Sue's issues that had compelled her to approach Lesley Norriss and demand my early return from the detachment. I knew that she had personal support on base through Mike & Siobhan Gault and there was a good and well-organised welfare set up to cater for such eventualities. She was not particularly forthcoming with information, and to this day, I have no real idea what had precipitated her action. The squadron executives were concerned, however, and encouraged me to take time out with my family to provide support for Sue and resolve any issues that might be present. As a result, I flew only twelve more sorties in a Buccaneer before I left the squadron in September 1983.

Even with all the acknowledged pressures on my home life, I was selected in mid-August to join the NATO TACEVAL Team once again. Entertainingly for me, it was at Spangdahlem and back to the 480th TFS. The Warhawks welcomed me with open arms, but there were to be no high jinks with Cluster J. Hartley the Third this time around. The squadron was in lockdown, no drinking was to be had and we, the TACEVAL Team, were living off base so as not to be contaminated by any prior engagements with this team of hardened drinkers! I flew twice in the F-4E as a TACEVAL chase aircraft with Captain Rice who, on climbing to medium level after a BAI mission in LFA 7, offered me control of his jet and encouraged me to fly formation on the leader of our section of two aircraft. Still smarting from the time I overstressed a Hunter on the OCU with another American in charge, I eased the aircraft gingerly towards our leader. 'Closer, closer!' encouraged Rice, as I stood my distance until in the end I had to ask him: 'Do you realise that I'm a WSO[36], not a pilot?'

'Holy Sheeeiiit!' he responded as we closed ever nearer and, with a yank of the joystick, he pulled us clear and back into Battle Formation. Poor chap; he was a recent arrival on the squadron and had not been present when 16 Squadron had been on exchange with the Warhawks in 1982. He'd never met me before!

The Buccaneer was now well within its last few months of its operational service in Germany and was to be replaced by the Tornado GR1 in early 1984. Minds began to focus on an 'end of era' extravaganza and much discussion of what we could do

---

36. Weapon Systems Officer; USAF equivalent of RAF navigator.

became regular bar talk. Jerry Witts and I were sharing such a conversation one Friday Happy Hour when we were approached by Graham Smart, the Laarbruch CO, who duly asked us what plans, if any, we had to, 'say goodbye to the Buccaneer'. We explained that there was much talk of a massive hangar party and that crews were thinking about exotic locations for their final Rangers. Graham listened and then, as he was about to depart, he threw down a challenge.

'Come up with something way out of the ordinary and tell me next Friday night!'

The following week Jerry and I met up in his office on the squadron and started to throw around a few ideas. We wondered whether there might be a possibility of running a, 'how far can you get in a Buccaneer' competition. We looked at exotic locations and we pondered the likelihood of obtaining various diplomatic clearances. We knew that fully laden with fuel, the Buccaneer would go a long way at high level and then we began to wonder just how far! We had proven its capability crossing the Atlantic unrefuelled in 1982 to get to Red Flag and had, only recently, done the same in reverse recovering aircraft from Maple Flag. Suddenly, I blurted out, 'Do you think we could get right round the world!' At first stunned at the notion, Jerry very quickly signed up to my idea and together we set about putting a sketch plan of our proposal together.

It was actually more than a sketch! I spent much of the following week squirreled away in the QWI office with the Planning Document[37]. I pored over charts of the Pacific Ocean, the Solomon Islands and the Indian subcontinent. I drew lines on En Route Charts. I measured the lines, calculated the flight times along the lines, worked out the fuel expended in the climb and descent for each destination, and applied the statistical meteorology figures to ensure that I had the very best 'guess' of just how much fuel we would have remaining at each destination if we departed on each leg with 23,000lbs of gas on board. My planning was comprehensive and included such detail as whether landing airfields had the appropriate arrestor gear should we suffer a hydraulic emergency on route. I was impressed with what I managed to achieve in a short space of time. Jerry was overwhelmed by my endeavour.

With the maps stuffed into the lower leg pockets of my flying suit, Jerry and I awaited the station commander's arrival in the bar at Happy Hour the following week.

'Well?' he asked as soon as he found us in the corner of the bar.

'Well, sir, how about this? Take two Buccaneers, three crews, a handful of ground crew and a supporting VC10 and spare parts around the world without AAR!' I responded.

His face was a picture. 'Are you serious? Can it be done?'

It was feasible. It could be done in the right weather conditions in an easterly direction. Granted there were some airfields in the Pacific that would have required significant efforts to gain Diplomatic Clearance, but that was not unachievable. The longest leg was the 2,300nm between Hickam AFB in Hawaii and McClellan

---

37. A navigator's bible! It gives almost all the information any aircrew man might need to plan a flight anywhere in the world including Statistical Meteorology (i.e. Statistical winds, temperatures at height, etc).

AFB near San Francisco which, with a strong prevailing westerly, would use about 20,000lbs of our maximum uptake. Should fuel become a problem we planned that San Francisco International, which we would overfly, was available as an on route diversion! The station commander was enthralled and very quickly signed up for the plan[38]. His last words were, 'Get on and plan it. You will fly with me, Dave, Jerry find yourself a navigator and a spare crew!' It was achievable and, it seemed, it was a goer.

It never happened! When the staff at HQ RAFG heard of the plan it was scotched straight away. There was no way that any staff officer was going to put his signature to a plan for a trans-Global flight by the Buccaneer when it was being replaced by the Tornado GR1 whose Radius of Action was never a match for the aircraft it replaced. OK! It was tight in some areas and weather delays may have jeopardised our plan for a thirty-day World Tour, but to dismiss it out of hand without asking any questions was inconsiderate. To cancel the hangar party similarly once the invitations had been sent out across NATO, however, was downright despicable and resulted in the CinC coming to the squadron for lunch one day to apologise on behalf of his staff – he had not been consulted and had he been, he would have been first at the beer barrel in the hangar on the planned date. It was a typical reaction by a raft of RAF staff officers who, throughout the Buccaneer's sterling service in the RAF, had always considered it to be a second-class citizen!

With the pending arrival of the Tornado GR1 in RAFG, XV Squadron was disbanded, and on 1 July 1983, Eddie Cox, the CO of XV, took command of the remaining Buccaneer aircrew and ground crew amalgamated under the banner of 16 Squadron. Peter Norriss and most of his executives departed Laarbruch and I began to consider my options for my next tour and to rebuild my family life.

As my experience had increased on the aircraft, and with greater maturity on the ground, my ACRs had improved since I had left 12 Squadron. After a couple of 'Not Yet Fit' for promotion, because of a lack of seniority as a flight lieutenant, my last report from 12 Squadron marked me as 'Recommended' – it was early days but it was a necessary upward trend if I wanted promotion. That trend had continued on the OCU staff with my first two reports showing 'Highly Recommended'. Then disaster! With the SNI convinced that I had only accepted a tour on 16 Squadron to allow me to buy a tax-free car, my last OCU report dropped me back to 'Recommended'. Not good!

Nick Berryman, from whom I had taken over as weapons leader on 16 Squadron, became my first reporting officer and wrote my first annual report on the squadron. He marked me 'Specially Recommended' for promotion to squadron leader. Peter Norriss and Graham Smart, in sequence, endorsed it, as did the 4th RO at HQ RAFG. There was no higher acclaim than a 'Spec Rec'. Whilst that might appear to the uninitiated as being the key to the door, to go from 'Rec' to 'Spec Rec' in one leap can be misinterpreted by the staff within PMA charged with managing an

---

38. The route was: Laarbruch; Decimomannu; Akrotiri (Cyprus); Luxor (Egypt); Bahrain; Bombay; Colombo (Sri Lanka); Singapore; Darwin; Sydney; Auckland; Fiji; Bucholz (Marshall Islands); Hickam; McClellan; Cold Lake; Trenton; Goose Bay; Keflavik; Laarbruch.

individual's career. However, when it is followed up with a 'High Rec' the following year it only serves to confuse! That 1983 report identified that there were problems at home and that fact had forced Nick to drop my recommendation. Note was made in the report that, as a flight lieutenant, I had struggled initially to secure the backing of my fellow junior officers in my new elevated role as the weapons leader. Surely, if the RAF was unable to provide a suitably ranked officer to fill the post, that was a fault of the system rather than of me I argued. However, more damning were the words that followed:

> '… *he was also unfortunately under increased domestic pressure from his wife and family.*'

Peter Norriss endorsed Nick's recommendation – I was on a backward slide. The report also recommended that I needed time out from flying to sort out my family issues and that a ground tour was the best option to allow me to consolidate. I had passed the C Examination and had re-enrolled in ISS. I wanted to be promoted. I wanted the additional responsibility. I needed to move forward if I was not going to stagnate. I had been a flight lieutenant for nine years. I needed to be promoted and I needed a challenge. It came in the form of a posting to a ground tour at HQSTC!

Of the ten Principles of War,[39] Concentration of Force and Economy of Effort are probably, but not exclusively, prime. From an Air Power perspective, however, they are most certainly key; as no government, no matter how flush they might be for cash, can afford to provide the absolute total resources necessary to cover all bases at all times. Consequently, every campaign plan must be rigorous in its management of its air assets. From a mud-moving standpoint it is imperative that assets in the shape of both delivery platforms and weapons are matched appropriately to the target in question. It is not, and has never been, the case that those who task aircraft at war do so on a whim. Specific targets have specific vulnerabilities to specific weapons. The task of the weaponeer is to know and understand those vulnerabilities and match suitable weapons in sufficient numbers to achieve the specific level of damage required against a nominated target. To do this, campaign planning staff require a weaponeer's bible and the weaponeer's bible in the Ministry of Defence in 1983 was SD–110A–0300–1G, *The Conventional Weapons Employment Manual.* It was hopelessly out of date!

On the face of it my task looked simple. Write a book! Write a book about air-to-surface weapons! Include current and future contracted weapon systems! Cover weapons effects! Incorporate a section on weapon effort planning! Finally, make it less scientific and more user-friendly! All of the above was well within my remit as a QWI and as a graduate of the Weapons Employment Course and I had been given two years, on my own, to complete the task. Once done, I was promised a posting to Tornado!

---

39. The Principles of War are: Selection and Maintenance of the Aim; Maintenance of Morale; Security; Surprise; Offensive Action; Concentration of Force; Economy of Effort; Flexibility; Cooperation; and Sustainability.

Now hang on just a cotton-picking minute! Was I not the poor unfortunate who had been struggling with ISS and had been criticised for my failings in written English! Yet PMA thought me an appropriate and suitable candidate to write a tome that would be published in large volume, was to be classified SECRET, and would be distributed to all squadrons, HQs and government agencies charged with the delivery and support of conventionally armed attack weapons from the air!

Irony – pure irony!

I flew my last operational Buccaneer sortie, appropriately, with Graham Smart on 8 September 1983 and, with our married quarter scrubbed to within an inch of its life, we all headed back to the UK for the next instalment in my career. I had achieved 2,165 hours and 15 minutes on the Buccaneer.

Nineteen months later I was at Cottesmore converting to the Tornado GR1.

Epilogue

The Buccaneer was finally withdrawn from military service on 31 March 1994. Having been brought into the RAF as a 'stop gap' to replace the much vaunted, but cancelled orders for TSR2 and the General Dynamics F-111, it had served faithfully for twenty-five years and fulfilled more than the expectations of those RAF top brass – very few, who had actually been behind the decision to acquire it. It was a robust airframe designed by Blackburns in the 1950s to do a particular job and it had done it outstandingly well. It had outlasted its forecast nemesis, the Soviet Sverdlov cruisers, and had been at the forefront of NATO's ASuW operations in both the FAA and the RAF for thirty-two years. It was more than just a ship-basher, however, and had proved itself within NATO and South Africa as a robust and exceptionally able platform in the overland role too. At Red Flag it had outfoxed the USAF and beaten them at their own game flying at heights around 100ft and at speeds in excess of 650 miles per hour. In the RAF it had flown on operations on three distinct occasions and most significantly, in its final years, it had been called upon to assist Tornados with their delivery of LGBs during the first Gulf War in 1991. Indeed, not only did the Buccaneers of 208 Squadron assist by designating targets for the Tornados' laser bombs, the aircraft was able to free the Tornado for other tasks when the operational commanders realised that the Buccaneer could actually self-designate its own bombs on to the target!

I consider myself distinctly privileged to have flown the Buccaneer for over half of its time in RAF service; as a result it has become very much a part of my soul. Aircrew, who were fortunate to be selected to fly it, share that feeling about the aircraft. We were a small band of professionals who worked hard, but, as you may have gathered, played hard too. It was not surprising, therefore, that there was a mass turnout of past and present Buccaneer aircrew at RAF Lossiemouth on 25 March 1994 for a 'Farewell to the Buccaneer' weekend that included a Friday night Happy Hour, a squadron 'Open Day' on the Saturday with a flying display and a 'no holds barred' airfield attack with every Buccaneer, still capable of flying, participating. If that was not enough, there followed a formal dinner in the officers' mess that went on into the small hours of the Sunday. Consequently, dawn came late on the twenty-seventh with sore heads catching the hair of the dog at midday in the bar before a Service of Thanksgiving in St Aidan's Church on base at 1300hrs. The festival closed at 1700hrs, which gave people just enough time to sober up before they headed south again and back to normality. It has often been described since as the 'Mother of All Parties'.

As I pondered the events of the weekend I subsequently realised just how monumental a relationship we Buccaneer aircrew had had with our aircraft. Many, both Royal Navy and Royal Air Force, had travelled across the world just to be at Lossiemouth for that weekend. The Buccaneer Spirit was high and the bond with each other strong. I decided that it would be wrong to let that spirit die just because our aircraft was no more and so formed the Buccaneer Aircrew Association in 1995. I was not surprised by the response and today, in 2017, despite a number of losses to the great white hangar in the sky, our membership stands at just short of five hundred – that includes some sixty from the South African Air Force. I took the role of Honorary Secretary, Graham Pitchfork became Chairman and Sir Michael Knight accepted our offer to be its first president. With the proceeds of the initial Life Members fees we purchased Buccaneer S2B, XX901, from the scrap merchant who was about to take his chainsaw to it, refurbished it and placed it on permanent static display at the Yorkshire Air Museum.

Despite the distance and never having met, we formed a very close bond with our South African cousins such that, in 2005, Sir Mike Knight and I were invited to attend their 40th Anniversary celebrations at Waterkloof AB near Pretoria. Sir Mike, you will recall from earlier in my tale, was the chap who, as my station commander at Laarbruch on my first tour, had written in my ACR:

> 'He is not ADC material (unless some senior officer is looking for a more than usually 'interesting' tour).'

Ironically, as BAA Secretary, I have been acting as his ADC now for over twenty years! But then Sir Mike is a man after my own heart who has always enjoyed a good party and a great laugh.

On our trip to South Africa I took along Jo, my second wife, to add beauty and common sense to a gathering that could otherwise have been more debauched than it actually was! It became quite obvious to me whilst in South Africa that there was a common bond between us and our South African Buccaneer aircrew hosts. Whether it was just that we were all aircrew, I doubt. Not all aircrew behave the same way as Buccaneer aircrew do! There had to be something else. These chaps could have put on a Brit flying suit, turned up in a Brit officers' mess and without any introductions whatsoever been taken for Buccaneer guys – which is exactly what they were, albeit they all had strange accents! It had to be the aircraft! It had to be the Buccaneer! It was the only thing we had in common. A life flying the best and last totally British built bomber! We were all Buccaneer Boys!

An excellent dinner was followed by much beer swilling and an international song contest! I say song contest! Of course it was nothing of the sort, but it soon became clear that these chaps had an alternative Afrikaans songbook and, as the beer flowed and their lungs oiled, they let rip. We, of course, joined in and when the opportunity arose Sir Mike and I gave them a resounding rendition of '*Give Me Buccaneers*' and '*When XV Came to Laarbruch*'! What a night, and after a 'survivors' barbecue' the following day, we, the UK contingent, felt quite at home. On the Monday we were on the road from Pretoria east through Gauteng heading for Mpumalanga and a three-day visit to the Kruger National Park. Jan Guyt, former Buccaneer pilot, retired

Brigadier General, and now my very good friend, and his wife Monika, led us on the most wonderful safari and tour through the Drakensburg Mountains that included stops at 'God's Window' and 'Pilgrim's Rest'. Throughout our time in Pretoria we were accommodated in the very welcoming Centurion Guest House and on the final night, before we departed for the UK, we returned the superb hospitality of our SAAF hosts by inviting them to 'drinks and supper on the Brits'. Over rather too many beers, the conversation drifted towards the 50th Anniversary, in 2008, of the first flight of the Buccaneer, and, before I knew it, I had agreed to a proposal that we should see if we could hold a joint reunion in Pretoria in three years' time. The SAAF membership of the BAA at that time was about seventy and I anticipated that any Brit contingent venturing south would probably be no more than forty strong.

In November 2008, having made all the in-country travel arrangements with my opposite number in South Africa, allocated UK individuals to tour buses, secured appropriate accommodation in Pretoria, collected and banked deposits and final payments and finalised the table plans, I led a one hundred and twenty strong contingent of RAF and RN Buccaneer aircrew and their ladies to Pretoria for a full weekend's reunion that included a Friday evening 'Meet & Greet', a SAAF Museum tour and a formal dinner at Swartkop AB on the Saturday, and, on Remembrance Sunday, a memorial service at the SAAF Memorial on Bay's Hill. To this were added tours to KNP, via 'God's Window' and 'Pilgrim's Rest', and for those who chose it, a tour of the Western Cape. It was in the Western Cape that I got the opportunity of a lifetime.

Whilst taking lunch in Simonstown, our tour guide announced that the next stop on our itinerary was a visit to Thunder City at Cape Town International Airport. At the time Thunder City operated a number of ex-military FJs and helicopters. Amongst its inventory were three Buccaneer S2s that had been purchased and flown south from Kemble, in Oxfordshire. Thunder City offered passenger flights through the Drakensberg Mountains in the rear seat of a Buccaneer for those who could afford the princely sum of twelve thousand pounds for the pleasure! We were going to meet the team who flew them and share a beer with them at that Friday's Happy Hour. However, delighted at the prospect of meeting 'real Buccaneer aircrew', the company had offered a 'no cost' flight to one lucky member of our tour group. Names were placed in a hat and our guide, Eugene Booysen of Cape Agritours, pulled the first name out of the hat. It was mine! I could not believe it! I was going to fly in a Buccaneer again! Then I looked in the hat. Every piece of paper had my name on it! My mates had decided that my organisational skills, and the effort I had put in to get them to and around South Africa, deserved a reward. I protested, I refused, I demanded another draw, but each and every one of them refused to participate further and insisted that I got airborne.

On arrival at Thunder City I was segregated from the rest of my group and issued with the bare necessities for a trip in a Buccaneer. Flying suit – check. Flying Boots – check. Flying helmet and O² mask – check and fitted! Flying gloves – nope! G-suit – nope! Flying socks – nope! No socks at all actually, as I had arrived at the airfield wearing sandals! So there I stood half-dressed for flying and clutching a bone dome when I was introduced to my pilot, a tall and rangy South African who introduced himself to me as Ian Pringle. A short briefing later and I found myself walking towards a Buccaneer with a plan to get airborne in it for the first time in twenty-five years! By way of conversation, I asked my new-found best friend what he had flown previously, to which I received the less than convincing answer: 'Best you ask me that after we have landed!'

XW986 had been a flight test aircraft at both Farnborough and Boscombe Down, and as a result, it did not have the navigation suite that I was accustomed to. Nevertheless, the rear cockpit had the same feel, the same smell and the same charm and atmosphere that I remembered as if it was just yesterday. It was still an ergonomic slum! At the sortie brief I had agreed with Ian that I would participate as fully from the back seat as I would have done had I still been an operational Buccaneer navigator. So he was mildly amused, therefore, when I started to read out the Pre-Take Off checks, challenge and response, as we taxied to the Marshalling Point for Runway 19; nobody had ever done that for him before! It all just came flooding back to me and it seemed the right and appropriate thing to do! I have to admit now that it was quite an emotional experience and as we started to roll for take-off I felt a tear fall from the side of my right eye. It was like a reunion with an old girlfriend – I was in love all over again.

As Ian shut down the engines after our short sortie I replaced my seat pins, unstrapped and stepped from the cockpit, elated that once again I had flown in a Buccaneer! It had only been a ten-minute sortie around the airport circuit, but it did include two 100 foot beat ups of the airfield at about 450kts. It was just ten minutes, but it was ten minutes that neatly rounded off my total flying hours to three thousand and eighty-eight exactly!

Glossary

AAR	Air-to-Air Refuelling
AB	Air Base
ACMI	Air Combat Manoeuvring Instrumentation
ACR	Annual Confidential Report
AD	Air Defence
ADC	Aide de Camp
ADD	Airstream Direction Detector
ADIZ	Air Defence Identification Zone
ADSL	Automatic Depressed Sight Line
AE	Aircraft Establishment
AEW	Airborne Early Warning
AFB	Air Force Base/Air Force Board
AFC	Air Force Cross
AFV	Armoured Fighting Vehicle
AGI	Auxiliary General Intelligence
AGL	Above Ground Level
AI	Air Interdiction
AIM	Air Intercept Missile
AIS	Airborne Instrumentation System
AMTC	Aeromedical Training Centre
ANS	Air Navigation School
AOA	Angle of Attack
AOC	Air Officer Commanding
AOR	Auxiliary Oiler Replenishment
AOTS	Aircrew Officer Training School
APC	Armament Practice Camp
APO	Acting Pilot Officer
AR	Anti-Radar
ARAM	Anti-Radar Acquisition Martel
ASAP	As Soon As Possible
ASI	Air Staff Instructions/Air Speed Indicator
ASP	Aircraft Servicing Platform
ASuW	Anti-Surface Warfare
ASW	Anti-Submarine Warfare
ATAF	Allied Tactical Air Force
ATC	Air Traffic Control
ATL	Above Target Level

ATM	Air Tasking Message
ATO	Air Tasking Order
AUW	All Up Weight
AVM	Air Vice-Marshal
AWACS	Airborne Warning and Control System
AWI	Air Warfare Instructor
AWOL	Absent Without Leave
AWTI	Air Weapons Training Installation
B/F	Before Flight
BA	British Airways
BAA	Buccaneer Aircrew Association
BAI	Battlefield Air Interdiction/ Buccaneer Attack Instructor
BAOR	British Army of the Rhine
BBC	British Broadcasting Corporation
BBT	Bomb Bay Tank
BDT	Bomb Door Tank
BEA	British European Airways
BEngO	Baby Engineering Officer
BFG	British Forces Germany
BFS	British Frontier Service
BFTS	Basic Flying Training School
BLC	Boundary Layer Control
BOAC	British Overseas Airways Corporation
BOQ	Bachelor Officer Quarter
BritMil	British Military
C to I	Competent to Instruct
C&RC	Control & Release Computer
CAOC	Combat Air Operations Centre
CAP	Combat Air Patrol
CARGRU	Carrier Group
CAS	Close Air Support
CASEVAC	Casualty Evacuation
CAVOK	Ceiling and Visibility OK
CBE	Commander of the British Empire
CBLS	Carrier Bomb Light Store
CBU	Cluster Bomb Unit
CCA	Carrier Controlled Approach
CCF	Combined Cadet Force
CFB	Canadian Forces Base
CFI	Chief Flying Instructor
CGI	Computer Generated Imagery
CHAG	Chain Arrestor Gear
CI	Chief Instructor
CinC	Commander in Chief

CO	Commanding Officer
Cockers P	Cocktail Party
CP	Critical Point
CQMS	Company Quarter Master Sergeant
CR	Combat Ready
CRT	Cathode Ray Tube
CSM	Company Sergeant Major
CT	Continuation Training
CW	Continuous Wave
D^2	Paul Dandeker
DCO	Duty Carried Out
DDR	Deutsch Democratic Republic
DFC	Distinguished Flying Cross
DFGA	Day Fighter Ground Attack
DIY	Do It Yourself
DM	Deutsch Mark
DMPI	Desired Mean Point of Impact
DoD	Department of Defense
DSO	Distinguished Service Order
ECM	Electronic Counter-Measures
ENDEX	End of Exercise
ESA	Explosives Storage Area
ETA	Estimated Time of Arrival
EW	Early Warning/Electronic Warfare
EWI	Electronic Warfare Instructor
FAA	Fleet Air Arm
FEAF	Far East Air Force
FIR	Flight Information Region
FJ	Fast-Jet
FL	Flight Level
Flt	Flight
Flt Lt	Flight Lieutenant
FNA	Fuel No Air
FOB	Flying Order Book/Forward Operating Base
FPB	Fast Patrol Boat
FRA	First Run Attack
FRC	Flight Reference Cards
FTS	Flying Training School
G&T	Gin and Tonic
GAT	General Air Traffic
GCA	Ground Control Approach
GCI	Ground Control Intercept
GCU	Ground Control Unit
GH	General Handling

GHS	Glasgow High School
GIB	Guy in the Back
GP	General Purpose
Gp Capt	Group Captain
GPS	Global Positioning System
GS	General Services
HAS	Hardened Aircraft Shelter
HE	High Explosive
HEMC	High Explosive Medium Capacity
HF	High Frequency
HMG	Her Majesty's Government
HP	High Pressure
HQ	Headquarters
HQ 1 Gp	Headquarters 1 Group
HQ 38 Gp	Headquarters 38 Group
HQSTC	Headquarters Strike Command
HT	High Tension
HYD	Hydraulic
IAS	Indicated Air Speed
ICAO	International Civil Aviation Organisation
IF	Instrument Flying
IFIS	Integrated Flight Instrument System
IFR	Instrument Flight Rules
IGB	Inner German Border
IMC	Instrument Meteorological Conditions
INAS	Inertial Navigation & Attack System
IP	Initial Point
IRE	Instrument Rating Examiner
ISS	Individual Staff Studies
ItAF	Italian Air Force
ITS	Initial Training School
JHQ	Joint Headquarters
JMC	Joint Maritime Course
JP3	Jet Provost Mk3
JP4	Jet Provost Mk4
JP5	Jet Provost Mk5
JT	Junior Technician
KNP	Kruger National Park
KOSB	Kings Own Scottish Borderers
LCR	Limited Combat Ready
LFA	Low Flying Area
LGB	Laser Guided Bomb
LLADSL	Low-level Automatic Depressed Sight Line
LLEP	Low-level Entry Point

LP	Long Playing/Low Pressure
LST	Landing Ship Tank
LTF	Lightning Training Flight
MAP	Manual Air Plot/Mental Air Picture
MARTEL	Missile Anti-Radar Television
MASB	Main Armament Safety Break
mb	Millibars
MCTU	Marine Craft Training Unit
MDA	Master Diversion Airfield
MDSL	Manual Depressed Sight Line
MEAF	Middle East Air Force
MI	Magnetic Indicator
MOB	Movement of the Body
MOD	Ministry of Defence
MOO	Movement of the Observer
MOU	Memorandum of Understanding
MP	Mission Planning
MPA	Maritime Patrol Aircraft
MPBW	Ministry of Public Buildings & Works
MPP	Mean Probable Position
MR	Maritime Reconnaissance
MRCA	Multi Role Combat Aircraft
MT	Motor Transport
NA.39	Naval Aircraft 39
NAAFI	Navy, Army and Air Force Institutes
NAS	Naval Air Squadron/Naval Air Station
NATO	North Atlantic Treaty Organisation
Nav	Navigator/Navigation
Nav Rad	Navigation Radar
NavAids	Navigational Aids
Navex	Navigation Exercise
NDB	Non-Directional Beacon
NEAF	Near East Air Force
NFTR	Nothing Further To Report
NLZ	No Lone Zone
NOTAM	Notice to Airmen
O Club	Officers' Club
O2	Oxygen
OASC	Officer and Aircrew Selection Centre
OAT	Outside Air Temperature
OC	Officer Commanding
OCA	Offensive Counter Air
OCT	On Call Tasking
OCU	Operational Conversion Unit

ODM	Operating Data Manual
Ops	Operations
OQ	Officer Quality
ORP	Operational Readiness Platform
PB	Practice Bomb
PC	Personal Computer
PD	Practice Diversion
PDQ	Pretty Damn Quick
PEC	Personal Equipment Connector
PEdO	Physical Education Officer
PFS	Primary Flying School
PI	Practice Intercepts
PIO	Pilot Induced Oscillation
Pk	Probability of Kill
PMA	Personnel Management Agency
PMC	President of the Mess Committee
PMRAFNS	Princess Mary's Royal Air Force Nursing Service
PMS	Personnel Management Squadron
PNR	Point of No Return
POW	Prisoner of War
PQ	Personal Quality
PR	Photographic Reconnaissance
PSO	Personal Staff Officer
PSP	Personal Survival Pack
PTI	Physical Training Instructor
QARANC	Queen Alexandra's Royal Army Nursing Corps
QFE	Airfield Pressure Setting
QFI	Qualified Flying Instructor
QNH	Regional Pressure Setting
QRA	Quick Reaction Alert
QRB	Quick Release Box
QWI	Qualified Weapons Instructor
R&R	Rest and Recuperation
RAF	Royal Air Force
RAFASUPU	Royal Air Force Armament Support Unit
RAFG	Royal Air Force Germany
RAS	Replenishment at Sea
RBSU	Radar Bomb Scoring Unit
RCAF	Royal Canadian Air Force
RCMP	Royal Canadian Mounted Police
RDAF	Royal Danish Air Force
RF79-1	Red Flag 79-1
RF82-1	Red Flag 82-1
RFA	Royal Fleet Auxiliary

RHAG	Rotary Hydraulic Arrestor Gear
R-Hour	General Release of Nuclear Weapons
RN	Royal Navy
RNoAF	Royal Norwegian Air Force
RO	Reporting Officer
ROE	Rules of Engagement
RP	Rocket Projectiles
RPM	Revolutions per Minute
RSO	Range Safety Officer
RTB	Return to Base
RV	Rendezvous
RWR	Radar Warning Receiver
SAAF	South African Air Force
SAC	Senior Aircraftman
SACEUR	Supreme Allied Commander Europe
SACLANT	Supreme Allied Commander Atlantic
SAG	Surface Action Group
SAM	Surface to Air Missile
SAR	Search and Rescue
SARBE	Search and Rescue Beacon Equipment
SASO	Senior Air Staff Officer
SBA	Sovereign Base Area
SD	Service Dress
SDO	Station Duty Officer
SEngO	Senior Engineering Officer
SFD	Strike Force Dispersal
SHAPE	Supreme Headquarters Allied Powers Europe
SID	Standard Instrument Departure
SLJ	Silly Little Job
SLR	Self-Loading Rifle
SMC	Station Medical Centre
SNEB	Societé Nouvelle des Etablissements Brandt
SNI	Senior Navigation Instructor
SOP	Standard Operating Procedure
SPINS	Special Instructions
SSA	Supplementary Storage Area
SSM	Surface-to-Surface Missile
STCAAME	Strike Command Air-to-Air Missile Establishment
Stn Int O	Station Intelligence Officer
STRIPRO	Strike Progression
SWP	Standard Warning Panel
T/R	Turn Round
TACAN	Tactical Air Navigation System
TACEVAL	Tactical Evaluation

TAP	Terminal Approach Procedure
TAS	True Air Speed
TFS	Tactical Fighter Squadron
Tgt	Target
TOD	Take-off Distance
TOT	Time on Target
TP	Tailplane/Terminal Phase
TVAT	Television Airborne Trainer
U/T	Under Training
UDI	Unilateral Declaration of Independence
UE	Unit Establishment
UHF	Ultra High Frequency
UK	United Kingdom
ULL	Ultra Low-level
UMO	Unit Medical Officer
UN	United Nations
UP	Unusual Position
USAF	United States Air Force
USMC	United States Marine Corps
USN	United States Navy
USSR	Union of Soviet Socialist Republics
UWT	Under Wing Tank
VFR	Visual Flight Rules
VHF	Very High Frequency
VMC	Visual Meteorology Conditions
VOR	Very High Frequency Omni-directional Range
VR	Velocity Rotate
Wg Cdr	Wing Commander
WP	Warsaw Pact
WSO	Weapon Systems Officer

Index